D1161958

THE NIGER JOURNAL OF
RICHARD AND JOHN LANDER

TRAVELLERS AND EXPLORERS

General Editor: Robin Hallett

THE
NIGER JOURNAL
OF
Richard and John Lander

EDITED AND ABRIDGED

WITH AN INTRODUCTION BY

Robin Hallett

FREDERICK A. PRAEGER, *Publishers*

NEW YORK · WASHINGTON

BOOKS THAT MATTER

Published in the United States of America
in 1965 by Frederick A. Praeger, Inc.
Publishers, 111 Fourth Avenue
New York 3, N.Y.

All rights reserved

© Robin Hallett 1965

Library of Congress Catalog
Card Number: 65–18460

916.62
L 25n

Printed in Great Britain

Travellers and Explorers

The Niger Journal of Richard and John Lander is the first volume in a series, TRAVELLERS AND EXPLORERS, designed to provide new editions of some of the great works of travel and exploration. Although the series has been newly planned, it is intended as a successor to THE BROADWAY TRAVELLERS, which ran to twenty-six volumes under the general editorship of two very distinguished scholars, the late Sir Edward Denison Ross and the late Eileen Power.

The last volume of that series appeared in 1937. In the generation that has passed since then, with the waning of European power and the emergence of the 'new nations' of Asia and of Africa, the world has been transformed. In nineteenth-century Europe the growth of nationalism was accompanied by a deepening and widening of historical studies; in the same way the revolutionary movements of the twentieth century have led people in Asia, Africa, and Latin America to look back on their own past, to discover anew the richness of their own heritage, and to challenge many of the preconceptions accepted by Europeans in the age of imperialism. Stimulated by this new tide of ideas, some Europeans—especially those with first-hand experience of the 'new nations'—have grown increasingly critical of the one-sidedness of much European historical writing. The expansion of Europe is perhaps the greatest single theme in modern history; yet Europe's expansion is a subject more complex than most European historians have assumed, a movement that can only be truly understood when looked at not only through European but also through Asian, African, or Latin American eyes. It is this exhilarating and revolutionary development in historical studies that gives to the works of early European travellers a new and deeper significance.

For at their best the European travellers of an earlier age were objective and sympathetic observers of the countries through which they passed. So their accounts can be regarded as historical documents of the greatest importance, throwing in many cases a flood of light on states and societies for which other forms of historical evidence—local chronicles, official records, and all the other types of material in which Europe is so rich—may be lacking. To Asian and African historians, in particular, as they attempt to unravel the past of their own countries, the accounts of early European travellers are likely to prove the most stimulating of sources.

89.8

FEB

HUNT LIBRARY
CARNEGIE-MELLON UNIVERSITY

Yet the appeal of the travellers of the past is not confined to scholars. Today the countries of the world are more closely involved in one another's affairs than ever before. A failure of understanding between one country and another may lead directly to faulty political judgments, to crisis and to conflict. It is never easy to acquire a sympathetic understanding of a nation other than one's own. But one way of doing so is by gaining some knowledge of another nation's history. Yet to the uninitiated many solid historical works can seem very dull. It is not perhaps the least of the uses of the works of early travellers that they can serve—for politicians as much as for undergraduates—as a vivid and engaging introduction to the history of countries beyond the bounds of Europe or North America.

Here one comes to the perennial appeal of the best works of European travellers of the past. From Herodotus onwards, their narratives may be commended simply because they make such good books, well-written, observant, entertaining, exciting, conveying, more obviously perhaps than any other form of literature, a sense of the amazing variety of life. Today some of the classics of travel and exploration are easily available, but others are now difficult to obtain, and there are some excellent works which have never been reprinted since they first appeared a century and more ago. The present series concentrates initially on those works likely to have the strongest appeal to the modern reader—the works of nineteenth century travellers in Asia and in Africa. As the series develops, it is intended to include works dealing with other continents and drawn from other centuries. The works of most travellers before the beginning of the twentieth century need editing if they are to be fully appreciated: an introduction to set the historical scene and to provide information on the life and character of the writer, footnotes to illuminate obscure points, and in some cases abridgment to cut down excessively bulky texts. The editors of the individual volumes of TRAVELLERS AND EXPLORERS have been chosen for their special knowledge of the country or the travellers concerned. In this way it is hoped to produce a series of volumes which will combine stimulus and satisfaction for the scholar with pleasure and information for the general reader.

R. H.

Contents

vii

CONTENTS

Illustrations

* These illustrations are taken from *A Narrative of the Expedition sent . . . to the River Niger in 1841* by Captain William Allen, R.N., and T. R. H. Thomson, M.D., R.N., London, 1848. All the other illustrations are from the Landers' *Journal.*

Maps

Introduction

I. THE RIDDLE OF THE NIGER

NO GREAT RIVER in the world follows so curious and unpredictable a course as the Niger of West Africa. Its head-waters rise amid the hills of modern Guinea, not far from the Sierra Leone border and little more than two hundred miles from the sea; but the stream does not finally merge with the ocean until it has flowed two thousand six hundred miles, its delta lying fifteen hundred miles to the east of its source. Its course runs first to the north-east, then to the east, then to the south-east, and finally to the south. In making this great bend, the river passes through every form of landscape that West Africa affords. At its northernmost point it sweeps the fringes of the Sahara; for more than half its length it flows through the bush-covered plains of Mali and Northern Nigeria; at the end it cuts through the rain-forest of Southern Nigeria, until its waters are dispersed among the labyrinthine channels of the mangrove swamp of its delta. But the Niger is not the only large river in West Africa. To its west, flowing into the Atlantic, lie the Senegal and the Gambia. Both rivers have their rise in the mountains of Futa Jallon, not far from the sources of the Niger; both rivers follow a curving course that takes them first to the north-west, then to the west. Of the Niger's tributaries the largest is the Benue. The Benue springs from the mountains of the Adamawa massif in modern Cameroun; it, too, makes a great bend, flowing north, then west through a gap in the Cameroon mountains, then south-west to merge with the Niger. At one point in its course the Benue is not far distant from the Logone, itself a tributary of the still larger Shari, which flows northwards to empty its waters into the great Lake Chad. The sources of the Shari lie far to the south-east, in the northern part of the Central African Republic, an area that forms a remarkable watershed, from which rise also streams that flow, some south to the Congo, others east

I

to the Bahr-el-Ghazal and the Nile. In its complexity then, even today when all is mapped and known, the geography of the river-system of Western Africa is difficult to grasp. How much more baffling did it appear to European geographers of an earlier age, as they tried, with nothing at their disposal but a few garbled and second-hand reports, to plot the main features of a continent whose 'darkness', whose 'mystery' was nothing innate, but merely a reflection of their own ignorance.

The first European to obtain a report of the existence of a great river in the interior of Africa was Herodotus. In the fifth century B.C. that insatiably curious Greek traveller picked up a remarkable story in the Greek North African city of Cyrene. A group of adventurous young Berber tribesmen had made, so Herodotus was told, a journey that took them across the burning wastes of the Sahara until they reached a fertile country where flowed a river from the west to the east, a river which Herodotus suspected might be the Nile. Four centuries later, Juba, a scholarly Berber king and a friend of the Emperor Augustus, described a river that rose in Mauretania—the modern Morocco—followed a subterranean course beneath the desert, and emerged as a great stream to flow eastwards to join the Nile. This river Juba called the Niger, a name derived not, it would seem, from the Latin word for 'black' but from a Tuareg expression *n'ger-n-gereo*, 'river of rivers', the Tuareg being a Berber people, some of whose tribes lived in the area of the Niger's bend.

Juba appeared then to confirm Herodotus. But Claudius Ptolemy, the best informed of all classical geographers, produced in the second century A.D. an account of the interior of Africa which accepted the existence of a river called Niger but showed it to have no connection with the Nile. Unfortunately Ptolemy's description of the river's course was phrased in so compressed and cryptic a manner that later scholars found it impossible to interpret coherently. A thousand years after Ptolemy the great Arab geographer, Edrisi, put forward a beguilingly simply account of the rivers of the interior of Africa. In the interior of east Africa Edrisi, basing himself on Ptolemy, placed a lake. Out of this lake flowed two great rivers, one northwards—and here Ptolemy again was his authority—to become the Nile of Egypt, the other, which Edrisi called 'the Nile of the Negroes', westwards across the breadth of the continent until it reached the Atlantic. The 'Nile of the Negroes' European geographers equated with the Niger; they saw in the Senegal and the Gambia the mouths of the great river; and they

INTRODUCTION

found confirmation that the Niger flowed to the west in the well-known account to the sixteenth-century Moorish traveller, Leo Africanus, for Leo had actually sailed on the river westwards from Timbuktu and stated categorically, if inexplicably, that his journey was made 'with the current'.

The concept of a westwards-flowing Niger entering the sea as the Senegal was almost ludicrously wrong; yet it was accepted by every European geographer of the seventeenth and eighteenth centuries—with one exception. In 1759 the masterly French cartographer D'Anville published an article in which he showed, by a careful analysis of all the existing information, that the Niger and the Senegal must be different rivers; but even he was not able to plot the course of the greater river with any assurance, for although, by the middle of the eighteenth century, Europeans had been trading along the coast of West Africa for nearly three hundred years, no European trader or traveller was ever thought to have set eyes on the great river of the interior;[1] nor had it occurred to the merchants who visited the African ports in the Bight of Benin that the rivers up which they sailed were not separate streams but part of the delta of one great river. To later observers the ignorance of eighteenth-century Europeans about the interior of a region with whose coast they had maintained so regular and vigorous an intercourse for many generations may seem an extraordinary phenomenon. It can be explained by a combination of factors: the opposition, based on sound economic arguments, of the coastal rulers to any attempt by Europeans to reach the rich markets of the interior; the physical deterrent of tropical diseases in all their deadly variety; finally, the lack of incentive for Europeans, their capital always in short supply, their coastal trade in slaves already yielding a satisfactory profit, to attempt to penetrate the difficult interior. This situation was to be transformed at the end of the eighteenth century.

In 1788 a small group of influential Englishmen came together to form the Association for Promoting the Discovery of the Interior Parts of Africa. Scientific curiosity was the motive that inspired them; their purpose was strengthened by a pride in the achievements of the times in which they lived, so that they could avow themselves 'desirous

[1] In fact, a number of Europeans must have seen the Niger before 1796, when Mungo Park reached the river. In 1591 Timbuktu was conquered by a Moroccan army, many of whose soldiers were renegades from Spain and Portugal. A century earlier the Portuguese had sent embassies to Mali and Timbuktu. In the first century A.D. a number of Roman military expeditions had crossed the desert, some of whose members may have reached the Niger.

3

of rescuing the age from a charge of ignorance, which in other respects belongs so little to its character'. The founders of the African Association were shrewd men of the world. Grandiose and amateurish may have been their first attempts at sponsoring exploration; but they were quick to appreciate the practical advantages of a better knowledge of the interior of Africa. By 1790 reports gathered from informants in North Africa had directed the attention of the Association to Timbuktu, and to other cities and states of the Western Sudan, places which maintained a lucrative commerce with Tripoli and Morocco, sending their slaves and their gold along the caravan trails of the Sahara. A glance at the map suggested that it should be possible to reach Timbuktu by a route that made the Gambia river its starting-point. Such a route could hardly fail to prove easier and more convenient than the gruelling journey across the western Sahara regularly undertaken by merchants from Morocco. Let this new route be pioneered by the Association's explorers. British merchants would be quick to follow in their train. A great new market would be open for the expanding manufactures of a country that was beginning to feel the first stimulating effects of the Industrial Revolution. Nor would the advantage be confined only to one side. The people of the Sudan would be able to purchase European products at a price much lower than that paid to the merchants of Morocco. More important, 'nations hitherto consigned to hopeless barbarism and uniform contempt'—such was the image Black Africa presented to contemporary Europe—would benefit from contact with the higher culture and superior technology that Europeans had evolved. This was a theme—Commerce and Civilization—that was to be repeated with ever-increasing assurance during the course of the next century.

In 1791 Major Daniel Houghton, a retired Irish Army officer in the Association's service, set out from the Gambia for the Niger; he died in mysterious circumstances before he had reached the great river. Four years later the Association sent out a young Scotsman, Mungo Park; his task was to gather information on 'the rise, the course and the termination of the Niger, as well as of the various Nations that inhabit its borders'. In 1797 Park returned to England with a tale of adventures so remarkable that his narrative immediately established itself as one of the classics of exploration. The hostility of the Moors and his own exhausted resources had prevented him from reaching Timbuktu; but he had attained the Niger and travelled for some distance along its banks. Thus he was able to assert beyond the possibility of contradiction that the river flowed to the east; many cartographers were forced to redraw their maps.

But if the Niger flowed east, where did it end? In the course of the next few years four different theories were devised to answer this question. James Rennell, the most eminent English geographer and the African Association's special adviser, was convinced that the Niger ended in a great lake or inland sea, which he placed approximately in the centre of the area that is now Northern Nigeria. He based his argument partly on a reading of Edrisi, who had mentioned lakes on the course of the Niger, partly on the reports of Park and other travellers, which seemed to suggest that there existed a great mountain range running parallel to the west Coast. In these mountains the streams that flowed into the Bight of Benin had their source; through these mountains it was impossible to conceive that the Niger could force its way. This theory Rennell maintained with formidable assurance for more than thirty years.

Two thousand years earlier Juba and Herodotus had said that the Niger joined the Nile. Their theory tallied with the answer given by many Africans when asked their opinion about the ending of the river; it won the support of a number of eminent European scholars and explorers. With so many confusing reports on the chain of rivers between the Niger and the Nile, it was by no means absurd that geographers should have sought some connection between the two great rivers.

A third theory was put forward in 1802 by an academic German geographer, C. G. Reichardt, then by a West Indian plantation manager, James Macqueen. Working independently of one another, both men came to the conclusion, after a careful examination of all the evidence, that the rivers that flowed into the Bight of Benin must in fact form the Delta of the Niger. They were, of course, absolutely right, but their ideas received little attention and no support until the end of the 1820s.

A final theory about the course of the Niger was first put forward by George Maxwell, an English merchant who had spent several years at the mouth of the Congo; it might have been ignored had it not been embraced with passionate conviction by no less well-qualified a person than Mungo Park. There was the Congo, Maxwell argued, a great river with an end but no beginning—for nothing was known of the river's course two hundred miles from the coast; and there was the Niger, whose higher reaches had been traced but not its lower; was it

THE NIGER JOURNAL

not reasonable to suppose that in fact the Congo and the Niger were one and the same river? Park at least was prepared to wager with his life that Maxwell was right.

In 1805 Park set out a second time for the Niger. He was in command of the first expedition of African exploration to be sponsored and financed by the British Government. Taking with him a force of fifty English soldiers, he set out from the Gambia. The overland march to the Niger, made at the height of the rainy season, became a nightmare—the most ghastly episode in the entire annals of African exploration. When at last Park reached the river all but a handful of his companions were dead, the victims of fever or fatigue. With iron resolution Park set about building a boat to sail down the river. 'Though all the Europeans who are with me should die,' he wrote in his last letter, 'and though I were myself half dead, I would still persevere, and if I could not succeed in the object of my mission, I would at least die on the Niger.' His words became a tragic prophesy. After sailing a thousand miles down the Niger, warding off as they went the attacks of the hostile Tuareg, Park and his companions were drowned in the rapids at Bussa.

Not until 1815 was Park's last journal published. It appeared at a propitious moment. In England the victorious ending of the long war with France created an atmosphere exceptionally favourable to the official support of exploration. In 1815 two large expeditions were organized. One, led by army officers, was to advance overland from the Gambia to the Niger; the other, under naval command, was to sail up the Congo. Both ended in utter failure. The hostility of powerful local rulers blocked the path of the overland force, while the naval expedition, unable to bring its boats through the rapids and gorges of the lower Congo, lost all its leaders from disease. Fortunately there existed another possible line of approach to the Niger and to the states of the western Sudan.

In 1798 Frederick Hornemann, one of the African Association's explorers, had travelled in Muslim disguise from Cairo to Murzuk, the capital of the oasis kingdom of the Fezzan, a kingdom that had recently become a dependency of the Pasha of Tripoli. In 1800 Hornemann crossed the desert from Murzuk to Bornu, only to disappear later without a trace, for it was not known until many years afterwards that he had died of dysentery in Nupe. In 1817, through the initiative of Colonel Warrington, the British Consul in Tripoli, and Captain Smyth, a naval officer engaged in the survey of the North African coast,

6

interest in the Tripoli route was revived. Assured of the Pasha's goodwill, the British Government sent an expedition to Tripoli in 1818. Unlike the two grandiose expeditions of 1815, it consisted only of two explorers, Ritchie and Lyon, and their servants. The expedition was unable to pass beyond the Fezzan; Ritchie died in Murzuk and Lyon returned to Tripoli. In 1822 a second British expedition, led by a doctor, Walter Oudney, assisted by an army officer, Dixon Denham, and a naval officer, Hugh Clapperton, set out on the same route. At last an expedition of African exploration was to prove a brilliant success.

Oudney died in the course of the expedition, but Denham and Clapperton returned to England in 1825, bringing with them a mass of information. Denham had spent more than a year in Bornu, with whose ruler, the Sheikh El Kanemi, he had come to establish a particularly cordial relationship. He had seen Lake Chad and travelled for some distance down the Shari, but he had not been able to gather any precise information on the countries to the east of the lake. In the meantime, Clapperton had visited Kano and Sokoto, the capital of the recently established Fulani empire, by whose ruler, Muhammad Bello, he had been accorded a courteous reception. Neither Denham nor Clapperton had been able to see for themselves either the Niger or the Benue, nor had they been able to gather any incontrovertible evidence about the course of the two rivers.

Clapperton was determined to return to Sokoto without delay. He had brought back with him a letter from Sultan Bello to George IV. Bello asserted that he was willing to establish friendly relations with the British. He was anxious to develop a trade that would bring him fire-arms and other munitions of war; in return he agreed to allow the establishment of a British consul in his domains, and he professed his willingness to prohibit the export of slaves to the coast. At a time when the British Government was actively concerned to suppress the West African slave trade, both by maintaining a naval blockade along the coast and by putting diplomatic pressure on powers engaged in the trade, this last point seemed of particular importance. In fact, it was an easy promise for Bello to make, for the Fulani of Sokoto carried on no direct trade with the coast.

Clapperton left England in August 1825. He was accompanied by another naval officer, Captain Pearce, who was to be installed as Consul, and two doctors, Dickson and Morrison. He took with him on his own account, to act as his personal servant, a young Cornishman,

Richard Lander. Bello had told Clapperton that he would send messengers to the sea-coast to conduct him to the capital. This seemed an excellent arrangement, for the journey from the coast to Sokoto was obviously much shorter than the arduous desert route from Tripoli. However, when Clapperton reached the coast between Accra and Lagos, there was no sign of Bello's messengers. Undeterred, Clapperton decided to make his own way to Sokoto. This was a formidable undertaking, for the hinterland of Lagos and Dahomey, most of it part of the extensive Yoruba empire of Oyo, was completely unknown to Europeans. Clapperton made the little port of Badagry, some miles west of Lagos, his starting-point. The political difficulties proved much less great than anyone, aware of the reluctance of coastal rulers to allow Europeans to visit the markets of the interior, might have anticipated. Indeed, from the hospitable Yoruba the white men received a heart-warming welcome. But the dreaded fevers of the coast crippled the expedition. Within a month Pearce and Morrison were dead of malaria, while both Clapperton and Lander were dangerously ill. Dickson, in the meantime, had been left behind in Dahomey; he died in mysterious circumstances on his way to Yoruba country. Despite these set-backs, Clapperton, with Lander as his only companion, succeeded in reaching Sokoto by a route that led through Borgu, Nupe, and Kano. From Bello he received a disappointingly cool reception. It was clear that there were powerful interests in Sokoto working against him. Traders from North Africa saw no reason to encourage commercial links between Britain and Sokoto. Nor was Bello himself uninformed of the activities of the French in North Africa—Buonaparte's conquest of Egypt left a deep scar on Muslim minds—or of the British in India. It was not unreasonable to suspect that Clapperton's mission, for all its lavish gifts, represented the thin end of the wedge of European imperialism. Clapperton was too impetuous a man fully to appreciate the reasons for Bello's evasions. The failure of his mission affected his already weakened constitution. In April 1827 he died in Sokoto.

Lander was now left with the daunting task of making his own way back to the coast, accompanied only by his African servants. Following much the same route as that which he had taken with Clapperton the previous year, he reached Badagry in November. The port was frequented by Portuguese slave-traders, who planned to cause his death. They accused him of plotting against the king. The king required Lander to clear himself by submitting to the ordeal of drinking poison.

By the prompt use of a powerful emetic Lander survived unscathed. Some weeks later he was rescued by an English ship. In May 1828 Lander was able to hand over to the Colonial Secretary all the possessions that his dying master had entrusted to his care. Despite his heroism and his remarkable adventures, Lander was received in official quarters with a remarkable lack of generosity; he was, after all, only a servant.

Lander had crossed the Niger twice between Borgu and Nupe, but he was not able to say with complete assurance where the river ended. In Africa, as he himself wrote later, 'theories respecting the Niger are even more various and contrary than the hypotheses of the learned of Europe on the subject'. To existing hypotheses a new addition was made some months after Lander's return, when a distinguished soldier, General Sir Rufane Donkin, published a dissertation intended to prove that the Niger reached the sea in the North African Gulf of Sirte, after passing through Lake Chad and flowing underground beneath the desert for more than a thousand miles. But though every possible variant had now been suggested, competent opinion had come to concentrate on two possible alternatives: either the river entered the Gulf of Benin, as Reichardt had originally suggested and as both Clapperton and Lander had been inclined to believe, or it flowed into Lake Chad as the Shari, the river whose lower course Denham had already traced. Which of these alternatives was the correct one could be settled only when a European traveller had traced the river from the point where Clapperton and Lander had crossed it to its mouth, wherever that might be.

In the autumn of 1829 Richard Lander volunteered to return to West Africa to search for the termination of the Niger. The high rate of mortality among African explorers—the death of Alexander Laing, murdered in 1826 shortly after reaching Timbuktu, had recently been confirmed—had produced in official circles a reluctance to risk more lives and waste more public funds. But Lander was evidently keen to go and asked for himself so modest a salary, while his brother John was prepared to accompany him without pay, that it seemed worth making one more attempt. Accordingly, Lander was given the limited amount of equipment that he needed, provided with a passage to the West Coast, and instructed to proceed from Badagry to Katunga, following the same route as that taken on his earlier expedition. Having reached the banks of the Niger, he was 'to follow its course, if possible to its termination, wherever that might be'.[1]

[1] Lander's instructions are given in full in Appendix I.

Of all the explorers who travelled in Africa in the years between 1788 and 1830, none fulfilled their instructions with such scrupulous exactitude as the brothers Lander. They left England in January 1830; seventeen months later they were back. They had reached the Niger at Bussa, procured a canoe, paddled down the river, passed another great river entering the Niger from the east (they called it the Tshadda; later it became known as the Benue), and finally, after many adventures, reached the sea.

By contemporaries the Landers' achievement could be regarded as 'perhaps the most important geographical discovery of the present age'.[1] The historian, with the advantage of hindsight, would confirm this view. Indeed, it may be said that of all the nineteenth-century feats of African exploration none—with the exception of Stanley's journey down the Congo from 1874 to 1877—was productive of such far-reaching political consequences as the Landers' modestly equipped expedition. For the brothers had proved that the Niger was indeed a great and easily navigable highway into the interior of West Africa. The first to appreciate the significance of this discovery was a group of Liverpool merchants who promptly established a company to send two steamships up the Niger. As a commercial enterprise, the venture was an utter failure; mortality among Europeans was appallingly high, and Richard Lander, who acted as leader of the expedition, lost his life in an unlucky skirmish in the Niger Delta.[2] But the experience gained paved the way for further activity. In 1838 a group of English Abolitionists, headed by Sir Thomas Buxton, began to put pressure on the British Government to finance a grandiose expedition; its object was to urge the rulers of the Niger states to abandon the slave-trade and at the same time to establish settlements on the Niger as centres both for legitimate commerce and for missionary enterprise. Superficially the expedition achieved nothing; it was withdrawn after a year, with its objects unfulfilled. Yet, as a Nigerian historian has recently pointed out, 'the 1841 expedition set the pattern for subsequent British operations in the Niger valley. Henceforth missionaries preaching the Gospel, merchants bearing manufactured goods and envoys concluding treaties with Nigerians became the major "civilizing" forces with which the British were to invade, and eventually to subjugate, the river basin'.[3] By the 1880s the Niger in its lower

[1] *Edinburgh Review*, Vol. 55, July 1832, p. 397.
[2] For an account of Lander's last expedition, see p. 290.
[3] Ifemasia, 1962, p. 310.

reaches was becoming an area of international rivalry. By 1903, with the overthrow of the Fulani empire of Sokoto following the establishment of the British Protectorate of Northern Nigeria, the last seven hundred miles of the great river were in British hands. Had Park not died at Bussa, had Clapperton not died at Sokoto, had the brothers Lander not followed the Niger to the sea, the interest of the British public and of those groups which influence official action might not have been brought so strongly to bear on the part of Africa that is now Nigeria. To have contributed in no small degree to the shaping of the modern face of Africa is one measure of the Landers' achievement.

2. RICHARD AND JOHN LANDER

Most of the men who won fame for themselves as African explorers stand out, cast in the heroic mould, as figures larger than life. One thinks of Livingstone's 'sublime obstinacy', of Burton with 'his almost insane hunger for excitement and fulfilment',[1] of Stanley's gargantuan egotism, of Abyssinian Bruce armoured in his arrogance with the qualities of the complete man, of Burckhardt and Barth, in their austere dedication the greatest scholars of them all, of modest Caillié with his obsession for Timbuktu, of Park with his conviction that he would acquire in Africa 'a greater name than any ever did'.[2] By contrast, the first and most striking impression left by Richard and John Lander is of a cheerful simplicity; it is an endearing quality. One may feel that there is no need to feel humbled or embarrassed in the presence of two such ordinary young men.

They were born into the lower orders of English society, working-class one might say, though Cornwall, the county of their birth, had not yet been touched by the Industrial Revolution. Their forbears must have been peasant-farmers; the only one to achieve any fame had been their grandfather, a noted wrestler from Land's End.[3] Their father kept a public-house, The Fighting Cocks, in Truro, where Richard, the fourth of sixth children, was born in 1804. John was born three years later.[4]

'My rambling inclinations,' Richard himself wrote in a brief account of his boyhood, 'began to display themselves in early youth. I was

[1] Moorehead, 1960, p. 165.   [2] Thompson, 1890, p. 165.
[3] Lander, 1830, I, p. 2.
[4] The Landers' associations with Truro are the subject of a series of articles by Ashley Rowe in *The West Briton* (Truro), January 1952. I am greatly indebted to Mr Ashley Rowe for showing me these articles.

never a great while together in one place, and used to delight to play truant and stroll from town to town, and from village to village, whenever I could steal an opportunity; as well as to mix in the society of boys possessing restless habits and inclinations similar to my own. I used also to listen with unmixed attention to old women's tales about the manners and ceremonies of the natives of distant regions of the earth. Their marvellous descriptions of monsters, existing, they affirmed, in remote lands, likewise conspired in me a longing to be a traveller.' 'These tales, how incredible so-ever they might have been, made a deep and permanent impression on my thoughts; and though so very young, I formed a resolution or rather felt a strong and violent inclination to become a wanderer, in order that the story of *my* adventures might one day rival in interest those to which I had listened with so devout an attention; perhaps also a childish feeling of pride entered my bosom as I used to say to myself: "And when I shall have returned from such and such a place, and seen all the strange sights in them, my former companions will look upon me with a mixture of wonder and admiration, and I shall excite the envy of the other boys."'[1] This blend of restlessness—of 'basic nomadism' as Alan Moorehead has recently called it[2]—and of ambition, of a desire to make a name for oneself, would seem to be a quality innate in all explorers. And yet for a man to achieve fame there is need for another gift from the gods, the luck of being in the right position at the right time.

Superficially Richard's early life was not a fortunate one; and yet in retrospect it seems the right preparation for the adventures of his maturity. When he was nine, 'a series of domestic misfortunes', which he regarded later as too 'unpleasant to particularize', forced him to leave home. Two years later a West Indian merchant took him out to St Domingo. There he spent three years and acquired his first experience of tropical diseases, for he nearly died of fever. There, too, he had an opportunity of enjoying the charm of African company, for he was nursed back to health by some 'benevolent and sympathizing Negro females'. In 1818 he returned to England and spent the next five years 'in the service of various noblemen and gentlemen', one of whom he accompanied on a Continental tour. In 1823 he offered his services to a certain Major Colebrooke who had been appointed to undertake a Commission of Inquiry in the new colony in South Africa and was looking for a servant to accompany him. The year he spent with his new master added to his store of adventures: the ship in which he

[1] Lander, 1830, I, pp. 3-5.   [2] Moorehead, 1960, p. 121.

sailed to the Cape was nearly ship-wrecked on three different occasions, while in South Africa he had the opportunity of visiting every part of the colony. In 1824, however, he decided to return to England, where he obtained a post in the service of a relation of the Duke of Northumberland. From the 'comparative indolence' of this easy, pleasant job, Lander was roused by the news of the return of Denham and Clapperton from their brilliantly successful expedition into the interior of Africa.[1]

Ever since the publication of Mungo Park's narrative of his first expedition to the Niger, spirited young men had dreamt of becoming African explorers. 'There was a charm in the very sound of Africa,' so Lander described his own emotions at the time, 'that always made my heart flutter on hearing it mentioned: whilst its boundless deserts of sand; the awful obscurity in which many of the interior regions were enveloped; the strange and wild aspects of countries that had never been trodden by the feet of a European, and even the very failure of all former undertakings to explore its hidden wonders, united to strengthen the determination I had come to, of embracing the earliest opportunity of penetrating into the interior of that immense Continent.'[2] Accordingly, no sooner had he learnt that Clapperton was to return at the head of another expedition than Lander called on the famous explorer and begged to be allowed to accompany his expedition in any capacity.

For Clapperton, sixteen years his senior, Lander's immediate emotion was hero-worship; 'the African traveller with his "keen, penetrating eye" struck him as 'the very soul of enterprise and adventure'.[3] On Clapperton the twenty-year-old Cornishman must also have made an instantly favourable impression; he engaged him on the spot to be 'his confidential servant'. The relationship thus hastily established was to be deepened by the ordeals that lay ahead. The annals of exploration are soured by frequent quarrels between explorers. Clapperton himself indeed had struck Denham, his companion on his first expedition, as intolerably brash, vulgar, and boastful. But Clapperton and Lander came to find themselves 'kindred spirits'.[4] Thrown by the death of their last European companions so intimately on one another's company that the position of master and of servant could no longer be maintained, there came to develop between them a friendship, as harmonious, affectionate, and heroic as any that the history of exploration affords.

[1] Lander, 1830, I, pp. 6–10. [2] *Ibid.*, pp. 11–12. [3] *Ibid.*, p. 10. [4] *Ibid.*, p. xv.

HUNT LIBRARY
CARNEGIE-MELLON UNIVERSITY

Of the qualities which Richard Lander revealed on his expedition with Clapperton the most remarkable was his extraordinary resilience. Within a few days of leaving the coast he suffered his first violent attack of fever. The methods used to relieve him served only to heighten his suffering 'to the utmost pitch of intensity' so that he became for a time 'completely delirious'. At one moment he heard Dr Morrison saying that he could not be expected to live through the night. The next morning, 'to the astonishment of all', he was able to 'sit up and converse rationally'; 'my health, in fact, seemed to return as rapidly as I had lost it'.[1] Later, on the road from Nupe to Kano, he was attacked with dysentery, 'a truly frightful disorder,' so he described it, 'that causes hope to die within the patient'. 'On the road my sufferings were too acute to be described; and it was not unusual for me to lag behind the rest of the party, and, dismounting from my horse, to roll myself in the dust, in the hope of relieving the agony of the moment.'[2] Finally, at Sokoto, after he had seen his master to the grave, Lander fell so ill that he came to abandon 'every hope of recovery', when 'in a manner as unexpected as strange' his health suddenly began to improve.[3]

No doubt this remarkable capacity for sudden recuperation could be explained in part by physiological causes, but Lander's natural robustness was clearly reinforced by an exceptionally buoyant temperament. He was by nature a cheerful extrovert. One characteristic incident throws a flash of light on his character. When the members of Clapperton's expedition were preparing to disembark from the warship that had brought them to Badagry the ship's officers showed themselves so 'deeply affected' at the parting that Lander found it hard to stifle his own emotion. So 'to dispel the gloom' he hastily shook hands all round, leapt into a canoe, and began playing on his bugle *Over the hills and far away*, as he was being rowed to the shore—a gesture that 'elicited the admiration of the sailors of the ship', so that he 'landed amidst the hearty cheers and acclamations of them all'.[4] Fortified with a strong sense of humour, Lander was able to find in the journey, despite all its hardships, 'a thousand amusing incidents'.[5] This sense of enjoyment was undoubtedly increased by the honour accorded to him in many of the African communities he visited as 'the astonishing "Nassarah Curramie" [little Christian] of Africa, the god, the prophet, the enchanter'. In England he was only a servant, a

---

[1] Lander, 1830, I, pp. 69–70.   [2] *Ibid.*, p. 195.   [3] *Ibid.*, II, p. 83.
[4] *Ibid.*, I, p. 40.   [5] *Ibid.*, p. x.

menial; in Africa 'he had shaken hands with majesty and lodged in the palaces of princes'.[1] Lander may have been critical of much that he saw in Africa, but he was never coldly condescending. His natural gaiety and ebullience must have served not only to strengthen his courage but also to win him many friends among the Africans whom he encountered on his journey.

Fat men are congenitally cheerful—Lander's figure was short and stout, 'as broad as he was long' in the words of a later acquaintance.[2] Yet one may feel that about Lander's cheerfulness there was nothing superficial; it rested on the foundation of a sure religious faith. 'A firm reliance on the goodness and mercy of the Divine Power,' Clapperton had written to him at a difficult stage of their journey, 'will inspire you with confidence, and bear you up with cheerfulness and courage even when all earthly enjoyments fail you.'[3] The truth of his master's words Lander proved to himself, when on his solitary journey back from Sokoto he made it his custom, before retiring to rest, 'to read aloud from a book of common prayer some portion of its contents', making his servants sit around him in a circle as he did so. 'By this pleasing exercise I felt unusual calmness and serenity steal over my mind; and I slept as soundly in the bosom of awful woods, amidst the howling of the tempest and the pelting of the storm—the yell of the tiger [sic] and the hollow roar of the crocodile—as if I had been reposing on a bed of down in my own country.'[4] To many twentieth-century readers the open profession and practice of a religious faith may seem a little strange; but about the Landers' piety—John was as devout as his brother—there was nothing strained or priggish. To possess a strong and natural belief in 'the goodness and mercy of the Divine Power' may well be thought for men faced with a long and solitary ordeal the most valuable gift of all.

When Richard Lander returned to England in the spring of 1828 there is nothing to suggest that he had any thought of revisiting Africa. He was still suffering from the effects of his journey, and his first wish was naturally to see his family. By the Government he was treated in a pretty shabby manner. Having been engaged as Clapperton's private servant, he had, of course, no claim on official funds; it was, however, agreed that he should be allowed the salary of eighty pounds a year originally intended for Columbus, a mulatto engaged as interpreter,

[1] Lander, 1830, II, p. 284.
[2] Macgregor Laird, in Laird and Oldfield, 1837, I, p. 73.
[3] Lander, 1830, I, p. 227.　　[4] Ibid., II, p. 158.

who had died at the start of the mission. This was the only official remuneration that he received; in these circumstances he can hardly have felt like pressing his services on the Government. Moreover, a few months after his return he married,[1] and thus had to apply himself to earning his living. Settling down in Truro, he obtained a post in the Excise Department. It proved quite unsuitable. In February 1829 he wrote to R. W. Hay, the Under Secretary at the Colonial Office, saying that he was suffering so badly from ague and rheumatism that his doctor had told him he would never be able to perform any duty that required him to be constantly out of doors. To his request for a post in any Department, 'where I may not be exposed to the inclemency of the weather',[2] Hay must have returned a dusty answer, for Lander wrote again two months later to say he would be glad of almost any indoor job. At the end of June—by which time his wife had given birth to a daughter—Lander had obtained another post, as a weighing-porter in the Customs; but the work was 'very laborious and much exposed to the weather', and the salary only fifty pounds a year.[3] In these depressing circumstances Richard's thoughts again began to turn to Africa and to the great problem of the Niger. Some time in the summer of 1829 he must have opened his mind to John Barrow.

Barrow, a senior civil servant at the Admiralty and himself a distinguished traveller, was the leading authority on African exploration. He had played a large part in the expeditions organized by the Government since 1815, and had been responsible for editing Clapperton's last journal. In his introduction to this work he had referred to Lander as an 'intelligent young man'.[4] On 18 September 1829 Hay, the Colonial Under-Secretary, sent to Barrow the plans he had received from two adventurous young men, Welford and Coulthurst, both of whom, quite independently one of another, were anxious to settle the question of the Niger.[5] Barrow was not impressed by their proposals, yet felt that something should be done. 'Would not Lander, who has been pressing to go again,' he suggested to Hay in a prompt reply, 'be the fittest person to send? No one in my opinion would make their way so well and with a bundle of beads and bafts and other trinkets, we

[1] The date of Lander's marriage is not known; he first refers to his wife in a letter written in April 1829. It seems most unlikely that he was married before going to Africa.
[2] C.O. 2/16, Lander to Hay, 14 February 1829, April 1829.
[3] *Ibid.*, 22 June 1829.   [4] Clapperton, 1829.
[5] C.O. 324/81, Hay to Barrow, 18 September 1829. Both Coulthurst and Welford attempted to carry out their plans, though without official support; both died at the start of their journeys, Coulthurst in Calabar and Welford in Sennar.

could land him somewhere about Bonny and let him find his way.'[1] Hay wasted no time in getting in touch with Lander. Lander's terms were extremely modest: he wanted no more than £100 for his wife, Harriet, during his absence, and a gratuity of the same amount for himself on his return.[2] He had, however, one special request to make: 'I should particularly wish,' he wrote to Barrow on 16 October, 'that my brother, John Lander, be permitted to accompany me on my lonely journey.'[3] Since John was willing to go without a salary, no objection could be raised to this modest demand.

John Lander was nearly three years younger than his brother. He had spent all his life in Truro, stayed on at school till he was fifteen, and been apprenticed as a compositor in the office of the *Royal Cornwall Gazette*.[4] From their portraits a certain family likeness—the same straight nose, the same curly hair—may be traced between the two brothers; but in character John, the taller of the two, was in some ways so different from Richard as to be almost his antithesis. In contrast to Richard, with his ebullient temperament and his breezy manners, John must have appeared pensive and indrawn; 'for the first five years of my life,' he confessed in his *Journal*, 'I have been told that I was never even seen to smile, and since that period, Heaven knows, my merriment has been confined to extraordinary and particular occasions only.' Richard, who had knocked around the world, took naturally to African society; John came to find African company distinctly tiresome, writing Africans down as 'savages' and 'barbarians' and feeling, at least at the start of his journey, 'a very considerable share of aversion towards their jetty countenances'. Richard's education had been sketchy in the extreme; content to take the world as his teacher, he had wasted no time over the formalities of book-learning.[5] John, on the other hand, was a naturally studious youth who lived with books and loved them and was not without the ambition to make a name for himself as a writer; he was already 'the author of several essays in prose and verse, by no means discreditable to his talents'.[6]

[1] C.O. 2/18, Barrow to Hay, 19 September 1829.

[2] C.O. 2/18, Lander to Hay, 13 November 1829.

[3] C.O. 2/18, Lander to Barrow, 16 October 1829.

[4] Mr Ashley Rowe, in his articles in the *West Briton*, January 1952, gives the date of John Lander's birth as 29 December 1806. In the minutes of the Cornwall Central School it is stated that John Lander was given a medal and prayer book on 1 April 1822.

[5] The earliest surviving manuscript in Richard Lander's hand—an account of Clapperton's instructions on his deathbed—has many spelling mistakes and no punctuation. (The original is in C.O. 2/16.) Richard's later letters show that his knowledge of English improved considerably, no doubt through contact with his brother.   [6] Huish, 1836, p. 430.

It was John's literary abilities that came to link his destiny with Africa. For when Richard decided to write a fuller account of his experiences than that contained in the section of his journal published by John Murray as a pendant to Clapperton's narrative, it was to his younger brother that he naturally turned. John indeed came to play the part of a 'ghost' writer. Richard acknowledged his help generously: 'having become impressed with my thoughts,' he wrote in the *Preface* of his book, 'he has "turned them to shape"', and, entering warmly into my feelings, he has depicted my emotions, even as I felt them.'[1] How warmly his younger brother had entered into his feelings, Richard could have realized only when he offered to accompany him on another expedition. By this time John must have been well aware of the dangers he would be called on to face. No doubt his 'exuberant imagination' cast a romantic glow over the enterprise; nevertheless, it was an act of very remarkable courage.

So it was that in the late autumn of 1829 these two young men started on the necessary preparations for their expedition. By the Government they were provided with far more equipment than the African Association had been able to put at the disposal of Mungo Park thirty-five years earlier; but compared to the paraphernalia and the funds allowed to other officially sponsored expeditions in the last ten years, the Landers could consider that the organization of their undertaking was extremely modest.[2] One fact must have been uppermost in the minds of their friends and relations as they said their good-byes: that of the white men who in the course of the last forty years had ventured into the interior of the mysterious continent, at least four in every five had paid for their audacity with their lives.

3. THE LANDERS' JOURNAL

The Landers' *Journal* may be commended to modern readers for three reasons. Most obviously, it is a splendidly exciting adventure story. Then it contains some descriptions of the African, more specifically the Nigerian scene, that for freshness, for vividness, for sheer literary skill have never been surpassed. Finally—a point of especial significance for African readers—the *Journal* is a historical document of particular importance.

To reach the Niger and sail down it to its termination: this objective,

[1] Lander, 1830, I, p. vix.
[2] Details of the Landers' equipment are given in Appendix II.

18

this purpose gives to the narrative, as Ithaca to Odysseus, its unity and its dynamic. The overland journey from Badagry through Yoruba country to Bussa on the Niger was made without excessive difficulty. But when the brothers set out to paddle their canoe from Bussa to the open sea they were attempting a feat no African even seems at that time ever to have undertaken. River-travel is the most soothing form of locomotion; but for the Landers their journey was constantly beset by dangers. Local rulers might detain them, sudden storms engulf them, crocodiles or hippopotami overturn them, bands of 'savages' assail them. And before the end the worst did happen: they were attacked, their canoe sent to the bottom, most of their possessions lost or stolen, themselves left to the mercy of a people more ferocious in manner than any they had yet encountered. At the very last, when they had succeeded in getting aboard an English ship, their perils were not at an end, for the captain revealed himself a brute and the ship escaped being wrecked in the fierce breakers of the bar by the slenderest of chances. Here, then, in its highlights are the ingredients of an adventure story in the classic tradition.

But the Landers' narrative is something more than a simple tale of adventure. In its variety of incidents and characters, it possesses something of the quality of a picaresque novel. The strange, the ludicrous, the unexpected, the entrancing is always happening. Take a chapter at random. The Landers leave Katunga; there is a violent row with the porters; a hideous female dwarf sends a shudder down John Lander's spine; the brothers are entranced by the beauty and kindness of some Fulani maidens; they play the doctor to the governor of a town, who rewards them by singing 'a ditty in praise of elephants'; they have a brief encounter with a band of 'very suspicious-looking fellows'; they travel through wild bush—John Lander rhapsodizing on the beauty of the evening—accompanied by a 'warlike and romantic escort' sent by the King of Kaiama.

> Sometimes they fell in our rear, and then again dashed suddenly by us with astonishing swiftness, looking as wild as the scenery through which their chargers bounded. The effect was rendered more imposing by the reflection of the moon-beams from their polished spears and the pieces of silver which are affixed to their caps, while the luminous fire-fly appeared in the air like rising and falling particles of flame.

This brief passage, describing the antics of the Kaiama escort, is a good sample of the charm of their style, fresh, vigorous, precise, with a poet's instinct for the striking, the life-enhancing image. The spontaneity of their writing ensures that their narrative embraces not only the grandeurs but also the miseries of their journey—the fever, the filthy huts, the poor food, the sleepless nights 'occasioned chiefly by exposure to damps, rains, and dews, mosquito attacks, frightful and piercing noises, and over-fatigue, or apprehension and anxiety of mind'. These are the routine discomforts of exploration; not all African travellers think them worthy of mention. The Landers—and especially the sensitive John—not being born to the tradition of the stiff upper lip, thought differently. 'Our journals,' the brothers wrote later, 'were invariably written on the spot at the close of each day';[1] by sticking so closely to this practice and by publishing their journals as they stood, they make it possible for their readers to share their experience in a way few other travellers have done.

Of all the men who set out to explore Africa in the nineteenth century, the Landers were among the least well qualified to report on their observations. They were not scholars, they possessed no scientific training, they seem to have shown no great linguistic ability (they could, of course, use their servants as interpreters, though Richard must from his earlier expedition have picked up some knowledge of Hausa). Of these limitations they were well aware. 'We are of opinion,' they wrote in Katunga, 'that it would require a long residence in this country and a perfect acquaintance with its language, to enable a foreigner to form a correct judgment of its laws, manners, customs, and institutions, as well as its religion and the form and nature of its government.' A modern social anthropologist would applaud this statement. As for themselves, they went on, 'We can only answer for what we *see*.' Fortunately they saw, they took in a great deal. Moreover, in their observations the brothers complement each other remarkably well, John with his romantic poet's eye dwelling enthusiastically on the landscape, the more sociable Richard sharply picking on the vagaries of African life.

To a modern reader familiar with the landscapes of the country through which the Landers passed, some of John's descriptions will seem a shade fantastic. Take, for instance, that valley in the rain-forest through which they passed soon after leaving Badagry: it was, for John, 'a deep glen more wild, romantic, and picturesque than can be conceived . . . overhung by trees of amazing height and dimensions. . . . Fancy might picture a spot so silent and solemn, as the abode of

[1] *Journal*, I, p. viii.

genii and fairies.' The sensibility of an age is revealed in its adjectives; no dead-pan modern writer would describe the foetid vegetation of the tropical forest in such terms. But it is in this particular brand of sensibility that one discriminating critic, Mr Morchard Bishop, has seen 'the essential and enduring merit of the Landers' book': 'in it we are able to see with extreme clarity what Africa looked like to a couple of eighteenth-century Cornishmen; to see, as it were, the eternal under the aspect of the temporal'. The phrase *eighteenth-century* Mr Bishop uses deliberately. 'Truro,' he points out, 'was then a long way from the centre of things, and the writers who had formed John Lander's mind were of an earlier and old fashioned sort. He had, one is sure, read his *Rambler* with attention, was deep in Pope and Thomson and Cowper. Nor were the characteristic accents of Sensibility absent.'[1] A modern traveller, blasé with the impressions gathered from half a dozen widely different countries, might respond to the Nigerian landscape with less fervour than provincial John Lander; he cannot say that Lander's descriptions are false or misleading. And indeed, infected by that romantic enthusiasm, reminded of 'the delicious fragrance shed around from trees and shrubs' in the bush at evening-time or urged to behold in the black inselbergs of northern Yorubaland 'mountains of granite of the most grotesque and irregular shape', he might find his own response quickened and enhanced.

The purple of John's landscapes will not be to every reader's taste; by contrast the passages in which the brothers describe the incidents of African life possess an instant appeal. How well they convey the texture of that life, its variety and its colour, the spectacular and the absurd, the gaiety and the fecklessness, the dignity and the squalor—a life, moreover, that seems in some respects, so a European who has lived in modern Nigeria may find himself thinking, to have changed remarkably little in the century and a quarter that has passed since the Landers wrote. Not many recent writers on West Africa have achieved the same quality of insight; nor is it difficult to understand the reasons for the inferiority of most modern accounts. The twentieth-century traveller in Africa moves encased in the shell of his own culture; he goes too fast, he eats his own sort of food, he sleeps in his own sort of bed. The Landers, slowly making their own way, alone and unprotected, were exposed to all the pressures of African life; it was an experience as exhilarating as it was exhausting.

Of all the passages in the *Journal* that are likely to stick in the

[1] Bishop, 1953, p. 21.

reader's mind, perhaps the greatest is the description of the festival at Bussa, followed immediately by the eclipse of the moon. So vigorous, so amusing—even if somewhat arch in its humour—so vivid in its details, so finely composed, it stands as a superb piece of English prose. And yet it is not an isolated peak. Both Landers, miraculously one may feel, were 'natural stylists'.[1] How often they produce a striking phrase —'the magnificent Niger slumbering in its own grandeur'; or an elegant period—the Nupe of Zagozhi 'made bold by freedom, affluent by industry and frugality, healthy by exercise and labour, and happy from a combination of all these blessings'. To write well is never an easy accomplishment; to write so well under 'the debilitating effects of the African climate' and 'a degree of languor which not even the warmest enthusiasm could wholly overcome'[2] is a quite extraordinary achievement, rendered the more astonishing by the fact that the writers were both young men of little formal education.

Their *Journal*, then, is not unworthy of a modest place in the annals of English literature. At the same time it is an historical document of especial importance to any student of West African history. For the Landers provide the first description ever composed of the states and peoples of the Niger valley. No doubt, if the Landers had never written, it would be possible to obtain from other sources, from oral tradition, for example, some impression of the state of this part of Africa in the first half of the nineteenth century. But the Landers' account puts flesh on to the dry bones of the king lists, the local chronicles. History is in part analytical, in part pictorial. For the historian concerned to study the relationship between the various states of the Niger area or the trade routes of the interior, the Landers provide valuable material. At the same time they present a splendidly animated picture of the past—kings and peasants, traders and priests, the marauding Fulani, the effete Yoruba of Old Oyo, the energetic Nupe, the vigorous canoemen of Aboh and of Brass. But to place these figures in their proper setting and at the same time to be able to follow clearly the Landers in the vicissitudes of their journey it is necessary for the modern reader to have clear in his mind a sketch of the state-system of what, for want of an exact, contemporary name, must be called the Niger Area.

[1] Bishop, 1953, p. 22.

[2] *Journal*, I, p. viii.

4. THE STATES OF THE NIGER AREA IN 1830

Today the country through which the Landers passed in the course of their journey from Badagry to Bussa and from Bussa down the Niger to the sea lies within the boundaries of the Federation of Nigeria. In 1830, however, the political geography of this part of Africa was infinitely more complex, for the area comprised by modern Nigeria covered three empires, many kingdoms or city-states, and a multitude of smaller, self-sufficient, independent communities.

Of the three empires the most powerful and the most extensive was that created by the Fulani, with its capital at Sokoto. The Fulani had been for centuries the most widely dispersed of all the peoples of West Africa, for they were to be found in all the countries of the Sudanic belt from the Senegal to the mountains of the Cameroons. Two things distinguished them sharply from their neighbours: one physical—a lighter skin and features differently shaped; the other social—the adherence to a pastoral way of life. Not all the Fulani, however, followed the ancestral pattern, tending their cattle in the bush; some had settled down near towns and villages, intermarried with people of darker complexion, and come to adopt the religion of Islam. From the Muslim Fulani had come a number of eminent and saintly scholars, one of whom, Uthman dan Fodio, was destined, as a revolutionary leader of a type particularly characteristic of Islam, to become one of the greatest figures in West African history. Uthman dan Fodio was born about the year 1754 in the Hausa kingdom of Gobir. The rulers of Gobir were nominally Muslim, but sanctioned many pagan practices. Uthman, widely esteemed both for his intellectual eminence and his personal holiness, became a powerful critic of the existing order; his sermons attracted to him many disciples, but drew down the wrath of the king of Gobir. In 1804 Uthman was forced to flee for his life. Gathering his disciples around him, he proclaimed the struggle with Gobir a *Jihad* or Holy War. The revolt spread; Uthman called on the Fulani of the other Hausa kingdoms to support him in his struggle; crusading zeal was aided by diplomatic intrigue. Within five years Uthman and his followers had achieved a remarkable act of conquest: having overthrown the rulers of most of the Hausa states, they had made themselves master of a great new empire, for which a capital was built at Sokoto.

Bornu, the second great empire, provided the most formidable opponent to the rising power of the Fulani. The empire, whose ruling dynasty could trace their lineage back over a thousand years, covered a wide stretch of territory to the west of Lake Chad. In 1808 and again in 1811 the Fulani invaded Bornu; they might have conquered the whole country, had not an effective resistance been organized by a

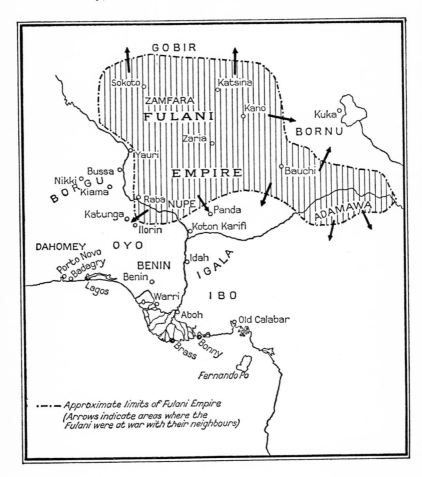

—·—·— *Approximate limits of Fulani Empire*
(Arrows indicate areas where the
Fulani were at war with their neighbours)

remarkable leader, the Sheikh Muhammad El Amin El Kanemi. El Kanemi preserved the ancient dynasty but established himself as *de facto* ruler and set about reforming the decaying empire. It was impossible, however, to restore completely the ancient prestige of Bornu; before the Fulani assault the Hausa kingdoms of Kano and Zaria—and even some more distant states—accepted the suzerainty of Bornu; by 1830 they were firmly held as part of the Fulani empire.

Richard Lander never visited Bornu, though in the course of his travels he heard much about the old empire. He was familiar, however, with the heart of the Fulani empire, for he had spent several months in Kano and Sokoto. On his journey down the Niger, as he touched on the country of Nupe, he had the opportunity of seeing something of the methods used by the Fulani in furthering their power. The people of Nupe had not been affected by the first stages of the Fulani *Jihad*. In 1810, however, there arrived in the country a certain Mallam Dendo, a Muslim Fulani, who, in the course of his travels as an itinerant preacher, succeeded in building up for himself a band of powerful supporters. His opportunity came ten years later, when Nupe was torn apart by civil war over a disputed succession. One of the rivals, Majiya, begged Mallam Dendo to assist him. Dendo became Majiya's most influential adviser and at the same time used his influence to strengthen the power of his compatriots. By 1830 it was clear that the Fulani were the effective rulers of Nupe: their tax-gatherers collected tribute from Nupe towns, their preachers brought Islam to hitherto pagan villages, their horsemen raided ever farther afield in their search for slaves and booty; arrogantly the Fulani could boast of the time when their empire would reach to the sea.

In one direction, however, the Fulani had achieved no success. The group of small kingdoms on either side of the Niger north-west of Nupe were always to remain free of Fulani rule. Yauri, whose capital of the same name was a town of considerable size and antiquity, being the nearest to Sokoto, had found it necessary to buy off Fulani attack with the payment of a modest tribute. But the people of Borgu, as the country on the right bank of the river was called, protected in part by the natural obstacles of river, swamp, and waterless bush, were never seriously molested by the Fulani. The Borguwa were organized into a loose confederation of city-states, three of which, Bussa, Wawa, and Kaiama, were visited by the Landers.

The third of the empires of the Niger area was that created by the Yoruba of Oyo. At its height in the eighteenth century Oyo covered an area comprising most of the western part of the present Western Region of Nigeria; it contained many substantial towns, though never a port on the sea-coast. By the beginning of the nineteenth century, however, the grip of the *Alafins*—such was the title of the rulers of Oyo—had weakened. Their decline, of which the Landers saw vivid evidence in the capital, Katunga, ushered in a long period of strife. The break-up of the empire was hastened by the revolt of one of the *Alafin's* most powerful subjects, a certain Afonja, who held the town of Ilorin. To provide himself with the army needed to gratify his ambitions, Afonja called to his standard all the Hausa slaves in the country. At the same time he accepted as his adviser a Fulani mallam named Alimi. Afonja's ambition brought about his downfall. About 1830—the exact date appears uncertain—the Hausa soldiers, with Alimi at their head, revolted against Afonja and killed him. Alimi became ruler of Ilorin and brought the province within the bounds of the Fulani empire.

From Ilorin and from Nupe the Fulani were to strike eastwards against the people of the Niger–Benue confluence. The most substantial state in this area had been formed by the Igala people with its capital at Idah; the *Ata*—such was the Igala ruler's title—of Idah controlled most of the country on the left bank of the Niger for about a hundred miles below the confluence. Two important towns, Panda (called by the Landers 'Fundah') and Koton Karifi, had been formed by descendants of the ruling house of Idah among the Igbirra, who lived north of the confluence. Both places were coming under Fulani attack by 1830. Between the confluence and the borders of Nupe was a country whose people had not yet been incorporated into the domains of their more powerful neighbours; the Landers were to visit one of these simple, independent communities, the Kakanda.

The valley of the Niger from a point south of Idah to the labyrinthine creeks and swamps of the delta was settled and dominated by the Ibo people. Unlike the Yoruba, the Ibo, whose country must then have been one of the most densely populated in Africa, had never formed a large political unit; they were dispersed among a great number of independent towns and villages. Aboh, the town visited by the Landers, occupied a peculiarly favourable trading position and was the most important Ibo settlement on the lower Niger; its ruling dynasty was of foreign origin, having come centuries earlier from Benin.

The influence of the kingdom of Benin reached not only eastwards into the Niger valley but also far to the west. Thus Lagos, then one of the lesser ports of the Slave Coast, was tributary to Benin, even as Badagry, the Landers' starting-place, was temporarily subordinate to Lagos. The Landers did not visit Benin; had they done so, they would have found another kingdom in decline.

In the sixteenth century Benin had been the richest state on the

Slave Coast. By 1800 its commercial importance had been eclipsed by the city-states of the Niger delta, Brass, Bonny, and farther east, on the Cross river, Old Calabar. The earliest inhabitants of the delta were the Ijaw people, whose villages the Landers must have passed on their journey from Aboh to Brass. But in the course of the past three centuries many of the inland people had moved south to take advantage of the opportunities for trade offered by European merchants, who from the end of the fifteenth century regularly visited the creeks and inlets of the delta. A majority of the migrants were of Ibo origin, except in Old Calabar founded by the Efiks. But other groups were involved, so that the mixed population of the city-states had come by the nineteenth century to form 'a people apart, the product of the clashing cultures of the tribal hinterland and of the Atlantic community to both of which they belonged'.[1]

From Badagry to Kuka, the capital of Bornu, or from Calabar to Sokoto was a distance of six or seven hundred miles. It is difficult to think of any other area of comparable size in the world that could have contained so great a variety of people. For the states of the Niger area could be distinguished one from another not only by their size and power but also by the political institutions, the economy, the religion, the culture, the character, or general temperament of their people.

'Despotic' was an epithet freely applied by the Landers and by other contemporary travellers to the rulers of African states; it is a misleading expression. The machinery of absolutism requires as its prerequisites an established revenue, a standing army, and an efficient bureaucracy. Such things were to be found—but only in a rudimentary form—in the states of West Africa. The problems African rulers had constantly before them were of a kind that would have been understood instinctively by the monarchs of medieval Europe—the rebellious over-mighty subject, the threat of invasion across ill-defined frontiers, the need to establish internal law and order, and to develop trade as a source both of revenue and of munitions of war. This was a world vastly different from the contemporary despotisms of an Ottoman Sultan or a Russian Czar. Moreover, every African monarch had to listen to his councillors and to conciliate his most powerful supporters.

Monarchy—the paramountcy, however limited, of a single king or chief—was the usual but not the universal system in the states through which the Landers passed. In Brass they were confused by the number

[1] Dike, 1956, p. 30.

27

of individuals who bore the title King; in Old Calabar they could have found a cluster of little republics, each with its own chief and council, united by the ties of a secret society; among the many Ibo communities a rich man—as in early medieval Europe—might acquire, through the help and protection he could afford to other members of his group, a position of authority. The complexity of the political structure of the countries through which they passed, the Landers could hardly be expected to unravel.

Easier to ascertain—for here the eye alone could act as a guide—were the economic differences revealed by various communities. At one extreme might be placed an entirely self-sufficient community, such as that settlement of Nupe refugees with whom John Lander spent a night on the road between Bussa and Wawa. At another the town of Brass, whose swampy surroundings produced nothing but plantains and fish, so that most of the food had to be imported; in this gloomy environment survival depended on a vigorous trade. The men of Brass were energetic middlemen; and yet the Landers were struck by 'the penury and wretchedness' of their town. The most substantial prosperity was achieved when trade and agriculture went together. Such was the case at Wawa, whose people, living in a fertile country-side and on one of the main trade-routes of West Africa, could enjoy 'plenty of the necessaries of life and a great many of the luxuries'.[1] Europeans are accustomed to assume that they have always enjoyed a higher standard of living than the people of Africa. It is worth reflecting that the inhabitants of a town such as Wawa must have enjoyed a much gayer, freer, and more comfortable life than the factory workers of the dismal cities of industrializing England or than the oppressed peasantry of Eastern and Central Europe.

Contemporary Europe—its pattern not yet simplified by the emergence of the modern nation state—could present as great a diversity of political units and institutions, could display an even greater range of economies, but it could not compare with West Africa in the variety of linguistic groupings. Had they been assiduous collectors of linguistic material, the Landers, in the course of their journey, would have been able to gather vocabularies from a dozen different languages. Yet the difficulties caused by this state of affairs should not be exaggerated. In most of the towns and villages of the Niger, from Yauri to Idah, Hausa, though nowhere the native language, was understood by some of the inhabitants; similarly in the Yoruba towns and even in Badagry,

[1] Clapperton, 1828, p. 93.

Hausamen or at least Hausa speakers were to be found. In the same way a knowledge of Ibo was diffused from Idah to Brass. But there were still some places where, in spite of the five different languages spoken by their servants, the Landers found great difficulty in making themselves understood.

Religion provided another, easily visible means of distinguishing state from state, at least in the distinction between animism and Islam. The range and variety of animistic belief the Landers were not in a position to grasp; they could only record outward ceremonies. But in their comments they provided valuable evidence of the spread of Islam. Islam had been brought to the states north of Lake Chad at a very early date by merchants from North Africa; in the fourteenth century Muslim missionaries from Timbuktu had come to the Hausa states; in the eighteenth century the first conversions had taken place among the Nupe. By 1830 a community of Muslims was even to be found, as the Landers noted, in Badagry on the sea-coast. Down the Niger, on the other hand, Islam had advanced more slowly; in Ibo-land Muslims were rarely, if ever, encountered. Islam is often represented as a militant faith; the Fulani *jihad* might seem to confirm this view, though after the first crusading zeal had evaporated the movement can be interpreted as the product either of the familiar dynamic of an advancing imperialism or of a simple desire for booty in a land where slaves constituted the surest form of wealth. Yet in the Landers' account one comes across no evidence of religious discord. Muslims were tolerated among the Yoruba, the Nupe, and the Igala, while in Bussa the king, himself a pagan, used Muslims to pray for his welfare and cheerfully participated in the festivals of Islam, thus making the best of both worlds.

The Muslim faith professed by the mallams of Nupe or Borgu was no doubt a simpler creed than that practised by the scholars of Sokoto or Kuka. But in whatever form it might be held, Islam had the power to affect men's way of life, influencing their dress, their manners, their superstitions, their education. Nevertheless, since none of the communities through which the Landers passed was completely Islamized, the new faith could represent only one strand in the pattern of culture. For the travellers housing and dress provided the most easily recognizable evidence of cultural differences. How sharp was the contrast between the curious huts of those islanders of the Niger, the Kamberri, and the elaborately carved dwellings of the Yoruba; or between the slovenliness of the same Kamberri with their taste for 'unbecoming and

29

singular ornaments', the simple grace and sobriety of the pastoral Fulani, and the penchant of some of the people of the lower Niger for articles of European attire.

From the complex intermingling of so many factors emerges the distinctive character of a people. Of the difference between people and people the Landers were keenly aware. Arriving in Kaiama from Katunga, they were immediately struck by the contrast between the Yoruba and the Borguwa—the former 'mild, unassuming, humble', the latter 'martial, passionate and proud'. Even the inhabitants of a single town could impress their character on the traveller's mind: thus the Nupe of Zagozhi stood out 'in this country of sluggards' for their industry and their love of liberty; by contrast, the Ibo of Aboh were written off as a set of ferocious drunkards. On images, on stereotypes such as these, tribal feeling—to which even Europeans in Africa are not immune—is built up.

Not all the states and peoples of the Niger area were fully aware of one another's existence. Between places so remote from one another as Yauri and Calabar there can have been no direct contact. Even among the Igala the Landers found that little appeared to be known of the country up the Niger. That isolated communities, ignorant of the outside world, should exist in this part of Africa is in no way surprising; even in parts of contemporary England lonely, indrawn, fiercely parochial villages were to be found. More remarkable was the degree of intercourse between people and people that the Landers were able to observe: thronged markets, busy roads, a multitude of canoes along certain stretches of the Niger. Of all this activity trade was the great generator. The Niger area was laced together by a network of trade routes that reached from the Mediterranean to the Atlantic.

Along the caravan trail that ran from Tripoli in North Africa through the Fezzan to Bornu the trans-Saharan trade was vigorously maintained. From Bornu a route ran westward to Kano, the most important commercial centre in the Fulani empire. From Kano traders could travel northwards through Air to the rich Saharan oases of Ghadames and Ghat, westwards to Katsina and Sokoto, southwards to Zaria and Nupe. From Nupe a much-frequented route ran westwards through Borgu to Gonja and Ashanti; from Borgu another route ran southwards to Katunga and on through the Yoruba towns to Badagry. From Badagry—and indeed from Whydah farther west—a canoe could travel along sheltered lagoons to the creeks of the Niger delta. These creeks led on to the main stream of the Niger, which provided a great highway into the interior; thus traders from Bonny could travel easily to the Igala country. This network of routes was not completely unified, but in fact embraced two systems, one geared to North Africa, the other to the Atlantic. Between the two systems, the former based on land routes, the latter on riverain traffic, a close connection had not yet been established. Raba, the important Nupe town on the Niger, was visited by North African traders; but North Africans were not to be found in Igala or Ibo territory. Between Igala and Nupe, indeed, there existed, though the river was still easily navigable, something of a no-man's-land, through which intercourse appears to have been limited. In taking a canoe from Bussa to the sea the Landers were making a journey that was exceptional even by African standards.

Slaves still constituted the most important of the Niger area's exports to the outside world. Two or three thousand slaves were sent each year across the desert to North Africa; a very much larger number passed through the delta ports to the slave-holding communities of the New World. Of the area's other commodities palm-oil, produced mainly in the Ibo country, had recently become the most valuable; with the demand of industrial England for a commodity so important in soap manufacture constantly rising, palm-oil was soon to replace slaves as the foundation on which the economy of the delta ports rested. In return for slaves and palm-oil and for a range of other products, timber, ivory, ostrich feathers, a little gold dust, the Niger area received a variety of manufactured goods. Cloth with fanciful trade names, bejutapauts or bandannoes from India, niccanees or cushtaes from Manchester, beads, earthenware—Clapperton came across a toby jug in Kaiama—iron bars, brass basins: these were in demand, though with local variations in taste, from Bonny to Bornu. For rum, as the Landers soon discovered, the ruling men of the coastal states had an insatiable thirst; in the Muslim kingdoms, on the other hand, alcohol was prohibited. But every ruler in the Niger area was anxious to obtain that most valuable of all European products—the fire-arm, a weapon whose possession could decide the destiny of a kingdom.

External trade was in itself dependent on a vigorous internal trade. European goods reaching the interior passed through the hands of many middlemen. But local products were also widely distributed. Cloth manufactured in Kano was sold even in distant Timbuktu. Natron from the desert found a market in Nupe. Kola-nuts, grown in

Ashanti, drew caravans of Hausa merchants to the entrepots in Gonja. The Brass people went inland up the Niger to purchase yams. There was much in the way of local traffic. The roads in Yoruba country were thronged with men and women on trading expeditions. Even the despised Kamberri were able to hold a market that attracted buyers from Yauri, Wawa, and Bussa.

On the life of the people of the Niger area European influence was still, except along the coast, indirect. In the coastal communities the marks of three hundred years of European intercourse could easily be observed: a widespread smattering of English or other European languages, a taste for the gaudier items of European apparel, an occasional preference for a certain European style of architecture, the ability possessed by a select few to read and write English. Away from the coast, as the Landers found, that incredible apparition—a man who was *white*—was to be conceived as a curiosity, a wonder, a magical being. But remote though the worlds of Europe and the Niger might seem from one another, the foundations of a profounder intercourse had already been laid. European traders had drawn the people of West Africa out of their isolation into the orbit of the Atlantic community. The revulsion against the slave-trade was to involve the English ever more deeply in the affairs of the area. British men-of-war cruising the waters of the Bight of Benin on the look-out for Spanish slavers provided the first effective manifestation of English power, even as the settlement in Fernando Po in 1828 marked the first establishment of a British base in the area.

In such a situation, with the Niger area coming to attract the scientific curiosity, the moral concern, and the economic interest of powerful groups in Great Britain, the two young Cornishmen on their mad, heroic journey down the Niger became the agents of history. Their achievement helped to pave the way to the eventual British conquest of this part of Africa. But for revealing, as they did, more clearly than ever before, the connections that could exist between the many indigenous people of the area, the Landers may also be accorded a place, not without honour, among the founders of modern Nigeria.

5. THE TEXT OF THE JOURNAL

The text of the Landers' *Journal* poses one or two problems that demand comment. From the start of the journey both brothers kept a separate journal, which they wrote up each day. In the disaster of the wreck of their canoe at Kirree, Richard lost the whole of his journal, 'with the exception of a note-book with remarks from Rabba to this place', John 'a small part of his journal', with 'memorandum, note and sketch books'. When the brothers came to prepare their journals for publication they were assisted by Lieutenant Becher of the Royal Navy, then working as a hydrographer at the Admiralty. Becher was a man of some literary experience, being the editor of the *Nautical Magazine*. According to the Landers, Becher was entrusted with 'the task of blending our journals into one'.[1]

'The first portion of the Journal,' Becher wrote in his Introduction, 'is from the observations of John Lander—those of Richard between their departure from England and Rabba having been lost. The remainder of it, to the conclusion, is from the journal of Richard Lander, assisted by that of his brother, part of the journal of the latter between Rabba and Kirree having been lost.' 'In preparing the journals for publication,' he explained, 'for the sake of clearness, as well as in pursuance of custom, Richard Lander has been considered as the principal, and the journal of John Lander, while they were separate from each other, is preserved in his own name.'[2] In fact, Becher proved an infuriating editor, whose search for clarity is only the cause of confusion. For except in the three places at Wawa, Kirree, and Brass, where the journal is specifically stated to be John's, it is not easy to tell which of the brothers is writing. Becher, so far as one can understand him, would have liked to have had one 'I' all the way through. This desire for uniformity soon produces difficulties. Most of the early chapters are, from the style, clearly the work of John, but on 18 April there occurs a passage (omitted in this abridgment) obviously written by Richard, since he refers in it to his earlier journey. On 19 April John falls ill, and for the next few days Richard writes the journal, until on 25 April John celebrates his recovery with a characteristically lyrical passage. Yet if Richard wrote the entries for the days when his brother was sick, then Becher must be wrong in stating that the first part of the entire work is from John's journal, unless by chance Richard made certain entries in his brother's journal-book. From Rabba onwards, according to Becher, Richard's journal is the source. Yet at one point in his Introduction, the editor states that 'the narrative is largely indebted to his (John's) observation' and that 'he (John) has enriched the Journal with much interesting and valuable information'.[3]

[1] *Journal*, Vol. I, p. ix.   [2] *Ibid.*, pp. lxii–lxiii.   [3] *Ibid.*, p. lx.

The only way in which it is possible to disentangle John's contributions from Richard's is by noting stylistic differences. Here is a passage that must have been written by Richard:

> Our track was through a narrow creek arched over by mangroves, so as to form a complete avenue, which in many places was so thick as to be totally impenetrable by the light above . . . The smell from decayed vegetable substances was sickly and exceedingly disagreeable.

And here is John's version of the same scene:

> Through those gloomy and dismal passages we travelled during the whole of last night, without stopping, unless for a few minutes at a time, to disengage ourselves from the pendent shoots of the mangrove and spreading brambles, in which we occasionally became entangled. These luxuriant natives of the soil are so intricately woven, that it would be next to impossible to eradicate them. Their roots and branches are the receptables of ooze, mud, and filth of all kinds, exhaling a peculiarly offensive odour, which no doubt possesses highly deleterious qualities.

The contrast is so sharp that it needs little comment. Richard's style is, as one would expect, simple and direct, John's elaborate and consciously literary. But there are many passages where one cannot be absolutely sure which of them is writing. According to the brothers' statement in their brief *Address to the Public*, 'since returning to our native country, we have made no alterations, nor introduced a single sentence in the original manuscript of our travels'.[1] But since the end of their Niger journey and their arrival in England, there was plenty of time for John to work on the Journal. This in fact he did; on 17 June 1831 *The Times* published a letter from John to a brother in Truro, in which he stated: 'Richard's Journal was lost in the Niger, but mine is preserved, which I have been busily engaged in copying during the voyage.' To imply that Richard's journal had been completely lost was somewhat misleading. But it is reasonable to assume that John, who had already experience of putting into literary shape his brother's journal from his expedition with Clapperton, spent a certain amount of time not only correcting the grammar but also polishing the style of his brother's entries. This is as far as it seems possible to take the matter. One day, perhaps, the original journals, which have disappeared without a trace will come to light and a more satisfactory edition be possible. As published in 1832, the Landers' *Journal* ran to about 175,000

[1] *Journal*, I, p. viii.

words. In the present edition it has been abridged to about 100,000 words. To the scholarly student of West African history no abridgment will ever seem satisfactory; but for all other readers there is a good deal to be said for shortening a lengthy work of travel. An abridgment can serve to give a greater pace to the narrative and at the same time to reveal more clearly some of its characteristic qualities. This abridgment has been made with three rules in mind: first, that it is essential to maintain the narrative flow, the sense of movement on a journey; second, that it is important to retain all facts of particular historical importance, for which the Landers serve as the only source; and thirdly, that it is desirable to give in full all the great passages of descriptive writing. The material that has been cut away falls into three categories: passages describing the routine of travelling, wearisome when constantly repeated; sections containing historical information, some of which has been condensed into a footnote, while others have been struck out because the information they contain is available from other sources; and finally—and most regretfully—a few of the incidents and characters met with on the course of the journey.

The Landers' *Journal of an Expedition to Explore the Course and Termination of the Niger* was published in three duodecimo volumes by John Murray in 1832; a second edition appeared the next year, an American edition in 1844, while translations were made into Dutch, French, German, Italian, and Swedish. For more than a century the work has remained out of print, though excerpts have been published in recent anthologies of exploration. So long a period of oblivion seems quite undeserved for a book that is surely one of the most entertaining narratives of travel ever written.

Glossary

Caffa	'A kind of pudding, made into little round balls, from bruised Indian corn, which is first boiled to the consistence of thick paste.'
Calavance	A kind of bean.
Coozie	Round hut.
Falatah	Fulani
Gafflie	Caravan.
Goora nut	Kola nut.
Haussa	Hausa.
Mallam	Muslim teacher.
Tobe	Long Muslim gown, the Hausa *riga*.
Trona	Natron.
Yarriba	Yoruba.

I

Portsmouth to Badagry

WE EMBARKED FROM PORTSMOUTH on the 9th January, 1830, in the brig *Alert*, Tyson master, for Cape Coast Castle, where we arrived on the 22nd of the following month. We should be sadly wanting in gratitude, if we were to omit acknowledging the truly handsome and gentlemanly treatment we experienced from Mr George Maclean, President of the Council at Cape Coast, who had been our fellow passenger in the *Alert*, as well as the merchants resident there, who welcomed us on our arrival.[1] Here we were fortunate enough to engage old Pascoe and his wife, with Jowdie, who had been employed on the last mission, together with Ibrahim and Mina, two Bornou men, who were well acquainted with English manners, and could converse in the Hausa language. These individuals promised to be very useful in the expedition, more especially old Pascoe, whose merits as an interpreter are unquestionable.[2]

[1] Strung out along the Gold Coast were more than twenty European 'forts', fortified posts for European traders. From 1750 to 1821 the British forts, of which Cape Coast Castle was the most important, had been administered by the African Company of Merchants. In 1821 the British Government took over the forts but decided to abandon them completely in 1828. British merchants protested, and a compromise was reached by which the administration of the forts was entrusted to a committee of three merchants nominated by the Government. George Maclean, (1801–1847), a Scotch army officer with previous experience of West Africa, was appointed as first President of the Council of Merchants. In the course of the next fourteen years Maclean was to bring about the remarkable achievement of establishing a British Protectorate over the petty states of the Gold Coast (Metcalfe, 1962).

[2] Pasko or Pascoe was an old hand at African exploration, with a remarkable career behind him. He was a Hausa from Gobir, with a Muslim name, Abubakr, though Lander considered that 'he knew nothing more of Islamism than its name, being in reality a Pagan'. He claimed to be a brother of the ruler of Gobir. During the Fulani wars he had been captured and sold to a merchant from Gonja. After being sold to another trader in Ashanti he came into the hands of a Portuguese slave-dealer at Whydah. The ship, bound

37

After remaining at Cape Coast Castle eight days, we accompanied Mr Maclean on a visit to Mr Hutchinson, Commandant at Anamaboo. Mr Hutchinson lives in his castle like an English baron in the feudal times, untinctured, however, by barbarism or ignorance, for the polished refinements of life have insinuated themselves into his dwelling, though it is entirely surrounded by savages, and though the charming sound of a lady's voice is seldom or never heard in his lonely hall. His silken banners, his turreted castle, his devoted vassals, his hospitality, and even his very solitariness, all conspire to recall to the mind the manners and way of life of an old English baron in one of the most interesting periods of our history, whilst the highly chivalrous and romantic spirit of the gentleman alluded to is strictly in unison with the impression.[1]

We abode at the fort till the 4th March, when we bade adieu to our kind host, and our much-respected friend Mr George Maclean, and embraced the opportunity of sailing in the *Alert* for Accra.

In two days we arrived opposite the British fort at Accra. Here we abode with Mr Fry, the commandant, a whole week. Accra is, without

[1] William Hutchinson had come out to the Gold Coast as a writer in the service of the Company of Merchants. In 1817 he had been a member of the first British mission to Ashanti and spent some months in Kumasi as British consul. He was now an independent merchant. On his position in 1830 see Metcalfe, 1962, p. 75.

for Bahia, in which Pasko was despatched, was caught by a British sloop of war. On being liberated, Pasko agreed to serve with the British as an ordinary seaman. In 1823 he agreed to accompany the Italian explorer, G. B. Belzoni, on his journey to Timbuktu. Belzoni made Benin his starting-point, but died a few weeks after his arrival. Pasko returned to the Navy until 1825, when Clapperton engaged him 'in the joint capacity of servant to Captain Pearce, and general interpreter to the mission'. He accompanied Clapperton to Sokoto, returned with Lander to Badagry, and later sailed with him to England. Pasko's 'thieving propensities' and 'tender regard for the softer sex'—the fellow was a complete Don Juan—caused Lander a great deal of inconvenience; but when Lander was desperately ill at Sokoto, Pasko had paid him the 'utmost attention'. In appearance Pasko was 'no more than five feet in height, with hands and arms disproportionately long'. His features were instantly striking: a huge mouth, set in 'a perpetual grin', to reveal 'large teeth of pearly whiteness'; a nose 'excessively broad and fat'; lips that 'resembled the famous German sausage ornamented'; cheeks furrowed with the eight broad scars of his tribal marks; 'an undefinable expression of low cunning in his dark, wandering eye, and an habitual restlessness in his manner which induced one to suspect that there was more of evil in him than he was willing should be detected, and which he strove to disguise under forced stupidity and carelessness which in reality did not belong to his disposition (Lander, 1830, I, pp. 203–12).

Jowdie was a young slave bought by Lander for seven dollars at Zaria to take the place of a servant whom he had dismissed. Pasko's wife was a slave woman Lander had obtained in Kano. Jowdie and Pasko's wife had been given their freedom on Lander's return to the coast and been given a plot of land at Cape Coast (Clapperton, 1829, p. 305; Lander, 1830, II, pp. 102, 281–2).

Richard Lander.

exception, the pleasantest and most healthy British settlement on the western coast of Africa. His Majesty's brig *Clinker* arrived the day before us.

On the 15th we embarked on board the *Clinker*, Lieutenant Matson commander, and having sailed direct for Badagry, we dropped anchor in the roadstead in front of that town on the 19th. My brother landed and was introduced to the chief by Mr Brown, master of the brig, on the following day, and everything having been arranged to our satisfaction, the luggage was safely landed on the 21st.[1]

From Lieutenant Matson we received a young man of colour named Antonio, son to the chief of Bonny, who eagerly embraced the opportunity of proceeding with us into the interior, being impressed with

[1] The log of H.M.S. *Clinker* is preserved in the Public Record Office: Adm 51/3130. On 22 March 'the King of Badagry was saluted with seven guns, his son being on board'.

the notion that he should be enabled to reach his home and country by means of the Great River, or Niger.

March 22nd.—Cheered by six hearty huzzas, good-naturedly given us by the crew of the *Clinker*, at the desire of her gallant commander, we sailed towards the beach in the earlier part of the afternoon, and having been taken into a canoe that was waiting at the edge of the breakers to receive us, we were plyed over a tremendous surf, and flung with violence on the burning sands.

Wet and uncomfortable as this accident had rendered us, we had no change of linen at hand, and we walked to a small creek about the distance of a quarter of a mile from the sea-shore, where we were taken into a native canoe, and conveyed safely through an extremely narrow channel, over-hung with luxuriant vegetation, into the Badagry river, which is a branch of the Lagos. It is a beautiful body of water, resembling a lake in miniature; its surface is smooth and transparent as glass, and its picturesque banks are shaded by trees of a lively verdure. We were soon landed on the opposite side, when our road lay over a magnificent plain, on which deer, antelopes and buffaloes are often observed to feed. Numbers of men, women, and children followed us to the town of Badagry, and they made the most terrific noises at our heels, but whether these were symptoms of satisfaction or displeasure, admiration or ridicule, we could not at first understand. We were soon, however, satisfied that the latter feeling was predominant; and indeed our clothing was exceedingly grotesque, consisting of a straw hat, larger than an umbrella, a scarlet Mohammedan tobe or tunic and belt, with boots and full Turkish trowsers. So unusual a dress might well cause the people to laugh heartily; they were all evidently highly amused, but the more modest of the females, unwilling to give us any uneasiness, turned aside to conceal the titter, from which they were utterly unable to refrain.

On our way we observed various groups of people seated under the spreading branches of superb trees, vending provisions and country cloth; and on our approach many of these arose and bowed, whilst others fell on their knees before us in token of respect. We reached the dwelling which had been prepared for us about three o'clock in the afternoon, but as the day was too far advanced to visit the chief or king, we sent a messenger to inform him of our intention of paying him our respects tomorrow morning.

March 23rd.—At nine o'clock this morning, we visited the chief at his residence. On our entrance he was sitting on a couple of boxes, in a small bamboo apartment, from whose sides were suspended a great quantity of muskets and swords, with a few paltry umbrellas, and a couple of horses' tails, which are used for the purpose of brushing away flies. King Adooley looked up in our faces without making any observation, and did not rise from his seat to congratulate us on our arrival. He appeared in deep reflection, and thoughtfully rested his elbow on an old wooden table, pillowing his head on his hand. One of the most venerable and ancient of his subjects was squatted at the feet of his master, smoking from a pipe of extraordinary length; whilst Lantern, his eldest son and heir apparent, was kneeling at his side, etiquette not allowing the youth to sit in the presence of his father. Everything bore an air of gloom and sadness totally different from what we had been led to expect. We shook hands, but the pressure of the chief was so very faint that it was scarcely perceptible; yet, notwithstanding this apparent coldness, we seated ourselves, one on each side, without ceremony or embarrassment. The conversation was commenced on our part by inquiring after the chief's health, which was answered only by a languid smile, and he again relapsed into his former thoughtfulness. We then displayed to the greatest advantage the presents we had brought for him from England; they were accepted, it is true, but without the slightest demonstration of pleasure or satisfaction; they were scarcely looked at, and were carried away by his attendants with real or seeming indifference. This was very mortifying, but we said not a word, though it was the easiest thing imaginable to perceive that all was not right. A reserve, the cause whereof we could not define, and a coldness towards us for which we could in no wise account, marked the conduct of the once spirited and good-natured chief of Badagry, and prepared us to anticipate various difficulties in the prosecution of our plans, which we are persuaded will require much art and influence to surmount. Adooley left us abruptly in the midst of the conversation, and did not return for some time.

Wearied at length with his long delay, we despatched a messenger to acquaint him that we were becoming impatient. On receiving this message the chief hastened back, and entered the apartment with a melancholy countenance, which was partially concealed behind large volumes of smoke from a tobacco-pipe which he was using. He seated himself between us as before, and gave us to understand in a very low tone of voice, that he was but just recovering from a severe illness, and from the effects of a variety of misfortunes, which had rendered him almost broken-hearted. His generals, Bombanee and Poser, and all his most able warriors, had either been slain in battle, or fallen by other violent means. The former in particular, whose loss he more particularly lamented, had been captured by the Lagos people, who were his most inveterate enemies. When this unfortunate man was taken prisoner, his right hand was immediately nailed to his head, and the other lopped off like a twig. In this manner he was paraded through the town, and exposed to the view of the people, whose curiosity being satiated, Bombanee's head was at length severed from his shoulders, and being dried in the sun and beat to dust, was sent in triumph to the Chief of Badagry. To add to his calamities, Adooley's house, which contained an immense quantity of gunpowder, had been blown up by accident, and destroyed all his property, consisting of a variety of presents, most of them very valuable, that had been made him by Captain Clapperton, and by European merchants and traders in slaves. The chief and his women escaped with difficulty from the conflagration; but as it was the custom to keep the muskets and other fire-arms constantly loaded, their contents were discharged into the bodies and legs of those individuals that had flocked to the spot on the first alarm. The flames spread with astonishing rapidity, notwithstanding every exertion, and ended in the destruction of a great part of the town. This accounted in some measure for the sad and grievous expression so strongly depicted on the chief's countenance, but still another and more powerful reason had doubtless influenced him on this occasion.[1]

On returning to our residence, a number of 'principal men', as they style themselves, were introduced, to compliment us on coming to their country, although their true and only motive for visiting our quarters was the expectation of obtaining rum, which is the great object of attraction to all of them. We have been annoyed during the

[1] Badagri, as the name is now spelt, developed as a commercial centre of importance in the slave-trade during the first half of the eighteenth century. Its population came partly from Dahomey, partly from Yoruba lands (Newbury, 1961, pp. 30-2). According to the Landers, whose account of Badagri history may briefly be summarized, the town was tributary to Lagos, even as Lagos was tributary to Benin. Adooley was the younger brother of the chief of Lagos. After his father's death he had quarrelled with his brother over the succession, been defeated and left Lagos, accompanied by many of his followers. On his arrival at Badagri, he had been invited to become chief of the town. In 1829 the death of his brother, the ruler of Lagos, had led Adooley to make an attack on the town. It was in the course of this campaign that he lost his two generals, Bombanee and Poser. In 1832 Adooley or Adele, as he was known in Lagos, succeeded in returning to Lagos and gaining the paramount title of *Ologun*. He died in 1834 (Newbury, 1961, p. 46).

better part of this day by a tribe of ragged beggars, whose importunity is really disgusting; and the number of old fat-headed and pot-bellied men, and skinny, flap-eared women of the last century, has been immense. To these garrulous ladies and gentlemen have we been obliged to laugh and talk, and shake hands, and crack fingers, and bend our bodies and bow our heads, and place our hands with solemnity on our hands and breasts; make presents, and cringe, fawn, and flatter up to the present moment, which is past bed-time.

Had Job, amongst his other trials, been exposed to the horrors of an interminable African *palaver*, his patience must have forsaken him. For my own part, I am of opinion that I shall never be a general favourite with this ever-grinning and loquacious people. If I laugh, and laugh I most certainly must, it is done against my inclination, and consequently with a very bad grace. For the first five years of my life, I have been told that I was never seen to smile, and since that period, Heaven knows, my merriment has been confined to particular and extraordinary occasions only. How then is it possible that I can be grinning and playing the fool from morning to night, positively without any just incentive to do so, and sweltering under a sun that causes my body to burn with intense heat, giving it the appearance of shrivelled parchment? Fortunately, these savages, for savages they most certainly are in the fullest extent of the word, cannot distinguish between real and fictitious joy; and although I was vexed at heart, and wished them all at the bottom of the Red Sea, or somewhere else, I have every reason to believe that my forced attempts to please the natives have so far been successful; and I have obtained the reputation, which I certainly do not deserve, of being one of the pleasantest and best tempered persons in the world.

March 24th.—One of the chief's messengers, who is a Haussa Mallam, or priest, presented himself at the door of our house this morning, followed by a large and handsome spotted sheep from his native country, whose neck was adorned with little bells, which make a pretty jingling noise. We were much prepossessed in this man's favour by the calmness and serenity of his countenance, and the modesty, or rather timidity of his manners. He was dressed in the Haussa costume, viz., cap, tobe, trousers, and sandals. He wore four large silver rings on his thumb, and his left wrist was ornamented with a solid silver bracelet. This is the only individual that has yet visited us purely with disinterested motives, as all the others make it a practice to beg

43

whenever they favour us with their company. But the Mallam is a Mussulman, and it is the fast of Rhamadan.[1]

A Falatah residing in the town has agreed to supply us with cow's milk every morning, as long as we may have occasion to remain; he is likewise a Mohammedan.

The chief's eldest son has been with us the greatest part of today. The manners of the young man are reserved, but respectful; he is a great admirer of the English, and has obtained a smattering of their language. Although his appearance is extremely boyish, he has already three wives, and is the father of two children. His front teeth are filed to a point after the manner of the Lagos people, but notwithstanding this disadvantage, his features bear less marks of ferocity than we have observed in the countenance of any one of his countrymen. When asked, whether if it were in his power to do so, he would injure us two, or any European that might hereafter visit Badagry, he made no reply, but silently approached our seat, and falling on his knees at our feet, he pressed me with eagerness to his soft naked bosom, and affectionately kissed my hand.

We have heard today that peace has been established between Porto Novo[2] and Badagry. This distracted country is ever at war with her neighbours, and consequently is always in a state of agitation and poverty.

Since our conference with the chief on Tuesday we have learned with surprise and sorrow, that a party of the populace have expressed themselves decidedly hostile to our projects, and that its leaders are continually with Adooley. They endeavour to persuade him to demand, ere he grants us leave to pass through his country, a sum of money, which they are all aware it is not in our power to pay, and therefore, they imagine we shall be compelled to abandon the undertaking. The first intimation we received of the effect of these insinuations on the mind of the chief was brought us this morning by one who pronounces himself to be on 'our side'. This man assured us with an ominous visage, that Adooley had declared in the hearing of all

[1] The Landers leant that a great number of Hausa mallams, who had been the slaves of Adooley's father, had accompanied Adooley, when he left Lagos. 'These men, though slaves to Adooley, are very respectable, and are never called on by their master except when required to go to war, supporting themselves by trading for slaves which they sell to Europeans.'

[2] At this time Porto Novo or Ardrah, whose people, the Gun, were independent of their powerful neighbour, the kingdom of Dahomey, was one of the most important ports on the Slave Coast. It lay about thirty miles west of Badagri.

the people, that the coat we had given him was intended for a boy, and not a man; it was therefore unworthy his acceptance as a king, and he considered that we meant to insult him. The coat alluded to is indeed extremely old-fashioned, and belonged to a surgeon in the navy about twenty years ago, notwithstanding which it is now almost as good as new, and was made very showy by the addition of a pair of tarnished gold epaulets. Nothing was so gladly received as this very coat two days ago. To counteract the effects of the malicious, we have been unusually busy today in sounding the dispositions of those, who, we are inclined to believe, from the fondness they evince for our rum, are favourable to our intentions.[1]

Two mulattoes reside in the town, one of whom, by name Hooper, acts as interpreter to Adooley, and shares a good deal of his confidence. He was born at Cape Coast Castle in 1780, and was for many years a soldier in the African corps. His father was an Englishman, and he boasts of being a British subject. He is excessively vain of his origin; yet he is the most confirmed drunkard alive, always getting intoxicated before breakfast, and remaining in a soaking state all day long. This does not, however, make him regardless of his personal interests, to which, on the contrary, he is ever alive. The other mulatto can read and write English tolerably well, having received his education at Sierra Leone; he is a slave to Adooley, and is almost as bad as Hooper as to drinking.[2] These political advisers of the chief we have had little difficulty in bribing over to our interests: we have likewise been tampering with several native chiefs, apparently with equal success. Unfortunately, every one styles himself a great and powerful man, and old Hooper himself calls a host of ragged scoundrels, 'noblemen and gentlemen'. Each of these he advises and conjures us to conciliate with presents, and especially spirituous liquors. There is hardly any knowing who is monarch here, or even what form of

[1] Richard Lander already possessed bitter experience of the hostility of certain of the inhabitants of Badagry. In 1827, on his return from Sokoto, he had been accused of plotting against the king and forced to submit to the ordeal by poison. He believed that this false accusation had its origin in the calumnies of the Portuguese slave-traders who frequented the town. Certainly anyone actively engaged in the slave trade had no cause to welcome the representative of a nation whose warships were constantly patrolling the coast in the search for slave-ships. The people of Badagry had another cause for distrusting the Landers' presence; as traders they were middlemen, much of the trade with Oyo passing through their hands. Should the English succeed in establishing a direct trade with Oyo, their economy would be threatened with ruin.

[2] This mulatto, whose name was probably Sam, was allowed by Adooley to accompany the Landers into the interior. His character and early life the Landers described later in their *Journal* (p. 160).

government prevails. Besides the king of kings himself, the redoubtable Adooley, four fellows assume the title of royalty; namely, the kings of Spanish Town, of Portuguese Town, or English Town, and of French Town—Badagry being divided into four districts, bearing the names of the European nations just mentioned. This evening we received an invitation from the former of these chieftains. He now lives in retirement, and subsists by purchasing slaves and reselling them to Spanish and Portuguese traders. In him we found a meek and venerable old man, of respectable appearance. A table was brought out into the court before the house, whereon decanters, and glasses, with a burning liquor obtained from the Portuguese, were placed. In one corner of the yard was a little hut, not more than two feet in height, wherein had been placed a fetish figure, to preserve the chief from any danger or mischief, which our presence might otherwise have entailed upon him. A portion of the spirit was poured into one of the glasses, and from it emptied into each of the others, and then drunk by the attendant that had fetched it from the house. This is an old custom, introduced, no doubt, to prevent masters from being poisoned by the treachery of their slaves. As soon as the decanters had been emptied of their contents, other ardent spirits were produced; but as my brother imagined that fetish-water had been mingled with it, we simply took about a tea-spoonful into our mouths, and privately ejected it on the ground.

We are most anxious to proceed on our journey, but the chief Adooley evades our solicitations to depart under the most frivolous and absurd pretences. Meantime the rainy season is fast approaching; and what makes us still more desirous to leave this abominable place, is the fact that a sacrifice of no less than three hundred human beings, of both sexes and all ages, is shortly to take place.

March 25th.—We had not finished breakfast this morning before Hooper introduced himself for his accustomed glass of spirits, to prevent him, according to his own account, from getting sick. He took the opportunity of informing us, that it would be absolutely necessary to visit the 'noblemen' that had declared themselves 'on our side'. We went in the first place to the house of the late *General* Poser, which is at present under the superintendance of his head man. Him we found squatting indolently on a mat, and several old people were holding a conversation with him. As the death of Poser is not generally known to the people, it being concealed from them for fear of exciting a commotion in the town, for he was universally loved and respected, we were not permitted even to mention his name, and the steward set us the example by prudently confining his conversation to the necessity of making him a present proportionable to his expectations. Gin and water were produced, and partaken of with avidity by all present, which being done, the head-man wished the 'Great Spirit' to prosper us in all our undertakings, and told us not to forget his present by any means. We resolved to pay our respects to Adooley, whom we had not seen for two days.

The chief was eating an undrest onion, and seated on an old table, dangling his legs underneath it with a vacant thoughtlessness of manner. He was full of good nature and promised to make my brother a present of a horse, which he had brought with him from Soccatoo on the former expedition; he added that he would sell another to me; and that he most particularly wished to examine the goods we intended taking with us into the 'bush', in order that he might satisfy himself we had nothing objectionable amongst them. During this palaver, the chief's sister and two of his wives were ogling at us, until the approach of the chief of English town and the rest of our party put a sudden stop to their entertainment. These men came to settle a domestic quarrel, which was soon decided by the chief, who, after receiving the usual salutation of dropping on the knees with the face to the earth, chatted and laughed immoderately. This was considered by us as a happy omen. Very little ceremony is observed by the meanest of the people toward their sovereign. They converse with him with as little reserve as if he were no better than themselves, while he pays as much attention to their complaints as to those of the principal people of the country.

This afternoon a herald proclaimed the approach to our habitation of the venerable chief of Spanish Town, with a long suite of thirsty followers. The old man's dress was very simple, consisting only of a cap and turban, with a large piece of Manchester cotton flung over his right shoulder, and held under his left arm. This is infinitely more graceful and becoming in the natives, than the most showy European apparel, in any variety of which, indeed, they generally look highly ridiculous. After we had made him and all his attendants nearly tipsy, the old chief began to be very talkative and amusing, not omitting to whisper occasionally to the interpreter by no means to forget, after his departure, reminding us of the present we had promised him. Our rum had operated so cheerily upon his followers in the yard, that fat and lean, old and young, commenced dancing, and continued performing the most laughable antics, till they were no longer able to stand. It amused us infinitely to observe these creatures, with their old solemn, placid-looking chief at their head, staggering out of the doorway; we were in truth but too happy to get rid of them at so cheap a rate.

Late in the evening we received the threatened visit from Adooley, who came to examine the contents of our boxes. He was borne in a hammock by two men, and was dressed in an English linen shirt, a Spanish cloak or mantle, with a cap, turban, and sandals. His attendants were three half-dressed little boys. One of them carried a long sword, another a pistol, and a third a kind of knapsack, filled with tobacco. We presented the chief with brandy; and he swallowed a large quantity of it with exquisite pleasure. The boys were permitted to drink a portion of the liquor every time that it was poured into a glass for Adooley; but though it was so very strong, it produced no grimace in these little fellows. The fondness of the natives, or rather their passion for strong waters, is astonishing, and they are valued entirely in proportion to the intoxicating effects they occasion. Adooley smoked nearly all the while he remained in our house. As each box was opened, however, he would take the pipe slowly from his mouth, as if perfectly heedless of what was going forward; and from the couch whereon he was reclining, regard with intense curiosity each article as it was held out to his observation. Everything that in his opinion demanded a closer examination, or more properly speaking, everything he took a fancy to, was put into his hands at his own request; but as it would be grossly impolite to return it after it had been soiled by his fingers, with the utmost *nonchalance* the chief delivered it over to the care of his recumbent pages, who carefully secured it between their legs. Adooley's good taste could not of course be questioned; and it did not much surprise, though it grieved us, to observe a large portion of almost every article in the boxes speedily passing through his hands into those of his juvenile minions. Nothing seemed unworthy of his acceptance, from fine scarlet cloth to a child's farthing whistle; in fact he requested a couple of these little instruments to amuse himself with in retirement! And although he has received guns, ammunition, and a variety of goods to the amount of nearly three hundred ounces of gold, he is so far from being satisfied that he is continually grumbling forth his discontent. Gratitude is unknown both to him and his subjects; the more one gives them, the more pressing are their importunities for other favours.[1]

[1] In addition to the presents made on their own behalf, the Landers found themselves obliged to meet a debt of one hundred ounces of gold, which Clapperton was said to have incurred in 1826 (C.O. 2/18. Lander to Maclean, copied to Hay, 21 March 1830).

March 26th.—Our rum, which had been kindly supplied us by Lieutenant Matson, we are happy to say, is now nearly all consumed, and the number of our general visitors has diminished in exact proportion to its decrease; so that we are beginning to feel the enjoyment of an hour or two's quiet in the course of the day, which is a luxury we could hardly have anticipated.

This evening Poser's head man, who we understand is one of the Chief's first captains, returned our visit of yesterday, followed by a multitude of friends and retainers. This great bully introduced himself into our dwelling—his huge round face inflamed with scorn, anger and 'potations deep'. He drank with even more avidity than his countrymen, but the liquor produced no good impression on him, serving rather to increase his dissatisfaction and choler. He begged everything he saw—and when we had gratified him to the best of our power, he began to be very abusive and noisy. He said he was convinced we had come into the country with no good intentions, and accused us of deceit and insincerity in our professions; or in plainer terms that we had been guilty of a direct falsehood in stating that we had no other motive for undertaking the journey than to recover the papers of Mr Park at Yaoorie. He was assured that we were afraid to tell the true reasons for leaving our own country. We withstood his invectives with tolerable composure, and the disgraceful old fellow left us in a pet about half an hour after his arrival.

It is really a discouraging reflection that notwithstanding the sacrifices we have made for the purpose of conciliating the good opinion of the people here, still some scoundrels are to be found hardened against us by hatred and prejudice. Pitiable, indeed, must the lot of that man be, who is obliged to drag on a year of existence in so miserable a place as this. Nevertheless we are in health and spirits, and perhaps feel a secret pride in being able to subdue our rising dissatisfaction, and in overcoming difficulties which at first glance seemed insurmountable. By the blessing of Heaven we shall proceed prosperously in our undertaking, for in the Divine goodness do we alone repose all our confidence and hopes of success. We may say that pleasure and enjoyment have accompanied us hither. The clearness of the sky is pleasant, and its brilliancy—the softness of the moon—the twinkling brightness of the stars, and the silence of the night—the warbling and the flight of birds, the hum of insects, and the varied and luxuriant aspect of beautiful Nature, are all charming to us. And what on earth can be more soothing or delightful than thoughts of home and kindred, and anticipations of a holier and more glorious existence? These are true pleasures of which the barbarians cannot deprive us.

Today the fast of the Rhamadan ends; and tomorrow will be held as a holiday by the Mohammedans of the place.[1]

Saturday, March 27th.—The noise and jargon of our guests pursue us even in sleep, and our dreams are disturbed by fancied palavers. Early this morning we were roused from one of these painful slumbers, to listen to the dismal yell of the hyena, the shrill crowing of cocks, the hum of night-flies and mosquitoes, and the hoarse croaking of frogs, together with the chirping of myriads of crickets and other insects, which resounded through the air as though it had been pierced with a thousand whistles.

Just after sunrise, two Mohammedans arrived at our house with an invitation for us to accompany them to the spot selected for the performance of their religious rites and observances. Here we observed a number of their countrymen sitting in detached groups, actively employed in the duties of lustration and ablution. It was a bare space of ground, edged with trees, and covered with sand. Groups of people were continually arriving at the spot, and these were welcomed to it by an occasional flourish of music from a native clarionet, etc. They were clad in all their finery, their apparel being as gaudy as it was various. Loose tobes, with caps and turbans, striped and plain, red, blue, and black, were not unpleasingly contrasted with the original native costume of figured cotton, thrown loosely over the shoulders, and immense rush hats. Manchester cloths, of the most glaring patterns, were conspicuous amongst the crowd; but these were cast in the shade by scarfs of green silk, ornamented with leaves and flowers of gold, and aprons covered with silver spangles. Very young children appeared bending under the weight of clothes and ornaments; whilst boys of maturer years carried a variety of offensive weapons. The Turkish scimitar, the French sabre, the Portuguese dagger, confined in a silver case, all gleamed brightly; and heavy cutlasses, with rude native knives, were likewise exhibited, half devoured by cankering rust.

[1] The festival that marks the appearance of the new moon that ends the month of fasting, Arabic *id al-fitr*, Hausa *salla*, is still commemorated by Muslims throughout West Africa in the same way as the Landers described the ceremony at Badagri. The appearance of the new moon 'is greeted with bursts of firing, beating of drums, and general rejoicing. About eight o'clock in the morning the festival prayer is held at a special praying-place outside the town where the men assemble by quarters. . . . Strict clergy disapprove of the drumming and dancing that goes on throughout the night' (Trimingham, 1959, p. 79).

Clumsy muskets and fowling-pieces, as well as Arab pistols, were also handled with delight by the joyful Mussulmen. In number the religionists were about a hundred and fifty. Not long after our arrival, they formed themselves into six lines, and having laid aside many of their superfluous ornaments, and a portion of their clothing, they put on the most sedate countenances, and commenced their devotional exercises in a spirit of seriousness and apparent fervor, worthy a better place and a more amiable creed. In the exterior forms of their religion, at least, the Mussulmen here are complete adepts; and the little we have seen of them has led us to form a very favourable opinion of their general temperance and sobriety. The ceremony was no sooner concluded, than muskets, carbines, and pistols were discharged on all sides; the clarionet again struck up a note of joy, and was supported by long Arab drums, strings of bells, and a solitary kettle-drum. All seemed cheerful and happy; and on leaving them, several, out of compliment I suppose, discharged their pieces at our heels; and were evidently delighted with themselves, with us, and the whole world. In the path we met a fellow approaching the scene of innocent dissipation, clothed most fantastically in a flannel dress, and riding on the back of what we were informed was a wooden horse. The figure itself was entirely concealed with cloth, which rendered it impossible to discover by what agency it moved. Some years ago, I saw a monster something similar to it with a company of mountebanks in a town in the west of England, which, amongst its other properties, used to swallow children. As soon as this party had joined the individuals assembled near the place of worship, a startling shriek of laughter testified the tumultuous joy of the wondering multitude. The sun shone out resplendently on the happy groups of fancifully-dressed persons, whose showy, various-coloured garments, and sooty skin, contrasted with the picturesque and lovely appearance of the scenery, produced an unspeakably charming effect. The foliage exhibited every variety and tint of green, from the sombre shade of the melancholy yew to the lively verdure of the poplar and young oak. For myself, I was delighted with the agreeable ramble; and imagined that I could distinguish from the notes of the songsters of the grove, the swelling strains of the English skylark and thrush, with the more gentle warbling of the finch and linnet. It was indeed a brilliant morning, teeming with life and beauty; and recalled to my memory a thousand affecting associations of sanguine boyhood, when I was thoughtless and happy. The barbarians around me were all cheerful and full of joy. I have heard that, like sorrow, joy is contagious, and I believe that it is, for it inspired me with a similar gentle feeling.

The 27th of March in this place is what May-day is in many country places in England, and it strongly reminded us of it. But here unfortunately there are no white faces to enliven us; and a want of the lovely complexion of our beautiful country-women, tinged with its 'celestial red', is severely felt; and so is the total absence here of that golden chain of kindness which links them to the ruder associates of their festive enjoyments. By and bye, doubtless, familiarity with black faces will reconcile me to them; but at present I am compelled to own that I cannot help feeling a very considerable share of aversion towards their jetty complexions, in common, I believe, with most strangers that visit this place.

Sunday, March 28th.—Luckily the inhabitants of this place consider this as a holiday; and their singing, dancing, and savage jollity have possessed greater charms for them than an empty rum cask, though it be backed by two white faces. This happy circumstance has afforded us opportunity and ample leisure for spending the Sabbath in a manner most agreeable to our feelings—by devoting the greater part of it to the impressive duties of our Divine religion.

Monday, March 29th.—The chief summoned us yesterday to settle the business relative to our journey into the interior, but we refused to have any disputes with him on the Sabbath, and promised to wait on him this morning instead. After breakfast, therefore, we redeemed our pledge, by paying him the promised visit. Adooley received us with his accustomed politeness and a gracious smile. He said he wished to inform us of his intention of detaining us at Badagry a day or two longer, the 'path' not being considered in a fit state for travelling. Now we well knew that the country was never in a more peaceable state than at the moment he was speaking; and are mortified beyond measure at the perpetual evasions and contradictions of this chief. When Adooley had made this declaration, he requested us to write on a paper in his presence for a few things which he wished to procure either from Cape Coast Castle, or from England, as a return for the protection he had promised us. Amongst other articles enumerated, are 'four regimental coats, such as are worn by the King of England, for himself, and forty less splendid than these, for the use of his captains; two long brass guns, to run on swivels; fifty muskets, twenty barrels of gunpowder, four handsome swords, and forty cutlasses'; to which are added, 'two puncheons of rum, a carpenter's chest of tools, with oils, paints and brushes', the chief himself boasting that he was a blacksmith, carpenter, painter, and indeed every trade but a tailor. Besides these trifles he wished to obtain a half-dozen rockets, and a rocket gun, with a soldier from Cape Coast, capable of undertaking the management of it. We asked, jocosely, whether Adooley would be satisfied with these various articles, when, having considered for a few moments, and conversed aloud to a few of his chiefs that were in the apartment at the time, he replied that he had forgotten to mention his want of a large umbrella, four casks of grape shot, and a barrel of flints, which having also inserted in the list, the letter was finally folded and sealed. It was then delivered into the hands of Adooley, who said that he should send it by Accra, one of his head men, to Cape Coast Castle, and that the man would wait there till all the articles should be procured for him. If that be the case, we imagine that Accra will have a very long time to wait.

During this long and serious conversation, we were occasionally enlivened by the music of three little bells, which were fastened to the tails of the same number of cats by a long string, and made a jingling noise whenever the animals thought proper to divert themselves. As an accompaniment to them, we were favoured with the strains of an organ, which instrument a little boy was placed in a corner of the apartment purposely to turn.

Tuesday, March 30th.—The pleasantest news we hear, is the fact of the king of Jenna having arrived at that town from Katunga. His messenger arrived here this morning, and came to see us in the afternoon. The chief sent for us again this afternoon, and summed up the measure of his exorbitant demands by requesting a gun-boat, with a hundred men from England, and a few common tobacco-pipes for his own private use. We could easily give a bill for the former; but the latter we dared not part with at any risk, because, considering the long journey before us, we are convinced we have nothing to spare; indeed it is our opinion that the presents will all be exhausted long before it be completed. We were most agreeably surprised by an assurance from the chief that we shall quit this place tomorrow afternoon with the newly-arrived Jenna messenger.

The soil of Badagry consists of a layer of fine whitish sand over loam, clay and earth. The sand is so soft and deep, that no one can walk on it without considerable labour and difficulty. The natives procure the necessaries of life chiefly by fishing, and the cultivation of the yam and Indian corn. In the former employment they use nets and spears, and likewise earthen pots, which they bait with the palm nut. Oranges, limes, cocoa-nuts, plantains, and bananas, are produced in abundance in the neighbourhood. The better sort of people are possessed of a small kind of bullock, with sheep, goats, and poultry; the chief himself is a driver and butcher, and when in want of money, he orders one of his bullocks to be slaughtered and publicly sold in the market. The dwellings of the inhabitants are neatly constructed of bamboo, and thatched with palm leaves. They contain several apartments, all of them on the ground floor. Some of the houses or huts are built in the coozie form, which is nearly round, and others are in the form of an oblong square; all have excellent yards attached to them, wherein lime-trees and others are planted in rows, and it gives one a pleasure to look at the cleanliness and taste which prevail in these courts. The land is excessively fertile; and if the inhabitants could only be induced to lay aside their habitual indolence, and the sluggishness of their characters, and devote a little more attention to the improvement of the soil, the country might soon be brought to an extraordinary pitch of perfection.

By some means many of the inhabitants have picked up a number of English words, which school-boys and children at home would style 'very naughty'; and these are made use of at all times without any particular meaning being attached to them. We have observed one virtue in the younger branches of the community—it is the profound respect and reverence which they entertain for their elders, and which has perhaps never been surpassed in any age or country, not even amongst the ancient Spartans themselves.

During our stay at Badagry, the thermometer of Fahrenheit has ranged between 86° and 94° in our hut, being oftener stationary nearer the latter than the former.

II

Badagry to Jenna

March 31st.—We bade adieu to the Chief of Badagry this morning, and repaired to the banks of the river at sun-set, expecting to find a canoe which Adooley had promised should be sent there for our use; but having waited above two hours, and finding it did not arrive, we placed the goods in two smaller canoes, which were lying on the beach. These soon proved to be leaky, and as no other resource was at hand, we were fain to wait as patiently as we could for the canoe promised us. In two hours more Hooper made his appearance in Adooley's war canoe, which he had prevailed on him to lend us. It was between ten and eleven o'clock at night when we were fairly launched out into the body of the river. The canoe was above forty feet in length; it was propelled through the water by poles instead of paddles, and moved slowly and silently along. It was a clear and lovely night; the moon shone glorious 'as a silver shield'; and reflecting the starry firmament on the unruffled surface of the water, the real concave of heaven, with its reflection, seemed to form a perfect world. The scenery on the borders of the river appeared wild and striking, though not magnificent. In the delicious moonshine it was far from uninteresting. The banks were low, and partially covered with stunted trees; but a slave factory and a fetish hut were the only buildings we observed on them.

We saw several small islands, covered with rank grass. They are inhabited by myriads of frogs, whose noise is more hoarse and stunning than ever proceeded from any rookery in Christendom. As we went up the river, our canoe-men spoke to their priests, who were invisible to us, in a most sepulchral tone of voice, and were answered in the same unearthly and doleful manner. These sounds formed our night's serenade.

E

April 1st.—At six a.m. we found ourselves still on the river, and our canoe gliding almost imperceptibly along. From half a mile in width, the river had narrowed to about twenty paces; marine plants nearly covered its surface, and marsh miasma, loaded with other vapours of the most deleterious quality, ascended from its borders like a thick cloud. Its smell was peculiarly offensive. An hour after we arrived at the extremity of the river, into which flowed a stream of clear water. Here our canoe was dragged over a morass into a deep but narrow rivulet. Shortly afterwards we found it to widen a little; the marine plants and shrubs disappeared altogether; and the boughs of beautiful trees shadowed us in their stead, forming an arch-like canopy impervious to the sun's rays. The river and this lesser stream abound with alligators and hippopotami; and wild ducks, and a variety of other aquatic birds, resort to them in considerable quantities. Monkeys and parrots inhabit the branches of the trees, and make an abominable chattering and noise between them all the day long. We landed in the sight of a great multitude.

Passing through a place where a large fair or market is held, we entered an extensive and romantic town called *Wow.* The major part of the inhabitants had never before had an opportunity of seeing white men, so that their curiosity was excessive. Two of the principal persons came out to meet us, preceded by men bearing large silk umbrellas, and another playing a horn, which produced such terrible sounds, that we gladly took refuge in the chief's house. After a formal and most ceremonious introduction, we were liberally regaled with water from a calabash, which is a compliment the natives pay to all strangers, and then shown into a very small apartment. Here my brother endeavoured to procure a little sleep, having remained awake last night; but we were so annoyed by perpetual interruptions and intrusions, the firing of muskets, the garrulity of women, the unceasing squall of children, the drunken petitions of men and boys; and a laugh (but it is quite out of my power to describe it—one that approximates more to the nature of a horse-laugh, than anything I know)—so that it was found impossible to close one's eyes.

The market of this place is supplied abundantly with Indian corn, palm oil, etc; together with *tron,* and other articles brought hither from the borders of the desert of Zaarha, through the medium of the wandering Arabs. By the regulations of the fetish, neither a white man nor a horse is permitted to sleep at Wow during the night season.

A Merry-Andrew at a country town in England never excited so

John Lander.

great a stir, as did our departure from Wow this afternoon. But it is 'fool's day', and some allowance ought to be made for that, no doubt. We had not proceeded more than a dozen paces from the outskirts of the town, when we were visited by a pelting shower, which wetted us to the skin in a moment. A gutter or hollow, misnamed a pathway, was soon overflowed; and we had to wade in it up to our knees in water, and through a most melancholy-looking forest, before we entered a village. The chief came out to welcome us and immediately introduced us into a long narrow apartment, built of clay, and furnished with two apertures to admit light and air into the room. One end of it was occupied with a number of noisy goats, whilst we took possession of the other. The walls of our apartment are ornamented with strings of dry, rattling human bones, written charms, or fetishes, sheep-skins, and bows and arrows. We did not repose near so comfortably as could have been desired, owing to the swarms of mosquitoes and black ants, which treated us very despitefully till morning.

April 2nd.—We continued our route through woods, and large open patches of ground, and arrived at the borders of a deep glen, more wild, romantic, and picturesque, than can be conceived. It is enclosed and overhung on all sides by trees of amazing height and dimensions, which hid it in deep shadow. Fancy might picture a spot, so silent and solemn as this, as the abode of genii and fairies; everything conducing to render it grand, melancholy, and venerable; and the glen only wants an old dilapidated castle, a rock with a cave in it, or something of the kind, to render it the most interesting place in the universe. There was one beautiful sight, however, which we would not omit mentioning for the world; it was that of an incredible number of butterflies, fluttering about us like a swarm of bees; they had chosen this, no doubt, as a place of refuge against the fury of the elements. They were variegated by the most brilliant tints and colourings imaginable—the wings of some were of a shining green, edged and sprinkled with gold; others were of sky-blue and silver; others of purple and gold delightfully blending into each other; and the wings of some were like dark silk velvet, trimmed and braided with lace.

To revert from insects to men: our followers formed a group at once savage and imposing. As they winded down the paths of the glen, with their grotesque clothing and arms, bundles, and fierce black countenances, they might be mistaken for a strange band of ruffians, of the most fearful character. Besides our own, we had hired twenty men of Adooley to carry the luggage. Being all assembled at the bottom of the glen, we found that a long and dangerous bog or swamp, filled with putrid water, and the decaying remains of vegetable substances, intersected our path. Boughs of trees had been thrown into the swamp by some good-natured people to assist travellers in the attempt, so that our men, furnishing themselves with long poles, which they used as walking-sticks, with much difficulty and exertion succeeded in getting over. For my own part, I was taken on the back of a large and powerful man, of amazing strength. His brawny shoulders supported me without any apparent fatigue on his part; and he carried me through bog and water in safety to the opposite side.

April 3rd.—We had made fires of dried wood and fallen leaves last evening, and had prepared to repose for the night under a canopy of trees, and were in fact actually stretched at full length on the turf for that purpose, when we were agreeably surprised by the arrival of four

of our men from the village with hammocks; for though sleeping in
the open air, with 'heaven for one's canopy', in a dark wood, and all
that, may be very pretty in description, yet in reality nothing can be
more disagreeable for the crawling of ants, black worms, etc, over
one's face, disperses the most enchanting reverie. These hammocks
were highly acceptable, and we were lifted into them with very
grateful feelings. It is pleasant, too, after a long day's journey on foot,
to be carried along so easily on one's back, to see parrots and other
solemn birds perched on the branches of very tall trees, whilst the trees
themselves seem tapering away from one most surprisingly.

After a charming journey of eight or ten miles, we entered the large
and populous town of *Bidjie*. As usual the natives testified the wild
delight they felt at our visit by clapping of hands and loud bursts of
laughter. The chief shook hands with us in great good humour, and
we remarked with pleasure, or fancied we could, that not only his
laugh, but that of his people, was a more social and civilized kind of
sound than what of late we had been accustomed to hear. Nevertheless
when I shook hands with the chief's son, which act is not very diverting
in itself, the bystanders set up so general a roar of laughter, that the
town rang with the noise; and when I ventured further to place my
hand on his head, they were yet more amazingly tickled, and actually

'Shriek'd like mandrakes torn out of the earth.'[1]

We were in momentary expectation of hearing some account of
our horses from Badagry. But just about sun-set two fellows arrived
from Badagry, with the mortifying intelligence that our horses would
not remain on the water in canoes, but having upset one of them,
had swam on shore and been led back to Badagry. We are persuaded
that this story has been made up for the occasion.

My brother has been amusing himself the greater part of this afternoon in teaching the simple-hearted chief to play on a child's penny
Jew's-harp; but his proficiency, owing to a wonderfully capacious
mouth, and teeth of extraordinary size, has not been near so flattering
as could have been wished.

Turnpikes are as common from Badagry to this place as on any
public road in England. Instead of horses, carriages, etc, people carrying burdens alone are taxed; but as we are under protection of the
government no duty has been exacted for any of our things.

Sunday, April 4th.—Many of the women of Bidjie have the flesh

[1] William Shakespeare, *Romeo and Juliet*, Act iv, Sc. 3, l. 47.

on their foreheads risen in the shape of marbles, and their cheeks similarly cut up and deformed. The lobes of their ears are likewise pierced, and the holes made surprisingly large, for the insertion of pieces of ivory and wood into them, which is a prevailing fashion with all ranks.

In the afternoon we departed from the town of Bidjie, accompanied by its good-natured happy governor, and reached the banks of a rivulet called *Yow* in a very few minutes. The Yow is an extremely narrow rivulet. Crocodiles are said to resort here in great numbers; the low bark or growl of these rapacious animals we heard distinctly. After we had been pushed along against the stream by poles for five or six miles, we landed at a narrow creek. We had not proceeded more than two hundred yards on the pathway when we were met by a messenger from Jenna, who informed us that the owners of all the horses in the town had rode out to welcome their chief, so that we should be obliged to walk the remainder of the way. A few minutes only had elapsed, before we descried a horse approaching us in the path. The horseman had an extravagant idea of his own consequence, and seemed a prodigious boaster. He wore abundance of clothing, most of which was superfluous, but it made him excessively vain. He informed us that he had been despatched by the King of Jenna to meet us in the path, and escort us to the capital; but understanding that Adooley had supplied us with horses, he did not conceive it necessary to send others. The messenger, however, dismounted and offered us his horse; and my brother and self agreed to ride him in turns.

It would require greater powers than we are in possession of to give an adequate description of the magnificence, solemnity, and desolate repose, of the awful solitudes through which we passed this evening. They were enlightened, however, at times by the appearance of glow-worms, which were so luminous that one could almost see to read by their golden splendour; and sometimes by the moonbeams, which trembled upon the leaves and branches of the trees. A fragrance also was exhaled from the forest, more odoriferous than the perfume of primroses or violets; and one might almost fancy, when threading his way through scenery which perhaps cannot be surpassed for beauty in any part of the world, that he was approaching those eternal shades where, in ancient times, the souls of good men were supposed to wander. The woods rang with the song of insects and night-birds, which saluted us with little intermission till about ten o'clock at night, when we entered *Laatoo*, a large and pleasant town. Here we were informed that no house would be offered us, the fetish-priest having declared that the moment a white man should enter the dwellings of the inhabitants, they would be seized by their enemies and enslaved.

April 5th.—Before sunrise this morning, we were all on the alert, and struck the tent at a very early hour. We then sent the carriers onward with the luggage, and hastily left the town after them; and in an hour's time reached the extensive and important town of *Larro*.

Public schools are established here for the avowed purpose of teaching the rising generation the rudiments of the Mohammedan religion.

The inhabitants possess horses, asses, and mules, though not in any considerable numbers; they have, however, great abundance of sheep and goats, which are bred in the town; and their yards and huts are the common place of resort for these animals—indeed they may be said to grow up and live with the children of their owners. Shrimps and fish, which are caught in the streams in the vicinity of the town, are daily exposed for sale; and the inhabitants appear to be in possession of a greater share of the necessaries and comforts of life than their neighbours of the sea-coast.

We have observed the country to be sensibly rising today; and agriculture appears to be conducted on a regular system, which is evident proof of the active and industrious habits of the people. The gloomy fastnesses and wildnesses of nature are less common as we advance; and open glades, with plantations of bananas, and fields of yams and Indian corn, all neatly fenced, met our view from the path yesterday and this morning. The inhabitants of Larro also exhibit greater cleanliness of person and tidiness of apparel than the tribes nearer the sea; and importunate beggars have disappeared entirely.

My brother and I begin already to feel the relaxing influence of the climate, but by the blessing of Heaven we hope that our progress through the country may not yet be impeded by sickness.

April 6th.—The sun had scarcely arisen, when we quitted the town of Larro. Three horsemen from Jenna followed us on the path, and we were enlivened by the wild jingling of their animals' bells, till we got within a mile of that town, where we alighted at a kind of turnpike, and fired a salute of two muskets. Here we were met by a parcel of fellows with horns; these men preceded us over a bridge, which is thrown across a moat that surrounds Jenna, into the centre of the town, where we awaited the chief's pleasure in an open shed. An immense crowd of people pressed in upon us on every side, subjecting us to the accustomed inconveniences of want of air, strong, unwholesome smells, and a confused hubbub that defies description. Never were people more eager to behold us. Altogether was formed a large amphitheatre of black woolly heads, and teeth set in jetty faces; and although we felt rather annoyed at their innocent curiosity, we could not help being highly diverted at the spectacle around us. The chief was clad in the prevailing finery of crimson velvet tobe and cap, both edged with gold lace. At his right hand sat his wives and women. The women sang the praises of their master in a loud unpleasant voice, in which they were assisted by the music (equally unharmonious) of drums, fifes, clarionets, and horns. The dignity of the newly-made governor seemed to sit rather awkwardly upon him, for he was shy and bashful as a maiden, and really appeared agitated and afraid of his white-faced visitants.

The former governor of Jenna died about fifteen months ago, and the King of Yarriba chose one of the meanest of his slaves as his successor. This is an invariable rule with the sovereigns of that country, of which Jenna is a province, for they fear that its distance from the capital being very great, a person of higher rank, if possessed of talents and spirit, could easily influence the natives to throw off the yoke, and declare themselves independent of Yarriba. The present governor is a Haussa man, and was raised to the dignity he now holds, in all probability, on account of his childish simplicity and artlessness, for a person with a countenance more indicative of innocence, and perhaps stupidity also, we never recollect to have seen. The qualities of his heart, however, are said to be excellent.

Showers are becoming heavier and fall more frequently than they did; and the rainy season may fairly be said to have commenced.

April 7th.—The fetish priest of the town came dancing into our hut this afternoon, looking exceedingly wild, and roaring as if possessed of an evil spirit. We paid little attention to the fellow's fooleries, who, not liking his reception, left the hut, after we had given him the accustomed fee of a few cowries. The man's person and dress, together with its whimsical ornaments, were admirably fitted to impose on the credulity and superstition of the inhabitants, although many of the town's people, influenced perhaps by the spreading doctrine of Mahomet, spoke their minds pretty freely, calling him a scoundrel and a devil. There was something peculiar in the priest's countenance that we could not define. On his shoulders he bore a large club, carved at one end with the figure of a man's head. A vast number of strings of cowries were suspended on this weopen, which were intermixed with bells, broken combs, small pieces of wood, with rude imitations of men's faces cut on them, large sea-shells, bits of iron and brass, nut shells, etc, etc. Perhaps the number of cowries on his person did not fall far short of twenty thousand; and the weight of his various ornaments almost pressed him to the ground.

April 8th.—The two messengers that arrived at Badagry whilst we were there, and stated that they had been employed for the purpose by the Governor of Jenna, were this morning discovered to be impostors, and put in irons accordingly. But as the poor fellows had really been of essential service to us, inasmuch as by their representations they prevailed on Adooley to give us leave to proceed on our journey much sooner than we ourselves could have done, we thought proper to intercede in their behalf, and although they were to have been sold as a punishment for their deception, they are now set at liberty. The person also that met us with a horse after crossing the river Yow, proceeded thither on his own account, without the knowledge or consent of the governor; but as he is a Falatah, and a respectable man, little has been said or done about that matter.

April 9th.—Since the demise of the last governor, it is calculated that Jenna has lost more than five hundred of its population, chiefly by wars, intestine broils, etc, and for want of a ruler.[1] It must not be imagined, however, that because the people of this country are almost perpetually engaged in conflicts with their neighbours, the slaughter of human beings is therefore very great. They pursue war, as it is called, partly as an amusement or 'to keep their hands in it'; and partly to benefit themselves by the capture of slaves. Success depends much more on the cunning and address of the parties, than on any extraordinary display of intrepidity; and living, not dead, subjects are sought after, so that it is their *interest* to avoid hard blows and enrich

[1] Clapperton reckoned that the population of Jenna might 'amount from 8000 to 10,000'. He had noted that the inhabitants were 'great carvers; their doors, drums, and every thing of wood is carved' (Clapperton, 1829, p. 13). T. J. Bowen, an American missionary who travelled in Yorubaland from 1849 to 1856 found that 'Ijenna (Jenna) was destroyed only a few weeks before my arrival in the country'. He also noted that 'of all the places visited by the Landers, only Ishakki, Igboho, Ikishi, and a few villages remain' (Bascom, 1960, p. 13). This destruction was brought about partly by the civil wars among the Yorubas that followed the decline of Oyo, partly by the devastating attacks launched by the rulers of Dahomey, who had themselves formerly been tributary to the *Alafins*. As a result the old trade route followed by the Landers came to be abandoned; its line 'now passes through some of the most sparsely populated parts of Yoruba country' (Allison, *Odu*, n.d.). The important Yoruba towns of Ibadan, Abeokuta, and (New) Oyo had not been founded when the Landers passed through the country.

themselves by the sale of their prisoners. Perhaps the extraordinary decrease in the population of Jenna has arisen from the desertion of slaves, who embrace the opportunity, whilst their masters are from home engaged in predatory excursions, of running away; and thus the latter frequently become losers, instead of gainers by their unnatural passion for stealing their fellow-creatures. The individuals captured are sent to the coast, and the chiefs of those unsettled and barbarous tribes that inhabit it are appointed agents to regulate the sale of them, for which they receive half the profits.

Late in the evening the young Falatah mentioned in yesterday's journal, paid us a visit, and offered his horse for sale. He is a Mohammedan priest and was accompanied by a countryman of the same persuasion; but neither of the holy men appeared in their dealing, to understand the meaning of truth or justice. An agreement was made, and we paid thirty dollars. The merchant implored us not to tell his father, who was the real owner of the horse, that he had sold him for less money than he had received. The Falatas are supposed to be spies from Soccatoo; but, although this is a very prevalent opinion, no measures whatever have yet been taken to watch their motions.

The women of Jenna employ themselves generally either in spinning cotton or preparing Indian corn for food. Much of the former material grows in the vicinity of the town, but the cultivation of the plant is not carried on with the spirit it deserves. Silk, which is brought over land from Tripoli, the inhabitants sometimes interweave in their cotton garments; but such, being very expensive, are only worn by the higher class of people. They have abundance of bullocks, pigs, goats, sheep and poultry, but they prefer vegetable food to animal; their diet, indeed, is what we should term poor and watery, consisting chiefly of preparations of the yam and of Indian corn, notwithstanding which a stronger or more athletic race of people is nowhere to be met with. Burdens with them are invariably carried on the head. The weight of a feather is borne on the head in preference to its being carried in the hand; and it not unfrequently requires the united strength of three men to lift a calabash of goods to the shoulder of one; and then, and not till then, does the amazing strength of the African appear.

April 10th.—It is the custom here, when a governor dies, for two of his favourite wives to quit the world on the same day, in order that it may have a little pleasant, social company in a future state[1];

---

[1] The 'honourable suicide' demanded of the governor's widow formed a modest parallel to the sacrifices that accompanied the death of the *Alafin*, the paramount ruler of

but the late governor's devoted wives had no ambition or inclination to follow their venerable husband to the grave, and went and hid themselves before the funeral ceremonies were performed, and have remained concealed ever since with the remainder of his women. Today, however, one of these unfortunates was discovered in her hiding-place at the present governor's, and the alternative of a poisoned chalice, or to have her head broken by the club of the fetish-priest, was offered her. She has chosen the former mode of dying, as being the less terrible of the two, and has come to our yard to spend her last hours in the society of her faithful slaves. These address their mistress by the endearing name of mother. Poor creatures! as soon as they learnt her misfortune, they dropped their spinning; the grinding of corn was also relinquished; their sheep, goats and poultry were suffered to roam at large without restraint; and they abandoned themselves to the most excessive, most poignant grief; but now the arrival of their mistress has added, if possible, to their affliction. There is not to be found in the world, perhaps, an object more truly sorrowful than a lonely, defenceless woman in tears; and on such an occasion as this, the distress is more peculiarly cutting. Females have been coming all day to condole with the old lady, and to weep with her; so that we have heard and seen nothing but sobbing and crying from morning till the setting of the sun. The principal males in the town have likewise been here to pay their last respects to their mistress; and so has her grave-digger, who has just risen from prostrating himself on the ground before her. Notwithstanding the representations and remonstrances of the priest, and the prayers of the venerable victim to her

---

Oyo. On the *Alafin's* death, several slaves were buried in his grave to be his attendants in the next world. At the same time certain members of the royal family, some of the King's wives and others who bore a special title signifying that they would die with the king, were required to commit suicide. 'The custom is that each should go and die in his (or her) own home, and among his family. The spectacle is very affecting. Dressed in their "death cloth" (a beautiful silk damask wrapper), they issue from the palace to their homes surrounded by their friends, and their drummers beating funeral dirges, eager crowds of friends and acquaintances flocking around them. . . . While the grave is digging, a parting feast is made for all the friends and acquaintances; and as they must die before sunset, they enjoy themselves as best they can for that day by partaking of the choicest and favourite dishes, appearing several times in changes of apparel, distributing presents with a lavish hand around, and making their last will disposing of their effects. When everything is ready, they then take poison, and pass off quietly. But if it fails or is too slow to take effect, and the sun is about to set, the last office is performed by the nearest relatives (by strangling or otherwise) to save themselves and the memory of their kin from indelible disgrace.' Those who were bound to die with the *Alafin* were his closest associates; 'to make their life dependent on his, therefore, is to ensure safety for him against the risk of poisoning, or the dagger of the assassin' (Johnson, 1957, pp. 55-7).

gods for fortitude to undergo the dreadful ordeal, her resolution has forsaken her more than once. She has entered our yard twice to expire in the arms of her women, and twice has she laid aside the fatal poison, in order to take another walk, and gaze once more on the splendour of the sun and the glory of the heavens, for she cannot bear the idea of losing sight of them for ever. Meanwhile her grave is preparing, and preparations are making for a wake at her funeral. She is to be buried here in one of her own huts the moment after the spirit has quitted the body. The poison used by the natives on this occasion destroys life, it is said, in fifteen minutes.

The *origin* of this abominable custom is understood to have arisen from a dread on the part of the chiefs of the country in olden time, that their principal wives, who alone were in possession of their confidence, and knew where their money was concealed, might secretly attempt their life, in order at once to establish their own freedom, and become possessed of the property. But why men also, who can have no interest to gain on the death of their prince, should be obliged to conform to the same rite, is not near so easily accounted for. The present governor of Jenna must of necessity go down to the grave on the first intelligence of the demise of the king of Yarriba; and as that monarch is a very aged man, the situation of the former is not the most enviable in the world.

Previous to her swallowing the poison, the favourite wife of a deceased chief or ruler destroys privately all the wealth, or rather money of her former partner, in order that it may not fall into the hands of his successor. The same custom is observed at Badagry also; and although the king's son may be of age at the period of his father's death, he inherits his authority and influence only. He is left to his own sagacity and exertions to procure wealth, which can seldom be obtained without rapine, enslavement, and bloodshed.

Whenever a town is deprived of its chief, the inhabitants acknowledge no law—anarchy, troubles, and confusion immediately prevail, and till a successor is appointed all labour is at an end. The stronger oppress the weak, and consummate every species of crime, without being amenable to any tribunal for their actions. Private property is no longer respected; and thus before a person arrives to curb its licentiousness, a town is not infrequently reduced from a flourishing state of prosperity and of happiness, to all the horrors of desolation.

Sunday, April 11th.—This being Easter-day, we have devoted it exclusively to religious purposes.

The old queen-dowager, like Prior's thief

'Often takes leave, but seems loth to depart;'[1]

although her doom is inevitably sealed, she has been more cheerful today than yesterday, and seems determined to spin out her thread of life to its utmost limit. Spies are now set over her, and she is not permitted to go out of the yard.

April 12th.—The principal people of the place, finding the old lady still obstinately bent on deferring her *exit*, have sent a messenger to her native village to make known to her relatives that should she make her escape, they will take all of them into slavery, and burn their town to ashes, in conformity to an established and very ancient law. They would therefore strongly advise the relatives of the old woman, for their own sakes, and for the sake of the public, to use all their endeavours to prevail upon her to meet her fate honourably and with fortitude. It is understood that she has bribed a few of the most opulent and influential inhabitants of Jenna with large sums of money, to induce them to overlook her dereliction from the path of duty, and that by their representations she has obtained the tacit consent of the King of Katunga to live out the full term of her natural life. But the people for many miles round, horror-struck at such impiety and contempt for ancient customs, have risen to enforce the laws of the country against her.

[1] Matthew Prior, *The Thief and the Cordelier*, v.

III

Jenna to Katunga

April 13th.—Last night we were visited by one of those terrific thunder-storms which are so prevalent in these latitudes. Our thatched hut afforded but an insecure and uncertain asylum against its fury; part of the roof was swept away, and the rain admitted freely upon our beds, whence the most awful lightning-flashes could be seen, making, as Milton says, 'the darkness visible'. It seemed as if the Genius of the Storm was driving through the murky clouds in his chariot of fire, to awaken the slumbering creation and make them feel and acknowledge his power. It is indeed a grand lesson to human pride, to contemplate the terrors of a tornado through the trembling walls and roof of a dilapidated hut in Africa. In civilized countries, when men are visited by an awful calamity of this kind, the distinctions of rank are levelled, and numbers flock together for the purpose of keeping each other in countenance, and strengthening each other's nerves; but here all is naked, lonely, and desolate.

Matters were arranged for our departure in good time this morning, and after breakfast we went to pay our last respects to the good governor. When the doors were opened, the band that was in attendance inside played a native tune as a token of welcome. We observed a greater number of drummers assembled than on any former occasion. Some of their instruments were something in the shape of a cone, and profusely ornamented with plates and figures of brass. On one of these was represented the busts of two men, with a tortoise in the act of eating out of the mouth of one of them. The tortoise had a cock by its side, and two dogs standing as guardian to the whole. These figures were all ingeniously carved in solid brass. Both ends of the larger drums were played on with the palms of the hand; hundreds of little

68

bells were suspended round their edges for ornament rather than use, for being without clappers they could produce no sound.

We were fortunate enough to meet with and purchase another horse this morning. Our pathway lay through a champaign country, partially wooded, and after a pleasant ride of three-quarters of an hour, we entered the small village of *Bidjie*. Here our carriers dropped their loads, nor could they be induced to resume them by the most pressing solicitations. Nor would the villagers, as their duty required, take them up, but when we begged them to do so, laughed at us, so that here we are compelled to remain till tomorrow. This is very provoking; and such is the tiresome mode of travelling through this country. No consideration will induce any of the natives to shake off their habitual indolence. Pleasure and sloth with them are synonymous words, and they are scarcely alive to any other species of gratification.

April 14th.—At an early hour this morning, to our infinite surprise and pleasure, the man from Badagry made his appearance with one of our horses and an English saddle. Paskoe, whose sagacity and experience have proved of infinite value to us, has been lamed in his endeavours to walk as fast as the rest of the party, and as he has also the misfortune of having one leg shorter than the other, he became the general butt and laughing-stock of his more robust companions. Today, however, we placed him on the back of the extra horse, from whence he has retorted their revilings.

We set off from Bidjie and arrived at *Chow* before eleven o'clock in the fore-noon.

Several strangers accompany us from town to town, in order to evade the duty which is exacted at the turn-pike gates, by stating themselves to be of the number of our attendants. Women have also placed themselves under the protection of our men from Cape Coast Castle, that they may enjoy the like advantage; in return for this favour they do us many little kind offices, and are useful in making fires, preparing food, etc, for our people.

The chief of Chow who entertained the last mission has been dead some time, and is succeeded by a humble, good-natured and active individual, who has treated us more like demi-gods than men.

In the evening the chief visited us with a present of provisions, and a few goora nuts. My brother took the opportunity of playing on a bugle horn in his presence, by which he was violently agitated, under the supposition that the instrument was nothing less than a snake!

April 15th.—The path today has winded through a country charmingly diversified by hill and dale, woods and open glades, and watered by streams flowing over beds of fine white sand. We found numbers of people of both sexes on the path, and several naked boys on their way to the coast, under the care of guardians. These are slaves, and will be sold most likely at Badagry. Women bore burdens on their heads that would tire a mule, and children not more than five or six years of age trudged after them, with loads that would give a full-grown person in Europe the brain fever.

We departed from Chow before sunrise; a surprising dew had fallen during the night, and distilled from the leaves and branches in large drops. With very trifling labour, the path, which is little better than a gutter, formed by repeated rains, might be converted into a good and commodious road; and were a tree simply thrown over them, the streams and morasses might be crossed with ease and safety. But the natives appear to have no idea whatever of such improvements; and would rather be entangled daily in a thick underwood, and wade through pools of mud and water, than give themselves any concern about repairing the road. Trees not infrequently fall across the pathway, but, instead of removing, the people form a large circuit round them, so inconsiderate and indolent are the natives in this part of the world.[1]

Many women with little wooden figures of children on their heads passed us in the course of the morning—mothers who, having lost a child, carry such rude imitations of them about their persons for an indefinite time as a symbol of mourning.[2] None of them could be induced to part with one of these little affectionate memorials.

We entered *Egga* in the early part of the afternoon. Egga is the principal market-town in this part of Africa, and is attended by buyers

[1] According to Samuel Johnson, the historian of the Yorubas, the state of the roads, before the break up of the empire of Oyo, was 'comparatively good'. The roads 'were annually repaired at the time of the drummers' and Egugun festivals. They were wide enough for the easy progress of the company of dancers at these festivals and also for nuptial processions. But they are now'—Johnson was writing in the 1890s—'neglected not only that they may impede the easy advance of invaders, but also to aid the concealment of the panic-stricken inhabitants, who at the first alarm disappear at once in the bushes surrounding their towns and villages' (Johnson, 1957, p. 93).

[2] 'When one or twin [*sic*] children dies, the mother has to make a wooden image of the deceased child and carry it about, otherwise evil will befall the surviving child or it will die and rejoin the company of twins in the spirit world' (Lucas, 1948, p. 193). The Landers must have been right in concluding (p. 72) that infant mortality was 'immense'; even with the extension of modern medical facilities, infant mortality still presents one of the most formidable problems affecting the life of the people of Nigeria.

and sellers for many miles round. Women here are the chief, if not the only traders; most of them are of graceful and prepossessing exterior, and they all practise those petty tricks and artifices in their dealings with which the market-women of more civilized countries are acquainted.

April 16th.—We found the path in much better condition than those behind it, and it lay almost entirely through plantations of yams, calavances, and pumkins, and three or four different varieties of corn, which a number of labourers were employed in weeding, etc. The hoe is the only implement of husbandry in use, and indeed they can well dispense with every other, because the soil during the rainy months is so soft and light that but very little manual exertion in working it is required. Population is abundant—labourers may be hired in any number—and in our opinion, the introduction of the plough would scarcely be a blessing—but on the contrary furnish new encouragement to the besetting sin of sloth.

Having crossed at noon a small but agreeable river, we entered the capacious and populous town of *Jadoo.*

The yard in which we reside is perfectly round, and walled with huts, all tenanted by the late chief's widows, who employ their time and earn their livelihood by spinning and weaving. Not less than a hundred of the king of Katunga's ladies are lodging in the yard with them. They have all passed the bloom of life, and arrived here lately with loads of trona and country cloth, which they barter for salt, and various articles of European manufacture, particularly beads. These royal ladies are distinguished from their countrywomen only by a peculiar species of cloth, which is wrapped round their goods, and which no one dares to imitate on pain of perpetual slavery. This severe punishment is often inflicted, for, as the king's wives pay no tribute or turnpike dues whatever, and must besides be entertained by the chiefs of every town through which they pass, strong inducements are offered for others to attempt to deceive by using the forbidden cloth, and hence examples are necessary.

It is now ten o'clock at night, and the women are sitting in groups round the several wood-fires. We ourselves occupy only a verandah, which is simply the projection of the roof of a thatched hut; our horses are fastened to wooden stakes in the centre of the yard; our men are lying round them, warming themselves at their own fires. Sheep, beautiful sheep, with tinkling bells hung round their necks, are chewing their cud in peace and happiness. But although it is the hour of

F   71

repose, the tongues of our female fellow-travellers are making a clatter which all the *Graces* of Billingsgate could not rival, and together with the squalling of brats innumerable, it spoils the emotions which the wild and pleasing scene around us would otherwise awaken in our hearts.

Sheep here are regarded with as much partiality, and treated much in the same manner as ladies' lap-dogs are in England. Great care is taken to keep them clean and in good condition; they are washed every morning in soap and water; and so greatly are they attached to their masters or mistresses, that they are constantly at their heels, following them in-doors and out, from town to town, and in all their peregrinations.

The inhabitants of Jadoo are, generally speaking, very tidily clad in cotton dresses, of their own manufacture. In their persons they are much more agreeable than those who reside nearer the sea. European goods are brought hither from Dahomey and Badagry, but more especially from Lagos. Several chiefs on the road have asked us the reason why the Portuguese do not purchase as many slaves as formerly; and made very sad complaints of the stagnation in this branch of traffic. Hippopotami abound in the rivers in the vicinity of the town; when young, the flesh and skin of these animals are sold as food; and whips and other articles are made of the skins of the old ones.

April 17th.—At the usual hour this morning we quitted Jadoo. The mortality of children must be immense indeed here, for almost every woman we met with on the road, had one or more of those little wooden images, we have spoken of before. Whenever the mothers stopped to take refreshment, a small part of their food was invariably presented to the lips of these inanimate memorials.

We continued our journey over gentle hills, and through vallies watered by streams and rivulets, so as to reach *Engua* in the afternoon. The soil is mostly dry and sterile; large masses of iron-stone presented themselves almost at every step. This day has been oppressively warm; and our skin was scorched and highly inflamed, so that we were very uncomfortable. For my own part, I was sore, tired, and feverish, and longed to lay myself down in a hut; but we were obliged to remain under a tree above three hours, because the chief of the town was engaged in making a fetish to counteract any evil intentions that we might entertain towards him.

Sunday, April 18th.—Our reception had been so truly inhospitable at Engua, that we arose and proceeded on our way by star-light. The country is partially covered with large and unshapely masses of granite. Mountains and elevated hills were observed to the right of us, whose sides were thickly wooded, and their summits reaching above the clouds. We entered the town of *Afoora* about mid-day. The governor gave us a hearty welcome. The best hut in the town was presently got ready for us, and we received a quantity of excellent provisions from the chief.

April 19th.—An easy, pleasant rise brought us to the first walled town we have seen, which is called *Assinara*. The wall is of clay, and so diminutive that a person might easily jump over it. Assinara has lately lost its chief in some battle, and all business is transacted by a benevolent, elderly man, who has volunteered his services till a successor shall be appointed. From him we have received the most hospitable treatment. The climate has already had a debilitating effect upon my brother, and from a state of robust health, he is reduced to so great a degree of lassitude that he can scarcely stand a minute at a time. He was attacked with fever this afternoon, and his condition would have been hopeless indeed, had I not been near to relieve him.[1]

April 20th.—My brother was much better, and free from fever this morning, but too weak to travel, and we shall therefore remain at Assinara till tomorrow. The acting governor visited us today with a long face and intreated us earnestly to discover a certain wizard whom he imagined to be concealed somewhere in the town. By this sorcerer's influence numbers of the people, it is said, pine away and die; and women with child are more especially the objects of his malevolence. These victims drop suddenly, without the slightest warning; and the deaths have lately been so numerous, that the old man himself is grievously alarmed, and begs a charm to preserve him and his family.

April 23rd.—My brother finding himself sufficiently recovered, we travelled onwards in excellent spirits and entered the town of *Accodoo* in the forenoon. At this time my brother enjoyed an unusual cheerfulness and buoyancy of spirits. In the course of a few minutes, however, his body was overspread with a burning heat, and he suffered under another attack of fever, more violent than any of the former. I resorted to the most powerful remedies I could think of at the time. I bled him and applied a strong blister to the region of the stomach, where the

---

[1] Though most of this part of the journal appears to have been written by John Lander, Huish's edition makes it clear that it was John and not Richard, whose illness is here described (Huish, 1835, p. 507).

disorder seemed to be seated. It was swollen and oppressed with pain, and he felt as if some huge substance lay upon his chest. His mouth being dry and clogged, and his thirst burning and unquenchable, he drank so much water, that his body was greatly swollen. In the evening his ideas were confused, and he became delirious. He afterwards described to me the horrible phantoms that disturbed him whilst in this state; and the delicious emotion that ran through his whole frame when the dreadful visions had passed away. Tears gushed from his eyes; a profuse perspiration gave him immediate relief, and he has since continued to improve.

Whilst my brother was so ill, the natives made a most hideous noise by singing and drumming in celebration of their fetish. I went out in the hope of inducing them to be quiet, but they only laughed at him [*sic*], and annoyed us the more; for they have no compassion for the sufferings of a white man, and if they can mortify him by any means, they consider it a praiseworthy deed. Yesterday was one of the hottest days we have yet felt, the thermometer at noon being 99° of Fahrenheit.

April 24th.—A hammock was prepared for my brother, because he was too weak to ride on horseback. We proceeded through large plantations of cotton, indigo, Indian corn, and yams, and over stony fields, till between ten and eleven, when we entered the town of *Chouchou*. We were almost immediately introduced to the chief, and from him into a ruinous hut, in a more filthy state than can be imagined. No pig-sty was ever half so bad.

Sunday, April 25th.—It rained heavily during the whole of last night; but our hut had a pretty good thatched roof, and sheltered us much better than we had expected. There are periods and seasons in our lifetime in which we feel a happy complacency of temper and an inward satisfaction, cheerfulness, and joy, for which we cannot very well account, but which constrain us to be at peace with ourselves and our neighbours, and in love with all the works of God. In this truly enviable frame of mind I awoke this morning to proceed onward on horseback; it was a morning which was fairly entitled to the epithet of 'incense-breathing'; for the variety of sweet-smelling perfume which exhaled, after the rain, from forest flowers, and flowering shrubs, was delicious and almost over-powering. The scenery of today has been more interesting and lovely than any we have heretofore beheld. The path circled round a magnificent cultivated valley, hemmed in almost on every side with mountains of granite of the most grotesque and irregular shapes, the summits of which are covered with stunted trees, and the hollows in their slopes occupied by clusters of huts, whose inmates have fled thither as a place of security against the ravages of the *war-men* that infest the plains. A number of strange birds resort to this valley, many of whose notes were rich, full and melodious, while others were harsh and disagreeable; but, generally speaking, the plumage was various, splendid, and beautiful. The modest partridge appeared in company with the magnificent Balearic crane, with his regal crest; and delicate humming birds hopped from twig to twig with others of an unknown species; some of them were of a dark, shining green; some had red silky wings and purple bodies; some were variegated with stripes of crimson and gold; and these chirped and warbled from among the thick foliage of the trees. It is the contemplation of such beautiful objects as these, all so playful and so happy—or the more sublime ones of dark waving forests, plains of vast extent, or stupendous mountains, that give the mind the most sensible emotions of delight and grandeur, leading it insensibly

'To look from nature up to nature's God.'

For myself I am passionately fond of them, and have regretted a thousand times over that my ignorance incapacitates me from giving a proper representation of them, or describing the simplest flower that adorns the plains, or the smallest insect that sparkles in the air. This consideration gives me at times many unhappy reflections, although my defective education arose from circumstances over which my boyhood had no control.

We rode into the town of *Gwendekki*, in which we purpose passing the night. Divine service was performed in the course of the day, as usual, and this is a duty which to persons in our situation is inconceivably pleasant. It renders us happy and resigned in the midst of our afflictions.

April 26th.—A thick mist obscured the horizon this morning, and hid in deep shade the mountains and hills; every object indeed was invisible except the pathway. It continued hazy for two hours after leaving Gwendekki, when the mist dispersed, and the atmosphere became clear. Preparatory to ascending a steep granite hill, we halted to refresh our horses under the branches of a high spreading tree. On attaining the summit of the hill, the *coup d'œil* was magnificent indeed, and the fog having been dispersed by the sun, the eye was enabled to range round an extensive horizon, bounded by hills and mountains of wonderful shape. Some of them bear a very striking resemblance to the Table Mountain, at the Cape of Good Hope. There was no continued range of hills, but numbers of single unconnected ones, with extensive vallies between them. In some places several were piled behind each other; and those most distant from us appeared like dark, indistinct clouds. Nothing could surpass the singularity, perhaps I may say the sublimity, of the whole view; and we contemplated it in silence for a few seconds with emotions of astonishment and rapture.

We continued our journey over a noble plain, watered with springs and rivulets; and in the afternoon entered *Dufo*, which is a most extensive and populous town. The inhabitants appear to be industrious and very opulent, as regards the number and variety of their domestic animals; we observed, for the first time, turkeys and Guinea fowl.

April 27th.—We were on horseback early this morning. The country seemed inferior indeed as to the boldness and beauty of its scenery to that traversed yesterday; but still it possesses features of no common interest. Ponderous masses of granite rock overhang the pathway; these were almost black, and seem to have been washed by the rains of thousands of years; in many of them were deep and gloomy caverns, which, were they in Cornwall instead of Africa, would, I am sure, be pointed out as the scenes of dark and bloody stories of the elder time. Hundreds of the natives followed us a long while, and annoyed us so much by their noises and curiosity that we were compelled to resort to violent measures to drive them away; but this is a line of conduct which we rarely adopt towards them, and never without extreme reluctance. We at length frightened them away, and we saw them no more. At a large straggling village we halted a little, as the path had been so stony, ragged and irregular. From this place the road became excellent, not at all inferior to a drive round a gentleman's park in England; and continued to be good till we came in sight of a capacious walled town called *Chaadoo*.

April 28th.—We have remained at Chaadoo today, to give the carriers with the luggage time to come up with us.

April 29th.—It commenced raining this morning at a very early hour. Before we quitted Chaadoo, the credulous governor, who in common with his people imagines that white men influence the elements, paid us a visit with a calabash of honey as a present, to thank us, he said, for the rain that had fallen, of which the country is greatly in want, and invoked blessings on us. The kindness of this good old man is remarkable. He never seemed weary of obliging us.

We traversed a mountainous country, intersected with streams of excellent water; and arrived towards evening at a capacious walled town called *Row*.

The governor of the town is a morose, surly, and ill-natured man. He sent us only a few bananas this evening, and a calabash of eggs, which were all stale and unfit to be eaten, so that our people were obliged to go supperless to bed.

April 30th.—It was between seven and eight o'clock before carriers could be procured this morning. At noon, we arrived at the foot of a very elevated hill, and perceived a town perched on its summit. We dismounted, and after a laborious ascent at length reached the top. The name of the town is *Chekki*.

People of both sexes, hereabouts, are infinitely more grave and serious in their manners than those nearer the coast and

'The loud laugh that speaks the vacant mind'[1]

we have not heard these many days.

May 1st.—In the cool of the morning we quitted Chekki, and rode on pleasantly, till we arrived at *Coosoo*,[2] a large and important town.

A company or *gafflie* of merchants from Hano [*sic*] are at present in the town, who have come thus far on their way to *Gonja*. Their merchandise consists chiefly of elephant's teeth, trona, rock salt, and country cloths. This, we are told, is a new route, the road formerly taken being considered unsafe. The *gafflie* consists of more than four hundred men.

The palm-tree becomes scarce, in proportion as we advance into the country, and consequently the oil is obtained hereabouts only in very small quantities. But Nature, ever bountiful, supplies its place with the *mi-cadania*, or butter tree, which yields abundance of a kind of vegetable marrow, pleasant to the taste, and highly esteemed by the natives. It is used for lights and other domestic purposes.

In the evening we received a fat goat, a basket of *caffas*, a calabash of bananas, a vast quantity of yams, and a bowl of milk, from the governor. He is a sober, kind and benevolent old man, and generally beloved by his people. He has informed us that the common path to Katunga is unsafe, in consequence of a serious quarrel between the inhabitants of Coosoo and those of a neighbouring town. 'Therefore,' said he, 'I entreat you to remain here with me tomorrow, in order that I may make arrangements to send you by a different road.'

[1] Oliver Goldsmith, *The Deserted Village*, l. 122.
[2] On the trade route from Kano to Gonja, see p. 96, n. 1.

The market, which is held this evening in the town, has an imposing and brilliant appearance, from the immense number of lamps used by the tradespeople.

Sunday, May 2nd.—A fetish priest came to see us this morning. His person presented a strange and singular appearance. The colour of his skin was like that of whitish brown paper; his eye-lashes and eye-brows were of a silvery whiteness, and his eyes of a bright blue; notwithstanding which, the negro features were strongly and distinctly marked on his countenance. The man's parents were both quite black, and we could not ascertain the reason of this extraordinary deviation from the common laws of Nature.[1]

May 3rd.—The path recommended by the friendly chief of Coosoo lies due east of this town; and we pursued our journey on it this morning by sunrise. Robbers were stated to be lurking about; we conceived it to be prudent, therefore, to take every precaution, and we loaded our own guns and pistols, and armed all our men with swords and muskets. With all these warlike preparations, a few harmless women, who were terrified at our appearance, were the only individuals met with on the path during a ride of two hours, which brought us to *Acboro.*

Shortly after our arrival, the governor sent us a sucking-pig. 'White men do nothing but good,' said he, 'and I will pray that God may bless you, and send more of your countrymen to Yarriba.'

May 4th.—We quitted the town by sunrise. At nine a.m. we arrived at *Cootoo.* After leaving Cootoo, the scenery became infinitely more pleasing. The soil was more rich and deeper; patches of verdure and cultivated land were more frequent, the latter being neatly fenced; fine handsome trees, with their spreading branches and thick foliage, embellished the country in every direction. One would be inclined to suppose that the trees had been carefully planted, for they grew at equal distances from each other, and none seemed to interfere with the order, beauty, and regularity of its neighbour. The soil between them was covered with a soft green turf. At length we came in sight of numerous herds of fine cattle, attended by little boys, and shortly after we arrived at a clean and neat Falatah village. We then crossed a small stream and entered a town of prodigious extent called *Bohoo.* Its immense triple wall is little short of twenty miles in circuit; but besides huts and gardens, it incloses a vast number of acres of excellent meadow land. By the hasty view obtained of it, the town is not much unlike

[1] The man was clearly an albino.

Kano. Bohoo was formerly the metropolis of Yarriba; but about half a century ago, the reigning prince preferring the plain at Katunga, the seat of government was transferred there, since which time Bohoo has materially declined, although it is still considered a place of great importance and the second town in the kingdom.[1] The land in the vicinity of the town presents a most inviting appearance, by no means inferior to any part of England in the most favourable season of the year. It seems to be duly appreciated by the Falatahs, a great number of whom reside with their flocks in different parts. These foreigners sell their milk, butter and cheese in the market at a reasonable rate.

I have been very ill all the evening with fever, accompanied by excruciating pains in the bowels, but my spirits are cheerful. We are thankful that we have not been both thus afflicted at the same time. As soon as one of us has in a measure regained his strength, his assistance has been required to minister to the wants of the other.

May 6th.—I am now so far improved in health, that I hope by tomorrow to be able to travel on horseback. Perhaps of all evils that can afflict a sick person, noises of any kind are the greatest. In Africa, whether one is ill or well, it is exactly the same, nothing like peace or quiet is anywhere to be found. Independent of the continual fluttering of pigeons, the bleating of sheep and goats, and the barking of numerous half-starved dogs, we are still more seriously annoyed by the incessant clatter of women's tongues, which I really believe nothing less than sickness or death on their part can effectively silence. A person in England might be inclined to think lightly of the matter; but it is indeed a grievance which can ill be borne by an invalid languishing under a wasting disease, and who has equally as much need of rest and silence as of medicine.

A company of Falatahs came to us in the evening, for they had never beheld a white man, and curiosity had led them to our habitation. They brought us a present of a little thick milk, and then went away highly gratified with the interview. The behaviour of the whole of them was extremely reserved and respectful; nothing in our persons excited their merriment; on the contrary, they seemed silently to

---

[1] Igboho, Landers' 'Bohoo' was founded by the *Alafin* Eguguoju and 'became the last resting-place of four Yoruba Kings before the government was again removed to the ancient capital' (Old Oyo or Katunga). The dates of Eguguoju are not known, but he appears to have reigned in the sixteenth century. Igboho would seem to have ceased to be the capital at a period considerably earlier than the 'half a century ago' suggested by the Landers (Johnson, 1957, p. 161).

admire our dress and complexion; and having looked well at us from a little distance, seemed grateful for the treat.

May 7th.—After we had retired to rest last night a Falatah woman came to our dwelling, bringing with her a quantity of eggs of the Guinea-hen, and a large bowl of milk fresh from the cow, as a return for a few needles we had given her in the afternoon. We relate this little circumstance simply to show the difference between the Falatahs and the Yarribeans, in point of gratitude for favours they may have received. The latter are seldom very thankful, and never acknowledge gratitude as a virtue; the indifference, unconcern, and even contempt, which they often evince on receiving our presents, is a proof of this; and, with very few exceptions, we never observed a Yarribean to be sincerely thankful for anything.

Three hours after leaving Bohoo, we arrived at *Jaguta*, which is a large and compact town.

We are daily assured that the path is rendered exceedingly dangerous by banditti. It will scarcely be believed, however, that this universal dread originates from a few Borgoo desperadoes, who, although only armed with powder and a few broken muskets, can put a whole legion of the timid natives to flight.

May 8th.—Extraordinary preparations were made by the governor of Jaguta to ensure our safety on the dreaded pathway; and a horseman, armed with a sword and spear, in company with four foot soldiers, who were equipped with bows and several huge quivers full of arrows, were in readiness to offer us their protection this morning. The horseman preceded our party, and played off a variety of antics, to our great amusement. He seemed not a little satisfied with himself; he flourished his naked sword over his head; brandished his spear; made his horse curvet, and bound, and gallop alternately; and his dress being extremely grotesque, besides being old and torn, gave him an appearance not unlike that of a bundle of rags flying through the air. But with all this display of activity and heroism, the man would have fled with terror from his own shadow by moonlight.

Our journey today has been vexatiously short, not having exceeded four miles. The town at which we are now halting is called *Shea*. It possesses a numerous population. A stranger, however, cannot give anything like a correct estimate of the population of any inhabited place in this part of Africa, for as he can only judge of it by the number of court-yards a town or village may contain, and as in one court-yard there may be residing at least a hundred people, and in the one next to it, perhaps, not more than six or seven, the difficulty will be immediately perceived. Generally speaking, the description of one town in Yarriba would answer for the whole. The form of the houses and squares is everywhere the same: irregular and badly built clay walls, ragged-looking thatched roofs, and floors of mud polished with cow-dung, form the habitations of the chief part of the natives of Yarriba, compared to most of which a common English barn is a palace. The only difference between the residence of a chief and those of his subjects, lies in the number and not in the superiority of his court-yards; and these are for the most part tenanted by women and slaves, together with flocks of sheep and goats, and abundance of pigs and poultry, mixed together indiscriminately.

Sunday, May 9th.—We arrived at the large town of *Atoopa.*

May 10th.—A village in ruins, and a small town called *Nama* were the only inhabited places we passed through during the day, till our entrance into the town of *Leoguadda,* in which we intend to pass the night.

In the centre of our yard, is a circular enclosure without a roof, within which is an alligator, that has been confined there seven years. This voracious animal is fed with rats only, and he generally devours five a day. One of the inhabitants volunteered to go to a river in the vicinity of the town, and to return in a few minutes with as many young crocodiles as I might wish for; but I declined the man's offer.

Leoguadda is almost surrounded by rugged hills, formed by loose blocks of granite; these, added to a quantity of tall trees, always green, and growing within the walls, render the town inconceivably pleasant and romantic.

May 11th.—We left Leoguadda early in the morning, and about the middle of the forenoon reached a walled town of some extent called *Eetcho.* The place is of importance on account of a large weekly market which is held there. Like most large trading towns, it is in as unsettled and filthy a state as can be conceived.

It will scarcely be believed, that not less than one hundred and sixty governors of towns and villages between this place and the sea coast, all belonging to Yarriba, have died from natural causes, or been slain in war, since I was last here; and that, of the inhabited places through which we have passed, not more than a half dozen chiefs are alive at this moment, who received and entertained me on my return to Badagry three years ago.

May 12th.—It rained so heavily this morning, that even if we had

81

not been obliged to remain in *Eetcho* today, it would have been next to impossible to have pursued our journey. The celebrated market of this place may be said to commence about mid-day, at which time thousands of buyers and sellers had assembled in a large open space in the heart of the town, presenting the most busy, bustling scene imaginable. To say nothing of the hum and clatter of such a multitude of barbarians, the incessant exertions of a horrid band of native musicians rendered our own voice inaudible. Country cloth, indigo, provisions, etc, were offered for sale, but we observed nothing in the market deserving particular notice.

May 13th.—We arose at a very early hour this morning to undertake the journey to Katunga. The air was cooler than we have felt it since landing from the *Clinker*, the thermometer being as low as 71° in the shade. The natives appeared to feel this severity of the weather most keenly, for though they huddled themselves up in their warmest cotton dresses, they were as yet shivering with cold. Hundreds of people, and perhaps if I were to say *thousands*, the number would not be overrated, preceded and followed us in the pathway; and as they winded through thick forests, along narrow roads, their blue and white clothing, contrasted with the deep green of the ancient trees, produced an eminently pleasing effect. We had not proceeded a great way when the escort from Katunga was descried at a distance, and approaching us at a rapid pace, joined the party in a few minutes. It consisted only of a few ragged individuals on foot, and eight on horseback.

I sounded my bugle, at which the natives were astonished and pleased; but a black trumpeter, jealous of the performance, challenged a contest for the superiority of the respective instruments, which terminated in the entire defeat of the African, who was hooted and laughed at by his companions for his presumption, and gave up the trial in despair.

The leader of our escort was a strange-looking, powerful fellow, and might very well serve the writer of a romance as the hero of his tale, in the character of keeper of an enchanted castle, when fierce, scowling looks, terrific frowns, and a peculiarly wild expression of countenance, are intended to be *naturally* described, for the man's stature was gigantic, his eyes large, keen, piercing, and ever in motion, his broad nose squatted over both cheeks—his lips immensely large, exposing a fine set of teeth; the beard was black, thick, and gristly, and, covering all the lower part of his face, reached to his bosom; the famous Blue Beard was nothing to him; and in gazing on his features one would almost be inclined to believe, that all the most iniquitous and depraved passions of human nature were centered in his heart. Yet with so unlovely and forbidding an appearance, the man is in reality as innocent and docile as a lamb. He wore on his head a small rush hat, in shape like a common earthenware pan inverted, or like the hats which are worn by the lower class of Chinese. His breast was enveloped in a coarse piece of blue cloth; from his left shoulder hung a large quiver of arrows; and in his right hand he held a bow, which he brandished like a lance; a short pair of trousers covered his thighs, and fantastically-made leathern boots incased his feet and legs. His skin was of jetty blackness, his forehead high; but his tremendous beard, which was slightly tinged with grey, contributed, perhaps more than anything else, to impart that wildness and fierceness to his looks which at first inspired us with a kind of dread of our leader.

Thus escorted, we travelled onwards; and after a hasty ride of six hours, beheld from a little eminence those black, naked hills of granite, at whose base lies the metropolis of Yarriba. About an hour afterwards we entered the gates of that extensive city. As is the custom, we stayed under a tree, just inside the walls, till the king and his eunuchs were informed of our arrival, which having been done, after a wearisome delay, we rode to the residence of *Ebo*,[1] the chief eunuch, who, next to the king, is the most influential man in the place. We found this personage, a 'great, fat, round, oily man',[2] airing himself under the verandah of his dwelling. Other eunuchs of similar appearance were sitting on the ground with him, and joined him in welcoming both of us (but myself more especially) to Katunga, with every appearance of sincerity, heartiness, and goodwill. We then walked all together to the king's house.

[1] Richard Lander knew Ebo well from his two earlier visits to Katunga in 1826 and 1827. On his first visit he had described Ebo as 'sly, lubberly, fat, monstrous' with a 'ravenous appetite' that was 'proverbial in the city'. 'That old gourmand had a paunch of a most awful size, which he contrived to keep in excellent condition by partaking largely of the good things intended for our use.' In 1827 Lander found on his return to Katunga that Ebo had been promoted 'to the highest offices of the state' (Lander, 1830, I, p. 109, II, p. 201). Eunuchs were 'generally chosen from boys bought with money, and employed first as pages to the King, or attendants on one of his wives'. The Eunuchs were known as *Iwefa*, 'lordlings of the palace'. They acted as 'guardians of the King's children', possessed 'the unenviable privilege of mingling with the King's wives' and had 'the exclusive right of seizing anything in the market with impunity'. The two chief eunuchs were the *Ona'efa*, who acted as legal adviser to the king, and the *Osi'efa* or *Olosi*, who 'represented the King on all occasions and in all matters civil as well as military' (Johnson, 1957, pp. 59–60).

[2] James Thomson, *The Castle of Indolence*, lxix:

A little, round, fat, oily man of God.

IV

Katunga

INFORMATION OF OUR COMING had been previously sent to the monarch, and we waited with much patience for a considerable period till he had put on his robes of state. Meantime, to amuse us and beguile the hour away, the head drummer and his assistant, with the most benevolent intention, commenced a concert of the most bewitching melody; and long drums, kettle drums, and horns, were played, with little intermission, till Mansolah made his appearance, when all noises were suddenly hushed, and we were desired to draw nearer to pay our respects to his Majesty. We did so after the English manner, much to the entertainment and diversion of the king, who endeavoured to imitate us, but it was easy to perceive that he is but a novice in the European mode of salutation, bowing and shaking hands. We have no doubt that it was owing to the rusticity and awkwardness of our address, that Mansolah's risible faculties were so strongly excited; but he laughed so long and heartily, and his wives, and eunuchs and subjects of all sorts, joined him with such good will, and such power of lungs, that we were constrained to unite our voices to the general burst of kindly feeling, although if we had been asked the cause of such jollity and obstreperous mirth, we should have been at a loss for an answer.

Mansolah's headpiece was something like a bishop's mitre, profusely ornamented with strings of coral, one of which answered the purpose of a ribbon, for it was tied under the chin, to prevent the cap from being blown off. His tobe was of green silk, crimson silk damask, and green silk velvet, which were all sown together like pieces of patchwork. He wore English cotton stockings, and neat leathern sandals of native workmanship. A large piece of superfine light blue cloth, given

84

the chief by the late Captain Clapperton, he used for a carpet. The eunuchs and other individuals who were present at the interview prostrated themselves before their prince, agreeably to the custom of the country, and rubbed their heads with earth two separate times, retreating at some distance to perform this humiliating and degrading ceremony, and then drawing near the royal person, to lie again with their faces in the dust. They saluted the ground also near which he was sitting, by kissing it fervently and repeatedly, and by placing each cheek on it. Then, and not till then, with their heads, and faces, and lips, and breasts, stained with the damp red soil, which still clung to them, they were allowed to seat themselves near their monarch, and to join in the conversation. Two or three inferior eunuchs, not satisfied with this servile prostration, began to sport and roll themselves about on the ground; but this could not be effected without immense labour and difficulty, and panting and straining, for, like Sir John Falstaff, they could be compared to nothing so appropriately as huge hills of flesh. There they lay wallowing in the mire, like immense turtles floundering in the sea, till Ebo desired them to rise.

The conference having ended, a kid, a calabash of *caffas*, and two thousand cowries in money were presented to us; and cheered by a flourish of music, we laughed in concert and shook hands with the king, and walked away towards our own dwelling, which had been repaired and thoroughly cleaned out for our sole use. In the evening the king returned our visit, and immediately took a fancy to my brother's bugle horn, which was readily given him. He was vastly pleased with the present, and by smiles and words, returned us many thanks for it; said he was quite delighted; and that it made his heart glad to see us; hoped we should make ourselves comfortable whilst we remained in Katunga; shook hands; made a bow, and 'smiling in heart and in soul content', the sovereign departed, followed by a suite of wives, eunuchs, and other attendants.

May 14th.—Accompanied by Ebo, and the other unwieldy eunuchs, my brother took a present to the king this morning, which was pretty well received, Mansolah, out of compliment I suppose, remarking that if we had not brought with us the value of a single cowry, we should have been favourably received at Katunga and well entertained at his own cost. We had previously sounded our friend Ebo on the subject of our journey to the Niger; but he strongly advised us by no means even to hint such an intention to the king, whose suspicions, he assured us, would immediately take the alarm, so that instead of being forwarded on our way thither, we should either be detained in the town for an indefinite time, or sent back again to the coast. We therefore conceived it prudent to give him the following statement only: 'That the king of England, anxious to procure the restoration of certain papers which belonged to a countryman of ours, who perished at Boossa about twenty years ago, which papers were supposed to be in the possession of the sultan of Yaoorie, we had been despatched hither by our sovereign, in the hope that the king of Katunga would forward us to the latter state, for the purpose of obtaining them from the sultan of Yaoorie, and taking them back to England.' Mansolah displayed neither eager curiosity as to our object in coming to his country, nor surprise when we had informed him of it; but very promptly observed, that in two days' time he would send a messenger to Kiama, Wouwou, Boossa, and Yaoorie, to acquaint the rulers of those provinces of our intention to pay them a visit; and that on the man's return we should have his permission to depart.

We intend, after leaving Yaoorie, to proceed direct to Guarie, the prince of which country will, no doubt, send us to Funda, from whence we must endeavour to discover the termination of the Niger.

May 15th.—Instead of the jarring noise of women's tongues, which had annoyed and followed us at every stage of our journey from Badagry, we at length enjoy as much of composure and tranquillity as we can well desire, for Ebo's wives residing at some distance from the part of the yard which we occupy, the shrill sounds of their voices are pleasant, contrasted with the former loud, discordant, and perpetual din which rang in our ears from morning till night. Our male visitors, likewise, are few and select, and do not remain with us any very considerable time together. An order has been issued by the king, that if any impertinent individual troubles us at any time with his company when it is not desired, Ebo is at liberty to behead him; and no one shall have the effrontery, says Mansolah, to tax the eunuch with injustice or cruelty in the performance of his duties. This proclamation, if it may so be termed, has had the desired effect, for dreading the even-handed Ebo, who is public executioner as well as chief eunuch, the inhabitants of Katunga have hitherto repressed their curiosity, and have confined themselves to their own abodes.

All seems quiet and peaceable in this large, dull city; and one cannot help feeling rather melancholy, in wandering through streets almost deserted, and over a vast extent of fertile land, on which there is no human habitation, and scarcely a living thing to animate or cheer the prevailing solemnity. The walls of the town have been suffered to fall into decay; and are now no better than a heap of dust and ruins; and such unconcern and apathy pervade the minds of the monarch and his ministry, that the wandering and ambitious Falatah has penetrated into the very heart of this country, made himself master of two of its most important and flourishing towns, with little, if any, opposition; and is gradually, but very perceptibly, gaining on the lukewarm natives of the soil, and sapping the foundations of the throne of Yarriba. The people cannot, surely, be fully aware of their own danger, or they never could be unconcerned spectators of events which are rapidly tending to root out their religion, customs, and institutions, and totally annihilate them as a nation.[1] But since they have neither foresight, nor wisdom, nor resolution, to put themselves in a posture of defence, and make at least a *show* of resistance, when danger, real or imaginary, menaces them; since neither the love of country, which stimulates almost all nations to heroic achievements in defence of their just and natural rights, and all that is truly dear to them in the world; and since neither affection for their defenceless wives and unprotected offspring, nor love of self, can awaken a single spark of courage or patriotism in their bosoms, can scare away that demon sloth from among them, or induce them to make a solitary

[1] The Landers' prophecy of approaching doom was to be fulfilled, when about the year 1837 Katunga was captured and destroyed by the Fulani from Ilorin. According to Samuel Johnson, the Yoruba historian, 'King Majotu [whom the Landers called Mansolah] was well advanced in age, before he was called to the throne, and consequently the business of state was for the most part left in the hands of the Crown Prince Adewusi; unfortunately, he was neither wise nor prudent but rather a dissolute and licentious prince, extravagant and cruel to a degree. He acted more like a monomaniac than like a rational being. His father was too old and weak to check him. . . . Added to the scourge of the sword, divine judgment fell upon the nation in famine also and pestilence. Towards the end of this reign there was a famine in the land for two years which obliterated every trace of the plenty they revelled in when there was peace and prosperity. . . . This calamity was followed by a pestilence called the Pehe, a disease of the respiratory organs; thousands were swept away by it, and king Majotu was among its victims.' Majotu was succeeded by Amodo, who 'came to the throne at a time when the kingdom was distracted by anarchy and confusion. None of the provincial kings now paid tribute to Oyo or acknowledged the authority of the King. He was virtually King of the capital only' (Johnson, 1957, pp. 213–17).

The site of Katunga or Old Oyo lies in an enclave of Western Region territory about thirty miles north-west of Ilorin. The site, which, lying more than ten miles from any road, is not easily accessible has been described by a recent visitor, as being 'so waterless that during the dry season even the wild game leave it for better watered areas. The area is overgrown with a dense growth of savannah woodland 30 or 40 feet high' (Allison, *Odu*, n.d.). A preliminary archaeological survey of the site was made by Mr Frank Willett in 1956/7 (Willett, 1960).

exertion to save themselves and posterity, from a foreign yoke; why then, they are surely unworthy to be called a people; they deserve to be deprived of their effects, children, and personal liberty to have their habitual sloth and listlessness converted into labour and usefulness, in tilling, improving and beautifying for strangers that soil, which they have neither spirit nor inclination to cultivate for themselves.

A market is held daily in different parts of Katunga, but twice in the week it is much larger, and better attended than on either of the other days. I visited one of the latter this morning, which is styled the 'Queen's market'; but as it is shifted to another place towards evening, it is then called the 'king's market'. The sellers were by far more numerous than the buyers; and, on the whole, the articles exposed for sale by no means realized the expectations which we had formed of them. Among them we observed three or four different kinds of corn; beans, peas, and vegetables in abundance; the mi-cadania butter; ground or guinea nuts; country cotton cloths, indigo, red clay, salt, and different varieties of pepper; besides trona, snuff and tobacco, knives, barbs, hooks, and needles, the latter of the rudest native manufacture. There were also, finger rings of tin and lead; and iron bracelets and armlets; old shells, old bones, and other venerable things, which European antiquaries would gaze on with rapture; besides native soap, little cakes of cheese and butter; an English common blue plate, a great variety of beads, both of native and European manufacture, among the former of which we recognized the famous *Agra* bead,[1] which at Cape Coast Castle, Accra, and other places, is sold for its weight in gold, and which has vainly been attempted to be imitated by the Italians and our own countrymen. Provisions also were offered for sale in abundance; and besides beef and mutton, which were made up into little round balls, weighing about an ounce and three-quarters each, and presented not the most delicate or tempting appearance, we observed an immense quantity of rats, mice, and lizards, dressed and undressed, all having their skins on, and arranged in rows.

I met with and purchased a very curious and singular kind of stone in the market. The natives informed us that it was dug from the earth, in a country called *Iffie*, which is stated to be 'four moons' journey

[1] The beads which the Landers called 'Agra' must in fact have been the famous *aggrey* or *akori* beads. According to the reports of Portuguese and Dutch writers in the sixteenth and seventeenth centuries the bead was in fact a stone, 'blue in colour but greenish in translucence', 'especially valued on the Gold Coast', and 'which European manufacturers had attempted with indifferent success to counterfeit in blue glass'. For a discussion of the archaeological problems presented by these beads see Fage, 1962.

from Katunga, where, according to their tradition, their first parents were created, and from whence all Africa was peopled.[1] It consists of a variety of little transparent stones, white, green, and every shade of blue, all embedded in a species of clayey earth, resembling rough mosaic work.

Sunday, May 16th.—We have been favoured with the company of several Haussa Mallams, who, notwithstanding the irksome restraint to which they are subjected by the jealousy of the king and his people, are content to remain so far from their native country, and reside among strangers and pagans as long as they live. Whether the priests have taken this step purely from religious motives, or, which is the more likely reason of the two, that they have exiled themselves from their home and families, for the mere purpose of being enriched at the expense of the credulity and ignorance of the inhabitants, we have been unable to discover.

May 17th.—Besides presents to the king and his chief eunuch, it is expected that something will be given to three 'head men', who advise with the prince, and lead his soldiers to battle.

We are of opinion, that it would require a long residence in this country, and a perfect acquaintance with its language, to enable a foreigner to form a correct judgement of its laws, manners, customs, and institutions, as well as its religion and the form and nature of its government. So innumerable are the mistakes which the smattering of ignorant native interpreters never fails to occasion, that we despair of getting much accurate information on any of these heads. We can only answer for what we *see*. Perhaps few despots sully their dignity by condescending to consult the inclination of their subjects, in personally communicating to them their most private as well as public concerns. Yet, the sovereign of Yarriba appears to be so obliging, as to make this a common practice. In return, however, the people are expected and compelled to satisfy the curiosity of their prince by adopting a similar line of conduct towards him; and all the presents they receive from strangers, how trifling soever they may be, are, in every instance,

---

[1] Ile Ife, the Landers' 'Iffie', is the most sacred place in Yorubaland. 'It was believed to be not only the centre of Yorubaland but also the centre of the world' (Niven, 1958, p. 9). Ife was not further from Katunga than Ijana.

The curious stone purchased by the Landers 'can be exactly matched in the collection of the Ife Museum. It is the incompletely remelted residue of mixed fragments of glass, looking quite opaque as melted glass does, from the bottom of a crucible, found originally in the Olokun Grove on the north side of Ife' (Willett, 1960 A, p. 234). I am most grateful to Mr Frank Willett for bringing this point to my attention.

taken to his residence for inspection. Every thing, indeed, that relates to their personal interests, and all their domestic concerns, he listens to with the most patriarchal gravity. Thus, our present to the king has been exhibited to his people two or three times; Ebo's also, and those of the head men, have been shown to them as well as to their sovereign. The common people were all anxious to know whether, among the other things, they had received, we had given their king or his ministers any coral; and their curiosity was immediately gratified without hesitation or remark.

May 18th.—Every one here appears uneasy at the very mention of Benin; and though we have endeavoured by various indirect means to ascertain the number of days it would take a person to travel thither from Katunga, evasive or equivocating answers are the utmost we can obtain; one of the people asserting that the journey might easily be accomplished in twelve days, and another declaring, a moment afterwards, that it would occupy a period of not less than four months. Nothing seems to be a greater grievance to the natives than the answering of any questions put to them, be they never so familiar and unimportant. They dislike, nay abhor to do it; and instead of satisfying the inquirer, they study to mislead him by falsehood and misrepresentation.

Katunga has by no means answered the expectations we had been led to form of it, either as regards its prosperity, or the number of its inhabitants. The vast plain also on which it stands, although exceedingly fine, yields in verdure and fertility, and simple beauty of appearance, to the delightful country surrounding the less celebrated city of Bohoo. Its market is tolerably well supplied with provisions, which are, however, exceedingly dear; insomuch, that with the exception of disgusting insects, reptiles, and vermin, the lower classes of the people are almost unacquainted with the taste of animal food.

Owing to the short time we have been in the country, the manners of the people have not sufficiently unfolded themselves to our observation; so that we are unable to speak of them with confidence; yet, the few opportunities we have had of studying their characters and dispositions induce us to believe that they are a simple, honest, inoffensive, but weak, timid, and cowardly race. They seem to have no social tenderness, very few of those amiable private virtues which would win our affection, and none of those public qualities that claim respect or command admiration. The love of country is not strong enough in their bosoms to incite them to defend it against the

irregular incursions of a despicable foe. To this unpardonable indifference to the public interest, and neglect of all the rules of prudence
and common sense, is owing the progress which the Falatahs have
made in gaining over to themselves a powerful party, consisting of
individuals from various nations in the interior, who had emigrated
to this country; and the great and uniform success which has attended
all their ambitious projects. They are now effectually and firmly seated
in the very centre of the kingdom; they have entrenched themselves
in strong walled towns; and have recently forced from Mansolah a
declaration of their independence, whilst this negligent and imbecile
monarch beholds them gnawing away the very sinews of his strength,
without making the slightest exertion to apply a remedy to the evil,
or prevent their future aggrandizement. Besides *Raka*,[1] which is
peopled wholly by Falatahs, who have strengthened it amazingly, and
rendered it exceedingly populous, another town of prodigious size
has lately sprung into being, which already far surpasses Katunga in
wealth, population, and extent. It was at first resorted to by a party
of Falatahs, who named it *Alorie*,[2] and encouraged all the slaves in
the country to flee from the oppression of their masters, and join
their standard. They reminded the slaves of the constraint under
which they laboured, and tempted them by an offer of freedom and
protection, and other promises of the most extravagant nature, to
declare themselves independent of Yarriba. Accordingly, the discontented many miles round eagerly flocked to Alorie in considerable

---

[1] 'Raka' is in fact the town called by the Landers later 'Rabba' (modern Raba). The
Landers were to have some dealings with Raba in the course of their journey down the
Niger (p. 193). Clapperton on his first visit to Sokoto had learnt that 'Rakah' was 'a
place of great trade between the interior and the coast'. Sultan Muhammad Bello had
agreed to allow British ships to come 'to the harbour of Racka' and a British consul to
reside there. This agreement he was not prepared to ratify when Clapperton returned to
Sokoto in 1826 (Denham and Clapperton, 1828, II 339, 420). Raba was originally a Nupe
town; the Fulani formed only a small proportion of the population.

[2] The Landers' account of the rise of Ilorin, 'Alorie', is misleading, as it makes no mention of the part played by Afonja. Afonja was one of the greatest war-lords of the *Alafin*
of Oyo, holding the title *Are-Ona-Kakanfo*, 'conferred upon the greatest soldier and
tactician of the day'. Basing himself on his town of Ilorin, he made himself independent
of the *Alafin*. 'In order to strengthen his hands, he invited a Fulah Moslem Priest named
Alimi to Ilorin to act as his priest. Alimi in responding to his call came with his Hausa
slaves and made Ilorin his home. These Hausa slaves Afonja found to be useful as soldiers.
All the Hausa slaves in the adjacent towns hitherto employed as barbers, rope-makers,
and cowherds, now deserted their masters and flocked to Ilorin.' Later—the exact date
is not certain, but the event must have taken place about 1830—the Hausa soldiery revolted against Afonja, killed him and accepted Alimi as their ruler (Johnson, 1957, 74,
189–200).

numbers, where they were well received. This took place as far back as forty years, since which, other Falatahs have joined their countrymen from *Soccatoo* and *Rabba*; and notwithstanding the wars (if mutual kidnapping deserves the name) in which they have been engaged in the support and maintenance of their cause, Alorie is become by far the largest and most flourishing city in Yarriba, not even excepting the capital itself. It is said to be two days' journey— that is, forty or fifty miles, in circumference, and to be fortified by a strong clay wall with moats. The inhabitants have now vast herds and flocks, and upwards of three thousand horses; which last will appear a very considerable number, when it is considered that Katunga does not contain more than as many hundreds. The population of Alorie has never been estimated, but it must be immense; lately, it has been declared independent of Yarriba; and its inhabitants are permitted to trade with the natives of the country, on condition that no more Falatahs be suffered to enter its walls. It is governed by twelve rulers, each of a different nation, and all of equal power; the Falatah chief not having more influence or greater sway than the others. *Raka* is but one day's journey north-east of Katunga; and *Alorie* three days' journey to the south-west.

May 19th.—The king has sent us nothing since the day of our arrival; and the present then given was disgraceful in the extreme, as coming from the monarch of a large and mighty kingdom. His treatment of the late Captain Clapperton was altogether the reverse of this: a bullock was sent him immediately after the first interview, and a live goat, or something equivalent, every day till his departure, which included a period little short of seven weeks. Nor, in other respects, has the conduct of Mansolah been such as to give us pleasure; but we can no otherwise account for this, than by supposing our present to have fallen far short of his expectations, and so failed to awaken those good-natured qualities which were displayed at sight of the infinitely more valuable as well as showy one of Captain Clapperton. But whatever may be the reason for it, certain it is that Mansolah and his subjects have seen quite enough of white men; and that the rapturous exultation which glowed in the cheeks of the first Europeans that visited this country on being gazed at, admired, caressed, and almost worshipped as a god—joined to the delightful consciousness of his own unmeasurable superiority, will, in the present age at least, never be experienced by any other. Alas! what a misfortune! The eager curiosity of the natives has been glutted by satiety—an

European is shamefully considered no more than a man! and hereafter, without doubt, he will be treated entirely as such; so that, on
coming to this city, he must make up his mind to sigh a bitter farewell
to goat's flesh and mutton, and familiarize his palate to greater
delicacies, such as lizards, rats, and locusts, caterpillars and other
dainties, which the natives roast, grill, bake and boil, and which he
may wash down, if he pleases, with draughts of milk-white water,
the only beverage it will be in his power to obtain.[1]

May 20th.—Last night, to our infinite surprise and pleasure, Ebo
entered our yard in a great hurry, with the agreeable information that
the king had consented to our departure on Friday morning. So con-
fident had we been that we should be unable to start hence for a month
to come, at the shortest, that we not only sowed cress and onion seed
the day after our arrival, which are already springing up, but had
actually made up our minds to abide here during the continuance of
the rains. But now we are in hopes of reaching Yaoorie in twelve or
fourteen days.

The old route to Kiama is considered so dangerous, that it is understood we are to be sent back to *Atoopa*, and thence proceed on a safer
path. Although we now require but five men, besides our own, to
carry the luggage, the king scruples and hesitates to supply us even
with these. We are told it is on account of the vast number of people
that have emigrated from Katunga to Raka and Alorie, that a sufficient number of carriers cannot be procured for us; but we suspect that
the real reason is the same original sin—the humble character of our
present.

May 21st.—Instead of a visit from the king, we were requested
this morning to repair to his residence. On our arrival, we were introduced, without any ceremony, into a private yard, wherein the king
had been patiently waiting our coming for some time previously.
He was rather plainly dressed in the costume of the country, namely,
a tobe, trousers, and sandals, with a cap very much resembling in
shape those which were worn by elderly ladies in the time of Queen

[1] When Richard Lander had passed through Yoruba territory with Captain Clapperton
in 1826 the mission was greeted with exceptional hospitality, for a belief was spread abroad
that the white men were coming as 'messengers of peace', 'charged with a commission to
make peace wherever there is war and to do good to every country' through which they
passed (Clapperton, 1829, p. 24). During their stay of seven weeks in Katunga, 'the king,'
Lander wrote, 'visited us almost every day, and never came without an acceptable present
of provisions; while his caboceers behaved with a still nobler generosity' (Lander, 1830,
I, p. 108).

Elizabeth, and which are still retained by some in the more remote parts of England. On his right the eunuchs were reposing their huge limbs on the ground, with several of the elders of the people; and his left was graced by a circle of his young wives, behind whom sat the widows of more than one of his predecessors, many of whom appeared aged. A good deal of discussion ensued, and much serious whispering between the monarch and his wives, in the course of which both parties quitted the yard two or three times to hold a private conference, followed by the eunuchs with their hands clasped on their breasts. Mansolah at length scraped together two thousand cowries (about three shillings and sixpence of our money), which he presented to the four men that had accompanied us from Badagry and Jenna as messengers, guides, etc, to enable them to purchase provisions on their journey homeward. This sum had been collected among the king's wives, each having contributed a portion, because their lord and master did not happen to be in a liberal mood.

Mansolah, after some time, beckoned to us to draw near him, for we were sitting at some distance on a bundle of sticks, and with a most benevolent smile playing upon his wrinkled features, he slowly, and with great solemnity, placed a goora nut in the right hand of each of us, and then asked our names. Richard and John, we replied. 'Richard-ee and John-ee,' said the king, for he was unable to pronounce our Christian names without affixing a vowel to the end of them, 'you may now sit down again.' We did so, and remained in that posture till we were both completely wearied, when we desired Ebo to ask the king's permission for us to go home to breakfast, which was granted without reluctance. So, having shaken hands heartily with the good old man, and wished him a very long and happy reign, we bade him farewell for the last time, bowed to the ladies, and returned with all haste to our hut.

V

Katunga to Kiama

WE LEFT THE CITY, and returned to *Eetcho* by the way we had come. The journey from Katunga is long, and, owing to the ruggedness of the path, is very fatiguing.

May 22nd.—The Katunga carriers all complained of pains in their limbs, and on reaching *Leoguadda* they placed their burdens on the ground, and, to a man, stoutly refused to take them any further till tomorrow. Our own men also, who were still more heavily laden than they, had suffered so much from the long and irksome journey of yesterday, particularly Jowdie, who is the strongest and most athletic of them all, that we greatly feared they would have been taken seriously ill on the road. We therefore lightened their burdens, and distributed a portion of what we had taken out of them, into the boxes, etc., of their already overladen Katunga associates, without, however, permitting the latter to know anything of the circumstance. Among the carriers was a very little man, called *Gazherie* (small man) on account of his diminutive stature; he was, notwithstanding, very muscular, and possessed uncommon strength, and bore a package, containing our tent, etc, which, though very heavy, was yet by far the lightest load of the whole. Conceiving that corporal strength should be taken into account, a bag of shot, weighing 28 lbs. was extracted from Jowdie's burden, and clandestinely added to his. The little man trudged along merrily without dreaming of the fraud that had been practised on him, till we arrived within a short distance of Leoguadda, when he discovered the cheat. He was much enraged and said he was resolved to proceed no farther than Leoguadda. He then succeeded in persuading his companions to follow his example, and thus a kind of combination was instantly formed against us.

We rested a while under a shady tree in Leoguadda, and here we were presently surrounded by the murmuring carriers, with the little man at their head. They were furious at first, and gave us to understand that they would go no further. Leoguadda contained no accomodations whatever for us; a storm seemed to be gathering over our heads; and Atoopa was the town in which the king of Katunga had advised us to spend the night. We resolved, therefore, to go on to that town, and strenuously endeavoured, by gentle means, to bring over the carriers to our views; but these failing, we resorted to their own mode of argument, namely, fierce looks, violent action, vociferous bawling, and expressive gesture, which intimidated them so much, that they snatched up their burdens without saying a word, and ran away with alacrity and good humour.

Sunday, May 23rd.—Though our horses were this morning in a very weak condition, yet we quitted Atoopa at an early hour and in good spirits. In two hours' time we entered a lively little walled town, called *Bumbum*, a great thoroughfare for *fatakies* of merchants, trading from Haussa, Borgoo, and other countries, to Gonja.[1] On quitting this town, our course altered to N.W., and continued so till our arrival at the large and important town of *Keeshee*, which is on the frontiers of the kingdom. Before entering this place, we passed through a clean, extensive, and highly flourishing Falatah village, called *Acba*.

In the centre of the town there is a high stony hill, almost covered with trees of stunted growth, to which, in case of invasion by an enemy,

[1] One of the most-frequented trade-routes in West Africa passed through Borgu. It linked the Hausa cities with Gonja, a country to the north of Ashanti. Kola-nuts, grown in Ashanti, were exported from Gonja to many countries in the western and central Sudan. Lander, on his first visit to Kiama, had met a Hausa caravan returning from Gonja, consisting of 'about a thousand individuals of both sexes'. Of the kola-nut, he wrote on this occasion: 'This nut, which is in high esteem and general use all through the interior, is frequently applied to the same purpose as the calumet [tobacco-pipe] of peace amongst the North American Indians, and is likewise used on all public occasions to testify the good understanding that prevails in the assembly: when presented to private individuals, it signifies that there is peace between the donor and receiver. The kola is the fruit of a beautiful tree, growing in abundance on many parts of the coast, and is an agreeable bitter and astringent; it also produces a rich yellow dye, which is oftentimes used by the natives in the embellishment of their persons. In some districts the nut is exceedingly scarce, and fetches an exorbitant price; hence the traffic in it is carried on to an incredible extent, and yields an immense profit to those who are venturesome enough to risk the dangers of a long and perilous journey' (Lander, 1830, I, p. 126). Kola-nuts are still in great demand among the people of Northern Nigeria. The nuts no longer come from Gonja, but from Western Nigeria, being grown in the area south of Abeokuta, where the kola tree was introduced after the First World War. With the decay of the Kano–Gonja route, Borgu was left as one of the most isolated districts of Nigeria.

the inhabitants fly for refuge. As soon as they have reached its summit, it is borne, say they, by a supernatural power beyond the clouds, where it remains till the danger is over. Some years have elapsed since this miracle last took place, yet the story is told with a serious belief of its truth, and with the most amusing gravity.

A great number of emigrants from different countries reside here: there are not a few from Borgoo, Nouffie, Haussa, and Bornou, and two or three Tauricks, from the borders of the Great Desert. In no town through which we have hitherto travelled, have we seen so many fine tall men and good-looking women, as at this place; yet several individuals of both sexes are to be met with who have lost the sight of one eye, and others who have unseemly wens on the throat, as large as cocoa-nuts. We have likewise seen a female dwarf whose height scarcely exceeds thirty inches. Her head is disproportionately large to the size of her body; her features, like her voice, are harsh, masculine, and unpleasant in the extreme. There was an expression in her countenance so peculiarly repulsive, unwomanly, and hideous, that on her approaching our hut, I felt a very unusual and disagreeable sensation steal over me.

May 24th.—We have been compelled to remain here today, through the governor's inability to procure us carriers for the baggage.

A company of women and girls from the Falatah village of *Acba*, impelled by a curiosity so natural to their sex, came to see us in the afternoon. These females are so modest and so retiring, and evince so much native delicacy in their whole behaviour, that they excited in us the highest respect. Their personal attractions are no less winning. They have fine sparkling jetty eyes, with eye-lashes dark and glossy as the raven's plume. Their features are agreeable, although their complexions are tawny. Their general form is elegant, their hands small and delicate; and the peculiar cleanliness of their persons, and neatness of dress added to these, rendered their society altogether as desirable as that of their neighbours was disagreeable.

The Falatahs inhabiting Acba were all born and bred in that town. Their ancestors settled in the country at so remote a period, that not even a tradition has been preserved on the subject. These 'children of the soil' lead a harmless, tranquil, and sober life, which they never suffer passing events to disturb. They have no ambition to join their more restless and enterprising countrymen who have made themselves masters of Alorie and Raka, nor even to meddle in the private or public concerns of their near neighbours of Keeshee. Indeed they have kept themselves apart and distinct from all; they have retained the language of their fathers and the simplicity of their manners, and their existence glides serenely and happily away, in the enjoyment of the domestic pleasures and social tenderness which are found in civilized society, and which are unknown among their roving countrymen. They are on the best possible terms with their neighbours, and by them they are held in great respect.

The governor of Keeshee is a Borgoo man, and boasts of being the bosom friend of Yarro, chief of Kiama; but as the old man told us many wonderful stories of the number of towns under this sway, his amazing powers, great influence, and the entire subjection in which his own people were kept by his own good government, we are inclined to believe that the governor's pretensions are as hollow as they are improbable. Every one in this country displays this ridiculous vanity; and in most of the towns we have visited, it was the first great care of their chiefs to impress on our minds an idea of their vast importance, which in many instances was refuted by their ragged tobes and squalid appearance. After a deal of talking, the governor of Keeshee begged the favour of a little rum and medicine to heal his foot, which is inclined to swell and give him pain; and requested that we would repair a *gun* which had been deprived of its stock by fire. He then sang us a ditty in praise of elephants and their teeth, in which he was assisted by his cane-bearer, and afterwards took his leave.

May 25th.—Some Mallams, and others who wish to accompany us to Kiama, persuaded the easy-going governor last night to defer getting us carriers till tomorrow, because, forsooth, they are not prepared to travel today.

The governor solicited a charm of us today, to preserve his house from the effects of fire, and cause him to become rich; while one of his elderly wives made a doleful complaint of having been likely to become a mother for the last thirty years, and begged piteously for medicine to promote and assist her *accouchement.* We could satisfy the old man easily enough, but his wife's hypochondriacal complaint we conceived to be too dangerous to be meddled with by unprofessional hands. Poor woman, she is much to be pitied, for the odd delusion under which she has been labouring so long a time has given her considerable uneasiness, so that life itself has become a burden to her. All that we could do for her, was to soothe her mind, by telling her that her distemper was very common, and not at all dangerous, and promising, that on our return this way, should nothing transpire in her favour in the mean time, we would endeavour to remove the cause of her complaint. This comforted the aged matron exceedingly, and, in the fulness of her heart, she burst into tears of joy, dropped on her knees to express her acknowledgement, and pressed us to accept a couple of goora nuts.

May 26th.—We had the pleasure of receiving the morning salutation of our fair friends the Falatahs on bended knee. Resolved to have another and a last chat with the white strangers, these females had come for the purpose of offering us two calabashes of new milk. This, and former little acts of kindness, which we have received from these dark-eyed maidens, have effectually won our regard, because we know they were disinterestedly given; and the few minutes which we have had the happiness of spending in their company, and that of their countrymen, have redeemed many hours of listlessness and melancholy, which absence from our native country, and thoughts of home and friends, but too often excite in our breasts. It was therefore not without a feeling of sorrow that we bade them adieu. There was less of feeling and tenderness, certainly, though more words and much greater noise in taking our farewell of the two old messengers that had accompanied us from Badagry, and who, with the Jenna guides, will return homewards tomorrow. They have behaved themselves throughout to our hearts' desire; and because they had been our companions in a long and painful journey, and because their faces had become familiarised to us, we left them behind with sincere regret.

Although we left Keeshee between six and seven in the morning, we were obliged to seat ourselves on a green turf in the outskirts of the town, and wait there till a quarter after nine before the carriers with the luggage made their appearance. Here we were joined by a Borgoo *fatakie*, and our ears were saluted with the hoarse, dull sounds of their drum, which was played by a ragged one-eyed Yarribean long after we were on our journey. A company of merchants trading through the country has always a drummer in their pay, who walks at the head of the party, and performs on his instrument continually, be the journey ever so long, for the purpose of animating the slaves to quicken their steps.

Our route lay through a vast and lonely forest, infested by bands of robbers, and in which there is not a single human habitation. My brother went unarmed before the *fatakie*, and travelled alone, whilst I remained behind to defend the carriers in case of necessity. He had already rode some distance in advance of us, when about twenty very

99

suspicious-looking fellows, armed with lances and bows and arrows, suddenly made their appearance from behind the trees, where they had concealed themselves, and stood in the middle of the path before the men with the luggage, who were so terrified, that they were preparing to drop their burdens and run away. My gun being loaded, I levelled it at them, and had nearly discharged it at the leader, which intimidated them all so much, that they retreated again into the heart of the forest.

We journeyed fifteen miles through this dreaded forest. We then arrived at the *Moussa*, which is a rivulet separating the kingdom of Yarriba from Borgoo.

When travelling in the bush, several men in the train of a *fatakie* wear a large iron ring on the thumb and middle finger. To the latter a piece of plate iron is attached, with which they make signals to each other and the *fatakie* when apart by clinking the rings. This method of communication is very significant, and it is understood as well, and is as promptly answered or obeyed, as our boatswain's whistle. The collision of the rings produces a harsh, grating noise, loud enough to be heard at a considerable distance.

The mere crossing of a little stream has introduced us into a country very different from Yarriba, which is inhabited by a different people, who speak a different language, profess a different religion, and whose manners, customs, amusements, and pursuits, are altogether different. The village in which we are stopping is called *Moussa*, after the river.

May 27th.—There is a sweetness in the mountain air and a dewy freshness in the morning, which we experienced today with considerable pleasure on ascending the hills which border the northern side of the pretty little *Moussa*. When wild beasts, tired with their nightly prowlings, seek retirement and repose in the lonely depths of these primeval forests, and when birds, perched on the branches of trees over our heads, warble forth their morning song, it is the time that makes up for the languid, wearisome hours in the heat of the day, when nothing can amuse and nothing interest us. It is in the earlier part of the morning, too, or in the cool of the evening, that nature can be leisurely contemplated and admired in the simple loveliness of a verdant plain, a sequestered grotto, or a rippling brook; or in the wilder and more mysterious features of her beauty in the height of a craggy precipice, the silence and gloom of vast shady woods, or when these woods are gracefully bending to the passing gale.

Our path lay through a rich country, covered with luxuriant grasses and fine trees, but very little underwood could be seen. It abounds plentifully with deer and antelopes, and other wild animals of a more ferocious nature, such as the lion, the leopard, the elephant, the wild ass, etc; but the solitary lowing of a buffalo was the only sound that we distinguished in the forest, and we had not the pleasure of meeting even with this animal.[1]

At eleven o'clock we entered a very small and cleanly-looking village, where we halted for the day. At sunset, not having anything to eat, I went out into the wood with my gun, and was fortunate enough to shoot a few doves; and Pasko, who went in a different direction, shot a Guinea hen, which made us an excellent supper. Hunger had driven back our Keeshee carriers, and therefore we have been obliged to send a messenger to Yarro, for men to supply their place.

May 28th.—In the forenoon, the musical jingling of little bells announced the approach of a body of horsemen, who in less than a minute galloped up to our hut, and saluted us one after another with a martial air, by brandishing their spears, to our great discomforture, within a few feet of our faces. The carriers who had arrived from Kiama, had preceded them on the road, and the whole of the men now sat down to partake of a little refreshment. It was twelve o'clock exactly when we set out on our journey. Ant-hills were numerous in the road; and a few paces from it, we observed little cone-shaped mud-buildings, erected by the natives for the purpose of smelting iron-ore, which is found in abundance in different parts of the country. At sunset we arrived at a village called *Benikenny*. We fully expected to have slept there, for the afternoon had been excessively warm, and we were all much fatigued. But our armed escort encouraged us to proceed. The moon and stars supplied us with a cooler and more agreeable light; and we journeyed on through the forest more slowly than before. In spite of our fatigue, we could not help admiring the serenity and beauty of the evening, nor be insensible to the delicious fragrance shed around from trees and shrubs. The appearance of our warlike and romantic escort was also highly amusing. They were clad in the fashion of the East, and sought their way between the trees on our right and left; but sometimes they fell in our rear, and then again dashed suddenly by us with astonishing swiftness, looking as wild as the scenery through which their chargers bounded. The effect was rendered more

[1] Borgu, with its wide stretches of almost waterless bush, is today one of the most thinly populated districts of Northern Nigeria and one of the few parts of the country where wild animals are still to be seen. For a well-illustrated account of a recent journey through Borgu, Campbell, 1955.

imposing by the reflection of the moon-beams from their polished spears and the pieces of silver which are affixed to their caps, while the luminous fire-fly appeared in the air like rising and falling particles of flame.

About eight o'clock Kiama appeared before us, and in a few minutes we entered the city, and rode directly to the king's house. He came out to receive us, and welcomed us with much satisfaction and good will. He is an elderly man, almost toothless, and has a beard as white as wool. His first question was concerning the health of our sovereign, and his second and last respecting our own welfare. He seemed to be exceedingly well pleased at seeing me again.[1] No sooner were we securely housed, than half a dozen of the king's wives introduced themselves with huge calabashes of sour milk, fried pancakes, and beef stewed in rice, the first we have yet seen. Various coloured mats of excellent workmanship were afterwards brought for our use; and with thankful hearts and comfortable feelings, we lay down to rest.

[1] Lander had been hospitably entertained by Yarro, the king of Kaiama, when he passed through Borgu in 1826 and again in 1827. He described Yarro then as 'an eccentric and facetious character; but without exception the finest and handsomest man I ever saw in Africa, or perhaps in any country' (Lander, 1830, II, p. 181). In the Kaiama king-list, Yaru Iloride is given as the ruler from 1827 to 1830. Kaiama is stated to have been founded in the latter half of the eighteenth century (*Kontagora Gazetteer*, pp. 28, 29).

VI

Kiama

May 29th.—Just before sunset, my brother selected a present, consisting of the following articles, for the king, viz. six yards of red cloth, a quantity of printed cottons, a pair of silver bracelets, a looking-glass, two pairs of scissors, a knife, two combs, and a tobacco-pipe. The goods having been properly secured, we repaired with this present to the king, who received it with much apparent satisfaction.

Yarro professes the Mohammedan faith, yet it is easy to perceive the very slender acquaintance he has obtained of the precepts of the Koran, by the confidence which he still places in the religion of his fathers, in placing fetishes to guard the entrance of his houses, and adorn their naked walls. In one of his huts we observed a stool of very curious workmanship. The form of it is nearly square; the two principal sides are each supported by four little wooden figures of men; and another of large dimensions, seated on a clumsy representation of a hippopotamus, is placed between them. These images were subsequently presented to us by Yarro, and we learnt that the natives, before undertaking any water excursion, applied for protection from the hippopotami and other dangers of the river to the principal figure, which is represented as mounted on one of those creatures. This important personage is attended by his musicians, and guarded by soldiers, some armed with muskets, and others with bows and arrows, who formed the legs of the stool. In the annexed sketch, which is about one-seventh the size of the original, he has been placed on the top of the stool, that the view of him might not be interrupted.

In an inner apartment we discovered Yarro sitting alone on buffalo hides. The walls of this apartment were adorned with very good prints of our most gracious sovereign George the Fourth, his late royal brother the Duke of York, Lord Nelson, the Duke of Wellington on horseback, together with an officer in the Light Dragoons, in company with a smartly dressed and happy-looking English lady.[1] Opposite to them were hung horse accoutrements; and on each side were dirty scraps of paper containing select sentences from the Koran. On the

floor lay muskets, several handsomely ornamented lances, and other weapons, all confusedly heaped together by the side of a large granite stone used for pounding pepper.

[1] These prints had been presented to Yarro by Clapperton in 1826. Clapperton was struck by the large number of articles of English manufacture to be found in Kiama, far more than in the Yoruba country; among the articles shown to him was an earthenware jug, 'representing old Toby Philpot with a flowing jug of ale in his hand' (Clapperton, 1829, pp. 67–8).

When we spoke of proceeding to Yaoorie by way of Wowow and Boossa, the king objected to our visiting the former state under any consideration, alleging that three of the slaves who carried the goods for Captain Clapperton had never returned to him again, but had remained at Wowow, where they were protected by the governor Mohammed; and that if he should send others with us to that place, they might do the same. He therefore promises to send us to Boossa in four days' time by another road. Independently of the above consideration, the king is highly incensed against the ruler of Wowow for harsh treatment of the widow Zuma, who is his friend and relative, and who has lately fled to Boossa for the purpose of claiming the protection of the king of that country.[1]

It is said that Yarro's father, the late king of Kiama, during his lifetime, enjoyed the friendship of an Arab from the desert, which was returned with equal warmth and sincerity. A similarity of dispositions and pursuits produced a mutual interchange of kind actions; their friendship became so great, that the king was never happy except when in the Arab's company; and as a proof of his esteem and confidence, he gave him his favourite daughter in marriage. The fruit of this alliance is the restless widow Zuma, and hence her relationship to the present monarch of Kiama. To return to his father and the Arab: their friendship lasted until the death of the latter. The king, however, was inconsolable for his loss, and looked around him in vain for some one to supply the place of his friend; but the ardour of his affections was too strong, and led by the hope of following his friend to another world, he committed suicide. Yarro is much attached to the widow Zuma; and she would have fled hither, instead of going to Boossa, if her intentions had not been suspected, and her actions narrowly watched by the ruler of Wowow.

Sunday, May 30th.—Unwilling as we always are to break the proper

---

[1] The widow Zuma had played an amusing role in Clapperton's and Lander's first visit to Wawa. The appearance of this middle-aged Arab lady was immediately striking: 'immensely fat'—Clapperton called her 'a walking water-butt', she dyed her hair 'a rich and vivid blue', stained her hands and her feet in streaks of yellow and red, and adorned her naked bosom with necklaces of coral and gold. Captivating—at least in her own eyes, wealthy—the owner of a thousand slaves, and restlessly ambitious, she had fallen in love first with Lander, then, on being rejected by him, with his master. Her affections were cunningly deployed, for she hoped to use the two white men as her allies in a revolution to overthrow the king of Wawa. From this embarassing situation, Clapperton extricated himself with masterly diplomatic skill. The whole episode is one of the most hilarious in the annals of African exploration (Clapperton, 1829, pp. 81, 85–6, 110–15; Lander, 1830, I, pp. 150–71, II, pp. 166–75).

observance of the Sabbath, we were nevertheless compelled this forenoon to submit to the mortification of cleaning and polishing a sword
and a pistol, which were sent us for that purpose by the king against
the approaching Mahommedan festival.

May 31st.—It is supposed that the ruler of Wowow will make war
on this state as soon as he shall be made acquainted with the fact of our
being in Borgoo without having visited him. Although it is within the
dominions of the King of Boossa, who is acknowledged to be the

Figure from a Kiama stool.

greatest of the sovereigns of Borgoo, Wowow is reported to have
lately received a body of Nouffie horse soldiers, consisting of eight
hundred men, which has rendered its chief more powerful than either
of his neighbours. These soldiers are the remnant of the army of
Ederesa, who is the rightful heir to the throne of Nouffie: they deserted
him in his misfortunes, and sought a refuge in Wowow from the fury
of their successful countrymen, leaving their leader to his fate. Ederesa
is said to have found an asylum with one of the chiefs of a state near
the kingdom of Benin.[1]

[1] On the death of the *Etsu* Ma'azu, the nineteenth ruler of Nupe, a civil war broke out
between Jimada, Ma'azu's son and the legitimate heir, and Mayija or Magia, Ma'azu's
brother's son. Majiya built himself a capital at Raba on the Niger; with the help of Mallam
Dendo, the leader of the Fulani in Nupe, he succeeded in defeating and killing Jimada
about the year 1820. Ederesa or Idirisu, Jimada's son, fled across the river to Egga, 'where
he stayed, an exile and fugitive, powerless against Majiya's army' (Nadel, 1942, 78).

We receive visits almost every hour of the day from a number of Mohammedan Mallams residing at Kiama. Of all the vices of which these Mohammedan priests are guilty (and by all accounts they are not a few), slander and defamation of character appear to be by far the most general. Never do we hear a Mallam speak of his neighbours in terms of common respect. By his account they are all the vilest creatures under the sun, not one escaping the lash of his censure. 'Avoid that man,' said a complacent and comfortable-looking old Mahommedan last night, pointing to one of his companions as he quitted the hut (he had just blessed him in the name of Alla), 'for, believe me, he will take every opportunity of deceiving you.' The venerable speaker had a quantity of gilt buttons, nearly new, in his possession, which we had given him to sell, for we were frequently obliged to make such shifts for a meal, and when his invective was finished, he arose to take his leave: but the self-righteous priest had neglected, in the hurry of discourse, to secure a few buttons which he had purloined, for as he stood up they dropped from the folds of his garment on the floor. The man's confusion was immediately apparent, but we did not wish to punish him further by increasing his shame. Gilt buttons fetch a high price here (from two to three hundred cowries each); and as we have a great quantity of them, it is likely that from henceforth they will be of infinite service to us. Women use buttons to ornament their necks, fingers and wrists; and they imagine that the brightest of them are made of gold.

June 1st.—This is the eve of the 'Bebun Salah' or 'Great Prayer Day', and is generally employed by the Mussulmen in Kiama in making preparations for a festival which will commence tomorrow, and be continued till the evening of the next day. Every one here, who possesses the means, is obliged to slaughter either a bullock or a sheep on the anniversary of this day.[1]

June 2nd.—The threatening appearance of the weather prevented the Mohammedans from repairing to the spot which they had selected for the purposes of devotion, so early in the morning as they could

[1] 'Bebun Salah' is the Hausa *Babbar Salla*, arabic *id-al-kabir*, the greatest festival of the Muslim year. The *Salla* is still vigorously celebrated by the Muslims of Nigeria; the ceremonies that accompany the *Salla* in the larger towns of Northern Nigeria are as exhilarating and as spectacular as those described by the Landers. In the Muslim kingdoms or emirates of Northern Nigeria the festival has more than a religious significance; 'the elements of worship and secular display, inextricably fused, and supported by the stimulus of mass experience,' serve, as Nadel has pointed out, 'to mobolize periodically sentiments of loyalty and the consciousness of unity' (Nadel, 1942, p. 144).

have wished; but the clouds having dispersed, they had all assembled there between the hours of nine and ten. The worshippers arranged themselves in six lines or rows, the women forming the last, and sat down on as many ridges of earth, which had apparently been thrown up for the purpose. The chief Mallam no sooner began a prayer, than the talking and noise of the multitude ceased, and the deepest attention seemed to be paid by every one, though the substance of what he said could only be guessed at, because it was in Arabic, which none of them understand. When the usual form of prayer had been gone through, the head Mallam placed himself on a hillock, and for about five minutes read to the people a few loose pages of the Koran. After he had finished reading, the priest descended from the hillock and, with the help of his assistants, slaughtered a sheep which had been bound and brought to him for sacrifice. The blood of the animal was caught in a calabash; and the king and the more devoted of his subjects washed their hands in it, and sprinkled some of it on the ground. This conclusion of the ceremony was announced by the discharge of a few old muskets; and with drums beating and fifes playing, the people returned to their respective homes.

In the afternoon all the inhabitants of the town assembled to witness the horse-racing, to which every one had been looking forward with impatience. Previous to its commencement, the king, with his principal attendants, rode slowly round the town, more for the purpose of receiving the admiration and plaudits of his people than to observe where distress more particularly prevailed, which was his avowed intention. A hint from the chief induced us to attend the course with our pistols, to salute him as he rode by.

The race-course was bounded on the north by low granite hills; on the south by a forest; and on the east and west by tall shady trees, among which were habitations of the people. Under the shadow of these magnificent trees the spectators were assembled, and testified their happiness by their noisy mirth and animated gestures. When we arrived, the king had not made his appearance on the course; but his absence was fully compensated by the pleasure we derived from watching the anxious and animated countenances of the multitude, and in passing our opinions on the taste of the women in the choice and adjustment of their fanciful and many-coloured dresses. The chief's wives and younger children sat near us in a group by themselves; and were distinguished from their companions by their superior dress. Manchester cloths of inferior quality, but of the most showy patterns, and dresses made of common English bed-furniture, were fastened round the waist of several sooty maidens, who, for the sake of fluttering a short hour in the gaze of their countrymen, had sacrificed in clothes the earnings of a twelve-month's labour. All the women had ornamented their necks with strings of beads, and their wrists with bracelets of various patterns, some made of glass beads, some of brass, others of copper; and some again of a mixture of both metals: their ancles also were adorned with different sorts of rings, of neat workmanship.

The distant sound of guns gave notice of the king's approach, and every eye was immediately directed to the quarter from whence he was expected. The cavalcade shortly appeared, and four horsemen first drew up in front of the chief's house, which was near the centre of the course, and close to the spot where his wives and children and ourselves were sitting. Several men bearing on their heads an immense quantity of arrows in huge quivers of leopard's skin came next, followed by two persons who, by their extraordinary antics and gestures, we concluded to be buffoons. These last were employed in throwing sticks into the air as they went on, and adroitly catching them in falling, besides performing many whimsical and ridiculous feats. Behind these, and immediately preceding the king, a group of little boys, nearly naked, came dancing merrily along, flourishing cows' tails over their heads in all directions. The king rode onward, followed by a number of fine-looking men, on handsome steeds; and the motley cavalcade all drew up in front of his house, where they awaited his further orders without dismounting. This we thought was the proper time to give the first salute, so we accordingly fired three rounds; and our example was immediately followed by two soldiers, with muskets which were made at least a century and a half ago.

Preparations in the mean time had been going on for the race, and the horses with their riders made their appearance. The men were dressed in caps and loose tobes and trowsers of every colour; boots of red morocco leather, and turbans of white and blue cotton. The horses were gaily caparisoned; strings of little brass bells covered their heads; their breasts were ornamented with bright red cloth and tassels of silk and cotton; a large quilted pad of neat embroidered patchwork was placed under the saddle of each; and little charms, inclosed in red and yellow cloth, were attached to the bridle with bits of tinsel. The Arab saddle and stirrup were in common use; and the whole group presented an imposing appearance.

The signal for starting was made, and the impatient animals sprung forward and set off at a full gallop. The riders brandished their spears, the little boys flourished their cows' tails, the buffoons performed their antics, muskets were discharged, and the chief himself, mounted on the finest horse on the ground, watched the progress of the race, while tears of delight were starting from his eyes. The sun shone gloriously on the tobes of green, white, yellow, blue, and crimson, as they fluttered in the breeze; and with the fanciful caps, the glittering spears, the jingling of the horses' bells, the animated looks and warlike bearing of their riders, presented one of the most extraordinary and pleasing sights that we have ever witnessed. The race was well contested, and terminated only in the horses being fatigued and out of breath; but though every one was emulous to outstrip his companion, honour and fame were the only reward of the competitors.

A few naked boys, on ponies without saddles, then rode over the course, after which the second and last heat commenced. This was not by any means so good as the first, owing to the greater anxiety which the horsemen evinced to display their skill in the use of the spear and the management of their animals. The king maintained his seat on horseback during these amusements, without even once dismounting to converse with his wives and children who were sitting on the ground on each side of him. His dress was showy rather than rich, consisting of a red cap, enveloped in the large folds of a white muslin turban; two under tobes of blue and scarlet cloth, and an outer one of white muslin; red trousers, and boots of scarlet and yellow leather. His horse seemed distressed by the weight of his rider, and the various ornaments and trappings with which his head, breast, and body, were bedecked. The chief's eldest and youngest sons were near his women and other children, mounted on two noble looking horses. The eldest of these youths was about eleven years of age. The youngest being not more than three, was held on the back of his animal by a male attendant, as he was unable to sit upright in the saddle without this assistance. The child's dress was ill suited to his age. He wore on his head a tight cap of Manchester cotton, but it overhung the upper part of his face, and together with its ends, which flapped over each cheek, hid nearly the whole of his countenance from view; his tobe and trowsers were made exactly in the same fashion as those of a man, and two large belts of blue cotton, which crossed each other, confined the tobe to his body. The little legs of the child were swallowed up in clumsy yellow boots, big enough for his father; and though he was rather pretty, his whimsical dress gave him altogether so odd an appearance, that he might really have been taken for anything but what he really was. A few of the women on the ground by the side of the king wore large white dresses, which covered their persons like a winding-sheet. Young virgins, according to custom,[1] appeared in a state of nudity; many of them had wild flowers stuck behind their ears, and strings of beads, etc, round their loins; but want of clothing did not seem to damp their pleasure in the entertainment, for they appeared to enter into it with as much zest as any of their companions. Of the different coloured tobes worn by the men, none looked so well as those of a deep crimson colour on some of the horsemen; but the clean white tobes of the Mohammedan priests, of whom not less than a hundred were present on the occasion, were extremely neat and becoming. The sport terminated without the slightest accident, and the king's dismounting was a signal for the people to disperse.

We then paid our respects to the chief as usual, but our reception was formal and chilling, though nothing could have been more gratifying to him than our attendance on the present occasion. We had half a mind to be vexed at this mortifying repulse, but consoled ourselves with the reflection that we had no right to expect anything more than common courtesy and politeness. Besides this, he was surrounded by the loveliest of his women and the most warlike of his subjects, and being a rigid Mohammedan when it suits his convenience, he might have considered us as the enemies of his religion. To have shown, therefore, too great familiarity with us in the sight of his people, would perhaps have been unbecoming the dignity of the Chief of Kiama.

We have here endeavoured, to the best of our ability, to describe an African horse-race, but it is impossible to convey a correct idea of the singular and fantastic appearance of the numerous groups of people that met our view on all sides, or to describe their animation and

[1] On his first visit to Kiama, Lander had noted that 'Yarro entertains the whimsical notion, that as females came into the world naked, naked they ought to live in it till their death. "Man," said the king, "is the nobler animal, and wears clothing in token of his superiority over the weaker part of the creation"; and, in accordance with this singular doctrine, none of his wives ever dare to approach his presence with any other dress than that which nature has supplied them with' (Lander, 1830, II, pp. 181–2). Clapperton described how the king, on important occasions, was accompanied by 'six naked young girls', each carrying three light spears: 'their light form, the vivacity of their eyes, and the ease with which they appeared to fly over the ground, made them appear something more than mortal as they flew alongside of his horse, when he was galloping, and making his horse curvet and bound' (Clapperton, 1829, p. 72).

delight; the martial equipment of the soldiers and their noble steeds, and the wild, romantic, and overpowering interest of the whole mass. Singing and dancing have been kept up all night, and the revellers will not think of retiring to rest till morning.

June 3rd.—We have been detained in Kiama thus long, by reason, it is alleged of the holidays. We expected, naturally enough, that plenty of good provender, and a few days' rest, would recruit the strength of our horses; but, unfortunately, a contrary effect has been produced. My brother's more especially, has fallen away to a perfect skeleton.

Figures from a Kiama stool.

June 4th.—Perhaps no two people in the universe residing so near each other, differ more widely in their habits and customs, and even in their natures, than the natives of Yarriba and Borgoo. The former are perpetually engaged in trading with each other from town to town; the latter never quit their towns except in case of war, or when engaged in predatory excursions: the former are pusillanimous and cowardly; the latter are bold and courageous, full of spirit and energy, and never seem happier than when engaged in martial exercises: the former are generally, mild, unassuming, humble and honest, but cold and passionless;—the latter are proud and haughty; too vain to be civil, and too shrewd to be honest; yet they appear to understand somewhat of the nature of love and social affections; are warm in their attachments, and keen in their resentments.

A very old and respectable Falatah, the chief of a village at a short distance from Kiama, came to see us with several of his people. This singular race are dispersed all over the Borgoo territories, where they have resided from time immemorial. The Falatahs in Borgoo maintain no intercourse whatever with their countrymen in Haussa; and in order to prevent mischief and disturbances from taking place, none of them are permitted, on any consideration, to wear a sword, or carry about his person any offensive weapon.

VII

Kiama to Boossa

June 5th.—We were on horseback between seven and eight o'clock this morning; and proceeded towards a town called *Kakafungi.* Kakafungi is a straggling, but extensive and populous town, and is delightfully situated on an even piece of ground. The inhabitants are so clean and well-behaved, and their dwellings so neat and comfortable, that before we had spoken many words to one of them, we were pre-possessed in favour of all.

Late in the evening, when our people were asleep, the sound of singing tempted my brother to go out alone, and he soon discovered a little group of thoughtless, happy creatures, amusing themselves by dancing in the moonlight to the sound of a large drum. He described their dance as being very different from that practised in Yarriba; their motions being sometimes swift and violent, and sometimes slow and graceful; their gestures expressive of mild delight rather than vehe-ment passion, and remarkable for propriety.

Sunday, June 6th.—I found my brother in a high fever this morning, and so ill that he was obliged to lie on his mat till the carriers were ready to depart.[1]

We quitted Kakafungi about two p.m., by a path which lay in a northerly direction, through a perfect wilderness, some part of which was more stony and barren than anything we remember to have seen. The few stunted trees that we found, afforded us a very indifferent shelter from the heat of the sun, which was almost insufferable; and this, with the length of the journey, and the speed with which we were obliged to travel, greatly increased my brother's fever. He was oc-casionally obliged to dismount and lie down on the ground for relief, being lifted off and replaced on his horse by our attendants. We saw the sun set behind some magnificent clouds, whilst we had yet a great way

[1] Huish's edition makes it clear that it was John Lander who fell ill on the journey from Kiama to Bussa (Huish, 1835, 587). The entry for June 5th appears from the style to have been written by John, for June 6th and the succeeding days by Richard.

HUNT LIBRARY
CARNEGIE-MELLON UNIVERSITY

to go; and the narrow footpath, which was here overgrown with bushes and rank grass, was hardly discernible by the light of the moon; In the afternoon all had been silent in the forest; but in the evening the jackal, the hyena, and the baboon had forsaken their retreats, and mingled their dismal howl with the sprightly chirping of innumerable insects.

My brother and I were far behind the rest of the party, because he had been unable to keep pace with them, and we discharged a pistol every now and then as a signal to the carriers of our approach. As each report echoed through the forest, it was answered by the increased howling of wild animals, till at length we gladly saw the gleam of a large fire, and arrived at the encampment which had been prepared for us. Here we took possession for the night of a few deserted huts, which were falling to decay.

June 7th.—The rest which my brother had obtained during the night seemed to have revived him. At eight a.m., after bathing, we crossed the river *Oly* in a canoe, which we found tied to a tree.

After a long and tiresome journey under a burning sun, we pitched our tent in the evening near a small stream. My brother was very ill, his fever having returned with increased violence; but he took no other medicine than a common soda powder, as I was fearful of our progress being retarded. A storm gathered over our heads a few minutes after the tent had been fixed, and presently burst with terrific violence. While it lasted we were occupied with the thoughts of our forlorn condition. The deafening noise of the thunder as it echoed among the hills, the overpowering glare of the lightning, the torrents of rain, and the violence of the wind, were truly awful. The whole of our party, amounting to twenty, were collected in the tent for shelter from the storm, and in spite of the water which ran through it, contrived to sleep till morning.

June 8th.—We were obliged to lie in our wet clothes all night, and the effects of this were visible on my brother this morning. I endeavoured, in vain, to rally him, but he was scarcely able to stand. The carriers hastened onwards as fast as they could, for the provisions were consumed. This proceeds from Paskoe's negligence in having obtained only provisions enough for one day instead of three. My brother and I lingered behind with old Paskoe and another of our men, and proceeded on at a very slow pace, as our horses were worn out with fatigue, and my brother's was quite lame. As we advanced he became worse, till at length he was completely overcome, and, to prevent falling off his horse, dismounted, and laid down. There was no tree near us that would afford shelter from the sun, so with the assistance of our people I obtained some branches, and formed a sort of bower. During the rest of the day my brother became worse, but the coolness of the evening appeared to revive him a little. I went into the wood, and shot the only bird I saw, which was about the size of a sparrow. With this I returned, made a fire, and prepared a little soup in a half-pint cup. The soup was rather unsavoury, from want of salt, nevertheless it was of service to my brother; the flesh of the bird I divided between myself and my man, as we were both weak from want of food. We lighted large fires to keep away the wild beasts. But neither of us could sleep, for, independent of his illness, we were attacked by myriads of mosquitoes and buzzing flies.

June 9th.—Notwithstanding his bad night's rest, my brother had little fever on him this morning. We proceeded on our journey; and in an hour's time we descried Paskoe approaching us with five men, who brought us corn and milk, and little cakes made of pounded corn and honey. The Governor of *Coobly*, the town to which we were going, had also kindly sent us a horse and a hammock for my brother. We arrived near Coobly shortly after sunset. We repaired to a hut that was assigned to us, where soon after my brother was seized with a return of the fever, more severe than the former.

June 10th.—I administered ten grains of calomel to my brother after which he fell into a kind of stupor and an insensibility to surrounding objects, which did not leave him till this afternoon, when his reason returned. Towards evening he became worse, and I expected every moment was his last. During the few intervals he had from delirium he seemed to be aware of his danger and entered into arrangements respecting his family concerns. At this moment my feelings were of too painful a nature to be described. The unhappy fate of my late master, Captain Clapperton, came forcibly to my mind. I had followed him into this country where he perished; I had attended him in his parting moments; I had performed the last mournful office for him which our nature requires, and the thought that I should have to go through the same sad ceremonies for my brother overwhelmed me with grief.[1]

June 11th.—Between eleven and twelve last night I rejoiced to find

[1] Clapperton had died in Lander's arms in Sokoto in April 1827, leaving him, as Lander wrote at the time, 'a hundred and fifteen days' journey from the sea-coast, surrounded by a selfish and cruel race of strangers, my only friend and protector mouldering in his grave, and myself suffering dreadfully from fever' (Clapperton, 1829, p. 278).

that my brother's illness seemed to take a favourable turn, and towards the morning he became tranquil and free from pain.

June 12th.—My brother's health is rapidly returning.

Sunday, June 13th.—My brother's health still continues to improve.

June 15th.—My brother, by the blessing of God, is now perfectly recovered from an illness that had nearly proved fatal to him. At an early hour this morning we quitted the town of Coobly. We travelled through a thick forest till noon, when we halted for the day amidst the ruins of a large town. A short time ago the town was taken by surprise and pillaged by a large party of Falatahs, who put to the sword all that made any resistance, and carried the remainder away with them as slaves. Here one of the horses died; the poor animal had been our fellow-traveller from Jenna.

June 16th.—We passed the ruins of two or three deserted villages; and entered a snug, pretty little town called *Zalee.*

June 17th.—Our course from Zalee was in a south-easterly direction. We came to a fine extensive plain. From hence we first beheld the city of Boossa. We entered the city by the western gateway, and discharge our pieces as the signal of our arrival.

We were introduced to the king, whom we found in company with the *Midikie,* the title bestowed on his principal wife or queen. They welcomed us to Boossa with every appearance of cordiality. They told us very gravely, and with rueful countenances, that they had both been weeping for the death of Captain Clapperton, whose untimely end they would never cease to lament. They might, it is true, have been thus engaged; but, as on our entrance we observed no outward signs of tears, we rather mistrusted their assertion.[1]

[1] Lander had been entertained with 'extraordinary kindness' by the ruler and his wife on his first visit to Bussa in April 1826. 'The features of the royal couple,' he wrote on that occasion, 'bore a closer resemblance to the European than the negro cast, and might be styled handsome, even in England; besides which an ineffable sweetness shone upon the countenance of Medaki, the queen, and there was an agreeableness in the innocent freedom of her deportment that captivated me at first sight' (Lander, 1830, I, pp. 163–4). 'Midikie' or 'Medaki' is the Hausa *mai-'daki:* literally 'owner of the house', the word is 'used by anyone when referring to his own wife' (Bargery, 1957, 197). According to Clapperton, the ruler, whose name was Mohammed, was 'a fine looking young man, about twenty-five or twenty-six years of age' (Clapperton, 1829, p. 99). The Bussa king-list gives the ruler of Bussa as Kitoro, 1793–1835 (*Kontagora Gazetteer,* p. 27). The king told Clapperton that 'his family were descended from the sultans of Bornou; and that they had paid the latter tribute until, of late years, the road had been shut up' (Clapperton, 1829, p. 103). According to a Bornu source, 'Sarkin Bussa used to send yearly presents to Sarkin Bornu, which consisted of 100 female slaves (concubines), 100 head of cattle, 100 horses, and 100 of everything which he could get.' A Bussa source gives a more modest list of the tribute paid by Sarkin Bussa (*Kontagora Gazetteer,* pp. 23, 25).

VIII

Boossa to Yaoorie

June 18th.—The noted widow Zuma visited us today. She related to us with great good humour her quarrels with her prince, the ruler of Wowow, and her consequent flight from that city to escape his resentment. She alleged that she had done nothing whatever to merit the displeasure of the Wowow chief, notwithstanding which he had robbed her of all her household furniture and a number of her slaves. But, from another quarter, we learn that one of her sons had committed a theft in the city, for which he would have suffered death, if he had not made his escape with his mother, who it is said had instigated them to the deed. The widow complained sadly of poverty and the hardness of the times; she had fought with the Yarribeans against Alorie; but instead of receiving a recompense for her bravery, she had lost half her slaves in an engagement, which so disgusted her with the military profession, that she immediately abandoned it and returned home. Yet, in spite of all her losses and misfortunes, she has gained so much in corpulency, that it was with the utmost difficulty she could squeeze herself into the doorway of our hut, although it is by no means small.

This morning we visited the far-famed *Niger* or *Quorra*, which flows by the city, and were greatly disappointed at the appearance of this celebrated river. Black, rugged rocks rose abruptly from the centre of the stream. The Niger here, in its widest part, is not more than a stone's throw across at present. The rock on which we sat overlooks the spot where Mr Park and his associates met their unhappy fate.[1]

[1] Near Bussa an outcrop of rocks across the bed of the river produces the most formidable rapids in the whole course of the Niger. It was here that H.M.S. *Joliba* had been wrecked and Park and his companions drowned in their journey down the river in 1806. For an excellent discussion of all the evidence relating to Park's death see Lupton, 1962.

June 19th.—This morning the king, accompanied by his consort, who is said to be his counsellor and only confidant, honoured us with a visit at our hut. They came without any kind of state or ceremony, and were both dressed more plainly than many of their subjects. The queen is the daughter of the last and sister of the present ruler of Wowow.

The demand for coral has been very great in every town of consequence which we have visited. All ranks of people appear passionately fond of wearing it, and it is preferred to every other ornament whatever. The midikie asked us, this morning, if we had brought any coral with us, and seemed rather disappointed, though not displeased, on being answered in the negative. She then pulled out a little box, made of sheep skin, which was filled with coral beads and little golden trinkets, and requested me to polish the latter for her. We offered her a few plated buttons, which we had just before been cleaning, and they were accepted with transport; but as their brightness had excited the admiration of her consort, a scramble took place as to which of the two should have them. After a long struggle, it ended in the triumph of the king, who first chose the largest and best for his own use, and then gave his spouse the remainder. The royal couple were like two great children, yet they were each well pleased with their own, and expressed their thankfulness with much warmth.

We imagined that it would have been bad policy to have stated the true reason of our visiting this country, knowing the jealousy of most of the people with regard to the Niger; and, therefore, in answer to the king's inquiries, I was obliged to deceive him with the assertion that our object was to go to Bornou by way of Yaoorie, requesting at the same time a safe conveyance through his territories. This answer satisfied the king, and he promised us every assistance in his power. Our visitors remained with us a considerable time, and in the course of conversation, one of them observed that they had in their possession a tobe, which belonged to a white man who came from the north many years ago, and from whom it had been purchased by the king's father. We expressed great curiosity to see this tobe, and it was sent us as a present a short time after their departure. Contrary to our expectations, we found it to be made of rich crimson damask, and very heavy from the immense quantity of gold embroidery with which it was covered. As the time when the late king is said to have purchased this tobe corresponds very nearly to the supposed period of Mr Park's death, and as we have never heard of any other white man having come from the north so far south as Boossa, we are inclined to believe it to be part of the spoil obtained from the canoe of that ill-fated traveller.

Sunday, June 20th.—Eager as we are to obtain even the slightest information relative to the unhappy fate of Mr Park and his companions, as well as to ascertain if any of their books or papers are now in existence at this place, we had almost made up our minds to refrain from asking any questions on the subject, because we were apprehensive that it might be displeasing to the king, and involve us in many perplexities. Familiarity, however, having in some measure worn off this impression, and the king being an affable, obliging, and good-natured person, we were emboldened to send Paskoe to him this morning, with a message expressive of the interest we felt on the subject, in common with all our countrymen; and saying that, if any books or papers which belonged to Mr. Park were yet in his possession, he would do us a great service, by delivering them into our hands, or at least by granting us permission to see them. To this the king returned for answer that when Mr Park was lost in the Niger, he was a very little boy, and that he knew not what had become of his effects; that the deplorable event had occurred in the reign of the late king's predecessor, who died shortly after; and that all traces of the white man had been lost with him. This answer disappointed our hopes, for to us it appeared final and decisive. But in the evening they were again raised by a hint from our host, who is the king's drummer, and one of the principal men in the country; he assured us, that there was certainly one book at least saved from Mr Park's canoe, which is now in the possession of a very poor man in the service of his master, to whom it had been entrusted by the late king during his last illness. He said moreover, that if but one application were made to the king, on any subject whatever, very little was thought of it; but if a second were made, the matter would be considered of sufficient importance to demand his whole attention—such being the custom of the country. The drummer therefore recommended us to persevere in our inquiries. At his own request, we sent him to the king immediately, desiring him to repeat our former statement, and to assure the king, that should he be successful in recovering the book we wanted, our monarch would reward him handsomely. He desired the drummer to inform us, that he would examine the man who was reported to have the white man's book in his possession, at an early hour tomorrow.

June 21st.—The city of Boossa consists of a great number of groups or clusters of huts, all within a short distance of each other. It is

I   119

bounded one side by the river Niger, and on the other by an extensive turreted wall, with moats, forming a complete semi-circle. Notwithstanding, however, its natural and artificial defences, Boossa was taken by the Falatahs many years ago; on which occasion its inhabitants fled, with their children and effects, to one of the little islands in the Niger. But the chiefs of Niki, Wowow, and Kiama, having been made acquainted with the circumstance, and having joined their forces with those of Boossa, drove the Falatahs, their common enemy, into the Niger, where many of them perished. Since that period the city has never been invaded, nor threatened with attack. The soil of Boossa is, for the most part, very fertile, and produces rice, corn, yams, etc, in great abundance. Very good salt is brought from a salt lake on the borders of the river, which is about ten days' journey to the northward of this place.[1] Guinea-fowl, pheasants, partridges, and a variety of aquatic birds are found here in the greatest plenty, and have afforded us excellent sport. Deer and antelope also abound near the city; but they are timid and shy, and rarely, if ever, caught by the inhabitants. The fish, with which this river abounds so plentifully, are eaten by all classes of people: they are tough, dry, and unsavoury; yet they form part of the daily food of the inhabitants, who appear exceedingly fond of them.

The Hausa language is understood by the generality of the natives of Borgoo, almost as well as their mother-tongue, and it is spoken by the majority of them with considerable fluency.[2] The government of the country is despotic; but this unlimited power, which is vested in the monarch, is almost invariably exercised with lenity and forbearance. All private disputes are settled by the king, and he punishes misdemeanours just as his inclination may lead him.

In the afternoon, the king came to see us, followed by a man with a book under his arm, which was said to have been picked up in the Niger after the loss of our countryman. It was enveloped in a large cotton cloth, and our hearts beat high with expectation as the man was

[1] The salt deposits were probably those of the Dallol Fogha, a dry river bed lying on the left bank of the Niger, just outside the present Nigerian boundary (Abadie, 1927, p. 277).

[2] Several languages are spoken in Borgu, none being related to Hausa. But 'the Hausa tongue', as Baikie, a traveller in the Niger area in the 1850s, noted, 'is the French of Central Africa, being very generally understood, and being the medium by which traders from different countries transact business in common. . . . African traders are in general good and ready linguists, speaking not infrequently three or four tongues; the speed, also, with which they translate a sentence, without almost a moment's consideration, is really surprising' (Baikie, 1856, p. 69).

slowly unfolding it, for by its size we guessed it to be Mr Park's journal; but our disappointment and chagrin were great, when, on opening the book, we discovered it to be an old nautical publication of the last century. The title page was missing, but its contents were chiefly tables of logarithms.[1] It was a thick royal quarto; between the leaves we found a few loose pages of very little consequence indeed; one of them contained two or three observations on the height of the water in the Gambia; one was a tailor's bill on a Mr Anderson; and another was addressed to Mr Mungo Park, and contained an invitation to dinner—the following is a copy of it:

'Mr and Mrs Watson would be happy to have the pleasure of Mr Park's company at dinner on Tuesday next, at half-past five o'clock.
    'An answer is requested.
'*Strand, 9th Nov.* 1804.'

The king, as well as the owner of the book, looked as greatly mortified as ourselves, when they were told that the one produced was not that of which we were in quest, because the reward promised would not of course be obtained. As soon as our curiosity had been fully satisfied, the papers were carefully collected and placed again between the leaves, and the book as carefully folded in its envelope as before, and taken away by its owner, who values it much as a household god.

June 22nd.—We brought three horses with us to Coobly from Jenna; two of them have died from fatigue, and the third is in so miserable a state, that he can be of no further service to us. The king paid us a visit this afternoon, and informed us that everything will be ready for our departure tomorrow. On this occasion he presented us with an excellent and handsome horse.

During the whole course of our journey we have nowhere experienced greater kindness, attention, and hospitality, than from the amiable ruler of this place, and his no less amiable companion, and we shall have occasion to remember their civility to us as long as we live.

Since we have been here the king has given us a horse, bullock, sheep, and turkey, which were all very valuable, while our present to him is considerably less than that which the King of Kiama received.

June 23rd.—At an early hour in the morning the king and queen

[1] Twenty-seven years later Bussa was visited by another English explorer, Lieutenant John Glover, R.N. Glover was shown a book of logarithms belonging to Mungo Park, which he was able to obtain with little difficulty in exchange for 'a spear-pointed knife about 8 inches long'. This book was later presented to the Royal Geographical Society, in whose museum it now reposes (Hastings, 1926, pp. 189–91).

paid us a farewell visit. An hour or two after they had taken their departure, we rode out of the city, accompanied by two horsemen as an escort, and a foot-messenger to the Sultan of Yaoorie. We journeyed along the banks of the Niger, and entered a pleasant little walled town, called *Kagogie*, peopled solely by the King of Boossa's slaves. We have been sent hither by land, because a canoe could not be paddled up the river without the greatest difficulty and danger, on account of the rocks.

June 24th.—Though the governor of Kagogie had been made acquainted with our intentions no less than three days before our arrival, yet no canoe had been got ready for our use; and this morning, when we expected to embark, the 'King of the Canoe', as the person who has the care of it is ridiculously styled, informed us with the utmost unconcern that it was out of repair, and that it would not be fit for our reception for some hours at least. The natives have no forethought, and imagine that all men value time as little as themselves; everything is deferred till the very last moment, and they look up into one's face with wonder when they see one anywise impatient.

Our horses were conveyed across from here to the opposite side of the river, from whence they will be taken to Yaoorie by land, because the canoes of the natives would be too frail a conveyance for them. These canoes are of great length, but the workmanship employed in making and fashioning them is exceedingly rude and careless. Owing perhaps to the want of proper trees of sufficient magnitude, they are made of *two* blocks of wood, which are sown together by a thick cord, under which a quantity of straw is placed, both inside and out, to prevent the admission of water; but the whole is altogether so clumsily executed, that every canoe in the country is always leaky.

About mid-day the workmen having finished our canoe, we embarked with our people, and were launched out into the river. We found it flowing from north to south, through a rich and charming country, which seemed to improve in appearance the further we advanced. Beautiful, spreading, and spiry trees adorned the country on each side of the river, like a park; corn, nearly ripe, waved over the water's edge; large, open villages appeared every half-hour; and herds of spotted cattle were observed grazing and enjoying the cool of the shade. The appearance of the river, for several miles, was no less enchanting than its borders; it was as smooth as a lake; canoes, laden with sheep and goats, were paddled by women down its almost imperceptible current; swallows, and a variety of aquatic birds, were sporting over its glassy surface, which was ornamented by a number of pretty little islands.

A little after eight, p.m., we landed on the eastern bank of the river, not far from a small village, and where we fixed our tent on a plot of rising corn, and, having nothing to eat, went supperless to bed.

June 25th.—A little before seven, a.m., our canoe was pushed off the sandy beach on which it had been secured last evening, and propelled down a very narrow channel, between a large sand-bank and the shore. This conducted us into the main branch of the Niger, and we again admired its delightful and magnificent appearance.

The river gradually widened to two miles, and continued so as far as the eye could reach. It looked very much like an artificial canal; the banks having the appearance of a dwarf wall, with vegetation beyond. In most places the water was extremely shallow, but in others it was deep enough to float a frigate. During the first two hours of the day, the scenery was as interesting and picturesque as can be imagined. The banks were literally covered with hamlets and villages; fine trees, bending under the weight of their dark and impenetrable foliage, everywhere relieved the eye from the glare of the sun's rays, and, contrasted with the lively verdure of the little hills and plains, produced the most pleasing effect. Afterwards, however, there was a decided change; the banks, which before consisted of dark earth, clay, or sand, were now composed of black rugged rocks; large sand-banks and islands were scattered in the river, which diverted it into a variety of little channels, and effectually destroyed its appearance.

About eleven o'clock, dark clouds from the west foretold an approaching storm; in a very few minutes it blew a hurricane, accompanied by thunder and lightning of the most awful description, and the rain fell in torrents. It became, besides, so dark, that nothing could be clearly distinguished at the distance of only a few yards. We were wetted to the skin in a moment; and our canoe was in danger of sinking as we came abreast of a little fishing village, on an island, close to the water's edge. We jumped on shore as soon as possible, and ran, without shoes or hats, into the first hut we came to for protection from the storm.

June 26th.—The tempest of yesterday was succeeded by a remarkably clear night. In the morning, on leaving the village, we were followed to the beach by a few of its inhabitants, and when the canoe was pushed off at seven o'clock, they cheered us loudly. These people are harmless and good-natured, but dirty in their persons and singular in their manners. Most of the villages on the islands, as far as Yaoorie, it is said, are inhabited by the same race of people, and they are also scattered on the banks of the river. The women daub their hair with red clay, but they are too poor to purchase many personal ornaments, and the men use none whatever. They appear to have the necessaries of life in abundance; they are partial to agriculture, and cultivate large portions of land with corn, rice, and onions; besides which fishing is carried on by them on an extensive scale, and numbers of the men go three days' journey up the Niger to catch fish. Situated between Boossa and Yaoorie, the inhabitants of most of the islands speak the language of those countries, but they have also one of their own, which nobody but themselves understand; a smattering of the Haussa tongue, which they have attained, is the only method of communication which is adopted in their trading transactions.

We had just entered into the main river, when we came to a spot where it spreads again into branches, and each channel was literally filled with dangerous rocks, sand-banks and low islands covered with tall rank grass. We were conducted up the main branch of the river, but were soon obliged to land with our people in order to lighten the canoe, which, after a great deal of exertion, was lifted over a ridge of rocks into deeper water. During the greater part of the morning, indeed, our canoe was continually striking against concealed rocks, or running on hidden sand-banks, but sustained no apparent damage on the concussion; the only inconvenience we experienced from it was the fatiguing one of being obliged to get out and in whenever it was found necessary. It therefore afforded us much pleasure to be landed, about two o'clock in the afternoon, on the left bank of the river, for we were heartily tired of our morning's work.

At a short distance from the water's edge the country was thickly studded with clusters of huts, which all together are called the village of *Sooloo*. The inhabitants resemble very much the islanders already spoken of. The only ornaments they wear are made of the back-bone of a certain species of fish, which are tied round the loins and other parts of the body. Besides corn, etc, the inhabitants also grow immense quantities of onions, and they have large store-houses full of these, ready to be exported to different parts of the continent.

We were treated this afternoon with much hospitality by them, and they did all in their power to render our short stay as agreeable as possible .

Sunday, June 27th.—We had heard so unfavourable an account of the state of the river at one particular place which we should have to pass, that our people were compelled to disembark and walk along the banks a considerable way till we had passed it, when we took them in again. On our arrival at this formidable place, we discovered a range of black rocks running directly across the stream, and the water, finding only one narrow passage, rushed through it with great impetuosity, overturning and carrying away everything in its course. Our boatmen, with the assistance of a number of the natives, who planted themselves on the rocks on each side of the only channel, and in the stream at the stern of the canoe, lifted it by main force into smoother and safer water. In a very little time we came to the termination of all the islands, after which, it is said, there is not a single dangerous place up the Niger. The river here presented its noblest appearance; not a single rock nor sand-bank was anywhere perceptible; its borders resumed their beauty, and a strong, refreshing breeze, which had blown during the whole of the morning, now gave it the motion of a slightly-agitated sea. In the course of the morning we passed two lovely little islands, clothed in verdure, which at a short distance looked as charming as the fabled gardens of Hesperia; indeed no spot on earth can excel them in beauty of appearance.

About eleven a.m. we landed at the foot of a little village on the east bank of the river, where our horses and men had arrived before us. Here we rested under a large tree an hour or so, awaiting the arrival of carriers from the city of Yaoorie. These men arrived in the village in the afternoon, and we immediately mounted and rode onwards.

We travelled over a sterile country, which was gradually rising at every step, and abounded plentifully in game. The soil improved greatly as we drew near Yaoorie; and immense patches of land, cultivated with a variety of corn, also with rice, indigo, cotton, etc, were visible on every side. Labourers were employed in these plantations, attended by a drummer, that they might be excited by the sound of his instrument to work well and briskly. On attaining the summit of a steep hill, we rode over a very narrow pathway. This led us to the wall of Yaoorie, and we entered the city through an amazingly strong passage, in which was an immense door covered with plates of iron, rudely fastened to the wood-work.

IX

Yaoorie

ALTHOUGH DURING THE DRY SEASON, no communication or intercourse is maintained by water between Boossa, and the countries or states
lower down the river, by reason of the dangerous rocks which have
been already alluded to; yet in the wet season, after the 'Malca'[1] (or
fourteen days' incessant rain) has set in, when all the rivers which are
dry during the remainder of the year, pour their overplus into the
'great Father of Waters', as the Niger is emphatically styled, then
canoes, it is said, pass to and fro, between Yaoorie, Nouffie, Boossa,
and Funda. It is immediately after the 'Malca' also, that the Niger, by
the depth and velocity of its current, sweeps off the rank grass which
springs up annually on its borders. Every rock and every low island
is then completely covered, and may be passed over in canoes without
difficulty, or even apprehension of danger. The enterprising Mr Park
must have had a thousand difficulties to overcome in his voyage down
the Niger. It was about this time of year that he arrived at Yaoorie,
and the river, it is said, was then about the same height as it is at present.
The canoe-men, who in all probability were his slaves, were said to be
chained to the canoe, in order to prevent their running away; his
pilot was unacquainted with the river any further, and therefore he
received his wages here in Yaoorie, and returned to his own country;[2]
and Mr Park, with a companion, and three white boys, continued

[1] Hausa *marka:* 'the period from the middle to the end of the wet season' (Bargery,
1957, I, p. 774).
[2] Park's guide, Amadi Fatoumi, had left him at Yauri. Amadi Fatoumi's account of the
disaster at Bussa, which he himself had obtained from an African slave, the sole survivor
of the shipwreck, provided the only evidence of Park's death, until Clapperton and
Lander visited Bussa in 1826. 'Amadi Fatoumi's Journal' is printed in the *Everyman's
Library* edition of Park's *Travels*.

126

their journey down the Niger without any person whatever to point out the safest channel, or warn them of the danger. When the accident happened at Boossa by which they lost their lives, it is said they preferred being drowned to avoid as they imagined a more dreadful death.

Many years ago, a large boat arrived at Yaoorie on a trading voyage from Timbuctoo. Having disposed of their merchandise, the boatmen returned to their country by land, because they asserted that the exertion of working their vessel back so great a distance against the stream, was too much for them, and therefore they left it behind at Yaoorie.

June 28th.—This morning we were visited by the chief of the Arabs of this city, who (if the title can be used with propriety) is Prime Minister to the Sultan. He is a very old man, as dark as a native; and was dressed in the costume of his countrymen, which is very becoming. His beard was long, and as white as snow, and a singular tuft of hair which was directly under the lower lip, did not look much unlike the tail of a white mouse. Though toothless, the old man was yet very communicative and intelligent, and among other things he informed us that Mr Park did not visit the city of Yaoorie, but remained in his canoe at the village where we landed yesterday, and despatched a messenger in his stead to the sultan, with a suitable present. The Arab had been sent by the sultan to the village with presents in return, and by his description of Mr Park's dress, he must have worn the laced tobe that we received of the King of Boossa, and which may account for the facility with which we obtained it, as well as the reluctance of the king to enter into an explanation of the manner in which his ancestor had got possession of it. Mr Park is stated to have been drowned in the same dress. The Arab informed us, that he had in his possession a cutlass and a double-barrelled gun, which was part of Mr Park's present to the sultan. We expressed a wish to look at these weapons, and they were immediately sent for. The gun was very excellent, and handsomely mounted; and we offered our own fowling-piece in exchange, which was cheerfully agreed to.[1]

June 29th.—This evening we went to pay our respects to the sultan. We soon arrived at the palace, which is a very large building, or rather a group of buildings inclosed by a high wall; and dismounting, we

---

[1] On Park's arrival off Yauri Amadi Fatoumi stated that he 'was sent on shore with a musket and a sabre, to carry to the chief of the village, also with three pieces of white baft for distribution. I went and gave the chief his present; I also gave one piece to Alhagi, one to Alhagi-biron, and the other to a person whose name I forget, all Marabous.' Park later gave some additional presents to the chief, 'five silver rings, some powder and flint' (Park, *Everyman's Library*, n.d., p. 318).

were presently conducted through a low avenue formed by pillars, which was as dark as a subterranean passage. This led to a large square yard, which we entered and found it to communicate with the sultan's apartments by the number of domestics that were hurrying about. Several people were sitting on the ground, but we were obliged to stand a long time, during which a profound silence was preserved, and no one was polite enough to offer us a mat to sit on. At length we received a summons to advance, and were introduced into another square, very much resembling a clean farm-yard. Here we discovered the sultan sitting alone in the centre of the square, on a plain piece of carpeting, with a pillow on each side of him, and a neat brass pan in front. His appearance was not only mean, but absolutely squalid and dirty. He is a big-headed, corpulent, and jolly-looking man, well stricken in years; and though there is something harsh and forbidding in his countenance, yet he was generally smiling during the conference. The conversation commenced in the usual complimentary way; and then our object in visiting Yaoorie was briefly and indirectly hinted at. When we asked him whether he did not send a letter to the late Captain Clapperton, in which he had affirmed that he had certain books and papers in his possession which belonged to Mr Park, he answered with an affected laugh, 'How do you think that I could have the books of a person that was lost at Boossa?' and this was all he said on the subject.[1] He subsequently wished to know the reason that Captain Clapperton refused to visit him when he had passed through the country; but more especially, why, after his death, I had not paid him that mark of respect on my return to the coast from Soccatoo. The sultan was more than half inclined to be angry with us; and we were not at all sorry to be reconducted into the open air.

June 30th.—This morning I carried the sultan's present to him; but it was very coldly received. I stated, that by reason of the selfishness and bad faith of the chief at the sea side, and the length of the journey from thence, the presents we had brought from England were nearly all expended; insomuch that we found it would be impossible to reach Bornou without receiving an additional supply of goods, which in our present situation we had no opportunity of obtaining; and that this being the case, we had no other recourse left but to get to the salt water,

---

[1] The ruler of Yauri had shown himself peculiarly anxious to persuade Clapperton to visit his kingdom. One of his messengers had told Clapperton that the king had in his possession two large printed books, which had belonged to the white men who had been lost at Bussa. Clapperton had refused to go to Sokoto by way of Yauri, as he had heard that there was war on the road (Clapperton, 1829, pp. 99, 122).

when our wants should be promptly supplied. I observed that going down the river in a canoe would be the easiest and best means of effecting this object, to which the sultan replied that the price of a canoe would be a hundred dollars; but he was told we had not property enough to purchase one. The road overland to Funda,[1] by way of Koolfu or Guarie, was then mentioned, and the sultan promised to send thither in two or three days.

July 1st.—This prince assumes more consequence than any chief or monarch that we have yet seen; he never receives a visit but he exacts from the visiter the most humiliating forms of address; and even when the Arabs themselves obtain an audience, they are obliged to deliver what they have to say to him on their knees. Perhaps he expected a similar servile position from us, for such his countenance seemed to indicate, but whatever might have been his expectation, we had no notion of demeaning ourselves so grossly in his presence. Since our arrival in this city, my brother and I have been very seriously indisposed, as might be expected, for the air is humid and unwholesome, being impregnated with all manner of noxious effluvia, from the swampy nature of the soil at this season of the year, and the number of large pools of impure water, which existed more or less in every quarter of the town.

July 2nd.—It is rather unfortunate for us, that so immense a quantity of needles was distributed through the country by the last mission; the market here is even now completely overstocked with them, so that we find it difficult to dispose of ours for a quarter of their value. Our best, and almost only resource, has been in the metal buttons attached to our English clothes. These, when polished brightly, look well and have completely won the people of all ranks, from the sultan to the slave. Our clothes are nearly all stripped of their buttons; and we now place our dependence for future support principally on a quantity of livery and soldiers' buttons, which are, however, rather dull and dirty, and will require many hours' labour before they attain any degree of brightness.

[1] On his return journey from Sokoto in 1827 Lander had been particularly anxious to reach Funda, which he had heard described as a place of considerable importance, only 'four days' sail' from 'the salt water'; he had been detained on his way to Funda by the governor of Zaria and found himself forced to continue his journey by way of Nupe and Borgu. Funda was in fact the Igbirra city-state of Panda, which lay about thirty miles north of the Niger–Benue confluence. Had he succeeded in reaching Funda on his first journey and passed on to the confluence, he would have seen that the Niger flowed south towards the sea.

THE NIGER JOURNAL

July 6th.—This forenoon we sent Paskoe with a message to the sultan, that we earnestly wished to receive a final and decisive answer with regard to the restoration of Mr Park's papers, which we declared to have been the sole object of our visiting him, and that it was our desire to quit Yaoorie immediately. This bold, and to us unusual language, seemed to have surprised and startled the sultan, and he instantly despatched the old Arab to inform us, that 'he declared to G–d, in the most solemn manner, that he had never had in his possession, nor seen, any books or papers of the white travellers who perished at Boossa'. His only motive for the dastardly conduct he has displayed, could have been neither more nor less than the hope of getting us into his power by misrepresentation and falsehood, in order to obtain some of the European articles which we had in our possession.

July 7th.—Yaoorie is a large, flourishing, and united kingdom. The crown is hereditary, and the government an absolute despotism. The former sultan was deposed by his subjects for his violent measures and general bad conduct; and the present ruler, who succeeded him, has reigned for the long period of thirty-nine years.[1] The sultan has a strong military force, which has successfully repelled, it is said, the repeated attacks which the ever-restless Falatahs for a number of years past made on the city and kingdom of Yaoorie; it is now employed in a remote province in quelling a rising insurrection, occasioned partly from the inability of the natives to pay their accustomed tribute, and partly from the harsh measures adopted by the sultan to compel them to do so. The city of Yaoorie is of prodigious extent and is supposed to be as populous as any other in the whole continent, or at least that part of it which is visited by the trading Arabs. Its wall is high and very excellent, though made of clay alone, and may be between twenty and thirty miles in circuit; and it has eight vast entrance-gates or doors, which are well fortified after the manner of the country.[2] The inhabi-

[1] According to one of the Yauri king-lists, Mohammadu dan Ayi (alias Basheru) was ruler of Yauri from March 1799 to November 1829. Another list gives the ruler's name as Basheru dan Amadu and his length of reign as 31 years 8 months. According to the second list, Basheru's predecessor, Gajeri, reigned for three years, and was then driven out (*Kontagora Gazetteer*, pp. 19, 20). In the letter which the ruler of Yauri gave Lander his name is shown as Mohammed Ebsheer (Lander, 1832, III, p. 341).

[2] 'Before the middle of the nineteenth century Birnin Yauri used to be the residence of the Emirs of Yauri. In those days it was an important town with a very large population. There is still evidence of its pristine glory in its great walls. These are over five miles in circumference, and even to the present day [1920] are 15–20 feet high and 25 feet thick. It is stated that they were built centuries before the advent of the Fulani era in Northern Nigeria. Since 1850 the Emirs of Yauri have not used this town as their headquarters

tants manufacture a very coarse and inferior sort of gunpowder, which, however, is the best, and we believe the only manufactory of the kind in this part of the country; besides which they make very neat saddles, country cloth, etc; and they grow indigo, tobacco, onions, wheat and different kinds of grain; and vast quantities of rice of superior quality. The inhabitants have likewise horses, bullocks, goats, etc, but notwithstanding their industry and the advantages which they enjoy, they are very poorly clad, have little money, and are perpetually complaining of their bad condition.

The better sort of women, or those that can afford time and money for the purpose, wear their hair plated [*sic*] very ingeniously, and dyed blue with indigo; their lips are likewise stained yellow and blue, which gives them an inexpressibly odd appearance; and their eyes are blackened with powdered antimony, or something of the same nature and properties, which is imported from a place called *Jacoba*.[1] This is in general use, not only here, but in every other place which we have visited.

The use of hennah is as general in Yaoorie as elsewhere; the more opulent females make use of this most beautiful dye in profusion: they simply apply the pounded leaves of this plant to the teeth, and to the fingers and toe nails.

July 8th.—The sultan has sent to inform us that he will be occupied three days in writing to the king of England an explanation of his conduct with respect to Mr Park's papers.[2]

Sunday, July 11th.—Having been sent for, I visited the sultan today with a piece of red cloth, two pair of scissors, a quantity of buttons, and a canister of powder. I found him cheerful and merry, and his good humour continued throughout our interview. He observed, that the war which was just terminated had cost him a great deal of money, so that he regretted his inability to pay so large a sum for the articles as I had demanded. At length, after a little civil contention on both

[1] *Jacoba:* the name applied to the province of Bauchi after its first ruler, Yakubu. Bauchi had not yet been visited by any European, but Lander had made the acquaintance of 'the King of Jacoba', possibly Yakubu himself, on his journey from Sokoto to Kano in 1827 (Lander, 1830, II, p. 96).

[2] The letter which the ruler eventually gave Lander contained no more than formal greetings written in singularly bad Arabic. The Landers included a translation of the letter as an appendix to their journal.

owing to internal dissensions and fear of Umoru Nagwamache and his son Ibrahimu, Emir of Kontagora' (*Kontagora Gazetteer*, p. 16). Yelwa, the present residence of the Emirs of Yauri, was founded at the end of the nineteenth century; it is situated on the banks of the Niger, a few miles to the north-west of the old capital.

sides, a bargain was made, by the sultan's agreeing to give twenty-five thousand cowries for the powder, scissors, red cloth, and two hundred cowries for every *little* button that we have, which he prefers to the larger ones.

July 13th.—The sultan told us today in plain and decisive terms, that he can send us neither by way of Koolfu nor Guarie, because the Falatahs, he affirms, are in both those places. Now we know very well that the Falatahs have neither the upper hand at Koolfu nor Guarie. The natives of the latter state in particular, not long since cut off the heads of all the Falatahs that could be found in their country, and from that time they have enjoyed the most perfect independence. The sultan of Yaoorie said further, that the best thing he could do was to send us back again to Boossa, and from thence he was sure we might have liberty to go any where. The moment we found that this was his intention, we returned to our house, and having formed our resolution, we instantly dispatched one of our men with a message to the king of Boossa, to the following effect:

'That finding our presents insufficient to defray our expenses on the road to Guarie and Bornou, we were under the necessity of returning to the salt-water, to obtain more. That the chief of Badagry had treated us so very ill, that he would detain us in his town for the remainder of our lives, if we were to return by the way we had come. Under these circumstances, we were extremely desirous of travelling to the salt-water by a shorter and safer route, and would therefore prefer going by Funda, as the easiest and likeliest means of accomplishing that end. But as we had heard that the road to that kingdom by land is infested with Falatahs, who live by plunder and violence, we should feel infinitely obliged to him (the king of Boossa), if he could either sell or lend us a canoe to proceed thither by water; and if so, that we would remunerate him to the utmost of our ability.'

July 16th.—Although the Falatahs have been so successful in Nouffie, and are gradually spreading themselves throughout the countries composing Western Africa, so as to be near the sea, where it is the great object of their ambition to get, they have within this year or two suffered many defeats, and lost much ground. Bello is at war with Bornou and some of the states of Haussa; and many thousands of his men, fearing no law, and having no ostensible employment, are scattered over the whole face of the country. They commit all sorts of crimes; they plunder, they burn, they destroy, and even murder, and are not amenable to any earthly tribunal for their actions.

The boasted good government of Bello does not extend beyond the precincts of Soccatoo. In other parts of his empire the civil department of his administration is most wretchedly conducted, and hence the predatory Falatahs which annually go forth to ravage the country.[1]

July 17th.—The Arabs in this place and all those that have passed through the city since our arrival in it, who have had no connexion whatever with each other, have assured us that the Niger flows from a place called Musser (query Mesr),[2] where silks and other fine articles are manufactured, and that the natives of that country trade to Timbuctoo in large vessels, carrying thither their silks and manufactures.

In this part of Africa not the slightest jealousy exists in respect to the Niger or any other river, for the people cheerfully answer every inquiry concerning what they may happen to know of its course, etc.

July 19th.—The premises which we occupy are situated at the northern end of the city. They form a little circular enclosure of huts, one of which is two stories high; and it has the convenience of three small yards, in which is good stabling for the horses. When we were introduced into them, one or two of the roofs were entirely wanting, and the rain, which fell daily, was freely admitted into all the remainder for want of repair, that with two stories alone being an exception. For our own comfort, therefore, we took possession of the upper room of this hut, which is a long, narrow and gloomy apartment, having a solid clay floor, and five or six small apertures, like pigeon-holes, for the purpose of admitting light and air.

As we have been unable, from the almost constant rain and the marshy nature of the soil of Yaoorie, to walk abroad, this room has been, in a great measure, our prison, for we have rarely stirred out of it. During the first few days and nights after our arrival we were pretty comfortable, and, every thing considered, we liked our quarters tolerably well; but an envious wind having blown a swarm of mosquitoes into our apartment, we have ever since been deprived of sleep at night. And as if this were not an evil sufficiently annoying, we are likewise visited by myriads of gnats, cockroaches, black ants, etc; besides a number of bats, which flutter even in our faces, and cause us much uneasiness. Other descriptions of animals and insects intrude into our apartment in the night season, which however do not molest us.

[1] Though this is a prejudiced view of the state of the Fulani empire, Sultan Bello is known, from other sources, to have had to face during his reign numerous revolts or attacks from the unsubdued remnants of the Hausa kingdoms. The people of Kebbi maintained a vigorous resistance only a few miles from Sokoto.

[2] I.e. Arabic *Misr:* Egypt (not Cairo, as the Landers wrongly state on p. 136).

Under this pressure of grievances, my brother and I, finding it impossible to sleep, either sit up or lie awake, and employ ourselves in doling away the long and wearisome hours of the night in chatting about indifferent matters, or in reading aloud, by lamp-light, some moral or religious work. As soon as the light or dawn of the morning penetrates our dismal chamber, our tormentors cease to molest us, and we generally find this the most favourable time for procuring a little sleep. But then the whole world is awake and abroad; and human visitors, whose society is scarcely less tolerable than the visitation of our nightly companions, intrude their unwelcome persons on our sleeping moments and compel us to listen and answer their vexatious nonsense. Deprived of our natural rest, the day is spent with scarcely more enjoyment than the night; we are heavy, languid, peevish, and uncomfortable, and wholly unfit for exertion of any kind. The happy freedom from such torture as this in Old England, can only be appreciated by those who have experienced it; even an hour of such relief now would be worth more than we could express.

This forenoon our Boossa messenger returned, and, to our unspeakable joy, informed us that the king had consented to procure for us a canoe, to proceed to Funda, provided the road by land could not be depended on. He candidly stated, however, his inability to protect our persons from insult and danger beyond his own territories; and that we must solicit the good-will of the prince of Wowow and the other rulers on the banks of the Niger; and further, that our own men alone must manage the canoe, because no one at Boossa would be willing, for various reasons, to accompany us in this journey. We are therefore in a fair way of accomplishing the object of the expedition; and though we are convinced that we shall be beset with dangers from the shore, yet we are in high spirits, and humbly hope that, by attending the necessary precautions, we shall be able to overcome them.

July 21st.—The sultan of this place puts off our departure from day to day, and from week to week, under a variety of nonsensical excuses; and we are persuaded that it is his intention to detain us here till he has drained us of everything we have.

July 26th.—For the last five days my brother has been laid up with an intermittent fever. Today, to our surprise and pleasure, a messenger from the king of Boossa arrived in this city to request our immediate release. One of the *inducements* urged by this monarch for our longer stay with him, is rather whimsical. He has made us a present of a quantity of worthless feathers, which he had caused to be plucked from the body of a live ostrich; and because he entertained an opinion that if others were added to them they would altogether form a very acceptable present to our gracious sovereign, he informed us that it would be necessary we should wait till such time as the ostrich should regain its plumage, in order for that part of its body which had not previously been plucked to undergo a similar operation; for the weather, he asserted, was much too cold for the bird to lose all its feathers at one and the same time. And further, to encourage their growth, he would order that two thousand cowries worth of butter (about twelve pounds weight) should be diligently rubbed into the skin of the animal. This money has actually been deducted by the sultan, for this express purpose, from the sum which he was indebted to us, because he said he did not approve of paying for the butter from his own pocket.

July 29th.—The sultan has been complaining sadly of poverty these two days, and has begged us to accept a female slave of him in lieu of the money he owed us, and which he has declared his inability to pay. We hesitated a good deal at first about the matter, but we soon felt convinced it would be useless to demur, for the sultan was fixed in his determination, and we have taken the girl, who is become Paskoe's wife.

Sunday, August 1st.—This morning the sultan sent a messenger to inform us that we were at liberty to pay our respects and take our farewell of him. We presently obeyed the summons; and on our arrival at the sultan's residence, we were introduced into a large, gloomy, uncomfortable apartment, wherein the monarch generally receives his more distinguished visitors. A number of naked girls and boys, his domestics, were continually passing through it to other parts of the building, carrying dirty calabashes in their hands; a quantity of swallows' nests were attached to the ceiling of the room (for neither here nor elsewhere are these birds ever molested), and their twittering owners, which were flying about in all directions, fed their young without interruption, and added not a little filthiness to the unswept and unclean apartment. In the centre and opposite the door-way, the ruler of Yaoorie was squatting on a platform, which was covered with faded damask, and smoking from a pipe of huge dimensions. On each side of him was a large pillow; and behind him, affixed to the wall, was a large square piece of ancient-looking figured silk, very rich and of various colours, with a beautiful deep fringe. It was, however, a little tarnished, owing to the length of time it has been in the sultan's possession. This once splendid and valuable article is said to have been brought from the celebrated *Musser* (the *Cairo* of Europeans), a place of which everyone here speaks in the most rapturous and extravagant terms. The dress of the sultan corresponded with the dirtiness of the apartment. Just before our introduction we had been cautioned not to offer to shake hands with him, for that would be considered too familiar on our parts, and would be rejected by the monarch. Our compliments were therefore confined to simple inquiries after his health. The conversation during the interview was as uninteresting and spiritless as our conversations with other native rulers have always been—a description of one being a sample of the whole. The most important points were an urgent request on the part of the sultan for one of our lancets which he had seen, and the promise of a calabash of honey, which we received in the evening. We then took our leave and returned home. Here we were soon intruded upon by the sultan's daughters and friends, who, finding that we were actually to go on the morrow, had come to purchase buttons, beg medicine, and pay their last respects; and we were not only subjected to the most wearisome and provoking ceremonies in the world during the remainder of the Sabbath, but we were likewise compelled to be bartering and wrangling with a parcel of noisy women till sunset, when we ungallantly drove them away.

During our stay at Yaoorie, the thermometer of Fahrenheit has ranged from 75° to 94° in our dwelling.

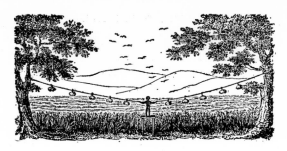

Bird-scaring

X

Yaoorie to Wowow

August 2nd.—All was hurry, bustle, noise, and confusion, at a very early hour in the morning, in getting our things ready for starting; but we had to wait a long time outside our house, for the sultan's long-expected letter to our most gracious sovereign. A mallam was at length perceived hurrying towards us with it; and after him came, mounted on a large bony horse, the venerable Arab chief. His appearance was stately and patriarchal in the extreme. But this crafty old man was not our friend, for he had misrepresented us and our goods to his master; and we had enjoyed an innocent kind of revenge, in administering to him, after repeated applications, a powerful dose of medicine, which, though harmless in its effects, had yet been very troublesome to him. Indeed it was not till we had 'jalaped' the sultan, his sister, and all the royal family, that we were permitted to take our farewell of Yaoorie.

It is pleasant, very pleasant, after an imprisonment of five weeks in a close, dark, and unwholesome chamber, subject to every kind of inconvenience and much anxiety, to be set at liberty; to know and feel that one is free; to admire again the beauties of God's creation, and enjoy once more the cheering freshness of the country. It is only in health that such feelings can either be excited or indulged. Objects ever so charming are looked on with indifference by an invalid. For our parts, we had entered Yaoorie in sickness, and had suffered much in that city; but we left it in all the strength and vigour of health. During our residence there, the growth of vegetation had been astonishingly rapid; the face of the country wore an aspect entirely different and improved; the trees and shrubs had put on a greener and lovelier 'livery'; the grasses, stunted as they were before for want of moisture, had sprung up to the surprising height of ten or twelve feet; and the corn and rice had grown up with no less vigour.

About mid-day we arrived at the walls of a pretty considerable town, called Guada, and halted near a small creek entering the Niger a little lower down. Here we embarked in two canoes, which were each paddled by four men. These canoes are about eighteen or twenty feet long, and formed from a single log of wood, unlike those of Boossa.

On entering the Niger, we found it running from two to three miles an hour, and with trifling labour on the part of the canoemen, we could have journeyed very rapidly; but the whole of them were so obstinately indolent, that we travelled very slowly indeed. The canoes, however, were passing along almost close to the shore, and we saw a woman at the water's edge who had a quantity of cheap country beer for sale, and thinking it might animate the men to a little more exertion, we purchased as much as they could drink, which in a few minutes completely metamorphosed them. The meekness, innocence, and composure of their listless countenances soon passed away; their heavy eyes sparkled with fire and animation; they trembled all over with anxiety to display their strength, dexterity and vigour; and each being emulous to rival his companions, they snatched up their paddles, and by their united efforts the canoes glided through the water with inconceivable velocity, even to the danger of upsetting. Thus we proceeded down the river till the sun had set, and the moon was shining beautifully on the water, as we drew near to a small Cumbrie village, where we landed and pitched our tents.

August 3rd.—On all the borders of the numerous branches of the river, as well as on its small islands, vast quantities of corn were growing; and it being near the time of harvest, it was nearly ripe, and waved over the water's edge very prettily. Platforms were everywhere erected to the height of, or rather above the corn, which grows as high as ten or twelve feet. People were stationed on these to scare away the numerous flights of small birds, which do great mischief, and would, without this precaution, destroy the hopes of the cultivator. A boy or girl, and in many cases a woman with a child at her breast, and even a whole family together, we observed on the platforms, amusing themselves in this manner, without the slightest shade or covering of any kind to shelter them from the fierceness of the sunbeams. Several of the watchers were furnished with slings and stones, in the use of which they seem to be very skilful; besides these, pieces of rope were fastened from the platform to a tree at some distance, to which large calabashes were suspended, with holes in them, through which sticks were passed, so that when the rope is pulled they make a loud clattering noise. To this is often added the hallooing and screaming of the watchers, which is dismal enough to frighten an evil spirit, and it rarely fails to produce the desired effect.

The inhabitants of many of the numerous walled towns and open villages on the banks of the Niger, and also of the islands, we find are for the most part Cumbrie people—a poor, despised, and abused, but industrious and hard-working race.[1] They are but too often oppressed and persecuted by their more fortunate and powerful neighbours, who affirm that they are fitted by nature only for slaves, and are therefore invariably treated by them as such.

The Cumbrie also inhabit many parts of Haussa and other countries; they speak different languages, but they have all the same pursuits, superstitions, amusements, and peculiar manners, to which they firmly and scrupulously adhere, both in good and bad fortune, in sickness and in health, in freedom and slavery, at home and in foreign countries, notwithstanding the scorn and derision to which it subjects them; and they are known to cherish and maintain them to the end of life, with as much pertinacity as the Hebrew does his faith and national customs. Inheriting from their ancestors a peaceful, timid, passionless, incurious disposition, they fall an easy prey to all who choose to molest them; they bow their necks to the yoke of slavery without a murmur, and think it a matter of course; and perhaps no people in the world are to be found who are less susceptible of intense feeling and the finer emotions of the human mind, on being stolen away from their favourite amusements and pursuits, and from the bosom of their wives and families, than these Cumbrie people, who are held in such general disesteem. Thousands of them reside in the kingdom of Yaoorie and its province of Engarski; and most of the slaves in the capital have been taken from among them.

The tribute, or rather rent which they pay to the sultan for the land they cultivate, consists of a quantity of corn, about the size of a bundle as much as a man can carry, for every plot of land, whether it be large or small. When, however, the harvest fails, they are at liberty to give

[1] The 'Cumbrie' are now known as the Kamberri. For an account of the Kamberri see Temple, 1922, pp. 198–204.

a certain number of cowries in lieu of the accustomed duty of corn. If the poor have no means of paying their rent when it becomes due, the sultan immediately despatches a body of horsemen to their villages, with a command to seize and carry away as many of the people as they may think proper. It sometimes happens, however, that the sultan of Yaoorie pulls the reins of oppression with too tight a hand; and as cowards, when driven to desperation, often give specimens of extraordinary courage and resolution, so the negligent and despised Cumbrie, writhing under the lash of injuries which they have never deserved, defend themselves with extraordinary determination and bravery, and not unfrequently come off victorious from the conflict. The benefit which results to them from these advantages is an exemption from the payment of rent for two or three subsequent years.

The most unfavourable trait in the character of the Cumbrie is the extreme dirtiness they display in their habits generally. Most of them are rather slovenly about their persons, and make use of few ornaments, and even these are of the commonest description. They bore immense holes in the lobe of the ear for the admission of bits of fine coloured wood; and the soft part of the septum of the nose is perforated in like manner, through which is thrust a long piece of blue glass. When the females have a mind to appear with unusual smartness and effect, a crocodile's tooth is inserted through both lips, and projects upwards as far as the nose. These useless, unbecoming, and singular ornaments impart to the countenance an unnatural and barbarous expression, which is very far from agreeable, and produces an unpleasant and painful emotion in the mind of the beholder. In *our* intercourse with the Cumbrie, they appeared mild, innocent, and even amiable in their manners; and they behaved to us with all the civility, hospitality, and kindness of their natures, untinctured by insincerity or lukewarmness.

The annexed sketch is a representation of the sleeping hut of these people. The doorway, which is the only opening they have, is closed by a mat which is suspended inside. They have no steps to enter by, but scramble into it as well as they can. The common coozie hut is used by them for ordinary purposes, such as cooking, etc, during the day, but never at night. These sleeping huts are about seven or eight feet wide, they are nearly circular, are made of clay, and thatched with palm leaves; they are elevated above the ground so as to secure the inmates from the annoyance of ants, snakes, and the wet ground, and even for protection from the alligators which prowl about at night in search of prey. We were informed of instances where these creatures have carried off the legs and arms of natives, who have incautiously exposed themselves to their attacks. The huts will hold about half a dozen people. Sometimes the pillars supporting the huts are walled round, but this is not often done, as they generally appear as in the sketch.

The natives frequently kill the alligators by means of a heavy spear ten feet long. One end is furnished with a heavy piece of iron-wood to give it force, and the other with a sharp-pointed barbed iron. It is attached to the bow of their canoe by a piece of grass rope, which is fastened to the upper end, and is a formidable weapon. A smaller spear of the same description is used by these people for killing fish, in which occupation they are very expert.

As we proceeded down the Niger by a different channel from that by which we had ascended it to Yaoorie, we had fresh opportunities of remarking the more striking features on its banks. The river is much swollen, and its current more impetuous than when we passed up on our voyage to Yaoorie; and many of the stones and rocks which then annoyed us, are now under water, and completely hidden.

August 4th.—The inhabitants of the village wherein we slept last night had nothing to offer us to eat either then or this morning; but we had the good fortune to shoot a partridge, and we had it dressed for breakfast. But it was, like many others, a most unsavoury repast, for we had nothing to eat with it, not even a little salt; the people of the village, as well as most of their countrymen, making use of a quantity of wood-ashes instead, which contains saline particles, because salt is too expensive an article for these simple villagers to purchase for their own consumption! We had everything conveyed to the canoes at an early hour, and at seven o'clock a.m. we were once more upon the Niger.

About noon we observed a herd of Falatah cows grazing on the banks of the river; and in the water a little way from them, we saw an immense crocodile floating on the surface like a long canoe, for which it was at first mistaken, and watching an opportunity to seize one of them and destroy it by dragging it into the river. As soon as he was perceived by the canoemen, they paddled as softly as possible towards him, intending to wait at a short distance till the crocodile should have accomplished his object, when they agreed to pull rapidly towards the shore, and reap the fruits of the reptile's amazing strength, by scaring him off from his prey, or destroying him with harpoons, for the skin of a crocodile is not considered impenetrable here. Their intentions, however, were frustrated by the sudden disappearance of the crocodile, which dived the moment he perceived the canoe so near him, making a loud plashing noise, and agitating the water in a remarkable manner in his descent. We waiting in vain for him to rise again. A very short time after this the canoemen landed at *Warree*, which is the most celebrated market town in the dependency of Engarski. The market is attended by many thousands of people from different parts of the country, besides Yaoorie, Boossa, and Wowow, yet nothing peculiar to Engarski is exposed to sale in it; and the cheapness at which the productions of the country are disposed of, is most likely the principal inducement for buyers to resort to Warree. Vast numbers of canoes, filled with people and goods, were passing from one side of the Niger to the other during our limited stay outside the town, and the countenances of both buyers and sellers betrayed a very anxious and businesslike expression. We also crossed over to the Boossa side of the river, and landed at a small walled town called *Garnicassa*, situated about five miles north of the city of Boossa.

Shortly after our arrival, when we were making some allusion to the river to one of the inhabitants, a Falatah hearing us came forward and made the extraordinary assertion, that instead of running to Funda, it took a turn to the eastward, and disembogued itself into the lake Tshad in Bornou. But theories respecting the Niger are even more various and contrary in this country, than the hypotheses of the learned of Europe on the subject. Scarcely two people are to be found that agree in the same opinion, and their suppositions are not confined to the course and termination, but include also the source of this mysterious river; yet, with all their talk, it is easy to perceive that the natives are entirely ignorant of the matter.

The earlier part of the evening, after our arrival at Garnicassa, was calm, serene, and delightful; and the silvery moon shone with unusual resplendence. It was a favourable time for the inhabitants of the town to enjoy themselves; and accordingly they were thus employed in good earnest. Singing, dancing, and music-playing, are the only divertisements with which the generality of the Cumbrie are acquainted; and though this people are even more despised than the slothful Hottentots of the southern part of the continent, though their rights are unheeded and their liberties abused, yet these considerations do not seem to impress them with gloomy reflections; and they trifle away their leisure hours in play with as much zest and thoughtless jollity as though they were the most favoured people in the world.

A sudden and confused noise of merriment awoke me from a pleasing kind of reverie in which I was indulging in the moonshine. I went out instantly to ascertain the cause of such obstreperous mirth, and discovered a number of young girls, and married women with children on their backs, dancing, singing, romping, and clapping their hands, after the manner of the country; and a group of their male relatives standing beside them as judges and spectators of their proceedings. The dance (if it deserve the name) commenced with the whole of the females, married and single. They first formed themselves into a circle, holding fast of each other's arms, and then moved round very slowly without lifting their feet from the ground. This exercise seemed to have occasioned them much exertion and difficulty, if we might be allowed to judge from the violent and peculiar manner in which they shook and twisted their bodies, as well as from the failure of several of the younger girls, who were obliged to quit the ring almost as soon as it was formed. This slowness of motion was gradually succeeded by a sprightlier movement, till they ran round so swiftly, that the circle was suddenly broken, and many of the women were thrown with violence to the ground. The singing, or rather screaming, and clapping of hands, together with other noises, more vociferous and wild than these, were continued till the approach of morning, when a heavy shower drove every one home. Nothing, perhaps, in this country is more capable of producing a wild, romantic, and pleasing effect than such a spectacle as this, and at such a time. In front of us lay the celebrated Niger, reflecting from its unruffled surface the splendid canopy over our heads, with the radiant clouds of departing day. On each side of the river Nature had scattered with a lavish hand the most lovely of her gifts; and verdant trees cast their tall shadows on the water. Almost close to the place where we stood, was a circle of naked savage women, all black as a coal, who were performing the oddest antics imaginable; and still nearer stood a wild-looking group of their male companions, resting on their tall spears and participating in the frolic with all their hearts. A three-cornered rush or straw hat, having a high peak, but without a brim, was the only article of dress worn by these men. Altogether, as we have already said, the scene was such as to fill the mind with the highest gratification and delight. To us it was irresistibly charming, and we contemplated it a long time with emotions of the most pleasing descriptions.

August 5th.—After an hour's ride we drew near to the walls of the city [Boossa], and soon arrived at the drummer's house, which had been our former residence. Here we found the Midiki on her knees to receive and welcome us back again to Boossa in the name of the king. But we were not permitted to enter and take possession of our old apartments, for the queen conducted us to other huts, which form part of a cluster inhabited by Falatahs, and emigrants of both sexes from Yarriba and Nouffie, who are mostly slaves to the king. It has been told us that the drummer's wife had excited the envy of the queen by wearing round her neck a smart gilt button which we had given her; and that this is the only reason that we are not allowed to occupy our former lodgings in her house. Yet, to be even with her *fair* rival, the queen had extracted from her little sheepskin box, wherein they had been confined for a quarter of a century, a small number of round and flat golden ornaments, with which she has adorned her sable bosom, and thereby totally eclipsed the transitory splendour of the button belonging to the drummer's wife.

On our arrival in Boossa, the face and hands of both my brother and self were much swollen and highly inflamed by exposure to the sun, and this circumstance, simple as it was, excited the queen's sympathy to tears.

August 6th.—In a conversation with the king this morning, he intimated that it would be necessary for us to visit Wowow, previous to our going to Funda, because the prince of that state, he said, had already made war on Kiama on our account, and captured a few of its people. The king has himself repeated to us the promise which he made to our man, of furnishing us with a canoe sufficiently large to contain the whole of our people and ourselves, and whatever goods we may have left; and in order to bind him to his word, we have given him our tent and the horse which was lately his own; so that, deprived of these, we shall not have the means of travelling on land, and shall therefore of necessity be obliged to proceed by water. Thus far everything is favourable to our enterprise, yet doubts sometimes arise in our minds; and should a canoe be denied us after all that the monarch of this place has said, we are determined, when the time draws near for our departure, to take a canoe of our own accord, and steal away from Boossa by night. 'Falatahs,' said the king today with much seriousness, 'reside on each side of the river in considerable numbers, and I begin to fear that they will endanger your personal safety.' But answers Paskoe, our interpreter, 'Englishmen are gods of the water, and no evil can befal them in boats, even though all Africa, or the whole world, should fight against them.' 'I will, however,' said the king in reply, 'go down and ask the *becken rouah* (dark or black water, which the Niger is everywhere emphatically styled) whether it will be prudent and safe for the white men to embark on it or not.' Tomorrow morning, we understand, he intends making this singular experiment.

Today when we ascertained that it was the actual intention of the king to supply us with a canoe, we thought proper to present him, in the name of our sovereign, with one of those beautiful silver medals which were cast during the American war, for the purpose of distributing amongst those Indian chiefs who were favourable to the English interests.[1] A large and valuable chain of the same metal was attached to it, and nothing which we had previously given him pleased him so much as this medal and chain.

August 7th.—Just after we had risen this morning, the king came to us with joy beaming in his countenance, and quickly informed us that, according to his promise, he had been down to the Niger with his mallam or priest, and that the result of his visit was highly favourable to our wishes as well as his own—'the river having promised to conduct us in safety to its termination'. He likewise observed that the canoes of the chief of Wowow were much superior to his own, and that he should therefore request him to sell us a large and good one, made of a single trunk, instead of one joined in the middle, which he said would not be either so strong or so safe.

[1] This medal is still in the possession of the Emirs of Bussa. Local tradition assets that the medal was given to the ruler of Bussa by a white man coming down the river, i.e. Mungo Park. Recently, however, this legend has been disproved, for it has been shown that the medal is of a type first struck in 1814, eight years after Park's death (Lupton, 1962).

August 9th.—The king is one of the tallest and finest men in the country, as well as one of the most active and industrious. He is often-times unwell, owing, according to his account, to having, many years ago, swallowed a quantity of poison which had been administered to him as an excellent medicine by one who sought his destruction. Other chiefs and 'great men', not only in Borgoo, but in every place that we visited, either doze and sleep away the greatest part of their lifetime, or spend it in the most childish and frivolous pursuits; whereas his majesty of Boossa, when he is not engaged in public affairs, usually employs all his leisure hours in superintending the occupations of his household and making his own clothes. The Midiki and he have distinct establishments, divided fortunes, and separate interests; indeed, they appear to have nothing in common with each other, and yet we have never seen so friendly a couple since leaving our native country. The manners of the Africans, too, are hostile to the interest and advancement of woman, and she is very rarely indeed placed on an equality with her husband.

The kings of Boossa have the reputation of being the greatest monarchs, next to the sovereigns of Bornou, between that empire and the sea; and this enviable distinction is acknowledged by every rival chief. Yet it cannot be owing to their power, their state, or their opulence, for of all the Borgoo rulers, they are perhaps the poorest and feeblest. The superior dignity of the kings of Boossa, and the honour and reverence which are universally paid them, have arisen, it is said, from the respectability of their origin, for they are believed to be descendants of the oldest family in Africa,[1] which in ancient times, long before the introduction of the Mahomedan religion, was the great head of the fetish; hence the profound respect which is yet shown them by the professors of the new faith, and those who still cling to the superstitions of the old, and the influence which they exercise as far as their name is known.

August 10th.—The Midiki sends us a bowl of bruised corn, boiled in water, which is called *tuah*, twice a-day for our people; and the king

---

[1] The rulers of Bussa claim descent from the legendary Kisra. Kisra is said to have lived in Mecca, where he set up a different religion from that of Muhammad and gathered many followers around him. He and his followers were eventually driven out of Mecca and made their way to Bornu. From Bornu they passed on to Bussa, where they settled. According to some versions of the legend, the Muslims, who were still in pursuit of Kisra, used their magic to transform the Niger, which was then a little stream, into a great river, so that Kisra should never be able to cross it and return to the east. Nikki and other towns in Borgu were said to be founded by the sons of Kisra (*Kontagora Gazetteer*, pp.

sends daily a little rice and dried fish, seasoned with pepper, salt, and palm-oil, for our own consumption. But we find this insufficient for our people, who are eight in number, and ourselves. Guinea-fowl and partridges, which we used to shoot here in great quantities, and which formed the principal part of our food, are now procured with the greatest difficulty and fatigue, owing partly to the prevalence of heavy rains, which have rendered the ground soft and boggy, and partly to the surprising height and stiffness of the corn-stalks, between which these birds always shelter themselves. We are, therefore, often much perplexed about the means of procuring a meal. With buttons the market is already overstocked; needles are unsaleable; we have disposed of all our bits of coloured cloth, and common red stuff, tea canisters, powder canisters, and almost everything indeed that *would* sell, reserving the very few articles of greater value which are left, for presents to the different chiefs along the banks of the Niger. Amongst other trifles disposed of were several tin-cases, which contained worthless and unpalatable portable soups, etc. These were labelled with slips of tin, which though rather dull and dirty, nevertheless attracted the admiration of many; and we have been highly diverted to see one man in particular walking at large, and strutting about with 'Concentrated Gravy', stuck on his head in no less than four places. He appeared quite proud and vain of these ornaments, and was simpering with pleasure wherever he went.

Our men bear fatigue and hunger extremely well, yet when they have food in abundance, they eat, or rather devour it voraciously. Having also two women (Paskoe's wives) in our train, we think it will be no easy matter, at a future period, to supply them even with the bare necessaries of life, more especially after our embarkation in the canoe.

August 11th.—We prepared ourselves early this morning to depart for Wowow. The path was filled with holes and pits, and overgrown with grass, so tall, that it reached far above our heads, and sprinkled a shower of water on our persons. Small rivers, rushing along with the impetuosity of a torrent, and their rugged and almost perpendicular sides, conduced to render travelling dangerous and even dreadful.

When the most difficult part of the journey had been accomplished

---

23–5). The Kisra legend must contain a core of historical fact. The original Kisra may have been a Muslim heretic or the descendant of some defeated Muslim dynasty from Egypt or Arabia, who sought refuge in the Sudan. But neither his identity nor even the date of his migration have ever been satisfactorily established.

we halted at a farm belonging to the king of Boossa. In the course of the day's journey we observed traces of lions and elephants. The latter animals infest the woods between Boossa and Wowow in incredible numbers, and by the impression of their feet on the pathway, their size must be prodigious.

August 12th.—After a very pleasant ride over an excellent footway, we entered the city of Wowow. We galloped swiftly towards the king's residence, and fired off a couple of pistols as a signal of our arrival. He presently came out to see us; but as the messenger from Boossa was not at hand, the old chief awaited his coming with much patience for more than half an hour. In the wall on each side of the entrance of the town is a large niche, in one of which the king stood fixed and motionless, with his hands clasped under his tobe, and supported on his bosom; and round a pole which had been placed erect in the other niche, a naked youth had entwined his legs, remaining in breathless anxiety to be a spectator of the approaching interview. No two human beings ever bore a more striking resemblance to statues than these; the deception was indeed complete.

The Boossa messenger at length arrived, and the spell which had bound everyone to the spot was dissolved in a moment. We were then conducted to the king, and formally introduced to him; but the grave, eccentric old man shook hands with us without taking them from the tobe in which they had been enveloped, or even condescending to look in our faces, for he never makes it a practice to raise his head above a certain height; fearing he should discover the person to whom he may be conversing gazing full in his countenance, to which he has a very strange but unconquerable antipathy.[1]

[1] Clapperton and Lander had been hospitably entertained by Mohammed, the ruler of Wawa, when they visited the city in 1826. On their arrival, the king had shown the same unwillingness to shake hands. 'The King, being a Mohammedan, fancied that the touch of a Christian would defile him; but this stiffness wore off on a more familiar acquaintance, and he subsequently displayed the characteristic virtues of Africans—generally hospitality and benevolence' (Lander, 1830, I, p. 131). Describing Wawa on the occasion of his first visit, Lander wrote: 'The city lies on a beautiful rising ground with gentle hills on every side; and may contain, on a hasty computation, perhaps twenty thousand inhabitants. It is surrounded by a high and substantial mud wall, and broad deep trench. The houses in it are circular, and the streets spacious and airy: and it is without exception the neatest, most wholesome, and best regulated town of any in the interior' (Lander, 1830, I, pp. 132–3). Wawa declined during the nineteenth century; in 1920 its population was 1049 (*Kontagora Gazetteer*, p. 38).

XI

Wowow

August 13th.—Today is the Mahomedan Sabbath, which is constantly kept as a holiday by the inhabitants for public recreations and festivities. The king's musicians were engaged in playing a very few simple airs during the whole of the morning. For native music it was certainly excellent; elsewhere we have heard nothing equal to it, not even at Katunga, Kiama, or Yaoorie. Boossa seems to have little music, and few amusements of any kind—no city is so dull and lifeless as that. In the evening, the weekly horse-racing commenced by a run of eight or ten ponies, as handsome as they were swift, and the competiton between them was most spirited.

The king's head drummer, a little Nouffie man, came to see us this afternoon. He stated, in answer to our inquiries, that the *Tshadda* (Shary) flows into the Niger at Funda, and a regular intercourse is kept up with the natives on its banks, for the purpose of trade, by means of very large canoes. The sheikh, he said, resided very near the *Tshadda*, which, in Bornou, spreads into a large body of water. He further informed us, that canoes, capable of containing five hundred men in each, and having 'thatched houses' in them, are taken to *Binnie* (Benin), with great quantities of cotton cloth, etc, by his countrymen, who sell them to the natives; and that Funda is very near the salt water; yet the drummer appears to know nothing of *any* river which runs to Bornou.[1]

[1] This account illustrates the degree of confusion that existed with respect to the course of the Benue, a river not yet seen by any European traveller. In 1824 Denham had seen the River Shari flowing into Lake Chad. From the information that he obtained, he assumed that the Shari flowed from the west and was possibly the same river as the Niger. Laird, the first European traveller to visit Funda, was informed that the Shari, as he called the Benue, came from Lake Chad (Laird and Oldfield, 1837, I, p. 224). The 'sheikh', in the

This morning, I carried the few things, which we had brought from Boossa for that purpose, to the king. The monarch appeared well pleased and cheerful, and expressed himself perfectly satisfied with the present. In compliance with my request, the king informed me, that he would sell us a canoe with the greatest pleasure. He was convinced, he said, that we should return in safety by the way of the Niger. He had heard of the refusal of the prince of Kiama to send us by the road of Wowow to his friend the king of Boossa, and his recommending us a path through a dreary wilderness, in which we ourselves had narrowly escaped with life. He had felt for us in that situation, and his heart had been touched with grief at the recital of our misfortunes. After the rains should be over, he was determined to resent the affront which had been thus offered him by the ruler of Kiama, and make him repent his cruelty. He rejoiced, however, to see us, because it would convince his neighbours that the white men neither disliked nor despised him.

August 14th.—Yesterday morning a messenger was despatched in haste to Inguazhilligie, which is a town and ferry on the banks of the Niger, where the king's boats are kept, to ascertain if a large canoe can be appropriated to our use. This morning he informed us, that we should be able to have the best and most commodious canoe in the place.

This day a long and gay procession, formed by the female followers of the ancient religion of the country, passed through the town, walking and dancing alternately, with large spreading branches of trees in their hands. The priestess had just swallowed fetish-water and was carried on the shoulders of one of the devotees, who was assisted by two female companions, supporting the trembling hands and arms of their mistress. Her body was convulsed all over, and her features shockingly distorted, whilst she stared wildly and vacantly on the troop of enthusiasts and other objects which surrounded her. The priestess was then believed to be possessed with a demon; indeed, to us they all appeared to be so, for not one of them seemed in their sober senses, so indescribably fantastic were their actions, and so unseemly did they deport themselves. The whole of the women forming this strange procession might amount to between ninety and a hundred; they were clad in their 'holiday best': their motions were regulated at times by the sound of drums and fifes, and to this music they joined

Nupe man's report, is El Kanemi, the ruler of Bornu, whose capital, Kuka, lay only a few miles to the west of Lake Chad.

their wild shrill voices. They presented one of the most extraordinary and grotesque spectacles that the human mind can conceive.

Sunday, August 15th.—I was seized with giddiness of the head and other symptoms, which are the usual precursors of fever. We had left our medicine-chest behind at Boossa. My brother agreed that it would be advisable for me to return without delay, and leave him here to settle the business respecting the canoe. My brother furnished me afterwards with the following account.

'About mid-day the female worshippers of the ancient gods performed a second mystical ceremony. The religion which these enthusiasts profess, and which was not long since the prevailing religion of the country, is still held in great reverence here; so much so indeed, that the king's daughters were early initiated into its mysteries, and invariably attend the celebration of all its superstitious rites and ordinances. Their parent also is still favourable to the religion of his fathers, which is blended with the Arab fables and traditions (for the Mahomedan creed in its purity is unknown here), and these form the foundation and superstructure of his faith.

'The priestess and her followers believe in the existence of a God, and a heaven wherein he resides; but this glorious and almighty Being superintends the destinies of man in this life, and in a future one rewards or punishes him according to his deserts. Yet of a hell or a place of eternal torment they have no idea whatever. The souls of good men, say they, are translated into a tranquil, happy, and beautiful region, wherein but one monkey is permitted to reside, and where they may remain for ever; whereas the wicked, before they can be allowed to participate in so much felicity and enjoyment, are forced to endure sorrow, pain, and punishment: a variety of tortures is in store for them, such as scourging and beating, till it is considered sufficient punishment has been inflicted for their misdeeds, when they are exalted to a happier state of being.

'Others, who waver between the Mahomedan religion and the ancient faith, believe that at the end of the world a voice will sound from heaven to invite all black men to the world of bliss, but that these will be too much unconcerned and too lazy to embrace the offer—a second voice will then proclaim the same invitation to white men, who will spring up with alacrity and transport, and enter the celestial regions before them with books in their hands. They profess to believe also that two men were originally created, one black and the other white, from whom the whole world is descended.

'The professors of the ancient superstitions sacrifice a bullock, a sheep, or a black goat to their divinities, but they shudder at the very idea of a human offering.

'*August 16th.*—The king of Wowow daily inquires after my health, and sends me a quantity of yams, milk, and eggs, every morning. Although this old chief has received a present infinitely smaller than we have given any other ruler, yet his treatment of us has been more generous than that of all of them together.

'*August 17th.*—In the evening one of our men arrived from my brother at Boossa; he informed me by letter of his convalescence. The letter further stated that the Midiki would settle with her brother, the prince of Wowow, for the canoe which he has promised to sell us.

'*August 19th.*—I have learnt with some surprise today, that Boossa and Wowow are not considered as being in the empire of Borgoo, but that they actually form a separate and distinct country, where a different language is spoken and different manners prevail. The principality of Kiama, however, is included by the natives in the former country, but owing to the long-continued and unceasing intercourse which has been maintained between it and Boossa, etc, the original Borgoo language has given place to the Boossa and Wowow tongue; and the customs and amusements of the people likewise bear at this time so great a similarity to those of their neighbours as not to be distinguished from them. Yet a stranger can scarcely fail to remark a surprising difference between the demeanour of the more respectable inhabitants of Kiama, and the behaviour of the same class of people at Boossa and Wowow. The former are bold, haughty, fierce, and rapacious, the latter are mild, humble, and sedate; the former are held in no better light by merchants and traders, than a band of robbers, whereas the latter are respected everywhere, and held in high reputation for honesty, integrity, and honour. Kiama, it is said, formerly paid a tax to the king of Niki, but now it has sworn allegiance to the Falatahs.[1]

'Niki is the largest and most powerful of the Borgoo states. Its capital, which is extremely populous, is of the same name, and though

---

[1] Richard Lander had described the people of Wawa in 1826 as 'a cheerful, thoughtless set of people, yet fonder of music, carousing, singing, and dancing, than any people we ever met with in Africa'. 'Drunkenness is their besetting sin'; 'chastity itself is barely acknowledged by them as an excellence'; 'nevertheless the people of Wow Wow have many substantial virtues and agreeable qualities, which one can hardly help loving them for. Their generous hospitality is unbounded, and a parcel of more merry, facetious, happy scoundrels than the generality of them is not to be found in the world' (Lander, 1830, I, pp. 133–4).

unwalled, it is of immense extent, and said to be of equal size to the city of Yaoorie. Its monarch has a thousand horses, which are all his private property, and he is, in other respects, wealthy and affluent. His soldiers, who form a good part of the population of the capital, are reputed to be brave, bold, and enterprising men; those on foot have one side of the head shaved to distinguish them from their fellow-subjects. Niki is almost the only country in the west, against which the Falatahs have not yet dared "to lift the spear".[1]

'There is reported to be not less than *seventy* considerable and important towns dependent on the state of Niki, all of which have several smaller towns and villages under their control and management. The chiefs of each of these large towns present to their sovereign, once in their lifetime, a young and pretty woman to be his wife, by which means his seraglio is always kept full. This is an odd and singular kind of tribute but it is slight, and the inhabitants of the "seventy" pay no other.

'This evening, the king's messenger returned from Inguazhilligee, and has succeeded in obtaining a large new canoe for our use, which it is understood will be sent up the river to Boossa as soon as the queen shall have paid the purchase-money to her brother, the chief of Wowow. We had much rather bargain for it ourselves, but the desires of the meddling Midiki are imperious, and it would not be prudent on our part to balk her wishes.—Very unwell all day.

'*August 20th.*—I felt considerably better this morning, and therefore determined to remain no longer in Wowow. Accordingly I went to the king to pay my respects and take my farewell of him before my departure. The monarch was unwilling to part with me so easily, and detained me in his company rather longer than I liked. I related to him, at his own request, an account of the power, the riches, and the glory of England, and kept him in an ecstasy and silent wonderment for some time. "Is all this true?" said the old man to Paskoe, who was at my side. "It is true," answered Paskoe, "for I have seen it." "Wonderful people!" said the king.

'Before I was suffered to leave him, he endeavoured with energy to impress upon my mind the high sense he entertained of Europeans, who were so widely different, he said, from the Arabs; so much kinder, so much better, so much superior in every way. He loved white men

[1] Nikki now lies within the borders of Dahomey. In 1894, during the era of the scramble for Africa, Nikki was the cause of a diplomatic crisis between Britain and France, in which Captain (later Lord) Lugard played an important part.

of the west, because good fortune was always sure to attend their footsteps wherever they went; all lands which they had visited had been blessed in them; and he had no doubt that after our departure Wowow would be similarly favoured. Having taken my farewell, I rode out of the city.

'The journey was long and irksome; but at three o'clock in the afternoon we halted for awhile under a tree at a rural little village embosomed in magnificent trees, which is peopled with emigrants from Nouffie, and as I was too unwell to travel further, we agreed to tarry here for the night. The poor harmless villagers, loving quiet and tranquillity, fled some few years ago from all the horrors of a civil war, which was ravaging their country like a consuming fire, and sought refuge in this peaceful village, which lies on one of the most sequestered vallies in the world. They have now sons and daughters, who seem to enjoy with them the delights of privacy and retirement which they had been so solicitous to obtain; for here these simple blessings are in their fullest perfection. They seldom see the face of a stranger, because their hamlet is situated at a good distance from the road-side; nevertheless a traveller sometimes strays to their dwellings, and when that is the case they receive him with hospitality, and endeavour to make him comfortable by kindness. A river flows near the village, which is said to be full of fish, and this is a source of employment to some of its inhabitants, and of advantage to all. The men are not only skilful fishermen, but they understand husbandry as well as their neighbours; they cultivate large quantities of grain, and grow beans, indigo, and yams in abundance. They likewise keep poultry, and have flocks of sheep and goats: so that though their dress be poor and mean, yet they are rich as regards the necessaries of life, and have the means of enjoying a few of what are considered in this country as its luxuries.

'In the evening, when the sun was going down, the elders of the village assembled under the spreading branches of a noble tree to spend an hour or two in familiar chat. To promote their cheerfulness and assist their conversation, large calabashes of strong home-brewed beer were placed by the side of them. Having swallowed two or three large draughts, the old men drew close to each other, and the venerable chronicler of the hamlet, in an under tone, started a conversation respecting their guest, the fearful white man of the west; and various and horrible were the conjectures of each on the cannibalism of his countrymen; their mysterious supernatural powers, and their partiality for the blood of black men in particular. Their conversation became more serious as the beer began to operate on the old men, and as the dusk of evening came on, they drew still closer together; their legs, which had before been stretched out carelessly and comfortably at full length on the ground, were now gathered up under them; and every now and then they ventured to look back over their shoulders to steal a glance at me, for I was not far off, but this only seemed to inspire them with greater fear than before. The younger natives were about this time returning to the village from their usual occupations by the river side, and in the fields, and they stopped to join the company of the old men. The latter were almost naked, and the young men and girls were perfectly so, as well as the children of both sexes, which had been attracted to the party, and stood listening to the tales of horror which were related. One of our men had been sitting all the while with them, partaking of their beer, and had been silent till he conceived it almost time to retire, when he endeavoured to undeceive them in regard to their opinion of the unnatural propensities of white men, and to overthrow all the visions of bloody adventures which they had imbibed in their infancy, and cherished in their old age, and which had this evening been strengthened almost to realities by my presence, assisted by the effects of the beer they had drunk. But their love for the marvellous could not so easily be eradicated from their minds, and they turned a deaf ear to his remarks. The children shunned my hut as if it contained a serpent or a scorpion, and one or two of them that met me by accident, started, then looked anxiously, eagerly, and entreatingly at me for a moment, as if overcome by terror, and then shrieked aloud and ran away.

'The elderly men of the village perform no manner of work, but reserve it for their children and grand-children, who labour for them without reluctance. The former lounge away their existence, chiefly under the large tree afore-mentioned, where they may be seen at all hours of a fine day, sitting in a group, the very picture of indolence, ease, peace, and comfort and where they chat away the hours as thoughtlessly as if they were to live in this world for ever. They have no troubles, no difficulties, and no cares to interrupt their enjoyment. With what tranquillity and happiness does their life pass away! How smoothly and serenely do they go down to the grave!

'*August 21st.*—Between eleven and twelve o'clock we came in sight of the walls of Boossa. I was rejoiced to find my brother perfectly recovered from his indisposition, and we felt as much pleasure in the meeting as friends that had long parted.'

XII

Boossa

August 23rd.—It was the earnest and oft-repeated desire of the chief of Wowow that we should return from Boossa and spend the approaching holiday with him, to which we thought proper to accede; indeed the old man had behaved so well to us, that we did not like to make him an ungrateful return. But his sister, the Midiki, is already jealous of her brother, because, perhaps, we have given him so good a character, and she says that she is apprehensive he may procure from us more than she is willing that he should have; and so she has not only set her husband's mind against the measure, but she has slandered and defamed the character of her brother to us most shamefully.

This is positively the worst trait in the character of the queen, for in other respects she is an amiable good kind of woman enough. This despicable vice of slander is universal in Africa; the people all speak ill of each other, from the monarch to the slave.

This afternoon the expected messenger arrived from Wowow, with full power to treat with the Midiki for the purchase of our canoe; and though we are the parties most concerned in this business, we are not allowed to say anything at all about it. We have just learnt that the bargain has been concluded; we are to give both our horses for the canoe.

August 24th.—Accounts have reached Boossa of the total discomforture of the Falatahs in the kingdom of *Catsheenah*, where, it is said, there had lately been much fighting; and that every Falatah has been expelled from the city of Catsheenah.

The reverses of the Falatahs have not ended here, for the people of the little but fertile kingdom of Zaria, of which Zeg Zeg is the capital, have also, with the assistance of the Bornouese, risen against their conquerors, defeated them in two or three engagements, driven out the Falatahs, and returned to the allegiance of their own native Prince, who was formerly, and will be again, tributary to the sheikh of Bornou.[1]

August 25th.—We despatched one of our men, named Ibrahim, this morning to Coulfo, with our ass, and a quantity of needles to sell. With him the king has sent a messenger, who has been commissioned to visit all the towns and villages on the Nouffie side of the Quotra, as far as the Falatah town of *Rabba*, and to request their chiefs and governors, in the name of the king of Boossa, to suffer us to pass down the river without inquiry or molestation. The messenger is not expected to return for a fortnight, for the journey is long and disagreeable.

August 31st.—A messenger with a canoe arrived today from the king of Wowow, but it is so very small that it is wholly inadequate for our purpose. Between the chief of Wowow and his sister, the Midiki, we have been completely taken in. Boats of a considerable size, are kept, it is said, at a small town on the banks of the Niger, called *Lever*, and thither we have resolved to proceed as soon as the Boossa messenger shall have returned from Rabba. The horses given in exchange to the prince of Wowow are large, handsome, and superior animals, worth in England at least sixty pounds, and their value here is little less; yet this canoe, which has been sent us is scarcely worth as many pence. There is infinitely more difficulty, and greater bustle and discussion in simply purchasing a canoe here, than there would be in Europe in drawing up a treaty of peace, or in determining the boundaries of an empire, such vast importance do the people attach to the most trifling matters in the world.

This is the eve of the much talked of Mahomedan festival,[2] and the

---

[1] These reports of Fulani reverses were undoubtedly exaggerated, but rested on a certain basis of fact. After the capture of Katsina by the Fulani the members of the ancient Hausa dynasty retreated northwards to Maradi, which they used as a base for constant attacks on Katsina. In Zaria the old dynasty had retreated southwards to Abuja. There is no record in the histories either of Abuja or of Zaria that the Fulani suffered a decisive defeat at this period.

[2] 'The first event of the Islamic year is the 10th night of Muharram (the Ashura) to which African practices connected with the New Year have cohered, although, since it is continually moving round the year, it has been disconnected from the agricultural season. The pious fast for from one to three days and most prepare for it by a short fast, ablutions, and a purge to purify the body. Symbolic rites to ensure prosperity during the new year are universal. When the sun has set everyone eats all he possibly can and poor people are invited to participate, for no one must go empty that night so that a prosperous new year may be ensured. After the feast many have torchlight processions and contests between age-groups' (Trimingham, 1959, pp. 76–7).

inhabitants of the neighbouring towns and villages, resolving to enjoy themselves in the holidays, are already resorting here in great numbers. The disposition of every one appears to be softened into good nature, by the bare anticipation of the festival, and joy beams from their countenances. The very dogs, which at other times receive unkind treatment, and are always badly used, now run about wagging their tails with an air of cheerfulness and courage. Men and women, elated with the thoughts of the pleasure which awaits them tomorrow, are enjoying themselves in singing and dancing, and are seen talking and laughing in every corner; while the younger children, quite naked, are as frolicsome as their grandmothers, and are either rolling on the ground or skipping along the turf like 'little playful fawns'.

September 1st.—Day was drawing to a close, when the king came out of his residence to show himself to his people. He was attended by a number of his head men, with whom he perambulated the town; and afterwards proceeded outside the gate to offer up a short prayer with them to the gods of his religion, for he is still a pagan, as all his fathers were, though he employs Mahomedan priests to pray for his welfare, and intercede with their prophet in his behalf, agreeably to their form of worship. Several musicians were in attendance with drums, fifes, and long Arab trumpets of brass; these men preceded their sovereign, and played lustily on their instruments all the while he was returning to his house. He shortly came out again, and rode slowly up the race-course, attended by people of both sexes most uncouthly dressed, singing and dancing before him, and followed by a party of well-dressed men mounted on mettlesome horses, and equipped as if for war. On our saluting him, the monarch stopped and sent us a goora-nut, which, on such an occasion as this, is considered as a mark of great condescension, and a sign of peculiar favour; and he stayed opposite us at least ten minutes, to give us a fair opportunity of admiring his grandeur, and diverting ourselves by the frolicsome gambols of his attendants. Smiling at our wonderment, and gratified with the respect we paid him by discharging our pistols close to his person, he nodded and passed on. The king was mounted on a fine handsome grey horse, sumptuously caparisoned, while he himself is a noble and commanding figure on horseback, and was dressed extremely well, in a red cap and large turban of the same colour, a silk damask tobe of green and crimson, made full and flowing, red cloth trousers and Arab boots. Groups of well-dressed individuals were seated under every tree with spears, quivers of arrows, long bows, and ornamented cows' tails.

These latter were flourished about as the people sang; their owners
threw them high into the air, and danced at the same time in the most
extraordinary manner, and flung their limbs about as though they had
been actuated by a supernatural power. Every one was exhilarated and
in motion—both horseman and footman, woman and child. The
musicians also, not satisfied by making the whole of Boossa echo with
the most grating and outrageous sounds conceivable, both sung, or
rather screamed and danced, twisting their mouths, with their exertions
into all manner of wry and comical shapes. The spectacle altogether
was odd and grotesque beyond description, and such an one could
never enter into the dreams or waking visions of an European. Guns
were fired by the king's followers, and other obstreperous and astonishing noises were made by the people. Never did we see the king in
a happier mood; his satisfaction seemed to be quite complete. He smiled
graciously on all around him; and bestowed many an arch and significant look upon us, as if he would have said, 'Can *your* sovereign boast
so splendid a retinue as mine, or display so much regal splendour?'

The ceremony was long and fatiguing; and though the king was
screened from the sun's rays by two large ponderous umbrellas, and
though two men were standing by, constantly fanning him, yet
perspiration stood in large drops upon his forehead, and he appeared
nearly exhausted. After our curiosity had been amply gratified, the
king rode away, preceded by his singing and dancing women, his
musicians, his bowmen, and his spearmen, with all their noise and
clamour, and instantly began to make preparations for a horse-race.
The course was short, rough, and uneven, and the competition between
the riders by no means animated. Indeed the race was of short duration,
and very inferior to the horse-racing of either Kiama or Wowow. The
king is a graceful rider, and displayed his horsemanship to much
advantage by galloping up and down the course; and, owing to his
advantageous stature, his appearance was very becoming. The sun
was then setting, and as soon as he had disappeared, the amusements
ceased. The people, both strangers and inhabitants, were then collected
together before the king's house, for the purpose of hearing an oration
from their monarch; for, in pursuance of an ancient and established
practice, the king of Boossa annually harangues his people on the
celebration of this festival. The sovereign is at least a head taller than
any of his subjects, so that he was a remarkable and conspicuous object
to every one of his audience. If such a comparison may be ventured
on, the commencement of his speech was in its nature not much unlike

that delivered on the opening of parliament by his Majesty of England. The king of Boossa began by assuring his people of the internal tranquillity of the empire, and of the friendly disposition of foreign powers towards him. He then exhorted his hearers to attend to the cultivation of the soil, to work diligently, and live temperately; and concluded with an injunction for them all to be abstemious in the use of beer. He declared that too much indulgence in it was the source of much evil and wretchedness, and the cause of most of the quarrels and disturbances that had taken place in the city. 'Go; retire to rest soberly and cheerfully,' said the king, 'and do as I have requested you, when you will be an example to your neighbours, and win the good opinion and applause of mankind.' The king's speech lasted for three-quarters of an hour. He spoke vehemently and with much eloquence; his language was forcible and impressive, and his action appropriate and commanding; and he dismissed the assembly with a graceful and noble air. Instead of a sceptre the monarch flourished the tuft of a lion's tail.

While the king was haranguing his subjects, and while all of them were listening with respect and attention to the precepts of morality and virtue which he recommended, two of our own men, one of whom was intoxicated, were fighting and blustering and making a great uproar among the people: my brother endeavoured to separate them, but all his efforts were unavailing and abortive, and he only received severe blows on the breast for his pains. The fight was observed by the king, who seemed distressed and angry, and rode up to the men three different times, and commanded them to forbear and be quiet, but his interference was regarded with no more respect than my brother's. My brother and I, perceiving that the principal of the fellows would not be pacified by any other means, gave directions that he might immediately be secured. But the people of Boossa are gentle and compassionate in their disposition, and they not only regretted that the man was to receive punishment, but were actually afraid to come near him, for he was wild as a maniac, and our men were obliged to lay hold of him, and attempted to bind him with ropes. This was no easy matter, for he struggled hard with them; but after an hour's desperate resistance, they succeeded in securing him, and he was subsequently confined in irons for the night, much against the wishes of the king and his people. This individual, whose name I forbear to mention, is a mulatto, and was born in the British colony of Nova Scotia, from whence he was removed in his childhood, with his parents, to Sierra Leone. While yet a boy, he was sent to sea; and before he had attained to maturity, he had filled the different characters of a slave, a seaman, a pirate, and the master of a vessel. He afterwards volunteered into the British navy, and became a man-of-war's man; but for a serious misdemeanour, he was flogged through the fleet in the Mediterranean, and deserted in consequence. We found him at Badagry, where he had suffered a fortnight's imprisonment by order of Adooley, for theft. When we first saw him, he told us a long and pitiful story, of his having been born a British subject, but falling sick on board of a merchant vessel, he was set on shore about five years ago by orders of his captain, and from that time up to the period of his joining our party at Badagry, he had been a slave to Adooley, for the captain had left him to his fate. As we knew the man would be extremely useful in a canoe, to the management of which he has been accustomed from his infancy, and that he also understood the cleaning and repairing of guns, besides other useful matters, and as we likewise believed his artful tale, we obtained the consent of the Badagrian chief, whose slave he was, to part with him, provided we would pledge ourselves to bring him back with us in safety. In Yarriba, we could by no means complain of his general conduct; he was always willing to do everything we required of him, and was by far the most diligent and useful man of the party. At Boossa and at Yaoorie, however, his evil propensities and bad conduct began to display themselves: he became idle, drunken, and careless, and purloined several little articles, which, intrinsically, were of no value; but in the reduced state of our finances, they were of great consequence to us. Besides which, he is one of the most abandoned creatures in the world; and it was a common practice with him to absent himself from our party several days together, so that we saw nothing of him, and when he returned, was accompanied by complaints from the native women. This man's conduct has given us both much uneasiness, anxiety, and apprehension; we scarcely know what to do with him, he is so profligate and vicous: we thought of sending him back to Yarriba by a party of men who will leave hence for Keeshee in a day or two, but they dread the thought of his company, and refuse to take him along with them for any consideration. He had already threatened the lives of more than one of our men, and they begin to tremble with apprehension for their personal safety. In his sober moments he is quiet, orderly and good natured; and it is only when his furious passions are excited by drinking, that he becomes altogether ungovernable, and displays all his fiend-like disposition, to the danger of our lives. We are likewise apprehensive that the natives of the country will entertain but a despicable opinion of us, when they reflect upon the outrageous conduct of this man, for his features are cast in the European mould; he dresses in English costume, like ourselves; he speaks our language with readiness, and writes with facility.

September 2nd.—Yesterday was considered as a day of amusement and recreation for men on horseback only; but this has been devoted almost exclusively to dancing and singing, and other trifling diversions, which are more generally relished by people of all ranks, and of both sexes. At an early hour in the morning, the people of the city, with musicians in their train, assembled in large groups, and continued parading the streets all day, and singing and dancing were kept up without intermission till four o'clock in the afternoon. Nothing could surpass the hilarity and general good humour which prevailed among the people during the day. The features of every one were animated with joy. Theirs was no ordinary mirth; for being naturally of a warm-hearted, sanguine disposition, they entered into the sports of the day with a fervency which displayed itself in all manner of extraordinary tricks, gestures, and movements. This was a holiday for all, from the king to the meanest of his subjects. The old seemed to have forgotten their weight of years, the young knew no restraint, and those who before had talked of love in secret, now openly exchanged with each other

> Quips and cranks, and wanton wiles,
> Nods and becks, and wreathed smiles.

A short relaxation from this tumultuous pastime was now obtained by some in making preparations for joining the king's party, which was fast collecting at his house. Such diversions as theirs, so highly exciting and gratifying, are nevertheless wearisome to the strongest frame, and in this sultry climate must be particularly so to them. When they had assembled, they presented a singular, grotesque and striking appearance. A cluster of between sixty and seventy Falatahs, men, women, and children, were some standing and some sitting in front of the door-way, leading to the interior apartments. Their dresses were remarkably clean, neat, varied and becoming; the long black hair of the women was ingeniously and prettily braided, and confined in nets and caps; and their flowing garments of striped cotton swept along the ground: the men wore red caps, loose white tobes, and full trousers; and their little children were pleasingly clad and decorated with all the finery and ornaments which their parents had been able to bestow on them. These well-looking Falatahs formed the most interesting and agreeable assemblage of the whole; they had likewise more vivacity in their looks, and more quickness of action than any of their companions. To the right of them, in an enclosure of mud, was seated the Queen of Boossa, dressed loosely, though not inelegantly, in rich English silks, as spectatress of the amusements; behind her were the king's other wives, and her own female slaves, who were pretty numerous. They formed also a cleanly, decent group inferior only to the former. On each side of the Falatahs, and behind them, was a great number of other spectators, of all ranks, many of whom were standing, and many sitting on the turf and reclining against the trunks of trees. Most of the men were clad in the Mahomedan costume, with cap, tobe, and trousers; and the majority of the women were dressed in neat and durable country-cloths, which were thrown carelessly over the left shoulder, and reached to the ground, leaving the right arm and shoulder, and part of the right leg, uncovered. A few among them, however, wore common Manchester cottons, of a large, showy, and vulgar pattern, which were infinitely surpassed by their own country cloth.

Although the king had not made his appearance, the amusements were carried on with much animation; and the dancers, far from being tired, seemed to imbibe fresh vigour and renewed activity; whilst the drummers, eight in number, with a fifer as an assistant, continued playing to them. A man first started from the crowd with a bundle of rushes in his hand, like a German broom, which he flourished over his head with inconceivable dexterity. After dancing awhile, he was joined by two Falatah women, who imitated his actions, and partook of his glee. One of them held a little girl by the hand; and the whole four individuals, man, women, and child, continued the dancing till they were completely fatigued, when they were succeeded by another party of three or four, and then another in like manner, so that there was not a moment's pause in the dance at any time. They kept good time with the music and singing. But instead of the quick, lively motion which is generally observed on similar occasions, the dancers moved with a slow and measured step, in which there was nothing unbecoming or improper, and all seemed consistent with the rules of delicacy. For want of a proper fan, the females used neat round mats of various colours; and it afforded us no little entertainment to see them placed before the mouth whenever they wished to hide their faces, or attempt to conceal their laughter.

Meanwhile, the king was expected by every one with much anxiety and impatience, for as yet he had not been present to witness the diversions of his people; and it was not till past four in the afternoon that he showed himself from one of his huts. His arrival was welcomed by a spirited rally upon the drums, while he took his seat on a stool between the queen's station and the group of Falatahs, and perceiving us amongst the crowd, he invited us to place ourselves near his person. Several attendants who had followed their master stood on each side of him, forming, if it may so be called, a 'guard of honour'. One of these men held two large bundles of spears, whose points or barbs were confined in caps of burnished brass, on which he rested his head with much solemnity, and with a slight inclination of the body; while from his temples was suspended a huge and enormous hat, made either of grass or rushes, which reached to the ground, and covered him like a shield. Others held loose bundles of spears, fans, and arrows, with the two prodigious Arab trumpets which have before been casually alluded to. Thus attended, the king entered into the spirit of the performances with a merry heart, and a determination to be pleased with them. He appeared to be by far the most delighted spectator of the whole, and signified his approbation by encouraging words and glances to those who danced or sung to his satisfaction. A cheerful smile animated his countenance during the whole time, and caused his features to assume an expression of good humour which it is a particular custom in him never to display so fully except on occasions of public festivity and enjoyment, though he is one of the pleasantest and best-tempered men that we have met with in Africa.

There was an elderly female who danced alone before the king, and by the peculiarity of her looks, and her ludicrous and uncommon gestures, afforded us very great amusement. This woman is a tall, awkward, masculine, and uncomely figure; yet she endeavoured to look so serious at the same time with so arch a countenance, and with a half-averted glance smiled with so much artfulness and loving-kindness on her sovereign and his attendants, dancing at the same time with such an extraordinary motion of her person, that she obtained universal applause. This was a fair challenge to the king; and as soon as she had finished, the monarch himself arose and stepped into the ring to display his acquirements in the art. Every one stood on his legs, out of respect to their sovereign, as well to applaud his dancing, as to obtain a fairer opportunity of beholding his person; and a great press was made by the crowd in consequence, that they might gain a better view of him.

The king moved with much stiffness and stateliness, which is at all times unbecoming in a dance; but the populace expressed their admiration of his abilities in shouts of joy, and certainly his attempts to please and amuse them deserved the full extent of their applause. To us, however, it does not appear that Nature, which has been so bountiful to this beloved monarch in other respects, has fitted him for so active an amusement as this; for though his size approaches to the majestic, though he walks and rides with equal ease, and though the exercise by no means requires the greatest flexibility of body, his dance to us at least was a complete failure; for he has a foot which may be compared to that of a dromedary in point of size, and his toe is anything but 'light and fantastic'. When his first dance, which was much the same as that performed by his people, was concluded, the king began a second by imitating the canter of a native horse when going to war. This, as may be supposed, was an inexpressingly odd and whimsical experiment, but it lasted a short time only; for in a very few minutes he disappeared from the spectators by cantering into one of his huts, followed by the cheers of admiration and the acclamations of every one present.

The sun had now set, and with the departure of the prince the singing and dancing ceased for the evening; nevertheless all the people patiently awaited his return to the spot. Now, of all the celebrated dancers in the country, none can excel or equal the king of Wowow in grace, elegance and vivacity; and the fame of his skill in this amusement, which is thought so much of in this country, is gone abroad into all lands: every one, even his enemies, acknowledge his superiority in this polite accomplishment; and the envious and malicious are compelled to own that he is without a rival from Bornou to the sea. Yet, notwithstanding his renown as a dancer, the chief is a very aged man, having a most solemn and forbidding aspect; and though he has evidently, to use a common expression, one foot in the grave, he is as active as a boy, and indulges largely in this his favourite amusement every Friday. It was in order for us to witness his elegant dancing, we have been told, that he pressed us with so much earnestness and importunity to spend the holidays at Wowow, which we should certainly have consented to, but for the discouragement our project received from the king of Boossa, who was envious of his celebrity, and therefore compelled, rather than enticed us to remain here, that we might see his personal accomplishments to advantage, witness the public gaiety and festivities of his people, and in his imagination be struck with astonishment and admiration at his own perfection in the art of dancing.

The Boossa people did not wait long for the reappearance of their monarch, for shortly after he came out to them, followed by a boy with two calabashes full of cowries, which were to be distributed among the multitude. But first of all the king took up a handful, and gave to each of the singers, dancers, and musicians, that had contributed so essentially to his entertainment; nor was the tall old woman forgotten, who had danced alone before him, for she received a double allowance. We were rather pleased at this, for she is our next-door neighbour, a poor old woman, who is very chatty and flippant, and has fallen in love with one of our young men, named Antonio. The remainder of the cowries were scattered by the king's own hand among the crowd to be scrambled for, which occasioned the most animated and amusing sight that can be conceived. Parents and children, brothers and sisters, strangers and friends, were scrambling and tumbling over each other, some on their faces and some on their knees, both giving and receiving cuffs and kicks in the scuffle to get at the money. This scramble lasted about ten minutes, when the party before the king's house broke up; but the good-natured monarch, to show his affection for his subjects, whom he indeed regards with as much tenderness as if they were his children, was unwilling to send them to their homes without giving them another last treat, so he danced sideways half way up the race-course and back again to his residence with much stateliness. This was indeed a royal attempt; the midiki smiled with pleasure that she had *such* a spouse; the people were louder than ever in their shouts of approbation; all was noise, tumult, and confusion; their sovereign was more beloved than ever he had been; and as the evening closed in, silence was gradually restored, and the people retired to their houses. This was the last of the holidays, and the proceedings of this day have concluded their festivities.

About ten o'clock at night, when we were sleeping on our mats, we were suddenly awoke by a great cry of distress from innumerable voices, attended by a horrid clashing and clattering noise, which the hour of the night tended to make more terrific. Before we had time to recover from our surprise, old Pascoe rushed breathless into our hut, and informed us with a trembling voice that 'the sun was dragging the moon across the heavens'. Wondering what could be the meaning of so strange and ridiculous a story, we ran out of the hut half dressed, and we discovered that the moon was totally eclipsed. A number of people were gathered together in our yard, on dreadful apprehension that the world was at an end, and that this was but the 'beginning of

sorrows'. We learnt from them that the Mahomedan priests residing
in the city, having personified the sun and moon, had told the king and
the people that the eclipse was occasioned through the obstinacy and
disobedience of the latter luminary.

While our informant was yet speaking to us, a messenger arrived
at our yard from the king, with an invitation to come to see him
immediately. Slipping on the remainder of our clothes, we followed
the man to the residence of his sovereign, from outside of which the
cries proceeded, and here we found the king and his timid partner
sitting on the ground. Their usual good spirits and cheerful behaviour
had forsaken them entirely; both appeared overwhelmed with apprehension, and trembled at every joint. Like all their subjects, in the
hurry of fear and the suddenness of the alarm, they had come out of
their dwellings half dressed, the head and legs, and the upper part of
their persons, being entirely exposed. We soon succeeded in quelling
their fears, or at least in diminishing their apprehension. The king then
observed, that neither himself nor the oldest of his subjects recollected
seeing but one eclipse of the moon besides the one he was gazing at;
that it had occurred exactly when the Falatahs began to be formidable
in the country, and that it had forewarned them of all the wars, disasters,
and calamities, which subsequently took place.

We had seated ourselves opposite to the king and queen, and within
two or three feet of them, where we could readily observe the moon
and the people without inconvenience, and carry on the conversation at
the same time. If the royal couple shuddered with terror on beholding
the darkened moon, we were scarcely less affected by the savage
gestures of those within a few yards of us, and by their repeated cries,
so wild, so loud, and so piercing, that an indescribable sensation of
horror stole over us, and rendered us almost as nervous as those whom
we had come to comfort. The earlier part of the evening had been
mild, serene, and remarkably pleasant; the moon had arisen with uncommon lustre, and being at the full, her appearance was extremely
delightful. It was the conclusion of the holidays, and many of the
people were enjoying the delicious coolness of a serene night, and
resting from the laborious exertions of the day; but when the moon
became gradually obscured, fear overcame every one. As the eclipse
increased, they became more terrified. All ran in great distress to inform
their sovereign of the circumstance, for there was not a single cloud
to cause so deep a shadow, and they could not comprehend the nature
or meaning of an eclipse. The king was as easily frightened as his

people, being equally simple and ignorant; he would not therefore suffer them to depart. Numbers sometimes beget courage and confidence, he thought; so he commanded them to remain near his person, and to do all in their power to restore the lost glory of the moon.

In front of the king's house, and almost close to it, are a few magnificent cotton-trees, round which the soil had been freed from grass, etc, for the celebration of the games. On this spot were the terrified people assembled, with every instrument capable of making a noise which could be procured in the whole town. They had formed themselves into a large treble circle, and continued running round with amazing velocity, crying shouting, and groaning with all their might. They tossed and flung their heads about, twisted their bodies into all manner of contortions, jumped into the air, stamped with their feet on the ground, and flourished their hands above their heads. No scene in the romance of Robinson Crusoe was so wild and savage as this; and a large wood fire, with a few men spitted and roasting before it, was alone wanting to render it complete! Little boys and girls were outside the ring, running to and fro, clashing empty calabashes against each other, and crying bitterly; groups of men were blowing on trumpets, which produced a harsh and discordant sound; some were employed in beating old drums; others again were blowing on bullock's horns; and in the short intervals between the rapid succession of all these fiend-like noises, was heard one more dismal than the rest, proceeding from an iron tube, accompanied by the clinking of chains. Indeed, everything that *could* increase the uproar was put in requisition on this memorable occasion; nor did it cease till midnight, when the eclipse had passed away. Never have we witnessed so extraordinary a scene as this. The diminished light, when the eclipse was complete, was just sufficient to enable us to distinguish the various groups of people, and contributed in no small degree to render the scene still more imposing. If an European, a stranger to Africa, were to be placed on a sudden in the midst of the terror-struck people, he would imagine himself to be among a legion of demons, holding a revel over a fallen spirit; so peculiarly unearthly, wild, and horrifying was the appearance of the dancing group, and the clamour which they made. It was perhaps fortunate for us that we had an almanac with us, which foretold the eclipse; for although we neglected to inform the king of this circumstance, we were yet enabled to tell him and his people the exact time of its disappearance. This succeeded in some measure in suppressing their fears, for they would believe anything we might tell them; and perhaps, also, it has procured for us a lasting reputation 'and a name'. 'Oh,' said the king, 'there will be sorrow and crying this night from Wowow to Yaoorie. The people will have no one to comfort or condole with them; they will fancy this eclipse to be the harbinger of something very dreadful; and they will be in distress and trouble till the moon shall have regained her brightness.' It was nearly one o'clock when we left the king and queen, to return to our hut; everything was then calm and silent, and we lay down to rest in peace.

September 6th.—It is time that we should leave Boossa, for in spite of the friendship of the king and queen, more especially of the latter, which is declining very fast indeed, their benevolent feelings are growing colder every day; our resources at the same time are diminishing rapidly, and when they are gone, we know not what we shall do. We now receive only a calabash of *caffas* (a kind of dough or paste) from the king once in three days, so that we are compelled to eat them, at times, either in a state of putridity, or go without; and our men are half-famished, from the careless inattention, or perhaps from the wilful negligence of the midiki; we cannot, like the camelion, live upon air, and we have not a single cowrie to spare to purchase provisions. Our powder is reduced to a very small quantity, and in all probability we have not half so much as we shall require on the Niger; so that for some time past we have relinquished our sporting excursions altogether, though these once afforded us an ample supply of game for the consumption of our whole party.

September 10th.—We have received two messes from the king lately, one consisting of a dish of stewed elephant's flesh, and the other of the flesh of an hippopotamus, which had been caught in the Niger a short time before. The latter was rank and fat, and bore a greater resemblance to pork than to any other meat with which we are acquainted, yet it is considered delicate and delicious eating.

Considering the vast numbers of elephants which inhabit the woods on the banks of the Niger hereabouts, it is singular that so few of them are annually destroyed by the natives. Perhaps one reason is the little encouragement they receive for their trouble; for the flesh of these beasts, except when very young, is almost unsaleable, by reason of its toughness and rancid nature; their teeth also are valueless here, no use whatever being made of them.

September 11th.—Perhaps it would be speaking within compass to say, that four-fifths of the whole population, not only of this country, but likewise every other hereabouts, are slaves. Many of them are permitted to roam at large, provided they attend upon their masters when called upon; these procure their own subsistence, and devote part of their time to the service of their owners: others reside in the houses of their masters as domestic servants, and are likewise expected to contribute towards their own support. The Queen of Boossa has a great number of Falatah slaves; the men are constantly employed in taking care of her herds, and milking the cows, and the females dispose of the milk; half of the money obtained by this means, the Falatahs keep to maintain themselves. Thus are the slaves treated in their native country—they enjoy much freedom; are never overworked; have plenty of leisure time, and are rarely punished, and even then but slightly. If a slave run away from his master, and is afterwards taken and brought back, he is simply confined in irons a day or two for his offence; but he is sold to another the first opportunity. The natives have a strong antipathy to flogging, or severe chastisement of any kind, and very seldom have recourse to the means of punishment which they have in their power to inflict.

Sunday, September 12th.—Our man arrived this afternoon from the city of Coulfo, but with very little money indeed, having disposed of the ass for less than half its value, and sold, comparatively speaking, a very small quantity of needles. The remainder, which were valued at thirty thousand cowries, were stolen from him, he asserts, a few days before his departure; but we strongly suspect that this is a falsehood, and that the fellow has converted them to his own use. Since the messenger to Rabba left Boossa on his errand, we have heard no intelligence whatever concerning him; and as everything is now ripe for our enterprise, we begin to feel impatient and uneasy at our long, and to us, unnecessary detention in this place, and the irksomeness of our present dependent situation.

September 18th.—During the last fourteen days my brother had been extremely indisposed from a slight attack of bilious fever, which has brought him to a very low and languid state, insomuch that I urged the king on Wednesday to send us away, to try if change of air and scene would not produce a beneficial effect on his health. The monarch, after many scruples and much hesitation, at length appointed the second day of the moon, that being, he pronounced, the happiest and luckiest of all days. He could not, however, forbear expressing his deep regret at our determination of leaving Boossa before the return of his messenger from Nouffie; it might be detrimental to our personal interests, and his own reputation also would suffer if any thing should

befall us on the river, but he had already given his word for our departure, and from this promise he could not swerve.

Sunday, September 19th.—Everything is now got ready for starting.
As it is not our present intention to call at many inhabited places on
the banks of the Niger, we have provided ourselves with a great supply
of provisions, which consists chiefly of three large bags of corn and
one of beans. We have likewise a couple of fowls and two sheep, so
that we are of opinion we shall have food enough for three weeks or a
month at least. To add to our stock, the king and midiki between them
have given us a considerable quantity of rice, honey, corn, and onions;
and two large pots of vegetable butter, which weigh not less than a
hundred pounds.

This afternoon, to our unspeakable joy, the long-expected and
wished-for messenger arrived in this city from Rabba, accompanied
by two messengers from the king of Nouffie, one of whom, a modest-
looking, respectable young man, is his own son. These men are to
be our guides as far as Rabba. 'The Magia,' says the Boossa ambassador,
'was delighted with the intelligence that white men were to honour his
dominions with their presence; he showed me the presents made him
by Captain Clapperton three years ago, and said a great deal in his
favour and commendation.[1] And as a proof,' continued the man, 'of
his friendly disposition towards you, and his interest in your welfare,
he has not only sent his son as your companion and guide, but he has
likewise despatched a messenger to every town on the banks of the
Niger, either considerable or unimportant, even as far as Funda, which
is beyond the limits of the empire.'

After some little consideration, we knew not whether we ought to
feel regret or pleasure at the arrival of these men; at present we can
only foresee that they will be a heavy burden on our funds. The king,
however, had but one feeling on the subject, and that was unbounded
delight. 'Now,' said he, 'whatever may happen to the white men, my

---

[1] Clapperton had visited the king of Nupe in 1826. 'He is one of the most beggarly
rogues I have yet met with; every thing he saw or heard that I was possessed of he begged,
not like a person that wished to have them because they were scarce or rare, but with a
mean greediness that was disgusting. Though I had given him a better present than he
had ever got in his life before, he told me that I said "No, no", to everything he asked
for. He has been the ruin of his country by his unnatural ambition, and by calling in the
Fellatas, who will remove him out of the way the moment he is of no more use to them;
even now he dares not move without their permission. Through him the greater part of
the industrious population of Nyffe have either been killed, sold as slaves, or fled from
their native country. To remove him now would be charity; and the sooner the better for
his country' (Clapperton, 1829, p. 128).

neighbours cannot but acknowledge that I have taken every care of them, treated them as became a king, and done my best to promote their happiness and interests.' And so he has, for though we have been his guests for so long a time, and been occasionally not a little troublesome, yet we have observed nothing either in his manners or character to condemn, but much, very much, to approve of and admire.

This evening an old Mahomedan priest, whose countenance seemed to radiate with meekness, simplicity, loving-kindness, and good-nature, entered our dwelling, and entreated us with earnest importunity to give him before our departure a quantity of deadly poison. The hoary old villain did not hesitate to confess, in confidence, that his motive for making this strange request arose from the desire he felt to administer the poisonous drug to a neighbour, whom he longed to put out of the world, because he had done him some slight imaginary wrong.

The Fetish at Patashie.

XIII

Boossa to Lever

September 20th.—About breakfast-time the king and queen arrived at our hut, to pay us a farewell visit, and bestow upon us their last blessing. We assured them, that should we be so fortunate as to return to England, it would be our first care to acquaint our countrymen of all their kindness to us, which we would remember as long as we lived. They were both touched with sorrow at our words, for they were the last which they would hear us utter; tears were glistening in the eyes of each as they were making an affecting and suitable answer; and the good couple walked out of our hut with heavy and mournful countenances, and immediately repaired to their own abode in order to make a powerful spell for our preservation and success.

When we ourselves quitted the hut, we found our yard filled with neighbours, friends and acquaintances, who all fell down on their knees to bid us good-bye. The eyes of many of them were streaming with tears, and all were more or less affected. As we passed by these poor creatures, we spoke to them all, and thanked them again and again for their good wishes.

When our people were all embarked on the Niger, and ourselves, we humbly thanked the Almighty for past deliverances, and fervently prayed that He would always be with us, and crown our enterprise with success.

At five p.m. we came to Inguazhilligee, the first town on the Wo-wow ground. Journeying along for a quarter of an hour without stopping here, we put into a market town, on a large and beautiful island called *Patashie*; here we shall be obliged to remain till the return of the messenger who we sent to Wowow for the purpose of informing the king of our intention to abide at Patashie till he chooses to send us the large canoe that we have purchased of him.

About twenty or thirty paces from the river's side, we discovered a great quantity of huge bones and skulls of hippopotami, piled up on a high platform which has been erected for the purpose. These, we under-stand, are preserved as trophies by the natives, on much the same prin-ciple as foxes' tails are kept by many country gentlemen in England. We were speedily introduced to the chief, who gave us a hearty wel-come, and who we found to be a little round, fat, jolly-looking old man.

September 21st.—Patashie is a large, rich island, unspeakably beautiful, and is embellished with various groves of palm, and other noble trees. The soil is so exceedingly fertile, and its inhabitants so industrious, that not an acre of ground in the whole island, it is said, is left without cultivation. Patashie is tributary to Wowow, though it is inhabited solely by Nouffie people, who are considered honest, active, laborious, and wealthy.

September 22nd.—In the morning we were favoured with a visit from the chief of Teah. He is a venerable-looking old man, of advan-tageous stature, and exceedingly corpulent. He expressed the utmost delight and satisfaction on seeing white men before he died, and de-clared it was a pleasure, which neither his father, mother, nor uncle, had ever enjoyed, and a gratification which his ancestors had never hoped for; he should therefore cherish the remembrance of it as long as he lived. We have with us a quarto edition of natural history, with plates; these, though incomprehensible to the natives of Yarriba, appear to be extremely well understood here, and have excited in the minds of those that have seen them the highest degree of admiration, rapture, and wonderment. The old chief of Teah gazed upon them in silent astonishment; but when we took out a watch and mariner's com-pass for his inspection, and their uses were explained to him, he became at first very uneasy, and afterwards perfectly wild with amazement. No one in the world could express more naturally or forcibly the emotion of wonder, or the passion of fear, which the countenance of this old man displayed as he looked at the watch; nor could he be persuaded for a long time but that it was in possession of life and being, and had the power of moving. After a long and friendly chat the good old chief saluted us, and took his leave.

Teah lies very near the island of Patashie, from which it is divided only by a very narrow channel.

In the evening a messenger arrived from the king of Wowow, with news not at all to our liking. He informs us that we were anxiously expected in that city from Boossa at the time of the holydays; and because we did not come agreeably to our promise, the prince could not conceal his chagrin. The messenger continued, that his sovereign had most certainly procured for us a canoe, which was laid up at *Lever*. 'It would not be paying him that respect,' he continued, 'which his rank and situation demanded, were the white man to leave his dominions and country altogether, without first coming to pay him their respects.'

September 23rd.—People here, of all ages, display the most anxious, though perhaps natural curiosity to see us: and large crowds of them assemble every day, and wait from morning till night, patiently, till they have gained the object of their visit. However, they are all as timid as hares, and if we happen to look fixedly at their faces for a moment, most of them, more especially the females, and the junior classes of both sexes, start back with terror, as if they had seen a serpent in the grass; and when we attempt to walk near any of them, they run away screaming, as though they had been pursued by a lion, or were in danger of falling into the jaws of a crocodile, so horrified are these poor people at the bare sight of a white man, and so frightful do their imaginations picture him to be.

The natives are subject to very few diseases, and those, generally speaking, are not of a dangerous or malignant tendency. Small pox is very prevalent, but we do not hear that it often terminates fatally. The Guinea-worm is frequently met with; ulcers, of that frightful description which prevails on the coast, are unknown; but agues and slight fevers are by no means uncommon; and of all complaints, sore eyes and affections of the bowels are by far the most general. Properly speaking, the natives have no active medicines of their own, though they boast an acquaintance with a variety of medicinal plants, which, as far as our observation extends, are wholly inefficacious; they likewise ascribe the most wonderful healing properties to a quantity of roots and fibres of trees, which are sought after and vended by a number of idle, lazy fellows who pretend to be Mahomedan priests:

however, from our experience, these do neither good nor harm, being perfectly innocent in their effects, and altogether useless. From the Arabs the natives obtain great quantities of *trona*, which is a fossil alkali, and is found on the borders of the desert. It is a strong and active aperient, and possesses other medicinal properties which are understood by the people. It is taken by all ranks in every complaint, of whatsoever nature it may be.

September 24th.—The Boossa canoemen, who have been intoxicated every day since they have been here, returned to their homes this morning in a state of ebriety, having received a shilling each and a few needles, as a reward for their labour. Shortly after their departure, I landed for the purpose of proceeding to Wowow. The King of Wowow's messenger accompanied me.

September 27th.—I returned from my visit to Wowow, with no less than three men as messengers from the king, the whole of whom are to accompany us to Lever.

It was not till the 26th, that the king granted me an audience, and then he said, with the greatest indifference, 'I have not yet been able to procure you the canoe which I promised to get; but I have no doubt that the ruler of Patashie will have it in his power to supply you with one to your satisfaction, for which purpose I will send an express to that island without delay, whom I will furnish with the necessary instructions to effect an immediate purchase.' Thus, with as much discussion as would fill a volume, continued with little or no intermission for seven weeks, between the sovereigns of two countries, who during that period were sending messengers to each other continually, the mighty business which had employed all their thoughts, and in which they were unceasingly engaged—the simple purchase of a canoe, is even now left unfinished; in fact, up to the present moment, no more has been done in the matter, than when we first made known our intentions and wishes to the king of Boossa from the city of Yaoorie two months ago. So much for the expedition with which Africans usually transmit their affairs. The king took the opportunity of informing me, that he should by and by set about erecting a suitable building for the reception of our countrymen, whenever it should please them to come up the river to trade: for the old man cherishes the belief, in common with other rulers on the banks of the Niger, that numbers of Europeans will, some time or other, certainly visit his country for the purposes of traffic.

Before my departure, the monarch showed me, in compliance with my request, the whole of his collection of charms, which are written on sheets of paper, glued or pasted together. Amongst them I discovered a small edition of 'Watts's Hymns', on one of the blank leaves of which was written: '*Alexander Anderson, Royal Military Hospital, Gosport, 1804.*' Mr Anderson was the companion, and I believe a very near relative of the celebrated Mr Park.[1]

September 29th.—In the evening we were urgently solicited by the hospitable chief of Patashie, for a charm to render him successful in all his shooting excursions, and in hunting the hippopotamus. This request was soon followed by a similar one from his brother. For ourselves we are obliged to follow the current of opinion, or consent to lose our credit and be regarded with detestation; and as our charms are likely to be as effective as those of the Arabs, we sometimes oblige the natives in this respect.

September 30th.—Between eight and nine o'clock in the morning, horses were brought us from the chief and his nephew, to take us to the waters' side, where the luggage had been previously conveyed. Here we waited a good while till canoes were brought from another part of the island, there being but one got ready at the time of our arrival. While we stood near the water's edge, hundreds of people were collected there to look at us, and among them was a native Pagan priest, who was dressed more fantastically than any Merry-Andrew in Christendom. His clothing was manufactured almost solely of fine soft grass. His head and shoulders and part of his body were hid underneath an enormous thing, in shape like the roof of a hut, with a fringe and tassels of stained grass. A tobe, made also of grass, excellently woven and of various colours, encircled his body, and reached as far as the knee; and the man wore likewise trowsers of the same material, and plaited in a similar manner, but this was unstained, and of the colour of dried grass; it was turned up at the ankles, though a deep fringe hung to the ground. He approached several individuals that were sitting on the turf, and stooping over them, the priest enveloped the upper part of their persons in his uncouth head-dress; shook it over them, which produced a strange rustling noise; screamed in a most frightful and unearthly tone; and then arose to perform the same barbarous ceremony to others.

We came in sight of *Lever*, which was the place of our destination, after rather a short excursion from Patashie of three hours.

[1] Dr Alexander Anderson was Mungo Park's brother-in-law and second-in-command of the expedition. He died at Sansanding on the Niger, 28 October 1805.

Our surprise was great indeed, when, instead of the proper person whom we expected would have received us, we were welcomed on shore by a man called *Ducoo*, and who represented himself as agent and confidential friend of the prince of Rabba; but this surprise was not a little increased on learning that a party of forty or fifty armed Falatah soldiers were also in the town. Ducoo, who is a Bornouese, treated us with the courtly politeness of a Frenchman, and was equally lavish in his compliments and his offers of service; he walked with us to the chief of the town, to whom he took the liberty of introducing us, almost before he himself knew who or what we were; went himself and procured excellent lodgings for us, returned and sat down in our company to tell us some droll stories, and impart to us in confidence some very disagreeable news; then hastily rose up, went out, and came back again with a sheep and other provisions, which he had obtained by compulsion from the chief, and finally remained with us till long after the moon had risen, when he left us to our repose. A man of such excessive volubility we never recollect to have met with; but at the same time he seems to be a most useful fellow.

This *Lever*, then, after all, does not belong to the king of Wowow, though it stands on his dominions, nor has that monarch a single subject here, or a solitary canoe, so that we are as far from getting one as ever we were, and with the loss of our horses to boot. We have been cajoled and out-manoeuvred very prettily by those fellows of Boossa and its adjoining state, whom we falsely conceived to be our dearest and best black friends. They have played with us as if we were great dolls; we have been driven about like shuttlecocks; we have been to them first a gazing-stock, and are now no doubt their laughing-stock, perhaps their mockery. Why have they led us about as though we had been blind, only to place us in the very lap of what *they* imagine to be danger? For can it be possible that the monarchs of Wowow and Boossa were ignorant of the state of things here, which is in their own immediate neighbourhood, and which have continued the same essentially for these three years? Surely they have knowingly deceived us.

As soon as we were convinced that no canoe could be had in this place, as we have all along been led to expect, we conceived it prudent, under existing circumstances, to detain the two canoes which were lent us this morning by the chief of Patashie; one of them is tolerably large, and nearly new, but the other is of much smaller dimensions. However we are well aware that the king of Wowow has not yet paid for them, and we are afraid that he never will; and it grieves and saddens us beyond expression to do this thing; for the island ruler is a simple, kind-hearted, and good, very good old man. But what can we do? *We* have not the means of purchasing his canoes, for the king of Wowow has deprived us of them; our resources are nearly exhausted, and how should we be able to prosecute our journey? The Patashie canoemen stoutly resisted our claims. For our own parts we were actually ashamed to look them in the face; but our busy, restless friend, *Ducoo*, the priest, soon silenced their remarks by threatening to cut off the head of him who should presume from that time to set foot in either of the canoes. To give his menace the greater weight, he stationed two of his men, to guard the forbidden boats till the sun went down with drawn swords, and during the greater part of the night another of his men paraded up and down the banks of the river near the spot as a watch, and this man was continually playing upon a large drum.

After the departure of Ducoo in the evening, the chief of the town came to pay his respects and to wish us good night. He related to us a pitiable account of the evils which he and his people had undergone, and were still enduring from the selfishness and rapacity of the Fala-tahs; 'and they never pay us a visit,' said he, 'but my spirits droop within me, and my heart becomes heavy and sorrowful, for these foreigners come only to plunder and lay waste'.

Mount Kesa.

XIV

Lever to Zago̧hi

October 1st.—This town is called indiscriminately *Lever* and *Layaba*. Its population is great, and though it is very extensive, it has been built and occupied a few years only. Its inhabitants are all Nouffie people, and not long ago resided in a large village on the opposite side of the river; but on account of the civil wars which raged in their country, they were driven to seek an asylum here, where they fancied themselves out of the influence of these evils, and beyond the reach of the Falatahs, of whom they have an unconquerable dread. However, the poor people were not left a great while to enjoy unmolested the security which they had been in quest of, for three years ago their relentless enemies invaded their retreat, ransacked the town and destroyed their houses by fire. Fortunately for them the inhabitants had timely notice of the approach of these marauders, and succeeded in recrossing the river, just before their arrival, without the loss of a single man; nor could the Falatahs follow them there, because they had no canoes. But rather than be liable to continual irruptions of their enemies, after their return hither the people of Layaba consented to pay a certain tribute to the prince of the Falatahs at Rabba, independent of a kind of ground-rent or acknowledgement, which is paid to the owner of the soil; so that a double duty is by this means exacted from them. Nor is this all: for parties of Falatahs, which are without employment at home, are generally prowling about the country, and levying contributions on those villages which are too feeble to resist their claims.

Such is the case here at this moment; the Falatahs entered the town on Wednesday to take from its peaceful inhabitants whatever they thought proper. These men are all extremely well-dressed, and are armed with large swords, which are carried about their persons wherever they go.

October 2nd.—In the evening the inhabitants of the town assembled outside our house to amuse themselves by dancing and singing in the moonlight. Every dancer held in each hand a cow's tail; they were all dressed grotesquely, and a great quantity of strings of cowries encircled their legs and bodies, which made a loud rattling noise by the violence and celerity of their movements. They sang as they danced, and excited, by the oddity of their gestures, loud clappings of applause, and bursts of laughter from all the bystanders. The spectacle was exceedingly ludicrous; we have rarely witnessed so much jocularity and thoughtless gaiety; and we have seldom laughed so much at any native exhibition.

Like many of their countrymen, and like the natives of Yarriba, the inhabitants of Layaba appear to bestow scarcely a moment's reflection either on public misery or individual distress—upon their own misfortunes or the calamities of their neighbours. Nature has moulded their minds to enjoy the life they lead; their grief, if they grieve at all, is but for a moment; sorrow comes over them and vanishes like the lightning's flash; they weep, and, in the same breath, their spirits regain their elasticity and cheerfulness; they may well be said to drink of the waters of Lethe whenever they please. As long as they have food to eat, and health to enjoy their frivolous pastimes, they seem contented, happy and full of life. They think of little else—

'Thought would destroy their paradise.'[1]

[1]
> *Yet ah! why should they know their fate?*
> *Since sorrow never comes too late,*
> *And happiness too swiftly flies.*
> *Thought would destroy their paradise.*
> *No more; where ignorance is bliss,*
> *'Tis folly to be wise.*

Thomas Gray, *Ode on a Distant Prospect of Eton College*, ll. 91–6.

Sunday, October 3rd.—We were desired yesterday to get our things packed up, for that this morning we should quit the island to proceed on our journey. We had got all our luggage in readiness, and only the coming of the chief to take our departure, when one of his messengers entered our hut to apprize us that we should be unable to go away till tomorrow, his master having been dissuaded from his original purpose by the officious, bustling priest, our friend and enemy.

October 4th.—Our surprise and displeasure may be guessed, when, after our goods had been removed from our hut into the yard outside, we were informed that we should be compelled to abide in the town yet another day. Our patience was now completely exhausted. Repairing instantly to a hut, wherein we knew the chief passed most of his time, we discovered him sitting on the ground in company with the artful Ducoo. We spoke with much emphasis of the shameful manner in which we had been treated, and expressed our determination of leaving Layaba presently, in defiance of them and all their power. With the most insolent effrontery in the world, the priest smiled at us, and replied, that we were entirely in his power—that we should do as *he* liked, and quit the town whenever *he* thought proper, Such language as this we thought was rather too bold; we pretended to be in a violent passion, and quickly undeceived him in this point, threatening, that if he should attempt to hinder us from getting away from the town, we should feel no more hesitation or reluctance in shooting him than if he had been a partridge or a Guinea-hen! The priest was crest-fallen in a moment, and, from being one of the most boisterous and consequential fellows in the world, became quite passive; yet his presence of mind did not forsake him: he stammered out a kind of apology, attempted to soothe us by soft language and submission, and did all in his power to effect a reconciliation. Our luggage was then conveyed into the two canoes, and shortly afterwards we were supplied with three men to paddle them with the assistance of our own.

We ran down the stream very pleasantly for twelve or fourteen miles, the Niger, during the whole of the distance, rolling grandly along—a noble river, neither obstructed by islands, nor deformed with rocks and stones. Its width varied from one to three miles; the country on each side was very flat, and a few mean, dirty-looking villages were scattered on the water's edge.

At one o'clock, p.m., we landed at a considerably large and spacious town, called *Bajiebo*, which is inhabited by Nouffie people, though it is situated on the Yarriba side of the river. For dirt, bustle, and nastiness of all kinds, this place, we think, can scarcely be exceeded. The huts are erected so close to each other, and with so little regard to comfort and a free circulation of air, that there is scarcely a foot-path in the town wide enough for more than one man to walk on at a time; and not having the advantage of shady trees, the heat of the town is excessive and distressing.

We have seen today several large canoes, the bottom of which is made of a single tree and built up with planks to a considerable height. In many of them sheds, or houses as they are called, have been erected, which are thatched with straw, and in which fires are kindled, food prepared, and people sleep, and indeed live altogether. The roof is circular, and formed in much the same manner as the upper part of a covered waggon in England. These sheds are of the most essential service to the natives, as, with their assistance, merchants are enabled to travel with some degree of comfort, with their wives and household, several days' journey up and down the Niger, without being under the necessity of landing, except to purchase provisions, or whenever they feel inclined to do so. As the natives have nothing that equals or answers to pitch, hemp, or tar, they use iron staples for the purpose of repairing it and keeping the planks together when a canoe becomes leaky. We have seen an old canoe with no less than from eight to ten thousand of these staples driven into her sides and bottom.

October 5th.—Just below *Bajiebo* the Niger spreads itself into two noble branches, formed by an island. The island is small, but verdant, woody, and handsome; and we passed by the side of it with considerable velocity. It was then that both banks presented the most delightful appearance. They were embellished with mighty trees and elegant shrubs, which were clad in thick and luxuriant foliage, some of lively green, and others of darker hue; and little birds were singing merrily among their branches. Magnificent festoons of creeping plants, always green, hung from the tops of the tallest trees, and drooping to the water's edge, formed immense natural grottoes, pleasing and grateful to the eye, and seemed to be fit abodes for the Naiades of the river! Yet with all its allurements there is something wanting in an African scene to render it comparable in interest and beauty to an English landscape.

By secret charms our native land attracts.

There is nothing here half so attractive or inspiring, It is seldom, very seldom, that the morn is ushered in by the 'song of earliest birds'; which is so eminently enchanting at home, and which induces so much happiness and cheerfulness, benevolence and joy. Here there are no verdant fields, nor hedges, adorned with the jessamine, the daisy, the primrose, the blue-bottle, or the violet, and the hundred other pretty wild flowers, which please the sight, and exhale in spring-time, or summer the most grateful and delicious fragrance. No flowers here

Waste their sweetness in the desert air,[1]

for not a solitary one is any where to be seen. Besides, generally speaking, a loneliness, a solemnity, a death-like silence pervades the noblest and most magnificent prospects, which has a tendency to fill the mind with associations of sadness, and reflections of melancholy, very opposite to the silent cheerfulness, and that internal springing joy which we feel on contemplating those goodly and charming landscapes, which are the pride, the beauty, and the ornament of England. To look at the cleanliness of our cottages, and the tidiness of their occupants is pleasant; but when the dirty mud huts of the natives of this part of the world, with the people themselves do appear, in our opinion, they banish every favourable impression, and destroy the effect of all.

We arrived at the end of our journey between four and five o'clock in the afternoon, when we landed at a fishing-town on a small island, which is called *Madjie*.

October 6th.—On leaving the island we came suddenly in sight of an elevated rock, which is called *Mount Kesa* by the natives. It forms a small island, and is probably not less than three hundred feet in height, which renders it a conspicuous and remarkable object. It is excessively steep, and rising out of the river as it does, its appearance is irresistibly imposing and majestic beyond expression. Its base is fringed by venerable trees, and less magnificent vegetation, which also strives to spring forth from its barren and almost naked sides. The height of Mount Kesa, its solitary position, and the peculiarity of its form, distinguish it from every other, and render it an object of more than common interest. It is greatly venerated by the natives of this part of the country, and, as may readily be imagined, favours the superstitious notions which are attached to it by a simple and credulous

---

[1]
>   *Full many a flower is born to blush unseen,*
>   *And waste its sweetness on the desert air.*

Thomas Gray, *Elegy Written in a Country Churchyard*, xiv.

people, who, like the vulgar of Europe, are fond of the marvellous. The story attached to Mount Kesa is of a very romantic nature. The natives believe that a benevolent genius makes the mountain his favourite and continual abode, and dispenses around him a benign and heavenly influence. Here the misfortunes of the unhappy are alleviated, the wants of the needy supplied, and the lamentations of the mourner turned to joy: sin, sorrow, and suffering are unknown; solemnity gives place to merriment, and the solicitude of futurity to present enjoyment and thoughtless jocularity. But more especially, say the natives, the weary traveller here finds a refuge from the storm, and a rest from his toil; here he reposes in the delights of security, and revels in the comforts of ease. However, to obtain all this, he makes known his wants and desires to the spirit of the mountain by supplication and prayer, when they are instantly answered; he receives the most delicate and excellent food from invisible hands, and when sufficiently invigorated by refreshment, he is at liberty either to continue his journey or remain awhile to participate in the blessings of the mountain. Such is the story we received from these superstitious people of this celebrated mount.

At nine in the morning we landed near a small town to procure a fresh supply of canoemen. As soon as we had obtained them we journeyed along the eastern side of the river; and, at eleven a.m., perceived the smoke of the far-famed Rabba ascending many miles before us. In another half-hour we drew near an island, called *Belee*. Here we stopped at a large, but mean and dirty-looking town.

We were shortly introduced to the chief. He informed us, that Mohamed, the Magia's son, who had left us at Patashie, had returned from his father, and proceeded up the river to meet us. It was nearly evening before Mohamed returned. After the first salutations were over, he informed us of his visit to his father. The Magia had desired him to assure us of 'his best wishes in our welfare, and his determination to protect, support, and encourage us, as far as he was able'. Mohamed then drew our attention to a young man who had entered the hut with him, and introduced him as a messenger sent to us by the Falatah prince of Rabba. This man said that his master, named Mallam Dendo, had commissioned him to acquaint us, that he heartily concurred with the king of Nouffie, in the favourable opinions which the latter entertained for us. With respect to our visiting Rabba, which he understood we were very much disinclined to do, he should not urge us; and rather imagined that we should be more comfortable on an island on the opposite side of the river. The Falatah messenger concluded by observing that we should be visited on the morrow by the *'King of the Dark Water!'* who would escort us to the island in question, of which he is governor.

October 7th.—Between nine and ten a.m., we heard a number of men singing and keeping time to the motion of many paddles, but we could see no one. However, in a very few minutes, a canoe, which was paddled by a few men only, came in sight, and we knew by this that the Water King was approaching. It was instantly followed by another, and much larger one, propelled by above twenty very fine young men, whose voices we had been listening to just before, and who were still continuing their song. Their music was slower, but very similar to that which may be heard on many parts of the western coast. The *King of the Dark Water* was with them. As the canoe drew nearer we were not only surprised at its extraordinary length and uncommon neatness, but likewise at the unusual display of pomp and show which we observed in her. In the centre a mat awning was erected, which was variously decorated, and on the front of it hung a large piece of scarlet cloth, ornamented with bits of gold lace stitched on different parts of it. In the bow of the canoe were three or four little boys, of equal size, who were clad with neatness and propriety; and in the stern sat a number of comely-looking musicians, consisting of several drummers and a trumpeter, whilst the young men who had the management of the boat were not inferior to their companions in decency of apparel or respectability of appearance. They all looked in fact extremely well.

As soon as this canoe arrived at the landing-place, the 'Water King' came out from beneath the awning, and, followed by the musicians and a suite of attendants, walked to the hut wherein all public matters are transacted, and whither, in a few minutes, we ourselves were desired to repair. The chief of the island, with his elders and the more respectable of the people, were seated, on our entrance, on each side of their important visitor, and my brother and I, as a mark of distinction, were invited to place ourselves in front of him. When the usual compliments had passed on both sides, he informed us, with much solemnity, of his rank and title; he then alluded to the cause of his coming, which, he said, was to do us honour, and repeated what had previously been told us by the king's son. This being done, he presented us with a pot of excellent honey, and two thousand cowries in money, besides a large quantity of goora-nuts, which are cultivated in the country, and which are held in so great esteem, that the opulent and powerful alone have the means of procuring them. Having nothing further to say or do, we shook hands with his sable majesty, whose name is Suliken Rouah, expressed our acknowledgements for his handsome present, and returned to our boats.

The 'King of the Dark Water' is a fine-looking man, well stricken in years; his skin as black as a coal; his features are coarse but benevolent, and his stature advantageous and commanding. He was dressed in a full bornouse, or Arab cloak, of inferior blue cloth, underneath which was a variegated tobe made of figured satin, country cloth and crimson silk damask, all patched together, he likewise wore a cap of red cloth, Haussa trowsers, and sandals of coloured leather. Two pretty little boys, about ten years of age and of equal size, and who acted in capacity of pages, followed him into the hut. Their clothing was neat and becoming, and their persons nicely clean; each of them was furnished with an ornamented cow's tail, and they stood one on his right hand and the other on the left, to brush away flies and other insects from his person, and supply him with goora nuts and tobacco. The king was also accompanied by six of his wives, fine handsome jet-black girls, dressed in neat country caps edged with red silk.

To such a man as the 'Water King', with such a suite and such a title, the greatest honour is expected to be paid, and we therefore showed our respect by saluting him with a discharge from two or three muskets; and by waiting patiently his return from the council-hut, wherein he stayed two whole hours, during which we were sitting in our canoes, exposed to a very hot sun.

It was exactly mid-day when Suliken Rouah re-embarked in his princely canoe, and quitted the island of Belee. Determined for once to make an attempt at a more respectable appearance, for heretofore it had been extremely mean and homely, we hastily constructed an awning of our sheets. It was the first time we had made use of such a thing, though we are without umbrellas, and till then had nothing but slight straw hats to protect our heads from the sun. Above the awning we elevated a slender staff, on the top of which we fastened our national colours, the union flag, which was kindly given us by a gentleman on the coast, who was commandant at Anamaboo. When unfurled and waving in the wind, it looked extremely pretty, and it made our hearts glow with pride and enthusiasm, as we looked on this solitary little banner. We thought it would be of service to us also if we made as gay an appearance as the king and his followers; and accordingly I

put on an old naval uniform coat which I had with me for state occasions, and my brother also dressed himself in as grotesque and gaudy
a manner as our resources would afford. Our eight attendants also put
on new white Mahomedan tobes, so that our canoe, with its white
awning surmounted by the union flag, our canoemen in new dresses,
and ourselves appearing as officers, contributed not a little to the effect
of the whole scene. 'The august King of the Dark Water', with his
retinue in twenty canoes, condescendingly gave us the precedence, and
ours was the first that moved off from land, and led the way down the
river towards Rabba.

For a little while we continued to take the lead, but the chief soon
went before us, for two reasons: First, that he might have an opportunity of looking at us; and secondly, that we might have a fairer
chance of seeing him in all his state, for which purpose he had placed
himself outside his awning on an elevated and conspicuous seat. However he only wished to get a few yards before us, for his canoemen soon
lifted their paddles out of the water, and the boat fell back to its former
situation. This going before and falling behind was done repeatedly.
The musicians in the large canoe performed merrily on their instruments, and about twenty persons now sung at intervals in recitative,
keeping excellent time with their paddles.

A brisk wind sprung up the river full in our faces, relieving us from
the extreme heat of the weather, which was remarkably fine; the scene
before us was very animating, and the whole of us were in high glee
and spirits. Other canoes joined us; and never did the British flag lead
so extraordinary a squadron. The 'King of the Dark Water' might be
mistaken for a river god; and his wives now and then showing their
pretty black faces from under the awning, cast many an arch look at us
with their sparkling, jetty eyes. It was not long before our reverie was
interrupted by a great noise from the adjacent land; and on turning we
perceived the banks of an island, called *Zagozhi*, which were lined with
numbers of people, admiring our flag, and watching us very earnestly,
by which we guessed that this was the place of our destination. The
island is so uncommonly low, that the houses and trees appeared as if
they were standing in the water, as indeed many of them actually
were. Here we arrived, and landed between one and two p.m., having
enjoyed a pleasant excursion of eight or nine miles. Ours being the
first canoe, before we landed on the island we waited for the king to
precede us, and the moment he set his foot on shore, we fired a salute
of four muskets and three pistols. Suliken Rouah was rather alarmed

at this, and demanded whether we were going to make war on him. He was soon relieved from his fear, by being told it was an honour that we had been in the habit of paying to all the princes we had met in our travels; which he no sooner understood, than he expressed himself much gratified by our attention. Suliken Rouah went in person in quest of a dwelling-house, and led us to one of the best which the island affords; however, it is miserably bad; for, as the town is built on a marsh, every hut in it has the disadvantage, during the whole of the rainy season, of soft damp floors and uncomfortable roofs. Our own has positively pools of water springing up out of the ground, and on this we shall be obliged to sleep.

About seven in the evening, messengers arrived from Rabba, to inform us that they should come early in the morning for the presents we intended for the chief. They said that the king would not put us to the trouble of going to see him, as the town is full of Arabs, whose begging propensities would be very inconvenient for us.

Nouffie canoe.

XV

Zagozhi

October 8th.—Mallam Dendo, the cousin of Bello, we find is still living, but in a very old and feeble condition. He is besides nearly blind,
and thinks he has not many more years to live. Being a cautious, peaceful old man, his chief concern is to establish his son as his successor,
and fearing that there might be some dispute about it after his death,
has already given up to him the reins of government.

Early in the morning, the messengers from the chiefs arrived, bringing with them two fine sheep and a great quantity of rice. It appears
that we shall be required to give presents to nine persons before we
shall get away from this place.

Having prepared the presents, I collected the messengers and laid
out before each of them those that were intended for their masters. The
presents consist of a handsome looking-glass, with a gilt frame, a pair
of silver bracelets; a snuff-box, tobacco-pipe, knife, razor, two pair of
scissors, four new shillings, and a number of books on natural history,
with plates. Besides these, we sent the King of Nouffie a pocket com-
pass, and the Prince of Rabba a camera obscura, desiring each of the

messengers to inform their sovereign that the latter were invaluable, but that owing to the length of our journey, and the few things which were left us in consequence, we were compelled to part with them— only, however, till such time as we should return to the country again, when we hoped they would be given back to us, for a handsome present which we should bring for the purpose. The old 'King of the Dark Waters', and after him several of his people paid us a visit today, bringing with them an enormous quantity of bits of meat and pounded yam, boiled or stewed in palm oil, and abundance of less delicate provisions; and strong beer sufficient for a regiment of soldiers! A Haussa interpreter followed in his train, so that we had no difficulty in understanding each other; but those who subsequently visited our dwelling were not quite so fortunate, and we could not comprehend a single word which they uttered. Having brought their offering of provisions and beer in huge pots and calabashes, and laid it at our feet, they wished very much to enter into conversation with us, and were much confused and disconcerted at our ignorance of the Nouffie language, and our apparent dulness of comprehension; at first, they stared at us in vacant astonishment, then looked at each other very cunningly, and afterwards looked into our faces again. Finding at length that either we could not, or would not, understand their words and gestures, they burst into a loud laugh and went away, leaving their pots and calabashes behind them. These men were extremely well dressed, and respectable in their appearance.

October 9th.—A great number of Arabs are at present residing in Rabba; they have come from various parts, and trade with the natives in red caps, trona, small looking glasses of the most inferior description, red cloth, silk, etc, which they bring chiefly from Fezzan. Among these Arabs is a famous Sheikh, who, we understand, will set out in a few days on a journey to Timbuctoo and other places.

October 10th.—Mohamed the Magia's son and the Falatah messenger arrived at Zagozhi this morning. The former brought with him a fine sheep as a present from the Magia, and Mallam Dendo sent a large pot of honey by the hands of the latter. Both princes according to the accounts of their representatives, were mightily pleased with their respective presents, and expressed their acknowledgements in the warmest and most grateful terms; they repeated the encouraging promises with regard to our journey, and have commissioned the 'King of the Dark Water', under certain circumstances, to supply us with a commodious canoe, as excellent as our hearts can desire;

strongly recommending us to enter into arrangements with him, and deliver our two Patashie canoes, which are comparatively small and of little value, into his keeping till our departure from the country. A man is also to accompany us as far as the sea, to be our guide and interpreter on the voyage. This intelligence had made us quite easy in mind, and filled us with hope and joy.

October 11th.—Ali, an Arab, who introduced himself to our notice in Yaoorie, paid us a visit today from Rabba, where he has been residing some time past. In the course of conversation, he remarked, that it would be a good speculation to send some needles for sale at Rabba market, which is extremely large and well attended; therefore we took the hint, and sent Jowdie and Ibrahim, two of our men, with a certain quantity to dispose of, and they both returned in the evening with the fruits of their success, having obtained the sum of eight thousand cowries for them. This has given us fresh spirits again, for we had not a single cowrie to give our men.

It has been the policy of Mallam Dendo, who, by all accounts, is an an able and crafty chief, and a courageous man, to advance foreigners of all nations to certain lucrative and important posts, either about his person, in the army, or as governors of conquered towns; and by this means he conciliates, in a great measure, the black, or original population of the country, confirms his reputation, and establishes his sovereignty with little trouble over lands and districts which he may have subjugated and added to his dominions. It appears that the prince of Rabba is wholly independent of Bello, the sultan of Soccatoo, or at most that he pays only a nominal allegiance to that monarch, though an amicable intercourse is constantly kept up between them.[1]

Mallam Dendo, it is said, can send one thousand horse soldiers, well equipped and mounted on noble animals, to the field; and the

[1] 'While the Nupe kings were absolute masters in their own country, the Fulani Emirs were, in a loose sense, vassals of a larger state, the Fulani Empire of Gwandu. Beyond an annual tribute by Bida [the capital of Nupe from the mid-nineteenth century] to Gwandu and the merely symbolic confirmation by the Emir of Gwandu of every newly appointed king of Nupe, expressed in the traditional bestowal of a flag, the vassalship involved little interference with the internal government of Nupe' (Nadel, 1942, p. 89). In 1808 Uthman dan Fodio had divided the administration of the Fulani Empire between his son Bello and his brother Abdullahi. Abdullahi, who made his capital at Gwandu west of Sokoto, was responsible for the countries to the south and west. On Uthman's death, his son, Bello, was elected Sarkin Musulmi in succession to his father.

Though Mallam Dendo, the founder of Fulani power in Nupe, was still alive, he was, according to the account the Landers received, now living in retirement (p. 196). The 'Mallam Dendo', with whom the Landers had dealings, was probably the old Mallam Dendo's son and eventual successor, Usuman Zaki.

number of foot soldiers he has at his command is so great, that it is not known. All runaway slaves are encouraged to join the ranks on condition of receiving their freedom; and they are joined by a vast number from the surrounding country. The natives are commanded by captains from among their own countrymen, and the Falatahs also by theirs; the greatest good-will prevails among them, and we have nowhere observed quarrelling of any kind.

The Falatahs are now in possession of the whole of Nouffie. Yarriba will soon follow the condition of Nouffie, and the Falatahs, in the course of a few years, will reach the sea. An idea of their character may be formed from their usual boast, that they could conquer the whole world if the salt water did not prevent them.

October 12th.—Rabba market is considered by traders as one of the largest and best in the whole country, of which it may be styled the emporium; it is generally well supplied with slaves of both sexes. Yesterday, one of our men counted between one and two hundred men, women, and children, who were all exposed for sale in ranks or lines. These poor creatures have, for the most part, been captured in war; and, it is said, that the Falatahs rarely treat them with unkindness, and never with brutality. The price of a strong, healthy lad is about forty thousand cowries (£8 sterling); a girl fetches as much as fifty thousand, and perhaps more if she be at all interesting; and the value of men and women varies according to their age and abilities. Slaves are sometimes purchased at Rabba by people inhabiting a country situated a good way down the Niger, and from thence they are delivered from hand to hand till they at length reach the sea. Ivory is likewise sold, most likely to the same individuals, and large tusks may be purchased at a thousand cowries each, and occasionally at a much cheaper rate. We have eleven elephants' tusks of our own, which were presented to us by the kings of Wowow and Boussa [*sic*], but we have been unable to dispose of them at Rabba because no strangers are at present in the city.

Mallam Dendo sent for Paskoe this morning in a great hurry. We waited Paskoe's return with much anxiety, for we had no doubt whatever that we were principally concerned in it. When, however, he *did* come back, and enter our hut, he looked very wistfully, and informed us, with considerable agitation both of voice and manner, that Mallam Dendo had expressed to him the greatest dissatisfaction with the things which he had received from us as a present, declaring them to be perfectly worthless, and, with the exception of the looking-glass, 'fit only for a child!'; that he well knew we could have sent him something more useful and of greater value, if we had thought proper; but that if we persisted in our refusal to do so, he should demand of us our guns, pistols, and powder, before he would permit us to leave Zago-zhi. This news made us very uneasy and unhappy, and we sat down in gloom and thoughtfulness without uttering a word, for we believed this to be a death-blow to all our hopes. To part with the only defensive weapons in our possession, we felt determined not to do; it brought to our recollection the fable of the lion deprived of his teeth and claws. We knew that if we were deprived of these, we should be entirely in the power of a set of fellows who are remarkable neither for generosity nor nobleness of principle, without the means of helping ourselves; and we resolved never to part with our guns unless compelled to do so by force or from the most urgent necessity. At this moment we thought of Mr Park's tobe, which was given to us by the king of Boossa; and thought, that as it was the only thing which we had to offer, it *might* in consequence of the splendour of its appearance, and its intrinsic value, prove an acceptable present to the covetous prince, and we fondly hoped that it might be the means of a perfect reconciliation on both sides; therefore, under these circumstances, we immediately dispatched Ibrahim with it to Rabba, though our hearts misgave us at the time, that it would after all be thought lightly of, as an excuse for further extortions.

In less than two hours after his departure, Ibrahim returned from his errand with a quick step and cheerful looks, and informed us, that the tobe was accepted by the prince with rapturous admiration. By this present we had made him our friend for ever. 'Ask the white men,' said he, 'what they would desire, and if Rabba can supply them with it, tell them they shall always have it.'

October 13th.—In pursuance of the chief's arrangement, we sent Ibrahim and Paskoe to him this morning. He received them with civility, and wished to know in what manner he could best express his acknowledgements to us for the present we had made him, which he termed a 'princely gift', promising to make us all the return for it is in his power, by forwarding our departure. Paskoe made answer, and said, that our first wish was to obtain a large canoe, and pursue our journey on the Niger as fast as possible; that as we had little money, and but few presents, and as the 'King of the Dark Water' had refused to exchange a canoe of the above description, for those which we had obtained at Patashie, unless we would consent to pay him ten thousand cowries, we should be obliged to him to settle that little affair to our satisfaction. And that if the prince of Rabba approved of it, a few mats, tobes, or sandals, would be highly acceptable; and would be considered by us as a sufficient remuneration for the presents we had made him. This answer pleased the prince, and he cheerfully agreed to the whole of Paskoe's propositions.

A foot messenger from the King of Nouffie arrived at Rabba in the morning. His sovereign had despatched him privately to Mallam Dendo, with a insinuation to him, 'that if it met with his approbation, he (the Magia) would order us to be detained at Zagozhi until we should consent to make him a present of a certain number of dollars'. Perhaps it was well that we had presented the prince of Rabba with Mr Park's tobe, for he treated the message and its bearer with contempt, and answered energetically: 'Tell the Magia, your sovereign, that I would rebuke him for this expression of his sentiments; and that I reject his proposal with disdain. What could be a greater reproach than the infamy which would attach itself to our characters, and to our name, should we treat these poor, unprotected, wandering strangers, and white men, too, in the manner your monarch, the King of Nouffie, proposes? I have already given my word to protect them, and I will not forfeit that sacred pledge for all the guns and swords in the world.' The above answer was related to Paskoe by the prince of the Falatahs himself.

Several Haussa merchants arrived at Rabba this morning, with a number of fine horses for sale. They went to pay their respects to the prince, when Paskoe happened to be in his company. In allusion to us, they spoke very much in our praise, mentioned Captain Clapperton in terms of the highest admiration, and had seen with wonder the splendid and curious presents which he had made to Sultan Bello at Soccatoo.[1] 'I know the white men, too,' said the prince, 'they are good men, in fact I have reason to speak well of them, for I also am a white man, and therefore I am of opinion that they are of the same blood as ourselves.' It is in this manner that the Falatahs endeavour to claim relationship with Europeans, though these people are either of a swarthy complexion, or black as soot; and this passion to be considered fair is often carried to a most ridiculous height. White men, how sorry soever

[1] The presents handed over by Clapperton to Bello at Sokoto in 1826 had included a gold watch, 'one ream of English foolscap paper', various guns, 'coloured prints of the royal family, battles, and a plain journal book', a large quantity of cloth, and a number of books in Arabic (Clapperton, 1829, pp. 196–7).

their outward appearances may be, are certainly considered, not only by Falatahs, but by the native blacks, as a superior order of beings, in all respects more excellent than themselves. At Yaoorie we recollect having overheard a conversation between two men, who were quarrelling in the very height of passion. 'What!' exclaimed one of them to his fellow, 'thou pitiful son of a black ant! dost thou presume to say that a horse was my father? Look at these Christians? for as they are, I am; and such were my ancestors; answer me not, I say, for I am a white man!' The speaker was a Negro, and his skin was the colour of charcoal.

October 14th.—It is time that our journey should be completed, for our goods are very nearly exhausted. We have only needles and a few silver bracelets left to present to the chiefs whom we may reasonably expect to fall in with on our voyage down the Niger.

Old Mallam Dendo now sits, as the Arabs tell us, in one position every day from morning till night, with three large calabashes around him, one of which is kept constantly filled with *tuah*, another with cowries, and a third with goora nuts; and he revels in the delights which these calabashes afford him all day long. He has the reputation also, now that he is become old, of being both a miser and a glutton, He receives but few visiters, and those are of a particular description, whose company, equality of age, and a similarity in tastes and inclinations, have rendered desirable. Old Mallam Dendo is considered a very eccentric character and his singular manner of living is the common theme of conversation among all ranks. His son is said to inherit none of his father's foibles or propensities; he is revered as a leader, and beloved as a man, though the Arabs do not speak well of his consistency. For some reason, the report of the old man's death is industriously propagated.

October 15th.—*Rabba* appears from Zagozhi to be a considerably large, neat, clean, and well-built town, though it is unwalled. In point of rank, population, and wealth, it is the second city in the Falatah dominions, Soccatoo alone being considered as its superior. It is inhabited by a mixed population of Falatahs, Noufanchie, and emigrants and slaves from various countries. The Arabs and all strangers have an enclosure of dwellings to themselves, which is in the suburbs of the town. The inhabitants grow abundance of corn and rice. They possess large flocks and herds of the finest description, and their horned cattle are remarkable for their size and beauty. They have also a prodigious number of excellent horses, of which they take the greatest care, and they are universally admired for their strength and elegant proportions. These animals are used only for war, recreation, and in travelling. It is the pride and pleasure of the higher classes to dress well, and display their persons and their horsemanship to advantage, and it is gratifying to witness the grace and dexterity with which they preserve their command over these beautiful creatures. In the management of their horses, they are perhaps not inferior to the Arabs, from whom they have, in all probability, derived most of their lessons in the art. Rabba is not very famous for the number or variety of its artificers, and yet in the manufacture of mats and sandals they are unrivalled. However in all other handicrafts Rabba yields to Zagozhi.

Zagozhi has various inconveniences peculiar to itself. The town is built on a bog. So little regard do the natives appear to have for what is termed comfort, that they suffer the walls of their dwellings either to fall to pieces, or permit large chinks and holes to remain in them, which freely admit the wind and rain. The huts of the natives are infested with mosquitoes and other more disgusting insects, which abound indeed in millions.

In their huts the people exhibit no very favourable specimens of taste or cleanliness. However, in their persons they are by no means so negligent, for they always appear extremely well dressed; and we have rarely met with so large a number of tall, handsome, well-formed men and comely women, as in this place.

The care which the Falatah bestows, and the pride which he takes in his horse, are employed and indulged by the inhabitants of Zagozhi in an equal proportion in their canoes; the Niger is covered with these little vessels, and to be skilful in the management of them is their greatest boast. The chief of the island has about six hundred canoes. They are fond of aquatic occupations, even to a passion, and carry them to excess. All the trade by water in these parts is in their hands. They are also excellent fishermen, and, in fact, the population of Zagozhi are almost amphibious, so prone are they to be perpetually sporting in bogs or dabbling in water. But they do not confine themselves all the year round entirely to the river, for they cultivate the soil as well, and like their countrymen of Nouffie, in the manufacture of various articles they evince considerable ingenuity and expertness. The cloth which they manufacture in common with their countrymen, and the tobes and trowsers which they make, are most excellent, and would not disgrace an European manufactory; they are worn and valued by kings, chiefs, and great men, and are the admiration of the neighbouring nations, which vainly attempt to imitate them. We have also seen a variety of caps, which are worn solely by females, and made of cotton interwoven with silk, of the most excellent workmanship. The people here are uncommonly industrious, be they males or females, and are always busy either in culinary, or other domestic occupations.

In our walks we see groups of people employed in spinning cotton and silk; others in making wooden bowls and dishes, mats of various patterns, shoes, sandals, cotton dresses and caps, and the like; others busily occupied in fashioning brass and iron stirrups, bits for bridles, hoes, chains, fetters, etc; and others again employed in making saddles and horse accoutrements. These various articles, which are intended for the Rabba market, evince considerable taste and ingenuity in their execution.[1]

We have not seen a single public amusement since we have been among them. In this respect they are an example to their neighbours. They seem quite independent of all authority and above all restraint, except that of the legitimate *King of the Dark Water*, and their own interests induce them to obey him alone. They care as little for the Falatahs as the Falatahs for them; the peculiarity of their situation renders them secure from foreign invasion, and insensible to the calamities and distresses which overwhelm the natives of many parts of the continent. They have liberty stamped on their features, and lightness and activity, so rarely to be seen in this country of sluggards, are observable in all their actions. The generality of the people are well-behaved; they are hospitable and obliging to strangers; they dwell in amity with their neighbours, and live in unity, peace, and social intercourse with themselves; they are made bold by freedom, affluent by industry and frugality, healthy by exercise and labour, and happy from a combination of all these blessings.

We have received permission to quit Zagozhi tomorrow morning, to

[1] The Nupe are still celebrated for their industry and craftsmanship. Their crafts and commerce have been vividly described by S. F. Nadel, whose study of Nupe society, *A Black Byzantium*, is not only the most detailed account yet written of any people in Northern Nigeria but also one of the classics of social anthropology. Many of the Landers' observations would be true of the Nupe today. The village of Kutigi between Bida and Mokwa is famous for its mat industry. 'Every man and boy in Kutigi,' Nadel noted, 'works mats in his spare time—and spare time here means just as much the leisure season of the year as every hour that can be spared from farm-work. When sitting in front of their houses in the evening, even when walking home from the farms, the people are working: they carry a supply of dried grass dyed in different colours, in a kind of quiver under the arm and, while they walk or talk, their fingers are busy plaiting the grass into long, narrow strips' (Nadel, 1942, p. 287).

pursue our journey down the Niger. We have been busily employed in packing up. We are in hopes of having no difficulties about the canoe, and are desirous of obtaining one that will hold all of our party, as it will be more convenient than two small ones. The chief of the island promised to send a messenger with us as far as *Egga,* the last town down the river belonging to the Nouffie territory.

Leaving Zagozhi.

XVI

Zagozhi to Egga

October 16th.—We were up and stirring at a very early hour in the morning, packing up our clothes and getting our luggage ready for embarkation. But when this was all done we met with a sudden and unforeseen embarrassment—the sable 'King of the Dark Water' laughed at the idea of giving us a canoe on the faith of receiving payment from the prince of the Falatahs, and refused at first to deliver up to us our own, which we had obtained from Patashie. At length, after much importunity, we induced the chief to restore them into our hands.

When we were quite ready to start, the old chief came down to the water-side to bid us farewell, according to his avowed purpose, but in reality to offer us a commodious canoe in exchange for our own, if we would consent to give him ten thousand cowries in addition to them. This was agreed to on our parts after a little delay, for we considered that it would be infinitely more comfortable to have our people and all our things with us in the same canoe. We had fortunately realized a sufficient number of cowries from the sale of needles at Rabba.

The canoes made here are of a particular description, very much resembling what are called punts in England, but are perfectly straight and flat-bottomed. They are generally formed out of one log of wood, and are of an immense size. That which we purchased is about fifteen feet in length and four in breadth, but they make them nearly as large again.

As soon as all our goods were all transferred into the purchased canoe, which, after all, was not near large enough for our purpose, we found it to be extremely leaky, and patched up in a thousand places. We saw that we had been cheated by the artful 'King of the Dark Water', but rather than enter into an interminable dispute, we held our peace. And yet after we had all got into her, we waited till we were weary for the arrival of a messenger that was to have accompanied us a little way on our journey; but he did not come and we resolved to leave without him.

It is inconceivable what difficulties we have experienced in obtaining paddles for our canoe; no where have we found people willing to sell us any, and until we reached Zagozhi we could induce no one to spare us a paddle; they would not do it for the world. However at Madjie, and other places, we returned the hospitality which we received from the chiefs, by suffering our men to go out at night when it was dark, and when the villagers were asleep, and steal what we found an invincible difficulty in procuring by fairer means.

We made no stop whatever on the river, not even at meal times, our men suffering the canoe to glide down with the stream while they were eating their food. At five in the afternoon they all complained of fatigue, and we looked around us for a landing-place, where we might rest awhile, but we could find none, for every village which we saw after that hour was unfortunately situated behind large thick morasses and sloughy bogs, through which, after various tedious and provoking trials, we found it impossible to penetrate.

The day had been excessively warm, and the sun set in beauty and grandeur. Nevertheless the appearance of the firmament, all glorious as it was, betokened a coming storm; the wind whistled wildly through the tall rushes, and darkness soon covered the earth like a veil. This rendered us more anxious than ever to land somewhere, we cared not where. Accordingly, rallying the drooping spirits of our men, we encouraged them to renew their exertions by setting them the example, and our canoe darted silently and swiftly down the current. We were enabled to steer her rightly by the vividness of the lightning, which flashed across the water continually. But though we could perceive almost close to us several lamps burning in comfortable-looking huts, and could plainly distinguish the voices of their occupants, and though we exerted all our strength to get at them, we were foiled in every attempt, by reason of the sloughs and fens, and we were at last obliged to abandon them in despair.

Therefore, we resigned ourselves to circumstances, and all of us having been refreshed with a little cold rice and honey, and water from the stream, we permitted the canoe to drift down the current, for our men were too much fatigued to work any longer. But here a fresh evil arose, which we were unprepared to meet. An incredible number of hippopotami arose very near us, and came plashing, snorting, and plunging all round the canoe, and placed us in imminent danger. Thinking to frighten them off, we fired a shot or two at them, but the noise only called up from the water, and out of the fens, about as many more of their unwieldy companions, and we were more closely beset than before. Our people, who had never, in all their lives, been exposed in a canoe to such large and formidable beasts, trembled with fear and apprehension, and absolutely wept aloud; and their terror was not a little increased by the dreadful peals of thunder which rattled over their heads, and by the awful darkness which prevailed, broken at intervals by flashes of lightning, whose powerful glare was truly awful. Our people tell us, that these formidable animals frequently upset canoes in the river, when every one in them is sure to perish. These came so close to us, that we could reach them with the butt end of a gun.[1]

However, the terrible hippopotami did us no kind of mischief whatever; no doubt, at first when we interrupted them, they were only sporting and wallowing in the river for their own amusement; but had they upset our canoe, we should have paid dearly for it.

The eastern horizon became very dark, and the lightning more and more vivid; indeed, we never recollect having seen such strong forked lightning before in our lives. All this denoted the approach of a storm. At eleven p.m., it blew somewhat stronger than a gale, and at midnight the storm was at its height. The wind was so furious, that it swept the water over the sides of the canoe several times, so that she was in danger of filling. Driven about by the wind, our frail little bark became unmanageable; but at length we got near a bank, which in some measure protected us, and we were fortunate enough to lay hold of a thorny tree, against which we were driven, and which was growing nearly in the centre of the stream. Presently we fastened the canoe to its branches, and wrapping our cloaks around our persons, for we felt over-powered with fatigue, and with our legs dangling half over the sides of the little vessel into the water, which for want of room we were compelled

[1] 'The Hippopotamus,' according to a modern survey of Nigerian wild life, 'is found in the Niger, the Benue and Cross Rivers as well as in Lake Chad but is local in these and nowhere very plentiful; normally it is an inoffensive beast that adds to the picturesqueness of a trip down the rivers, but occasionally a 'rogue' will become a nuisance and a danger, upsetting canoes deliberately' (*Nigeria Handbook*, p. 212).

to do, we lay down to sleep. The wind kept blowing hard from the eastward till after midnight, when it became calm. The rain then descended in torrents, accompanied with thunder and lightning of the most awful description. We lay in our canoe drenched with rain, and our little vessel was filling so fast, that two people were obliged to be constantly baling out the water to keep her afloat. The water-elephants, as the natives term the hippopotami, frequently came snorting near us, but fortunately did not touch our canoe. The rain continued until three in the morning, when it became clear, and we saw the stars sparkling like gems over our heads. Therefore, we again proceeded on our journey down the river, and two hours after, we put into a small insignificant fishing-village, called *Dacannie*, where we landed very gladly. In the course of the day and night, we travelled, according to our own estimation, a distance little short of a hundred miles.

Sunday, October 17th.—While we were at breakfast, the promised messenger from Zagozhi arrived at the village, in a canoe of his own, and came up to us, and introduced himself. We found several Falatah Mallams on the island, who have been sent by the Chief of Rabba for the purpose of instructing the natives in the Mahomedan faith. The island is inhabited by Nouffie fishermen, a harmless, inoffensive race of men, who only a few weeks ago were obliged to abjure their pagan deities for the Koran, whether against their inclination or otherwise. This is another of the effects of the Falatahs' spreading their conquests over the country. Wherever they become masters, the Mahomedan religion follows.[1]

It was between nine and ten in the morning, when the guide desired us to proceed onward, and promised to follow us in a few minutes, With this arrangement we cheerfully complied, for, of all persons, a messenger is the most unpleasant companion; he is fond of procrastination, sullen when rebuked, and stops at every paltry village wherein he fancies that he can levy his contribution without the fear of interruption.

About the middle of the day we put in at a small village, situated on an island called *Gungo*. Here, for the first time since leaving the coast, we could not make ourselves understood, We could muster up five different languages spoken by the Africans,[2] but the Haussa language

[1] The spread of Islam by the Fulani was an act of political propaganda as well as of religious zeal. 'Teaching Islam means teaching the holy cause which sent the conquerors down to this country' (Nadel, 1942, p. 142).

[2] The language spoken at Gungo was probably a dialect of Nupe. Of the languages spoken by the Landers' African companions, Hausa was spoken by Paskoe and others,

was not even understood here, nor any other that we could speak; so we had recourse to signs and motions, and soon made the natives comprehend that we wanted something to eat, and a hut to sleep in for the night.

October 18th.—Having read prayers to our people, a custom which we have never neglected either morning or evening, we bade adieu to the Chief of Gungo and his people. We had not been on the water more than half an hour, before the wind rose to a gale, causing the river to be agitated like a sea, and our canoe to be tossed about like a cocoa-nut shell. It also rained heavily, and our canoe soon became half filled with water. We were then in the middle of the river, and in danger of sinking every instant. Our men struggled hard to pull the canoe among the rushes on the right bank, for the purpose of holding on by them till the wind and the rain should abate, and the water become smooth. No sooner had we got into the morass, and were congratulating ourselves on our deliverance, than a frightful crocodile, of prodigious size, sprang forth from his retreat, close to the canoe, and plunged underneath it with extraordinary violence, to the amazement and terror of us all: we had evidently disturbed him from his sleep. He was the largest I ever saw; and had he touched our canoe, would have upset it.

At Zagozhi, we had been strongly recommended to put into a large and important trading town, called *Egga*, which was reported to be three days' journey down the river from thence, and we had been promised a guide or messenger to accompany us thither, but we have neither heard nor seen anything of him since yesterday.

At four in the afternoon, our men were tired with their exertions, and complained sadly of fatigue and exhaustion, so that we were induced to put in at a small island called *Fofo*, where we resolved to sleep.

After we had landed, a man who asserted that he had just arrived from Funda, introduced himself to our notice: he states that it is three days' journey from hence down the Niger, to the frontiers of that kingdom; and that its metropolis, which is of the same name, is situated at an equal distance from the water-side; so that, if this information be true, it will be utterly impossible for us to visit the city of Funda, as it was our intention to do, for we are without horses, and the means of procuring them; and the attempt to penetrate so great a distance through the bush in our present languid and debilitated state, would be

Ibo by Antonio and Kanuri by Ibrahim. The other two languages were not mentioned by the Landers; possibly they were languages of the Gold Coast.

impracticable, and highly improper. Besides, what presents have we to offer to the king?

October 19th.—The banks this morning have exhibited a more beautiful appearance than we had observed for several days before; nevertheless, they wanted the charm of novelty to recommend them. Very elevated land appeared on each side of the river, as far as could be seen; which appeared to be formed of a range of hills, extending from north-east to south-west-west. At eleven o'clock we touched at a large village to inquire whereabouts Egga lay, and were informed that we had not a long way to go. We journeyed onwards for about an hour, when we perceived a large, handsome town, behind a deep morass. Several little inlets led through it to the town, distant about three miles from the bank of the river. It was the long-sought Egga, and we instantly proceeded up a creek to the landing-place. The town is upwards of two miles in length, and we were struck with the immense number of large, bulky canoes which lay off it, and which were filled with trading commodities, and all kinds of merchandise which are common to the country. They also had huts in them, like the canoes we had seen before. All of them had blood smeared on their sterns, and feathers stuck in it as a charm or preservative against robbers and the evil disposed.

We despatched Paskoe to the chief, to tell him whom we were, and what we wanted. He quickly returned, saying that the old chief was ready to receive us. In a few minutes we arrived at the *Zollahe*, or *Entrance Hut*, in which we found the old man ready to receive us. We discovered him squatting on a cow's hide spread on the ground, smoking from a pipe of about three yards long, and surrounded by a number of Falatahs, and several old Mallams. We were welcomed in the most friendly and cordial manner, and, as a mark of peculiar distinction, we were invited to seat ourselves near the person of the chief. He looked at us with surprise from head to foot, and told us that we were strange-looking people, and well worth seeing. Having satisfied his curiosity, he sent for all his old wives that they might do the same, but as we did not altogether relish so much quizzing, we requested to be shown to a hut. The chief is a very aged and venerable-looking man, with a long white beard, and of more patriarchal appearance, perhaps, than any one we have ever seen; yet he laughed, played, and trifled, like a child. A house 'fit for a king', to use his own expression, was speedily got ready for our reception, and as soon as he had learnt, with surprise, that we subsisted on the same kind of food as himself, we were led to our dwelling, and before evening, received a bowl of *tuah* and gravy from his wives. As soon as the news of our arrival spread through the town, the people flocked by hundreds to our hut, for the purpose of satisfying their curiosity with a sight of the white people. The Mallams and the kings had given us trouble enough, but the whole population of Egga was too much for us, so we were literally obliged to blockade the doorways, and station three of our people at each to keep them away.

October 20th.—Benin and Portuguese cloths are worn at Egga by many of its inhabitants, so that it would appear that some kind of communication is kept up between the sea-coast and this place. The people are very speculative and enterprising, and numbers of them employ all their time solely in trading up and down the Niger. They live entirely in their canoes, over which they have a shed, that answers completely every purpose for which it is intended, so that, in their constant peregrinations, they have no need of any other dwelling or shelter than that which their canoes afford them.

The curiosity of the people to see us is so intense, that we dare not stir out of doors, and therefore we are compelled to keep our door open all day long for the benefit of the air; and the only exercise which we can take is by walking round and round our hut like wild beasts in a cage. The people stand gazing at us with visible emotions of amazement and terror; we are regarded, in fact, in just the same light as the fiercest tigers in England. If we venture to approach too near the doorway, they rush backwards in a state of the greatest alarm and trepidation; but when we are at the opposite side of the hut, they draw as near as their fears will permit them, in silence and caution. But, from an insolent Falatah, and one or two troublesome head men, we have experienced infinitely more inconvenience—they have hunted us like evil spirits. These individuals enter our hut in the morning, and, whatever we may have to do, they squat themselves down on our mats with the most provoking effrontery, and are unwilling to leave us, except for a few moments at a time, till long after we lie down to rest.

Egga is of prodigious extent, and has an immense population.[1] Like many other towns on the banks of the river, it is not unfrequently inundated, and a large portion of it, as at the present moment, actually overflowed. No doubt the people have their reasons for building their habitations in places which appear to us so very inconvenient and un-

[1] In 1920 the population of Egga or Eggan was 1510; the town is still an important centre for local trade (*Ilorin Gazetteer*, p. 53).

comfortable. The soil in the vicinity of the town consists of a dark heavy mould, uncommonly fruitful, and produces in abundance and with trifling labour all the necessaries of life. Perhaps Egga can boast of having a greater number of canoes, both large and small, than any single town to the northward.

October 21st.—Though the venerable chief of Egga has to all outward appearances lived at least a hundred years, he is still active; and instead of the peevishness and discontent too often the accompaniment of lengthened days, possesses all the ease and gaiety of youth. He professes the Mahomedan religion; and it is his custom to arise every morning long before day-break, and having assembled all his priests round him, performs his devotions, such as they are, repeating his prayers in a loud, shrill tone, so that we can hear him in his pious employment. As soon as these devotional exercises have been gone through, several of his companions, with a disposition as thoughtless, as childish, and as happy as his own, get together in his hut, and squatting on the ground with the old chief, they form a circle, and beguile the time by smoking and conversing till long after sunset, and separate only for a few minutes at a time in the course of the day for the purpose of taking their meals. This company of grey-beards, for they are all old, laugh so heartily at the sprightliness of their own wit, that it is an invariable practice, when any one passes by, to stop and listen outside, and they join their noisy merriment with so much good will, that we hear nothing from the hut in which the aged group are revelling during the day but loud peals of laughter and shouts of applause. Much of this gaiety, however, must be affected, in order to gratify the ruling passion of the old chief for joke and frolic. Examples of this nature are uncommonly rare. Professors of Mahomedanism affect, generally speaking, the solemnity of the owl; and though they understand no more of their faith than of the doctrines of Christianity, they regard all natives of a different persuasion with haughtiness and disdain.

The old chief longed today to give us a specimen of his activity and the vigour which he yet possessed; and for this purpose, when the sun was going down, his singers, dancers, and musicians, assembled round our hut with a great concourse of people, who could not boast a proficiency in those refined attainments, but who came to witness the accomplishments of their aged leader. The old man advanced proudly into the ring, with a firm step and a smiling countenance, and casting upon us a glance full of meaning, as if he would have said, 'Now white men, look at me, and you will be filled with admiration and wonder'—

> He frisked beneath the burden of *five*-score;[1]

and shaking his hoary locks, capered over the ground to the manifest
delight of the by-standers, whose applauses, though confined, as they
always are, to laughter, yet tickled the old man's fancy to that degree,
that he was unable to keep up his dance any longer without the aid of
a crutch. With its assistance he hobbled on a little while, but his
strength failed him, and he was constrained for the time to give over,
and he sat himself down at our side on the threshold of the hut. He
would not acknowledge his weakness to us for the world, but endeavoured to pant silently, and suppress loud breathings that we might
not hear him. How ridiculous yet how natural is this vanity?

The chief has been soliciting a charm of us, to prevent the Falatahs
from ever again invading his territory. The old man's allegiance to
the king of Nouffie appears to us to be merely nominal. When we sent
word to the chief that we intended going tomorrow, he begged us to
remain at Egga a few days longer, and declared the banks of the river to
be inhabited by people who were little better than savages, and plundered every one that came near them. He assured us that they were
governed by no king and obeyed no laws, and that each town was at
war with the others. I asked him if he would send a messenger with us,
but he refused, saying, that the Falatah power and his own extended no
farther down the river; that Egga is the last town of Nouffie, and that
none of his people traded below it. 'If that is the case,' I said, 'it will be
as safe for us to go tomorrow as any other day'; and with this determination I left him.

I then proceeded to give directions for our people to prepare themselves for starting, when to my astonishment Pascoe, and the mulatto
so often alluded to, were the only two who agreed to go; the rest of
them refused to a man. I then found that the people of the town had
been telling them stories about the danger of the river, and that they
would all certainly either be murdered or taken and sold as slaves.
Nor could all I say to them change their determination. I talked to
them half an hour, telling them they were cowards, and that my
brother's life and mine were as good as theirs; till at length, tired of
them, and seeing that I made no impression on them, I told them to go

---

[1]
And the gay grandsire, skill'd in gestic lore,
Has frisk'd beneath the burthen of three-score
Oliver Goldsmith, *The Traveller*, l. 251.

away from our sight, and that we could do without them. But now they demanded their wages or a *book* to enable them to receive them at Cape Coast Castle, to which they said they would return by the way they had come here. This I refused instantly to comply with, and added that if they chose to leave us here, they should not receive a farthing; but if they would go on with us down the river, they should be paid. They were indignant at this, and went directly to the chief to lay down their case before him, and to induce him to detain us. The old man, however, would not listen to them, but sent them about their business.

The people of this town appear all very neatly dressed; the population is one-half of the Mahomedan religion, and the other the original Pagan. The streets are very narrow, and, like most places where there are large markets, are exceedingly filthy. The reason for building their houses so close together is, that the Falatahs may not be able to ride through them so easily and destroy the people; it is said that they have been expecting an attack from these people a long time. The Portuguese cloth which we observed here on our arrival is brought up the river from a place called *Cuttumcurrafee*, which has a celebrated market for Nouffie cloths, trona, slaves, Nouffie knives, bridles, stirrups, brass ornaments, stained leather, and other things.

Damuggoo.

XVII

Egga to Damuggoo

October 22nd.—At half past six this morning our people set about loading the canoe according to my expectations, but with a bad grace, and nothing but sulky looks, grumbling, and fearful apprehensions passed among them. They were, however, unwilling to lose their wages, and they seemed to have no wish to remain at Egga. Having no one to look to for protection, it is not improbable but that they would have been made slaves immediately after our departure, so that they had made up their minds to accompany us, although, when they took their paddles and we were fairly starting, they seemed to feel their situation more keenly than ever, and said that we were going to take them to a country where they would all be murdered. We endeavoured as much as possible to pacify their fears, but were obliged to have recourse to threats, and therefore said we would throw them overboard if they were not quiet and worked the canoe properly. This and other threats to the same effect silenced them.

At seven o'clock, all being ready, we bade farewell to the old chief, whose good humour had afforded us so much amusement, although his wives had nearly suffocated us, and on leaving the landing-place of Egga we fired off three muskets as a parting salute. A few miles from the town we saw, with emotions of pleasure, a sea-gull, which flew over our heads; this was a most gratifying sight to us. It reminded us forcibly of the object we had in view, and we fondly allowed it to confirm our hopes that we were drawing very near to our journey's end. We likewise beheld, for the first time, about half a dozen large white pelicans, which were sailing gracefully on the water.

At eleven a.m., we passed a very large market-town on our left. We observed an immense number of canoes lying off it, built in the same manner as those of the Bonny and Calabar rivers. A great many of them were moving to and fro on the river; some passed close to us, and their crews gazed at us with astonishment, but did not offer to interfere with us. It is a source of annoyance that we have no means of conversing with these people, and it may prove a serious inconvenience hereafter.

For many miles we could see nothing but large, open, well-built villages on both sides of the river. Yet we touched at none of these goodly places, but continued our journey till the sun began to decline, and the men to be fatigued, when we stopped at a small hamlet on an island, intending to sleep there. At first the inhabitants mistrusted our intentions, and were alarmed at our appearance. They no sooner saw us than they raised the war-cry, and every man and woman armed themselves with swords and dirks, bows and arrows, assuming a threatening and alarming position. We called out lustily to them in the Haussa language, but they were unable to understand either our words or gestures. Fortunately, in a few minutes, a woman, who could converse a little in the Haussa tongue, came down to us at the waterside, and we informed her that we were friends and Christians, travelling down the river to our native country, and that it was not our wish to make war with them. All this she repeated to those around her, and succeeded but partially, however, in removing their prejudices and suspicions. Had it not been for the timely arrival of this woman, we should certainly have had a volley of arrows among us, for we were taken for Falatahs at first, and we observed the woman persuading them to the contrary. Still the people could not, or rather would not, accommodate us with a lodging for the night. They were deaf to all our entreaties; but fearing that we could enforce our request, they did all they could to induce us to proceed onwards a little further, when we should arrive at a city of considerable importance, called *Kacunda*, at which place we recollected that the people of Egga had strongly advised us to stay.

Kacunda is situated on the western bank of the river; and at a little distance, it has an advantageous and uncommonly fine appearance. It was evening when we arrived there. The people at first were alarmed at our appearance, but we were soon welcomed on shore by an old Mahomedan priest, who speedily introduced us into an excellent and commodious hut, once the residence of a prince, but now the domicile of a school-master.

October 23rd.—Kacunda, properly speaking, consists of three or four villages, all of them considerably large, but unconnected, though situated within a very short distance of each other. It is the capital of a state or kingdom of the same name, which is quite independent of Nouffie, or any other foreign power.[1] Its government is despotic, and all power is invested with the chief or king, who exercises it with lenity: in all cases of emergency, he never depends upon his own judgement entirely, but consults the opinion of the elders of his people. Kacunda maintains little intercourse with Nouffie, or any other considerable nation, but confines its trade, almost exclusively, to divers people inhabiting the banks of the Niger to the southward; and slaves purchased here are said to find their way to the sea. The only dress that the natives wear, is a piece of cotton cloth round the loins. This is made by themselves, and dyed of various colours, according to the taste of the owner. The Nouffie language is not understood in Kacunda; but as in almost every place which we have visited, the Haussa tongue is spoken fluently by several individuals.

The chief excused himself from visiting us this morning, but sent his brother in his stead, to assure us of the pleasure he felt in our arrival.

At 11 a.m., a large double-bank canoe, paddled by fourteen men, arrived at Kacunda, and we shortly found that the king's brother had come in her to see us. The brother came, attended by a long train of followers, and in the name of the chief he presented us with a few goora-nuts, a goat, some yams, and an immense quantity of country beer. Our meeting was very cordial, and we shook hands heartily with, and immediately explained to him our business. I then took out a pair of silver bracelets, and begged he would present them to his brother, and tell him the reason we could give him nothing better.

[1] Baikie, who visited the Niger–Benue confluence in 1854, wrote: 'I believe that the term Kakanda embraces three distinct tribes, named respectively Bassa, Ishabe, and Bonu, differing from each other in language!' He was told that Igbido, 'the Kakanda of some charts, and the Budu of Captain Trotter's reports' was the chief town of the Ishabe (Baikie, 1856, pp. 271–2). The Landers' 'Kacunda' would seem to be identical with the modern Budon.

We had now become great friends, and he commenced giving us a dreadful account of the natives down the river, and would have us not think of going among them, but return by the way we had come. He said to us, with much emphasis, 'If you go down the river, you will surely fall into their hands and be murdered.' 'Go we must,' I said, 'if we live or die by it, and that also tomorrow.' 'If you will not be persuaded by me to turn back and save your lives,' he replied, 'at least you must not leave this by day-light, but stop until the sun goes down, and you may then go on your journey—you will then pass the most dangerous town in the middle of the night, and perhaps save yourselves.' We asked him whether the people he spoke of had muskets or large canoes? To which he replied, 'Yes; in great numbers—they are very large and powerful, and no canoe can pass down the river in the day-time without being taken by them and plundered; and even at night the canoes from here are obliged to go in large numbers, and keep close company with each other, to make a formidable appearance in case of their being seen by them.'[1]

We propose starting at half-past four tomorrow evening. I told the chief's brother of our intentions, at which he seemed quite astonished; and we have no doubt that this determined conduct, which we have everywhere shown, and apparent defiance of all danger, in making light of the dreadful stories we have heard, has had much influence on the minds of the people, and no doubt inspired them with a belief that we were supernatural beings, gifted with more than ordinary qualifications.

The few trifling things which we sent back to the chief were received by him in a much more gracious manner than we had anticipated. He besought us earnestly to write him a few charms—one of which is to insure a continuance of peace and prosperity to the kingdom; another to prevent quarrels, abuses, and disturbances in the market-place; to obviate the shedding of human blood therein, which has recently been of frequent occurrence; and to bring to the market a greater number of buyers and sellers, which would proportionately augment the amount of duty exacted from them. Another charm he wants of us is to possess the virtues of a panoply, for preserving all persons, whilst bathing from the fangs of the crocodiles, which infest the adjoining slough in great numbers, and which, it is said, have lately carried off and destroyed several children.

[1] The people living on the Niger between 'Kacunda' and the confluence with the Benue were Igbirra, a tribe to which later accounts ascribe no especial ferocity. Possibly the people of whom the Kakanda were afraid were the more formidable Igala from Idah.

All ranks of people are firmly persuaded that we are necromancers, or at least that we are capable of performing any miracle, and, therefore, they believe that the making of these charms is but a trifling effort, compared with what we *might* do, were we to exert the whole of our power. An attempt to undeceive the ignorant, credulous and deluded people, we know, would be unavailing and useless, and fear that it would be dangerous; therefore we dared not meddle with their superstitions or prejudices, but conform to their wishes, and let them enjoy their own opinions in peace.

We observe here, for the first time, that the natives have a custom of marking themselves, so that their tribe may be known from the rest. The distinguishing mark of the people of Kacunda is three cuts down the face from the temple to the chin, which gives them an odd appearance. They are a mild, harmless, and inoffensive race of people, and very industrious. Their huts are the largest and cleanest we have seen in the whole country. Our old friend the schoolmaster informs us that we shall very soon pass the *Tshadda* river. Canoes, he said, frequently go up the Tshadda to Bornou.

Sunday, October 24th.—The children of the more respectable inhabitants of Egga are placed at a very early age under the tuition of our friendly host, the schoolmaster, who teaches them a few Mahomedan prayers; all, indeed, with which he may be acquainted in the Arabic tongue. In this consists the whole of their education. The boys are diligent in their exercises, and arise every morning between midnight and sunrise, and are studiously employed by lamp-light in copying their prayers, after which they read them to the master one after another, beginning with the eldest. This is repeated in a shrill, bawling tone, so loud as to be heard at a distance of half a mile at least, which is believed to be a criterion of excellence by the parents; and he who has the strongest lungs and clearest voice is of course considered as the best scholar, and caressed accordingly.[1] The Mahomedans, though excessively vain of their own attainments, and proud of their learning, and intellectual superiority over their companions, are nevertheless conscious of the vast pre-eminence of white men over

[1] Despite the increase in Western-style education, first introduced by Christian missionaries, Koranic schools are still vigorously maintained by West African Muslims. In most such schools the content of education has not changed since the Landers' day. 'The object of the school is not primarily the initiation of the child into community life but simply memorization of the Qur'an by which power is gained in this world and reward in the next. This is accompanied by instruction in the formal duties of Islam' (Trimingham, 1959, p. 158). For an account of Koranic schools in Nupe see Nadel, 1942, pp. 378–81.

themselves, for they have heard many marvellous stories of Europeans, and their fame has been proclaimed with a trumpet-voice among all people and nations of the interior, insomuch that they are placed on an equality with supernatural beings. As an illustration of this, a priest, himself a writer of charms, made a pressing application today for an amulet from us, which he begged might possess properties so extraordinary and amazing, as to be the wonder of the whole country. He gave us a large pot of beer, and would not leave our hut until he had exacted a promise that we would give him the paper which he had craved so piteously. In all obstinate cases of this nature, we have found it expedient to follow the example of Mr Park, which is, to give the superstitious a copy of the *Lord's Prayer*, which, at least, can produce no mischievous effects.[1]

At three in the afternoon, we offered up a prayer to the Almighty Disposer of all human events, for protection on our future voyage, that he would deign to extend to us his all-saving power among the lawless barbarians it was our lot to be obliged to pass. Having done this, we next ordered Pascoe and our people to commence loading the canoe. I shall never forget them, poor fellows, they were all in tears, and trembled with fear. One of them, named Antonio, a native of Bonny, and son to the late chief of that river, was as much affected as the rest, but on a different account. For himself he said that he did not care, his own life was of no consequence. All he feared was, that my brother and I should be murdered: he loved us dearly: he had been with us ever since we had left the sea, and it would be as bad as dying himself to see us killed.

At half past four in the afternoon we bade adieu to the kind inhabitants of Kacunda. The poor natives gazed at us with astonishment, no doubt expecting that we should never be seen or heard of more.

We were now fairly off, and prepared ourselves for the worse. 'Now,' said I, 'my boys,' as our canoe glided down with the stream, 'let us all stick together. I hope that we have none among us who will flinch, come what may.' Antonio and Sam said they were determined to stick to us to the last. The latter is a native of Sierra Leone,[2] and I

---

[1] On his first expedition in 1796 Park was asked by his negro landlord in Sansanding, a town much frequented by Moors, for a saphie or charm. '"If a Moor's saphie is good (said this hospitable old man), a white man's must needs be better." I readily furnished him with one possessed of all the virtues I could concentrate, for it contained the Lord's prayer' (Park, *Everyman's Library*, p. 158).

[2] Sam must have been the mulatto, whose name the Landers had earlier in their journal (p. 160) refused to reveal on account of his reprehensible conduct.

believe them both to be firm fellows when required. Old Pascoe and Jowdie, two of my former people, I knew could be depended on; but the new ones, although they boasted much when they found that there was no avoiding it, I had not much dependence on, as I had not had an opportunity of trying them. We directed the four muskets and two pistols to be loaded with ball and slugs, determined that our opponents, whoever they might be, should meet with a warm reception; and having made every preparation for our defence which we thought would be availing, and encouraging our little band to behave themselves gallantly, we gave three hearty cheers, and commended ourselves to Providence.

Our little vessel moved on in grand style under the vigorous and animated exertions of our men. There were no tears now, and I thought, as they propelled her along with more than their usual strength, that they felt they were a match for any canoe that would dare attack us.

The evening was calm and serene, the heat of the day was over, the moon and stars now afforded us an agreeable light—everything was still and pleasant; we glided smoothly and silently down the stream, and for a long while we saw little or nothing to excite our fears, and heard nothing but a gentle rustling of the leaves, occasioned by the wind, the noise of our paddles, or now and then the plashing of fishes as they leapt out of the water.

About midnight we observed lights from a village, to which we were very close, and heard people dancing, singing and laughing in the moonshine outside their huts. We made haste over to the opposite side to get away, for fear of a lurking danger, and we fancied that a light was following us, but it was only a 'Will o' the wisp', or some such thing, and trees soon hid it from our sight.

October 25th.—At one a.m., the direction of the river changed to south-south-west, running between immensely high hills. At five o'clock this morning, we found ourselves nearly opposite a very considerable river, entering the Niger from the eastward; it appeared to be three or four miles wide at its mouth, and on the bank we saw a large town, one part of which faced the river, and the other the Quorra. We at first supposed it to be an arm of that river, and running from us; and therefore directed our course for it. We proceeded up a short distance, but finding the current against us, and that it increased as we got within its entrance, and our people being tired, we were compelled to give up the attempt, and were easily swept back into the

Niger. We conclude this to be the Tshadda, and the large town to be Cuttumcurrafee.[1]

At 10 a.m., we passed a huge and naked white rock, in the form of a perfect dome, arising from the centre of the river. We passed by it on the western side, and were very nearly lost in a whirlpool. It was with the utmost difficulty we preserved the canoe from being carried away, and dashed against the rocks. Shortly after, seeing a convenient place for landing, the men being languid and weary with hunger and exertion, we halted on the right bank of the river, which we imagined was most convenient for our purpose.

The spot, for a hundred yards, was cleared of grass, underwood, and vegetation of all kinds; and, on a further observation, we came to the conclusion that a market or fair was periodically held thereon. Very shortly afterwards, as three of our men were straggling about in the bush, searching for firewood, a village suddenly opened before them: this did not excite their astonishment, and they entered one of the huts which was nearest to them to procure a little fire. However it happened to contain only women; but these were terrified beyond measure at the sudden and abrupt entrance of strange-looking men, whose language they did not know, and whose business they could not understand, and they all ran out in a fright into the woods, to warn their male relations of them, who were labouring at their usual occupation of husbandry. Meanwhile our men had very composedly taken some burning embers from the fire, and returned to us in a few minutes, with the brief allusion to the circumstance of having discovered a village. We immediately sent Pascoe, Abraham [*sic*], and Jowdie, in company, to obtain some fire, and to purchase a few yams for us. In about ten minutes after, they returned in haste, telling us that they had been to the village, and had asked for some fire, but that the people did not understand them, and, instead of attending to their wishes, they looked terrified, and had suddenly disappeared. In consequence of their threatening attitudes, our people had left the village,

[1] The Landers were the first Europeans to set eyes on this great tributary of the Niger. Almost exactly twenty years later Heinrich Barth, travelling down from Bornu, saw the same river in its higher reaches as it flows through Adamawa. One of the riverain tribes, the Batta, called the river Benue, 'mother of waters'. This name, publicized by the publisher Petermann, soon came to be adopted for the whole river. 'That the river is anywhere really called Chadda, or even Tsadda,' Barth wrote, 'I doubt very much. I think the name Chadda was a mere mistake of Lander's, confirmed by Allen, who visited the area in 1834 and 1841, owing to their fancying it an outlet of Lake Tsad' (Barth, 1890, p. 453). The town at the confluence was not 'Cuttum-currafie' (Koton Karifi), which lies some distance up the Niger.

and rejoined us with all the haste they could. We did not, however, think that they would attack us, and we proceeded to make our fires and then laid ourselves down.

Totally unconscious of danger, we were reclining on our mats—for we, too, like our people, were wearied with toil, and overcome with drowsiness—when in about twenty minutes after our men had returned, one of them shouted, with a loud voice, 'War is coming! O war is coming!' and ran towards us with a scream of terror, telling us that the natives were hastening to attack us. We started up at this unusual exclamation, and, looking about us, we beheld a large party of men, almost naked, running in a very irregular manner, and with uncouth gestures, towards our little encampment. They were all variously armed with muskets, bows and arrows, knives, cutlasses, barbs, long spears, and other instruments of destruction; and, as we gazed upon this band of wild men, with their ferocious looks and hostile appearance, which was not a little heightened on observing the weapons in their hands, we felt a very uneasy kind of sensation, and wished ourselves safe out of their hands. Our party was much scattered, but fortunately we could see them coming to us at some distance, and we had time to collect our men. We resolved, however, to prevent bloodshed if possible—our numbers were too few to leave us a chance of escaping by any other way. The natives were approaching us fast. Not a moment was to be lost. We desired Pascoe and all our people to follow behind us at a short distance with the loaded muskets and pistols; and we enjoined them strictly not to fire, unless they first fired at us. One of the natives, who proved to be the chief, we perceived a little in advance of his companions; and, throwing down our pistols, which we had snatched up in the first moment of surprise, my brother and I walked very composedly, and unarmed, towards him. As we approached him, we made all the signs and motions we could with our arms, to deter him and his people from firing on us. His quiver was dangling at his side, his bow was bent, and an arrow, which was pointed at our breasts, already trembled on the string, when we were within a few yards of his person. This was a highly critical moment—the next might be our last. But the hand of Providence averted the blow; for just as the chief was about to pull the fatal cord, a man that was nearest him rushed forward, and stayed his arm. At that instant we stood before him, and immediately held forth our hands; all of them trembled like aspen leaves; the chief looked up full in our faces, kneeling on the ground—light seemed to flash from his dark, rolling eyes—his body was convulsed all over, as though he were enduring the utmost torture, and with a timorous, yet undefinable, expression of countenance, in which all the passions of our nature were strangely blended, he drooped his head, eagerly grasped our proffered hands, and burst into tears. This was a sign of friendship—harmony followed, and war and bloodshed were thought of no more. Peace and friendship now reigned among us; and the first thing that we did was to lift the old chief from the ground, and to convey him to our encampment. The behaviour of our men afforded us no little amusement, now that the danger was past. We had now had a fair trial of their courage, and should know who to trust on a future occasion. Pascoe was firm to his post, and stood still with his musket pointed at the chief's breast during the whole time. He is a brave fellow, and said to us, 'If the *black* rascals had fired at either of you, I should have brought the old chief down like a guinea-fowl.' As for our two brave fellows, Sam and Antonio, they took to their heels, and scampered off as fast as they could directly they saw the natives approaching us over the long grass, nor did they make their appearance again until the chief and all his people were sitting round us; and even when they did return, they were so frightened, they could not speak for some time.

All the armed villagers had now gathered round their leader, and anxiously watched his looks and gestures. The result of the meeting delighted them—every eye sparkled with pleasure—they uttered a shout of joy—they thrust their bloodless arrows into their quivers— they ran about as though they were possessed of evil spirits—they twanged their bowstrings, fired off their muskets, shook their spears, clattered their quivers, danced, put their bodies into all manner of ridiculous positions, laughed, cried, and sung in rapid succession— they were like a troop of maniacs. Never was spectacle more wild and terrific. When this sally of passion to which they had worked themselves had subsided into calmer and more reasonable behaviour, we presented each of the war-men with a quantity of needles, as a further token of our friendly intentions. The chief sat himself down on the turf, with one of us on each side of him, while the men were leaning on their weapons on his right and left. At first no one could understand us; but an old man made his appearance shortly after, who understood the Haussa language. Him the chief employed as an interpreter, and every one listened with anxiety to the following explanation which he gave us:

'A few minutes after you first landed, one of my people came to me and said, that a number of strange people had arrived at the market-place. Not doubting that it was your intention to attack my village at night, and carry off my people, I desired them to get ready to fight. We were all prepared and eager to kill you, and came down breathing vengeance and slaughter, supposing that you were my enemies and had landed from the opposite side of the river. But when you came to meet us unarmed, and we saw your white faces, we were all so frightened that we could not pull our bows, nor move hand or foot; and when you drew near me, and extended your hand towards me, I felt my heart faint within me, and believed that you were "*Children of Heaven*", and had dropped from the skies.' Such was the effect we had produced on him; and under this impression he knew not what he did. 'And now,' said he, 'white men, all I want is your forgiveness.' 'That you shall have most heartily,' we said, as we shook hands with the old chief, and having taken care to assure him we had not come from so good a place as he had imagined, we congratulated ourselves, as well as him, that this affair had ended so happily. It was a narrow escape; and God grant we may never be so near a cruel death again. It was happy for us that our white faces and calm behaviour produced the effect it did on these people—in another minute our bodies would have been as full of arrows as a porcupine's is full of quills.

The old chief returned to the village, followed by his people. They came back to us again in the afternoon, bringing with them a large quantity of yams and goora-nuts as a present.

October 26th.—Early in the morning the chief of the village, the old man that acted as interpreter, and a number of men and women visited our encampment, and behaved themselves in the most becoming and friendly manner. Not satisfied with what they had given us yesterday, the villagers offered us another large heap of yams, which, however, we refused to accept without making a suitable recompense.

We now learnt from the interpreter that buyers and sellers attend this market, [which is called *Bocqua*,] not only from places adjacent, but also from remote towns and villages, both above and below, and on each bank of the Niger.[1] The chief assured us that we had nothing

[1] According to Baikie, the name 'Bocqua' reported by the Landers was 'not known to the natives'. Baikie gives the name of the place as 'Ikiri or Okiri'. No place of this name is to be found on the modern map, but Iroko, which Baikie places a few miles north of Ikiri, is still marked. It is puzzling that Baikie should describe Ikiri as lying on the 'eastern shore of the river', while Lander's Bocqua is clearly placed on the opposite bank. Baikie noted that the market was held every ten days and was attended by traders from Kakanda to Aboh (Baikie, 1856, p. 65).

to fear, having passed all those places from which we might have expected danger and molestation during the night. A little below Bocqua, he said, on the left bank of the river, resides a powerful king, sovereign of a fine country, called *Atta*.[1] He said that the chief was a very extraordinary man, and if he had us in his power would detain us longer than we wished. We resolved to keep out of his reach by running along close to the shore on the opposite side of the water. The chief concluded by observing that in seven days we should reach the sea.

Having finished our usual scanty breakfast of a roasted yam and some water from the river, we commenced loading our canoe and preparing for our day's journey. The canoe being all ready, we shook hands cordially with our friend the chief, and the principal male and female villagers, and a few minutes after seven fired a salute of two or three muskets, gave three cheers, and departed from Bocqua.

Both banks of the river still continued hilly, and were fringed with primeval woods, which were bending over the water. At eleven a.m., we were opposite a town, which we supposed to be Atta. It is situated close to the water's edge on the south-east bank of the river, in an elevated situation, and on a fine green sward: its appearance was unspeakably beautiful. The town is clean, of prodigious extent, and ornamented with verdant shrubs and tall goodly trees. A few canoes were lying at the foot of the town, but we escaped observation, and passed on near the opposite shore. Afterwards the margin of the river became more thickly wooded, and more umbrageous than before; and for upwards of thirty miles not a town or a village, or even a single hut, could anywhere be seen. The whole of this distance our canoe passed smoothly along the Niger, and everything was silent and solitary; no sound could be distinguished save our own voices and the plashing of the paddles with their echoes; the song of birds was not heard, nor could any animal whatever be seen: the banks seemed to be entirely deserted, and the magnificent Niger to be slumbering in its own grandeur.

At about five in the evening, our people being tired, we descried a canoe and pulled towards it; but those that were in it were frightened on seeing us, and jumped out and hid themselves in the forest. In two or three minutes we perceived on the left bank a few dilapidated

---

[1] 'Atta' was not the name of the town, which was called Idah, or of the country, but the title, *Ata*, of the ruler. Lander was to visit Idah on his third expedition in 1833 (Epilogue, p. 293).

huts, and we pulled the canoe ashore, intending to remain there for the night. A number of women first observed us; they were also alarmed, and hurried away to an adjacent village, where we saw them providing themselves with muskets and other uncivil weopens, and very formidable Amazons they appeared to be. However we did not seem to regard them, but jumped on shore with our mats and sat down on the ground very comfortably under the branches of a cocoa-nut tree, the first that we have seen since leaving Yarriba. We had not been long seated before a number of people made their appearance, running hastily towards us with swords and muskets in their hands. Seeing that we were sitting down quietly, without making any hostile display, they hesitated and stopped at a short distance from us, and wished to know what we wanted at their town. We had recourse to our usual method of expressing ourselves by signs, and the natives finding that we were really harmless beings, ventured to draw nearer, and very soon became reconciled to us. Shortly after they were joined by some more of their companions, and among them was a young man who imperfectly understood the *Bonny* language; so that Antonio, one of our men, who is son to '*King Pepper*', chief of that country, was enabled to enter into conversation with him, and presently made him comprehend everything relative to us, which he repeated to the villagers. We had been thus employed a short time, and had become great friends with these people, the women chatting with a familiarity we had not been accustomed to up the country, when the chief, a tall, Herculean, awkward figure, with a sullen and most forbidding countenance, made his appearance. He introduced himself without the smallest ceremony, and very briefly desired us to accompany him to his hut in the principal village, which is called *Abbaȝacca*. On arriving there, a clean shed was prepared for us. Through the interpretation of Antonio we informed the chief who we were, and where we wished to go. He immediately said he would accompany us to a large town lower down the river, of which his brother was governor, and where we should meet with people from Bonny, Calebar, Brass, and Bini, which latter place we conclude is meant for Benin. The natives of all these places, he informed us, come up to his brother's town for the purpose of buying slaves, and we shall then be at liberty to accompany whichever party we please.

October 27th.—It was the avowed intention of the chief to send a man with us as messenger to a large town, of which he said that his brother was governor; but imagining, no doubt, that he would not be paid to his satisfaction, and that, should he accompany us himself, the reward would be greater, he changed his mind, and resolved on the latter expedient.

In consequence of the lightness of his canoe, and its superiority to our old one, the chief passed us with the utmost facility, and touched at various towns and villages, to inform their inhabitants that Christians were coming from a country they had never heard of. We were solicited to stop at one or two of these, in order to please the curiosity of the people, hundreds of whom ran out into the water to obtain a better view of our persons, but we did not get out of our canoe. These brought us presents of eggs, which we accepted very gladly, and passed on.

At two in the afternoon we came abreast of a village of pretty considerable extent, intending to pass by it on the other side. We had no sooner made our appearance than we were lustily hailed by a little squinting fellow, dressed in an English soldier's jacket, who kept crying out as loud as his lungs would permit him, 'Holloa, you Englishman! you come here.' However we were not inclined to obey his summons, being rather anxious to get to the town mentioned to us by the chief of Abbazacca, and as the current swept us along past the village, we took no notice of the little man; and we had already sailed beyond the landing-place, when we were overtaken by about a dozen canoes, and the people in them stopping us, desired us to turn back, for that we had forgotten to pay our respects to the king. The name of this village, we now find, is *Damuggoo*.[1] Ever willing to please and oblige all parties, as far as we are able, and being in no condition to force ourselves from the men that had interrupted us with so little ceremony, we pulled with all our strength against the current, and, after an hour's exertions, landed amidst the cheers and huzzas of a multitude of people. The first person we observed at the landing-place was our little friend in the red jacket, whom we found out afterwards was a messenger from the chief of Bonny. His business here was to buy slaves for his master.

My brother and I were instantly conducted over a bog to a large fetish tree, at the root of which we were made to sit down, and were shaded by its branches from an intolerably hot sun. Here we awaited the arrival of the chief, who made his appearance in a few minutes. We arose to salute him, and he shook hands with us, welcoming us

---

[1] The name 'Damuggoo' is given by later travellers (e.g. Baikie, 1856, p. 290) as 'Adamugu' and the name of the chief as 'Aboko'.

to his town with a reserved and sorrowful, yet friendly air. He requested us to stop a few days at his town, which we promised him we would do, having told him that we were going to the sea. The chief of Bonny's messenger, he said, was going there in a few days, and he would recommend us to remain with him till he went, that we might accompany him. We had no objection to this, and thought that the little squinting fellow, who was a very important personage in his own

The Chief of Damuggoo.

estimation, might be useful to us, and be some sort of protection to our party where he was known.

The chief put a great many questions to us respecting ourselves and our country, the places we had come from, their distance up the river, and also concerning the river itself, and was astonished at our answers. He told us that he had never heard of any countries higher up the river than Funda and *Tacwa*, by which latter we found he meant the Nouffie country. He said that he had never heard of Yarriba, Borgoo, or Yaoorie. A Mallam now joined our company, who appeared to be a respectable man. We found afterwards that he had been sent for by the chief of Damuggoo for the purpose of writing charms to protect him from all evil which might threaten him and his village.

At six in the evening, the chief sent us some fofo, and a quantity of stewed goat, sufficient for thirty persons. We were not a little surprised by the addition of a small case-bottle of rum—a luxury which we have

not known since we were at Kiama. It is long since we have tasted
tea or coffee; but the rum was a treat that we did not expect, although
it was the worst kind of trade rum I ever recollected to have tasted.

Here, to our infinite surprise, we saw, on landing, besides the little
man dressed in a soldier's jacket, several others partially clothed in
European apparel, all of whom have picked up a smattering of the
English language from Liverpool vessels which frequent the Bonny
river for palm-oil.

Fetish Deity of Damuggoo.

XVIII

Damuggoo to Kirree

October 28th.—At ten a.m., the chief visited us, accompanied by the Nouffie mallam. He brought with him some palm wine, eggs, bananas, yams, etc, and desired us to ask for anything we might want, telling us that we should have everything we wished that the town could afford. He told us that neither he nor his father had seen a white man, although they had much wished it, and that our presence made him quite happy. He then gave us a pressing invitation to come to see him, which we readily accepted. He seemed to be one of the worthiest fellows whom we have yet met.

We shortly after proceeded to the residence, and passed through a variety of low huts which led to the one in which he was sitting. He had a very handsome leopard's skin thrown over him. In his hand he held a staff, covered with the skin of a wild beast; and two pages, one on each side, were cooling him with circular fans, made of bullock's hide. He accosted us with cheerfulness, and placed mats for us to sit on; and rum was produced to make us comfortable withal. We again briefly related to him from whence we had come, where we had been,

226

and whither we were going. When Antonio, our interpreter, explained to him that we were ambassadors from the 'great king of the white men', he seemed to feel peculiar delight. 'Something must be done for you tomorrow,' said he, and left us to conjecture for a short time what that something would be; but we soon learnt that he intended to make rejoicings with all his people; that they would fire off their muskets, and pass a night in dancing and revelry. He told us that when we left him to go down the river, he intended to send one of his canoes, with nine people in her, to accompany us all the way to the sea. He requested us to wait eight days longer, when he expected his people back from the Bocqua market. 'I think,' he added, 'that the Chief of Bocqua's messenger and our people will be a sufficient protection for you.' We readily assented to his proposal, and told him that as our presents were all expended, we would send him some from the sea-coast, if he would allow a person to accompany us thither on whom he could depend, to bring them back to him. He expressed himself much gratified by our promises, and said that his own son should accompany us; and that although his people had never been lower down the river than to a place called Kirree, about a day's journey from hence, he had no doubt that we should reach the sea in safety.

October 29th.—The promise of 'something', which was made us yesterday, has been fulfilled today with great *éclat*. In the morning, a bullock, wild in the bush, was offered us, with a proviso that one of our party could shoot him. Pascoe, therefore, went out with his gun, and discovered the animal ruminating among the trees; and levelling his piece, he shot him dead the first fire. It is usual here for the cattle to run wild in the bush, being never admitted into the town; and when one is wanted for food, the natives go into the woods and shoot it.

At the back of our hut stands a fetish god, in a small thatched hut, supported by four wooden pillars, which is watched continually by two boys and a woman. We were desired to roast our bullock under him, that he might enjoy the savoury smell of the smoking meat, some of which he might also be able to eat if he desired. We were particularly enjoined to roast no yams under him, as they were considered by the natives too poor a diet to offer to their deity. The natives are all pagans, and worship the same kind of figures as those of Yarriba.

A feast and great rejoicings are to take place today, in consequence of our arrival, and the preparation of the bullock only seems to be the first step towards it. The natives are getting their muskets ready, and all the swivels in the town are brought and placed under the fetish tree we have mentioned.

At six in the evening the ceremonies were commenced, by a volley of musketry being fired off by command of the chief, and we were afterwards saluted by a discharge from the swivels. This was a signal for the inhabitants to come forward and follow the example of their monarch, which they did with so much spirit and effect, that continual firing was kept up till between eleven and twelve o'clock, at which time the people paraded the town for the remainder of the night, dancing, singing, and making merry. Pascoe tells us that every man has a musket. They must be very numerous, for the fire is as incessant as if we were in a field of battle, so that it is quite impossible for us to get any sleep while it is going forward.

October 30th.—From a conversation with a Nouffie man we learn that these muskets and guns have been procured from the coast in exchange for slaves and ivory. He informs us, also, that Bornou and Jacoba are at peace, and consequently that the road from Funda to *Kouka*, which is the metropolis of the Bornou empire, is now open and free from danger of any kind. The same individual assures us that a person can travel from one country to the other, by land, in seventeen days; but that to travel by water up the *Tshadda*, to Kouka, would be a journey of nineteen days.

Sunday, October 31st.—At ten in the morning, the chief sent for me to visit him, and I immediately obeyed his summons. I found him engaged in earnest conversation with his priests, and he no sooner saw me than he requested me to sit down by his side. He appeared very serious, but did not give me long to speculate on what was coming; for, turning towards me, he said, with a deep-drawn sigh, that the fetish which had been made yesterday for us, had not ended in our favour. He was sure, he said, that we would meet with many troubles before we reached the sea. All this was said with a great deal of earnestness, and his countenance was very expressive of sorrow. I desired that he would not feel hurt on our account, telling him that we were not afraid of anything; that we had done no one any harm in Africa, and we trusted in our God for protection. 'It is good,' said he; 'if my people return from Bocqua market tomorrow, you shall go in a few days.'

In the course of conversation this morning, the chief said that he cannot think of sending us away in an old leaky canoe, such as ours, and unprotected; that such would not be fitting our rank. He observed, that our canoe is what sailors would term not 'sea-worthy'; for, having been exposed to the heat of the sun, it had split in several places. These considerations had induced him to procure for us a far better canoe than our own.

A great part of the population of Damuggoo left the town this morning for the Bocqua market. They take thither powder, muskets, soap, Manchester cottons, and other articles of European manufacture, and great quantities of rum, or rather of rum and water; for not more than one third of it is genuine spirit, and even that is of the worst quality. These commodities are exchanged for ivory and slaves, which are re-sold to European traders.

The natives of this part of the country scarcely ever heard of the religion of Mahomet, and, therefore, they believe in all manner of gods and demons, as in Yarriba and other places. They have a variety of tutelary gods, and others whose business it is to watch over and protect the public interests. Their religious dances, and their songs or hymns, addressed to their divinities differ but slightly from those of other pagan countries, and the superstitious ceremonies of their faith bear the same close resemblance.

November 2nd.—The streets of Damuggoo are so muddy, owing to the nature of the soil, and to the rains which have recently fallen, that we cannot step outside the door of our hut without exposing ourselves to the inconvenience of being covered with black, filthy mud, so that we are obliged to stay within from necessity. Our hut does not exceed six or seven feet in diameter, and withal it is so very dark and dismal, that we can neither see to read nor write; added to which we are invaded, from the first peep of dawn to the close of day, by a host of impudent fellows, who plant themselves round the door-way, and in the passage, like as many blocks of marble, and remain there in spite of us, to the utter exclusion of every particle of air. The chief, to whom we have made a grievous complaint, tells us seriously to '*cut off their heads*'; but really we do not relish the idea of human heads, all so black and ghastly, tumbling down at our feet, and so we resort to a milder punishment, but, hitherto, this has not been attended with any good effect. When evening comes, and the moon shines brilliantly above our heads, like all nature, we seek the comforts of repose; but who can sleep when legions of mosquitoes come singing in your face, to tease and worry you without mercy? It is a fact, that the chief and his people are frequently driven, in the dead of night, to seek shelter from the attacks of these tormenting insects in the open air, or under the trees.

November 3rd.—The inhabitants of this town dress, generally speaking, in Manchester cottons (if a cloth confined to the waist, and extending below the knee, may be styled a dress). The neat and becoming tobe or shirt of the interior is worn only by the king and a few of the principal inhabitants. Indeed, the people appear to have little communication with the natives of the more inland provinces, and we have found the progress of civilization to be rapidly diminishing the nearer we approach the coast.

Those of the inhabitants who are not engaged in trading transactions, employ themselves in cultivating the soil. Yams and Indian corn form, we believe, the principal, if not the only vegetable food of the poorer classes, and they rarely eat anything else. The plantain and banana are imported from a neighbouring state; but these are beyond their reach, on account of expense; and form, in fact, with the exception of the cocoa-nut, the only fruits and vegetables with which they seem to be acquainted. Rice, which is grown so generally, and in such abundance, almost in their immediate neighbourhood, they have never seen. They confine their agricultural labours to cultivating maize, which is the hardiest of all grain, and the yam. The inhabitants of Damuggoo never saw a horse, nor have they the most distant idea of such an animal.

At five in the afternoon the people returned from Bocqua market, and the chief sent us word to be ready for leaving Damuggoo tomorrow evening. He continues to be very kind to us, and has allowed us to want nothing which his village could supply.

November 4th.—To ascertain whether or not we are to proceed on our voyage today the chief and his priests have been diligently employed in consulting the entrails of fowls, but the omens were pronounced to be very inauspicious. Our determination of departing, however, was not to be shaken by such means. By the chief's own arrangement our people were to embark in the leaky canoe, with the heaviest of the luggage; whereas my brother and I were to travel in one of his own canoes, and to take along with us whatever was of most consequence.

Long before five o'clock, everything, on our parts, had been got in readiness for quitting the town, and we sat in the canoe till after sunset, waiting the arrival of the boatmen, who did not seem at all disposed to hurry themselves in making their appearance. The chief could not be spoken with, because he was engaged in a religious rite with his priests. At length, when our uneasiness was at its height, we saw him coming towards us with a train of followers. The Mallam and all of his principal people were with him, bringing numerous jars of palm wine. A mat was spread near the water-side, whereon the chief sat himself, and we were instantly desired to place ourselves one on each side of his person. The palm wine circulated freely in the bowls, and the natives of the village, who witnessed all our proceedings, with no little anxiety, seemed to be greatly delighted at seeing their chief and the priests so familiar with the white men. Meanwhile several elephants' tusks, and a number of slaves and goats, were put into the canoe as presents for the chief of Bonny. A fatted goat was given us as a parting gift, and a small decanter of rum was thrust in my brother's bosom as a cordial during the night. We drank and chatted away until half past six in the evening, when we sent Pascoe on before us in charge of our old canoe, telling him that we should soon overtake him.

To our great mortification we were unable to follow him till eight in the evening, being detained by another fetish ceremony. It was dark when we jumped into the king's canoe which was waiting for us, and launched out into the stream. The canoe-men entertained us with their native songs, keeping time with their paddles, and every thing contributed to render the passage pleasant had we not been uneasy at our canoe with Pascoe being so far before us, without any messenger or guide.

November 5th.—We continued on our way down the river until two in the morning, when we arrived at a halting place, near a considerable village. Here our people landed to repose awhile under the branches of trees, and await the coming of our own canoe, which we had not seen during the night. Our lodgings were very far from agreeable; we were crammed, comparatively, into a small canoe, with a dozen people as companions, besides a number of goats, and six slaves, consisting of three women, two men, and a pretty little boy. Neither of these slaves seem to bestow a moment's regret on leaving their native country, though they know they are to be sold on the coast, and conveyed to a foreign and distant land, if we may except a troublesome female, who screamed by starts during the night; but her sorrow was evidently assumed, her object being to disturb her associates in misfortune, and give trouble to her keepers, rather than to give vent to her own feelings. The little boy above-mentioned, is intended as a present from the chief of Damuggoo to the king of Bonny; he is not placed on a similar footing to his companions, but treated with tenderness. The men and women slaves are fettered in the day-time, but their irons are taken off at night. These have been all free people; but having been found guilty of minor offences at Damuggoo, they are sentenced to perpetual slavery and banishment.

A market is to be held tomorrow in the village near which we are stopping, and several large canoes filled with people and goods are lying alongside of us. Others are constantly arriving from various quarters. Ours, with Pascoe and his companions, has just entered the creek.

We endeavoured to obtain a little rest, but found it quite impossible, and at five in the morning we arose wearied and fatigued. The heavy dew which has fallen wetted us completely through. At sunrise I joined our people in the old canoe, which contained the whole of our luggage, for the purpose of encouraging them to greater exertion, otherwise they would not keep up with the men of Damuggoo, and might loiter behind and lose themselves; and as my brother's canoe could easily overtake me, I proceeded onwards at five a.m. leaving him behind with the other.

I had left one trunk and one medicine-chest in my brother's canoe, and a couple of muskets, in case he might want them, and being very anxious to get down the river had started without breakfast, at which my people were very much dissatisfied. They complained of being tired very soon, and asked for their breakfast. I cheered them up all I could with the hopes of getting them on further before we stopped; and, taking the paddle myself, I set them the example in using it, at the same time singing 'Rule Britannia' to them, and telling them that in six or seven days we should reach the sea, when I would reward them all well. This had the desired effect, and although I could not but think that the poor fellows complained very justly, we continued on very pleasantly.

At seven a.m. we saw a small river enter the Niger from the eastward. Shortly after we observed a branch of the river running off to the westward. On the right bank of this river, close also to the bank of the Niger, we observed a large market, which I was informed is Kirree; and that the river, flowing to the westward past it, runs to Benin. A great number of canoes were lying near the bank. They appeared to be very large, and had flags flying on long bamboo canes. We took no notice of them, but passed on, and in a short time afterwards saw about fifty canoes before us, coming up the river. They appeared to be very large and full of men, and the appearance of them at a distance was very pleasing. They had each three long bamboo canes, with flags flying from them, one fixed at each end of the canoe, and the other in the middle. As we approached each other I observed the British Union flag in several, while others, which were white, had figures of a man's leg, chairs, tables, decanters, glasses, and all kinds of such devices. The people in them, who were very numerous, were dressed in European clothing, with the exception of trousers.

I felt quite overjoyed by the sight of these people, more particularly so when I saw our flag and European apparel among them, and congratulated myself that they were from the sea-coast. But all my fond anticipations vanished in a moment as the first canoe met us. A great stout fellow, of a most forbidding countenance, beckoned to me to come to him, but seeing him and all his people so well armed I was not inclined to trust myself among them, and paid no attention to him. The next moment I heard the sound of a drum, and in an instant several men mounted a platform and levelled their muskets at us. There was nothing to be done now but to obey; as for running away it was out of the question, our square loaded canoe was incapable of it, and to fight with fifty war canoes, for such we found them, containing each above forty people, most of whom were as well armed as ourselves, would have been throwing away my own and my canoe-men's lives very foolishly. In addition to the muskets, each canoe had a long gun in its bow that would carry a shot of four or six pounds, besides being provided with a good stock of swords and boarding-pikes.

By this time our canoes were side by side, and with astonishing rapidity our luggage found its way into those of our opponents. This mode of proceeding I did not relish at all; so as my gun was loaded with two balls and four slugs, I took deliberate aim at the leader, and he would have paid for his temerity with his life in one moment more, had not three of his people sprung on me and forced the gun from my hands. My jacket and shoes were as quickly plundered from me, and observing some other fellows at the same time taking away Pascoe's wife, I lost all command over myself and was determined to sell my life as dearly as I could. I encouraged my men to arm themselves with their paddles and defend themselves to the last. I instantly seized hold of Pascoe's wife, and with the assistance of another of my men dragged her from the fellow's grasp; Pascoe at the same time levelled a blow at his head with one of our iron-wood paddles that sent him reeling backwards, and we saw him no more.

Our canoe having been so completely relieved of her cargo, which had consisted only of our luggage, we have plenty of room in her for battle, and being each of us provided with a paddle, we determined, as we had got clear of our adversary, to cut down the first fellow who should dare to board us. This was not attempted; and as none of the other canoes had offered to interfere, I was in hopes of finding some friends among them, but at all events was determined to follow the people who had plundered us to the market, where they seemed to be going. We accordingly pulled after them as fast as we could. My men, now that the fray was over, began to think of their forlorn condition. All their things were gone, and as they gave up all hopes of regaining them, or being able to revenge themselves on the robbers, they gave vent to their rage in tears and execrations. I desired them to be quiet, and endeavoured all in my power to pacify them by telling them that if we were spared to reach the sea in safety, I would pay them for everything they had lost.

We were following the canoe that had attacked us as fast as we possibly could to regain our things, if possible, when some people hailed us from a large canoe, which I found afterwards belonged to the New Calebar river. One of the people, who was apparently a person of consequence, called out lustily to me, 'Holloa, white man, you French, you English?'—'Yes, English,' I answered him immediately. 'Come here in my canoe,' he said, and our two canoes approached each other rapidly. I accordingly got into his canoe, and he put three of his men into mine to assist in pulling her to market. The people of the canoe treated me with much kindness, and the chief of her who had hailed me gave me a glass of rum. There were several females also in the canoe who appeared to take a great deal of interest in my safety.

On looking around I now observed my brother coming towards us in the Damuggoo canoe, and the same villain who had plundered me was the first to pursue him. The following narrative of my brother's will give the reader an account of his proceedings to the time I saw him.

'My brother left the village nearly two hours before me, and therefore he was far in advance when the Damuggoo canoe, in which I had remained, was pushed off the land. Wishing to overtake him, for he had no guide, the men exerted themselves wonderfully to make amends for the time which they had trifled away, and it was really astonishing to see the rapidity with which the canoe was impelled through the water.

'After we had been in the canoe perhaps an hour, one of the men who happened to be standing in the bow, fancied that he could descry, in another canoe, then at a considerable distance before us, a sheep and goat, which my brother had taken away with him in the morning. All doubt as to the identity of the animals having been removed from his own mind and those of his companions—though for my own part I must own that my vision was not near keen enough to allow me to agree with them in opinion—we gave chase to the suspected canoe. The men summoned all their resolution and strength to the task, and, like an arrow from a bow, our narrow vessel darted through the water. We gained rapidly on the chase, and the people, perceiving our object and mistrusting our intentions, kept near the shore, and laboured hard to get away from us. They then entered a branch of the river which was running to the south-west, and sheltered themselves amongst a number of canoes that were lying alongside a large market-place, situated on the left bank.

'This did not damp the spirit of our men, or deter them from following the pursued: we succeeded in discovering their hiding-place; and at length, after much wrangling and many threats, the robbers (for such they proved to be) were compelled to restore the animals. But how my brother could have suffered two men to plunder his canoe, puzzled me exceedingly and I was totally at a loss to account for it. Nothing could exceed my surprise, on approaching the market, to observe, as I thought, large European flags, affixed to poles, and waving over almost every canoe that was there. On a closer examination I discovered them to be imitations only, though they were executed with uncommon skill and neatness. British colours apparently were the most prevalent, and among these the Union flag seemed to be the general favourite. Nor did my former surprise diminish in the least, when I landed, on finding that the market-people were clad in European apparel, though with the odd fancy which is remarkable among Indians, who have any intercourse with Europeans, none of them were dressed in a complete suit of clothes. One wore a hat only, with a Manchester cotton tied round his waist, another a shirt, another a jacket, etc. As all natives, with the exception of kings, are forbidden by law to wear trousers, a common pocket handkerchief was generally substituted for that article of dress. The multitude formed the most motley group we have ever seen; nothing on earth could be more grotesque or ridiculous. Many of the men had a smattering of the English and French tongues.

235

'The object for which we had stopped at the market having been effected to our satisfaction, we pulled out again into the main body of the river, and here we saw several canoes of amazing size coming towards us from the southward. Totally unsuspicious of danger of any kind from this quarter, astonishment at such a sight was the only emotion that entered my mind; and we resolved to pass in the midst of these canoes, that we might more conveniently look on each side of us, for the purpose of ascertaining whether they contained anything belonging to us. At the next moment, another *squadron* of the same description of vessels came in sight, in one of which I could discover my brother by his white shirt, and I fancied that he was returning to demand restitution of the animals of which he had been plundered, therefore I still felt perfectly easy in my mind.

'When we drew nearer, it was apparent that these were all war-canoes, of prodigious dimensions; immense flags of various colours were displayed in them, a six-pounder was lashed to the bow of each; and they were filled with women, and children, and armed men, whose weapons were in their hands. Such was their size, that each of them was paddled by nearly forty people. In pursuance of our arrangements we passed through the midst of them, but could see nothing; and we had advanced a few yards, when on looking behind us, we discovered that the war-canoes had been turned round, and were swiftly pursuing us. Appearances were hostile; the apprehension of danger suddenly flashed across my mind; we endeavoured and struggled hard to escape; but fear had taken possession of the minds of my companions, and as they were unable to exert themselves we did not get on; all was in vain. Our canoe was overtaken in a moment, and nearly sent under water by the violence with which the pursuer dashed against her; a second crash threw two or three of the Damuggoo people overboard, and by the shock of the third she capsized and sunk. All this seemed the work of enchantment, so quickly did events succeed each other; yet, in this interval, a couple of ill-looking fellows had jumped into our canoe, and in the confusion which prevailed, began emptying it of its contents with astonishing celerity.

'On finding myself in the water, my first care was, very naturally, to get out again; and therefore looking round on a hundred ruffians, in whose countenances I could discern not a single trace of gentleness or pity, I swam to a large canoe, apart from the others, in which I observed two females, and some little ones—for in their breasts, thought I, compassion and tenderness must surely dwell. Perceiving

236

my design, a sturdy man of gigantic stature, such as little children dream of, black as a coal, and with a most hideous countenance, suddenly sprang towards me, and stooping down, he laid hold of my arm, and snatched me with a violent jerk out of the water, letting me fall like a log into the canoe, without speaking a word.

'I soon discovered, and sat up with my companions, the women and children, and discovered them wiping tears from their faces. In momentary expectation of a barbarous and painful death, "for what else," said I to myself, "can all this lead to?" the scene around me produced little impression on my mind; my thoughts were wandering far away, and this day I thought was to be my last. I was meditating in this manner, heedless of all that was going on around me, and reckless of what came next, when I looked up and saw my brother at a little distance, gazing steadfastly upon me; when he saw that I observed him, he held up his arm with a sorrowful look, and pointed his finger to the skies. O! how distinctly and eloquently were all the emotions of his soul at that moment depicted in his countenance! Who could not understand him? He would have said, "Trust in God!" I was touched with grief. Thoughts of home and friends rushed upon my mind, and almost overpowered me. My heart hovered over the scenes of infancy and boyhood. O how vividly did early impressions return to my soul! But such feelings could be indulged only for a moment. Recollecting myself, I bade them, as I thought, an everlasting adieu; and weaning my heart and thoughts from all worldly associations, with fervour I invoked the God of my life, before whose awful throne I imagined we should shortly appear, for fortitude and consolation in the hour of trial. My heart became subdued and softened; my mind regained its serenity and composure; and though there was nothing but tumult and distraction without, within all was tranquillity and resignation.

'On account of the eagerness and anxiety with which every one endeavoured to get near us in order to share the expected plunder, and the confusion which prevailed in consequence, many of the war-canoes clashed against each other with such violence, that three or four of them were upset at one time, and the scene which ensued baffles all description. Men, women, and children, clinging to their floating property, were struggling in the river, and screaming and crying out as loud as they were able, to be saved from drowning. Those that were more fortunate, were beating their countrymen off from getting into their canoes, by striking their heads and hands with paddles, as they laid hold of the sides and nearly upset them. When the noise and disorder had in some measure ceased, my brother's canoe and that which I was in were by the side of each other, and he instantly took his shirt from his back, and threw it over me, for I was naked. I then stepped into his canoe; for whatever might be our fate, it would be a mournful kind of pleasure to comfort and console one another in the hour of trial and suffering. But I had no sooner done so, than I was dragged back again by a powerful arm, which I could not resist, and commanded by furious gestures to sit still on my peril.

'Unwilling to aggravate our condition by obstinacy or bravado, which would have been vain and ridiculous, I made no reply, but did as I was desired, and silently watched the motions of our keepers. Now there were still other canoes passing by on their way to the market-place, and amongst them was one of extraordinary size. Fancying it to be neutral, and hoping to make a diversion in our favour, I beckoned to those who were in it, and saluted them in the most friendly manner. But their savage bosoms were impenetrable to feeling. Surely they are destitute of all the amiable charities of life. I almost doubted whether they were human beings. Their hideous features were darkened by a terrible scowl; they mocked me, clapped their hands, and thumped upon a sullen drum; then with a loud and scornful laugh, the barbarians dashed their paddles into the water and went their way. This was a severe mortification; I felt confused and abashed; and my heart seemed to shrink within me. I made no more such trials.'

Seeing my brother swimming in the river, and people clinging on to what they could, I endeavoured all in my power to induce the people of my canoe to go to him. But all I could do was in vain. My feelings at that moment were not to be described; I saw my brother nearly exhausted, and could render him no assistance, in addition to our luggage being plundered and sunk; and I had just formed the resolution of jumping into the water after him when I saw him picked up.

The canoes near me, as well as mine, hastened to a small sand island in the river, at a short distance from the market, and my brother arrived soon afterwards. In a short time the Damuggoo people made their appearance, and also the chief of Bonny's messenger, having like ourselves lost everything they had of their own property as well as their master's. We were all obliged to remain in our respective canoes, and made rather a sorry appearance in consequence of the treatment we had received.

We had been lying at the island; but now the war-canoes were all formed into a line and paddled into the market-place, before alluded to, which is called *Kirree*,[1] and which likewise was the place of their destination. Here we were informed that a *palaver* would be held, to take the whole affair into consideration; and about ten in the morning, a multitude of men landed from the canoes, to 'hold a council of war', if it may be so termed. For our parts we were not suffered to go on shore; but constrained to remain in the canoes, without a covering for the head, and exposed to the heat of a burning sun. A person in a Mahomedan dress, who we learnt afterwards was a native of a place near Funda, came to us, and endeavoured to cheer us, by saying that our hearts must not be sore—that at the palaver which would be held, we had plenty of friends to speak for us. That all the people in the Mahomedan dresses who had come from Funda to attend the market, were our friends, besides a great number of females, who were well dressed in silk of different colours. These women wore large ivory anklets of about four or five pounds weight, and bracelets of the same material, but not so large. About twenty canoes full of Damuggoo people had arrived from the various towns near Damuggoo. These persons having heard how we had been treated, also became our friends, so that we now began to think there was a chance of our escaping, and this intelligence put us into better spirits.

A short time before noon, the river being pretty clear, several guns were fired as a signal for all the canoes to repair to the market and attend the palaver. Eager to learn the result of the discussion at the assembly, in which we were so intimately concerned, but without the means of gaining any intelligence, we passed the hours in fearful suspense, yielding by turns to the pleasing illusions of hope, and the gloomy forebodings of despair.

The heat of the sun to which we were exposed was excessive, and having no shirt on even to protect my shoulders from the scorching rays, I contrived to borrow an old cloth from one of the canoe-men, who spoke a little English. Some of the market-women came down to our canoe, and looked on us with much concern and pity, spreading their hands out, as much as to say, God has saved you from a cruel death. They then retired, and in a few minutes afterwards returned, bringing with them a bunch of plantains and two cocoa-nuts. This was

[1] The name 'Kirree' will not be found on any modern map, but it is clearly to be identified with Asaba (Baikie, 1856, pp. 52, 436). Today, the important road ferry across the Niger runs from Asaba to Onitsha.

an acceptable offering, and we gladly took it and divided it among our people and ourselves.

A stir was now made in the market, and a search commenced through all the canoes for our goods, some of which were found, although the greater part of them were at the bottom of the river. These were landed and placed in the middle of the market-place. We were now invited by the Mallams to land, and told to look at our goods and see if they were all there. To my great satisfaction, I immediately recognized the box containing our books, and one of my brother's journals. The medicine-chest was by its side, but both were filled with water. A large carpet bag, containing all our wearing apparel, was lying cut open, and deprived of its contents, with the exception of a shirt, a pair of trousers, and a waistcoat. Many valuable articles which it had contained were gone. The whole of my journal, with the exception of a note-book with remarks from Rabba to this place, was lost. Four guns, one of which had been the property of the late Mr Park, four cutlasses, and two pistols were gone. Nine elephant's tusks, the finest I had seen in the country, which had been given us by the Kings of Wowow and Boossa, a quantity of ostrich feathers, some handsome leopard skins, a great variety of seeds, all our buttons, cowries and needles, which were necessary for us to purchase provisions with—all were missing, and said to have been sunk in the river. The two boxes and the bag were all that could be found.

We had been desired to seat ourselves, which, as soon as we had done, a circle gathered round us, and began questioning us; but at that moment the sound of screams and the clashing of arms reached the spot; and the multitude catching fire at the noise, drew their swords, and leaving us to ourselves they ran away to the place whence it proceeded. The poor women were hurrying with their little property towards the river from all directions, and imagining that we ourselves might be trampled under foot, were we to remain longer sitting on the ground, we joined the flying fugitives, and all rushing into the water, sprang into canoes, and pushed off the land, whither our pursuers dared not follow us. The origin of all this was a desire for more plunder on the part of the Eboe people. Seeing the few things of ours in the market-place which had been taken from their canoes, they made a rush to the place to recover them. The natives, who were Kirree people, stood ready for them, armed with swords, daggers, and guns; and the savage Eboes finding themselves foiled in the attempt, retreated to their canoes without risking an attack, although we fully expected to have been spectators of a furious and bloody battle. The noise and uproar which this produced were dreadful, and beyond all description.

This after all was a fortunate circumstance, inasmuch as my brother and I, having unconsciously jumped into the same canoe, found ourselves in each other's company, and were thus afforded, for a short time at least, the pleasure of conversing without interruption.

At about three in the afternoon we were ordered to return to the small island from whence we had come, and the setting of the sun being the signal for the council to dissolve, we were again sent for to the market. The people had been engaged in deliberation and discussion during the whole of the day, and with throbbing hearts we received their resolution in nearly the following words: 'That the king of the country being absent, they had taken upon themselves to consider the occurrence which had taken place in the morning, and to give judgment accordingly. Those of our things which had been saved from the water should be restored to us, and the person that had first commenced the attack on my brother should lose his head, as a just retribution for his offence, having acted without his chief's permission; that with regard to us, we must consider ourselves as prisoners, and consent to be conducted on the following morning to *Obie*, king of the *Eboe* country, before whom we should undergo an examination, and whose will and pleasure concerning our persons would then be explained.' We received the intelligence with feelings of rapture, and with bursting hearts we offered up thanks to our Divine Creator for his signal preservation of us throughout this disastrous day.

It was, perhaps, fortunate for us that we had no article of value which the natives were at all solicitous about; and to this circumstance, added to the envy of those who had joined in the conquest, but who had not shared the plunder, may chiefly be attributed under Providence, the preservation of our lives. Our medicine-chest, and a trunk containing books, etc, which were all spoiled by the water, were subsequently restored to us; but our wearing apparel, Mr Park's double-barrelled gun, the loss of which we particularly regretted, and all our muskets, swords, and pistols, with those of our men, were sunk or missing. We likewise lost the elephant's teeth given us by the kings of Boossa and Wowow, a few natural curiosities, our compass and thermometers, my own journal, my brother's memorandum, note and sketch-books, with a small part of his journal and other books which were open in the canoe, besides all our cowries and needles, so that we are left completely destitute, to the mercy of we know not whom.

The object of the barbarians in coming so far from home was never correctly explained to us; but we have no doubt that it was from motives of plunder, which had our party been larger was to have been carried into effect on an extensive scale. But the capture of two white men supposed to have valuable goods with them, seems to have disconcerted all their plans for the present by producing division and distrust amongst them. However it was apparent to us that all these savage warriors had left their country not only to plunder whatever might happen to fall in their way, but likewise to attend two or three markets near *Kirree*, for the purpose of trading with the natives whenever they might fancy themselves not sufficiently powerful to take away their property without fighting and bloodshed. For this purpose they were amply furnished with various commodities, such as powder, muskets, cutlasses, knives, cotton cloths, earthenware, skins of wild animals, mats, sweet potatoes, cassada root, and a very large kind of straw hat which they would exchange for slaves, ivory, yams, and palm-oil. It was evident also at Kirree that more than one party of these robbers had made several attempts at plunder, and it was equally notorious that they had been many times repulsed. Hence the dreadful screaming at the market, and the state of hurry, tumult, and alarm that prevailed therein during the whole of the day.

In the evening, when everything was quiet, fires were kindled in all the canoes, for dressing provisions, and there being a vast number of them, the Niger was illuminated by streams of yellow light, which produced a highly romantic, but melancholy effect. It was a time fitted for adoration and thanksgiving to the benificent Creator and Monarch of all. But alas! how few hereabouts are bending the knee to him; how few are lifting up their hearts to his mercy-seat!

The Kirree people are a savage-looking race. They are amazingly strong and athletic, and are also well-proportioned. Their only clothing is the skin either of a leopard or tiger fastened round their waist. Their hair is plaited, and plastered with red clay in abundance, and their face is full of incisions in every part of it; these are cut into the flesh so as to produce deep furrows, each incision being about a quarter of an inch long, and dyed with indigo. It is scarcely possible to make out a feature of their face, and I have never seen Indians more disfigured. The Eboe women have handsome features, and we could not help thinking it a pity that such savage-looking fellows as the men should be blessed with so handsome a race of females. The mark of the Eboe people is the point of an arrow pricked in each temple, the end being near to the eye. We are informed that the leading man, who commanded the first canoe that attacked us in the river this morning, is confined in double irons, and condemned to die by the people who are friends at this place. It is said they have taken our treatment up with so much determination to do us justice, that if the king of Eboe, whose subject he is, refuses to put him to death, no more of his canoes will be allowed to come to this country to trade. His wives have been crying round him and making great lamentation.

Eboe canoe.

XIX

Kirree to Eboe Town

November 6th.—My brother felt quite feverish this morning, and I was very unwell, yet we had nothing to eat, nor anything to purchase it with. At sun-rise our canoe was taken from before Kirree market-place, to the little sand-bank or island in the middle of the river, where we waited till nine o'clock for the coming of two war canoes, which it has been resolved should convey us to the Eboe country. A head man from one of them stepped into ours, though as it was we had scarcely room enough to move a limb. The sunken canoe had been got up again; the Damuggoo people had regained their slaves, having lost only cloth and ivory, for which they are told they will be recompensed by the king of the Eboe country on arriving there; so that this circumstance seemed to have revived their hopes a little, and to have inspired them with fresh life and spirits, which one could scarcely expect from individuals who had so recently been half drowned, beaten, and otherwise ill-used. Nevertheless, though our loss far exceeded theirs, we were as cheerful as they. Our minds had been relieved from a painful state of anxiety; we now looked forward to our journey down the river with the most pleasing anticipations; and even in our forlorn condition we profited by the lesson we had received, and rejoiced that our situation was no worse. Our thoughts were once more turned on home; we quickly resumed our former cheerfulness; the freshness of the morning gave us new vigour, and we ardently wished to set out.

At seven in the morning we bade adieu to Kirree, the scene of all our sorrows, accompanied by six large war-canoes, and again took our station with the Damuggoo people. The canoe once more darted along at a great rate, the men, as they applied their whole strength to their paddles, gave us a song of their country, which seemed to animate them to still greater exertion. Our minds were well prepared to enjoy it; and in no part of the country have we listened to a native song with so much pleasure and gratification.

Besides our convoy, we had a *sumpter-canoe* in company, belonging to the Eboe people, from which the others were supplied with dressed provisions. For our own part, we had neither money nor needles, nor indeed anything to purchase a meal; and knowing this to be the case, our sable guardians neglected to take into consideration the state of our stomachs. However, we felt no very strong inclination to join them in their repast, though on one occasion we were invited to do so, for we felt an invincible disgust to it, from the filthy manner in which it had been prepared. Yams were first boiled, and then skinned and mashed into a paste, with the addition of a little water, by hands that were far from clean. As this part of the business requires great personal exertion, the man on whom it devolved perspired very copiously, and the consequences may easily be guessed at. This was the reason for the unconquerable aversion we felt to partake of their food. The natives, however, are not equally squeamish about such trifles, and compassionate our want of taste in not relishing their savoury banquet. With their yams they generally have a little fish, either smoked and dried, or fresh from the stream; but on very particular occasions, instead of fish, a young kid, roasted with its skin and hair, is substituted. In eating, they use the fingers only, and every one dips his hand into the same dish.

At four in the afternoon we halted to purchase yams at a town on the bank of the river, which was nearly hid from our sight amidst the trees and thick underwood. The canoes having reached the bank, five of the canoemen landed well armed, and proceeded to the town. They had been absent an hour, when they again made their appearance, followed by a great many people carrying bundles. They were also accompanied by one old woman, who appeared to be a person of consequence. It appears that the natives in this part of the river are such outrageous and lawless fellows, that they are mistrustful of each other even in the smallest communication, and we had an opportunity of seeing how far this was carried.

The object of our visit was to purchase yams, and our people had succeeded in getting the villagers to bring some down to the canoes. These people, however, had armed themselves either with a gun or sword, as well as our own, and had no women among them, excepting the old one above-mentioned. Having arrived at the bank of the river, the old woman directed all the yams to be placed in a row before our people, and in distinct and separate bundles, and the owners to retire to a short distance, which order was implicitly obeyed. The purchaser now inspected the bundles, and having selected one to his satisfaction, which might contain the finest yams, placed what he considered to be its value by the side of it, consisting of cloth, flints, etc. The old lady looking on all the time, if in her opinion it was sufficient to give, takes up the cloth and gives it to the owner of the bundle, and the purchaser likewise takes away the yams. But on the contrary, if the cloth, or whatever was thus offered by the purchaser, is not considered sufficient by the old woman, she allows it to remain a short time to give him an opportunity of adding something else to his offer. If this were not done, the owner of the yams was directed by the old woman to take them and move them back out of the way, leaving what had been offered for them to be taken away also. All this was carried on without a word passing between the parties, and the purchase of a sufficient number of yams by our people occupied three hours.[1]

This method of trading must have arisen either from the fear of quarrelling, or from not understanding each other's language, which is difficult to suppose; but it seems to have been instituted by mutual agreement, for both parties quite understood how they were to act. This is the first time we have witnessed it.

It was ten at night when we came abreast of a small town, where we stopped. Instead of making the canoes fast to the bank and landing,

---

[1] The 'silent trade', in which neither party came into direct contact with one another, was an African practice of great antiquity. Herodotus describes how the Carthaginians used this method when trading for gold with a people living on the Saharan coast of West Africa (Bovill, 1958, p. 25).

we lay out in the river at a short distance from it, in case of an alarm by strange canoes. It was long since we had tasted food, and we had suffered from hunger the whole day without being able to obtain anything. Soon after we had stopped for the night, our guards gave us each a piece of roasted yam, and our poor people had the good fortune to get some also, being the first they have had since leaving Damug-goo. The roasted yam, washed down with a little water, was to us as joyful a meal as if we had been treated with the most sumptuous fare, and we laid ourselves down in the canoe to sleep in content.

Sunday, November 7th.—At the dawn of day, our canoemen were busily employed in making preparations for departure. We had been unable to get much sleep, from having nothing to protect us from the cold, and the heavy dew, which had wetted us completely through. The morning was calm, and beautifully fine; and the clear, shrill whistle of the cheerful parrot echoed through the woods, breaking the stillness which had prevailed around, as we took a hasty leave of the few villagers who had assembled out of curiosity to see us, and pursued our course down the stream. The banks of the river have altered decidedly within these two days; its course is not so serpentine as it has been; the banks are so low and regular, that not even a simple rising can anywhere be distinguished to break their uniformity; and, for the first time, we have seen the fibrous mangroves interspersed among the other trees of the forest. Indeed they are beginning to present a degree of sameness little different from that which prevails on many parts of the sea-coast. Both banks, however, are pretty thickly inhabited, and villages are scattered every here and there; for though they are embosomed in trees, and invisible from the river, yet their situation might easily be known from the number of their inhabitants which appeared on the beach to trade with the canoemen. Plantains, bananas, and yams, are cultivated by these villagers to an almost incredible extent. They form, in fact, with the addition of the fish which they may happen to catch, their sole support, and the only articles of export. Many of them, though poor and wretched, are mild, and even timorous in their manners, and are said to be honest and upright in their dealings; but others again are bold, cruel, and rapacious, and are dreaded and shunned not only by their neighbours, but also by those whom business may lead this way, unless they go in large, strong, and well-armed parties. Ours was certainly one of this description; yet men were constantly appointed to keep a watchful eye on the bank, when we were compelled to pass it close, by keeping the channel, in order to guard against surprise by an ambuscade. For this purpose, two or three men stood up in the canoe for several hours at a time, with a musket and cutlass in each hand, to intimidate the natives, by convincing them that we were fully prepared for an attack.

At eleven o'clock at night we arrived at a spot which had been chosen as a place of rendezvous for the whole party, and here we slept in our canoes.

November 8th.—Long before sunrise, though it was excessively dark, the canoes were put in motion. It proved to be a dull hazy morning, but at seven o'clock, a.m., the fog had become so dense, that no object, however large, could be distinguished at a greater distance than a few yards. This created considerable confusion; and the men fearing, as they expressed it, to lose themselves, tied one canoe to another, thus forming double canoes, and all proceeded together in close company. We wished to be more particular in our observations of this interesting part of our journey; but were constrained to forego this gratification, on account of the superstitious prejudices of the natives, who were so infatuated as to imagine that we had not only occasioned the fog, but that, if we did not sit or lie down in the canoe (for we had been standing), it would inevitably cause the destruction of the whole party: and the reason which they assigned was, 'that the river had never beheld a white man before', and, therefore, they dreaded the consequences of our rashness and presumption in regarding its water so attentively.

We hung on by the shore till the fog had dispersed, when we were again allowed to see the river. We now found ourselves on an immense body of water, like a lake, having gone a little out of the road, and at the mouth of a very considerable river, flowing to the westward, it being an important branch of the Niger; another branch also ran from hence to the south-east, while our course was in a south-westerly direction on the main body; the whole forming, in fact, *three* rivers of considerable magnitude. The banks were all low and swampy, and completely covered with palm trees.

About mid-day, one of the Eboe men in our canoe exclaimed 'There is my country!' pointing to a clump of very high trees; and after passing a low fertile island, we quickly came to it. Here we observed a few fishing canoes. The town was yet, we were told, a good way down the river. In a short time, however, we came to an extensive morass, intersected by little channels in every direction, and by one of these we got into clear water, and in front of the Eboe town. Here we found hundreds of canoes, some of them even larger than any we had previously met with.[1] They are furnished with sheds and awnings, and afford commodious habitations for a vast number of people, who, constantly reside in them; perhaps one of these canoes, which is made of a single trunk, contains as many as seventy individuals.

The little we could see of the houses with which the shore is interspersed, gave us a very favourable impression of the judgement and cleanliness of the inhabitants of the town. They are neatly built of yellow clay, plastered over, and thatched with palm leaves; yards sprucely fenced are annexed to each of them, in which plantains, bananas, and cocoa-trees grow, exhibiting a pleasing sight, and affording a delightful shade. When we came alongside the large canoes already spoken of, two or three huge brawny fellows, in broken English, asked how we did, in a tone which Stentor might have envied; and the shaking of hands with our powerful friends was really a punishment, on account of the violent squeezes which we were compelled to suffer. The chief of these men calls himself *Gun*, though *Blunderbuss*, or *Thunder*, would have been as appropriate a name; and without solicitation, he informed us that though he was not a great man, yet he was 'a little military king'; that his brother's name was King *Boy*, and his father's King *Forday*, who with 'King *Jacket*', governed all the *Brass* country. But what was infinitely more ridiculous to us than this ridiculous list of kings, was the information he gave us, that, besides a Spanish schooner, an English vessel, called the 'Thomas of Liverpool', was also lying in the *first Brass river*, which Mr Gun said was frequented by Liverpool traders for palm-oil.

Full of joy at this intelligence, we passed on to a little artificial creek, so narrow that our canoes could scarcely be pulled along, and here we were desired to wait till the King's pleasure respecting us should be known. On the return of the messenger, we were drawn, in the canoe, over ooze and mud to a considerable distance, when we got out and walked to a house, similar to those which we have already mentioned as having seen from the river. There was a little verandah supported by wooden columns in front, and on the floor mats had

[1] At this time the town of Aboh, the Landers' 'Eboe Town', was the most important commercial centre on the Lower Niger. It occupied a 'strategic position' at 'the head of the three great outlets of the Niger—the Benin, the Bonny, and the Nun' (Laird and Old-field, 1837, II, p. 104). This position enabled the people of Aboh to exercise 'what amounted to a monopoly of trade up and down the Niger valley' (Dike, 1956, pp. 26-7).

been placed for our accomodation. Indeed its whole appearance was so clean and comfortable, and it likewise had such an appearance of neatness and simplicity about it, differing entirely from anything of the kind which we had seen for a long time, that we were quite pleased with our new abode; and if the countenance of our host had been at all in unison with the agreeableness of his dwelling, we imagined that we could live at ease in it for a few days at least. But it was not so. The harshness of this man's manners corresponded with his sulky, ill-natured face, and deprived us of a good deal of pleasure which we should have enjoyed in reposing at full length on dry, soft mats, after having been cramped up for three days in a small canoe, with slaves and goats, and exposed to the dews by night, and the sun by day.

An hour or two of rest invigorated and refreshed us extremely; and we then received a message from the King, that he was in waiting to see and converse with us. Having little to adjust in regard to our dress, we rose up, and followed the man immediately. Passing near the outskirts of the town, the man conducted us, by paths little frequented, to the outward yard of the palace, before the door of which was placed the statue of a woman in a sitting posture, and made of clay, very rude of course and very ugly. Having crossed the yard, in which we saw nothing remarkable, we entered by a wooden door into another, which was far superior. This formed an oblong square; it was cleanly swept and had a very spruce appearance, and each of its sides was furnished with an excellent portico. Near the doorway we saw, with surprize, a large heavy cannon, lying on the ground. From this enclosure we were led into a third, which, like the former, had its porticos, and in one of them a number of women were employed in manufacturing a kind of cloth of cotton and dried grass, which they wove together. Opposite the entrance, is a low clay platform, about three feet from the ground, which was overlaid with mats of various colours, a large piece of coarsened red cloth covering the whole, and at each of its corners we observed a little squat figure, also of clay; but, whether these were intended to represent males or females, it is impossible to conjecture. Here we were desired to place ourselves, among a crowd of half-dressed, armed men, who were huddled together on the left of the platform, some sitting, and others standing, and awaiting the coming of the Prince. Our friend Gun was with them, and he immediately claimed priority of acquaintance with us. He chatted with amazing volubility, and in less than two minutes he was on the most familiar footing, slapping us with no little force just above the knee, to give weight to his observations, and to rivet our attention to his remarks. Then, while we spoke, he would rest his heavy arms on our shoulders, and laugh aloud at every word we said; look very knowingly, and occasionally apply the palm of his hand to our backs with the most *feeling* energy, as a token of his encouragement and approbation. We wished to answer questions which concerned us nearly, but the only satisfaction which we received, was contained in the expression, 'O yes to be sure!' and this was repeated so often, with an emphasis so peculiar, and with a grin so irresistibly ludicrous, that, in spite of our disappointment, we were vastly entertained with him.

In this manner was the time beguiled, till we heard a door suddenly opened on our right, and the dreaded *Obie*, King of the Eboe country,[1] stood before us! And yet there was nothing so very dreadful in his appearance after all, for he is a sprightly young man, with a mild open countenance, and an eye which indicates quickness, intelligence and good-nature, rather than the ferocity which we had been told he possesses in an eminent degree. He received us with a smile of welcome, and shook hands with infinite cordiality, often complimenting us with the word 'yes!' to which his knowledge of English is confined, and which no doubt he had been tutored to pronounce for the occasion. Several attendants followed their sovereign, most of whom were unarmed, and almost naked, and three little boys were likewise in attendance, whose office it was to fan him when desired.

The dress of the King of the Eboe country somewhat resembles that which is worn, *on state occasions*, by the monarch of Yarriba. Its appearance was altogether *brilliant*; and from the vast profusion of coral ornaments with which he was decorated, Obie might not inappropriately be styled, 'the Coral King', such an idea at all events entered our mind, as we contemplated the monarch, sitting on his throne of clay. His head was graced with a cap, shaped like a sugarloaf, and covered thickly with strings of coral and pieces of broken looking-glass, so as to hide the materials of which it was made; his neck, or rather throat, was encircled with several strings of the same kind of bead, which was fastened so tightly, as in some degree to affect

---

[1] 'Obie' was not a name as the Landers inferred but a title. The title *Obi* is used by the chiefs of Aboh and of Onitsha, both towns in which the ruling dynasty claims to have come from Benin (Meek, 1937, p. 11). The 'Obie's' name was Ossai. In 1841 the *Obi*'s sovereignty was reported to be acknowledged 'for about fifty-five miles along both sides of the river' but his power did not 'extend much beyond the reach of his canoes' (Allen and Thomson, 1848, I, p. 233). He was, therefore, in no way ruler of the entire Ibo people.

his respiration, and to give his throat and cheeks an inflated appearance. In opposition to these were four or five others hanging round his neck and reaching almost to his knees. He wore a short Spanish surtout of red cloth, which fitted close to his person, being much too small. It was ornamented with gold epaulettes, and the front of it was overspread with gold lace, but which, like the cap, was entirely concealed, unless on a close examination, owing to the vast quantity of coral which was fastened to it in strings. Thirteen or fourteen bracelets (for we had the curiosity to count them) decorated each wrist, and to give them full effect, a few inches of the sleeves of the coat had been cut off purposely. The beads were fastened to the wrist with old copper buttons, which formed an odd contrast to them. The King's trousers, composed of the same material as his coat, stuck as closely to the skin as that, and was similarly embroidered, but it reached no further than the middle of his legs, the lower part of it being ornamented like the wrists, and with precisely the same number of strings of beads; besides which, a string of little brass bells encircled each leg above the ankles, but the feet were naked. Thus splendidly clothed, Obie, smiling at whose own magnificence, vain of the admiration which was paid him by his attendants, and flattered without doubt by the presence of white men, who he imagined were struck with amazement at the splendour of his appearance, shook his feet for the bells to tinkle, sat down with the utmost complacency, and looked around him.

Our story was related to the king in full by the Bonny messenger who had accompanied us from Damuggoo; and if we may be allowed to form an opinion, it was a fine piece of savage eloquence. This singular speech lasted, as near as we could guess, two whole hours, and produced a visible effect on all present. As soon as it was over we were invited by Obie to take some refreshment; being in truth extremely hungry at the time, we thankfully accepted the offer, and fish and yams, swimming in oil, were forthwith brought us on English plates, the king retiring in the meanwhile from motives of delicacy.

The oil was the commonest kind used in the lamps of warehouses in England, extremely unpalatable, and emitted so unsavoury a smell that we found it impossible to partake of it, so great was our disgust: Gun was of a different opinion, and declaring it to be the best Liverpool beef fat that he had seen for a long time, he soon made away with it. When Obie returned, a general conversation ensued, and he was engaged in talking promiscuously to those around him till evening, when the 'great palaver', as it is called, was formally prorogued till the morrow.

The people, with whom we had to wait the arrival of the king, pestered us with all manner of questions before he made his appearance. In answer to their interrogations, I told them we had come from a country called Yaoorie, and another called Boossa, where we had been to obtain the books of one of our countrymen who had been killed a long time ago by the people of the latter place. This answer was quickly followed by a question whether he went there in a ship? and I answered, 'No, in a large canoe.' 'Where is the canoe?' they asked; 'He ran it on the rocks,' I replied, 'and broke it.' They did not, however, seem to comprehend me, and imagined that I was speaking of a ship that was lost at sea on the other side of the land. The *little military king* of Brass-town told us that he had come here for the purpose of buying slaves for a Spanish vessel.

November 8th.—Two of our attendants who have accompanied us from Cape Coast Castle, and who, during their lifetime, have spent many years in Ashantee, declare that the buildings of the people here are nowise different from those at Coomassie, the capital of that kingdom, than in their size, which is much smaller. They certainly resemble the houses of the Yarribeans, but they surpass them in neatness, regularity, and cleanliness, and are besides much better secured from the rain. There is not a single round hut in the place. The Eboe people, like most Africans, are extremely indolent, and cultivate yams, Indian corn, and plantains only. They have abundance of goats and fowls, but few sheep are to be seen, and no bullocks. The city, which has no other name than the 'Eboe Country', is situated in an open plain; it is immensely large, contains a vast population, and is the capital of a kingdom of the same name. It has, for a series of years, been the principal slave-mart for native traders from the coast, between the Bonny and Old Calebar rivers; and for the production of its palm-oil it has obtained equal celebrity. Hundreds of men from the rivers mentioned above come up for the purpose of trade, and numbers of them are at present residing in canoes in front of the town. Most of the oil purchased by Englishmen at the Bonny and adjacent rivers, is brought from hence, as are nearly all the slaves which are annually exported from these places by the French, Spaniards and Portuguese.

About noon we were informed that our attendance was required at the king's house, Obie being fully prepared, it was said, to resume the hearing of our case. In less than half an hour, the monarch dressed in every respect as yesterday, entered the yard. His fat, round cheeks, were swelling with good humour, real or assumed, as he shook our hands with a sprightly air, when he instantly sat himself down in his chair to receive the prostrations and addresses of his subjects and others.

The business of the day was entered into with spirit, and a violent altercation soon arose between the Brass and Bonny people, but scarcely any part of the conversation was interpreted to us. Sufficient, however, was explained to put us in a very bad humour; for not-withstanding the opinion we had entertained of the benevolence of the chief, from his pleasing countenance joined to a mild and affable demeanour, we are assured that we shall never leave this country unless ransomed at a high price!

Bonny is now the place of our destination. We have with us a messenger from the present and a son to the late ruler of that state (King *Pepper*), and, as it has already been related, we had engaged some Damuggoo people to accompany and protect us thither. Whilst, on the other hand, we know nothing at all of *Brass*, never having heard the name of such a river in our lives before.

The discussion was violent and stormy, and the council did not break up till a late hour in the afternoon. They came to no decision, but will meet again tomorrow morning.

In the evening Antonio and five other Bonny people came to our hut with tears in their eyes. On asking them what was the matter, 'the chief,' they said, 'is determined to sell you to the Brass people, but we will fight for you and die rather than see you sold.' 'How many of you Bonny people are there?' I asked. 'Only six,' was the reply. 'And can you fight with two hundred Brass people?' I said; 'We can kill some of them,' they answered, 'and your people can assist.' 'We have all been to the chief,' Antonio added, 'crying to him, and telling him that black man cannot sell white man; but he will not listen to us; he said he would sell you to the Brass people.' Our poor canoemen on hearing this began to sob aloud, and continued lamenting their fate nearly all the night. My brother and I felt much hurt at our situation, for we did not expect it would be so bad as this; but we have made our minds up to prepare ourselves for the worst, for it is impossible to foresee the length to which these savages will go. We saw a Funda man at the chief's house, with whom we could have communicated in the Haussa language, but for some reason or other we were not permitted to speak to him.

November 10th.—Being taken very unwell with fever this morning, I was unable to attend the summons to the king's house, and requested my brother to go in my stead. The following is his account of what took place.

'On arriving there this morning, to my infinite surprize I found *King Boy* (Gun's eldest brother), with a number of his attendants already assembled. He was dressed in a style far superior to any of his countrymen, and wore a jacket and waistcoat over a neat shirt of striped cotton, to which was annexed a silk pocket-handkerchief, which extended below the knees. Strings of coral and other beads encircled his neck, and a pretty little crucifix of seed beads hung on his bosom. King Boy introduced himself to me with the air of a person who bestows a favour, rather than soliciting my acquaintance, and indeed his vanity in other respects was infinitely amusing. He would not suffer any one to sit between him and the platform, but squatted himself down nearest the king's seat, which as a mark or honour had previously been assigned to us; and with a volubility scarcely imaginable, he commenced a long narrative of his greatness, power and dignity, in which he excelled all his neighbours. To convince me of his veracity, he produced a pocket-book, containing a great number of recommendatory notes, or "characters", as a domestic would call them, written in the English, French, Spanish and Portuguese languages, and which had been given him by the various European traders who had visited the Brass river. Among others is one from a "James Dow", master of the brig *Susan*, from Liverpool, and dated "*Brass First River, Sept.*—1830," which runs as follows: "Captain Dow states, that he never met with a set of greater scoundrels than the natives generally, and the pilots in particular." These he anathematised as d—— rascals, who had endeavoured to steer his ship among the breakers at the mouth of the river, that they might share the plunder of its wreck. *King Jacket*, who claims the sovereignty of the river, is declared to be a more confirmed knave, if possible, than they, and to have cheated him of a good deal of property. The writer describes *King Forday* as a man rather advanced in years, less fraudulent, but more dilatory. *King Boy*, his son, alone deserved his confidence, for he had not abused it, and possessed more honesty and integrity than either of his countrymen. These are the rulers of the Brass country, and pretty fellows they are, truly. Mr Dow observes further, that the river is extremely unhealthy, and that his first and second mates, three coopers, and five seamen had already died of fever, and that he himself had had several narrow escapes from the same disorder. He concludes by cautioning traders against the treachery of the natives generally, and gives them certain directions concerning the "dreadful bar", at the mouth of the river, on which he had nearly perished. Another of Boy's papers informs us that the writer's name is "Thomas Lake, and that he is master of the brig *Thomas*, of Liverpool", which is now lying in the Brass river.

'This business had been no sooner settled than Obie entered the yard. After the customary salutations, Boy directed the monarch to appeal to me, that he might be satisfied in what estimation he was held by white men. Of course, I said a variety of fine things in his favour, which were received with a very good grace indeed; but that a piece of paper, simply, which could neither hear, speak, nor understand, should impart such information, was a source of astonishment and wonder to Obie and his train, who testified their emotion in no other manner than by looks of silly amazement, and repeated bursts of laughter.

'The king then said, with a serious countenance, "That there was no necessity for further discussion respecting the white men, his mind was already made up on the subject"; and, for the first time, he briefly explained himself to this effect: "That circumstances having thrown us in the way of his subjects, by the laws and usages of the country he was not only entitled to our own persons, but had equal right to those of our attendants; that he should take no further advantage of his good fortune than by exchanging us for as much English goods as would amount in value to twenty slaves. In order to have the matter fairly arranged and settled, he should, of his own accord, prevent our leaving the town, till such time as our countrymen at Brass and Bonny should pay for our ransom, having understood from ourselves that the English at either of these rivers would afford us whatever assistance we might require, with cheerfulness and alacrity. Concerning the goods of which we had been robbed at Kirree, he assured that he would use his utmost exertions to get them restored.'

'This final decision of the king is a bitter stroke for us. Heaven only knows whether the masters of English vessels at Bonny or Brass have the ability or will feel a disposition to ransom us.'

November 11th.—This morning my brother felt himself extremely unwell, but I am rather better. In truth we wonder much that our health, generally speaking, has been so good, when we reflect for a moment on the hardships and privations which we have lately undergone, the perplexities in which we have been entangled, and the difficulties with which we have to contend. After all of them, however, by the blessing and mercy of our God, instead of sorrow and suffering, we have enjoyed a lightness and even levity of spirits, which caused them to make but a feeble and transient impression upon our minds; but Nature, though she make extraordinary efforts for a time, will at last be crushed by repeated disappointments, cares and vexations, unless she be supported by the vigour of health, and encouraged by the excitement of powerful feelings.

During the few days that we have spent in this place, we have been sadly perplexed for want of provisions. Obie has been in the habit of sending us a fowl, or a yam or two every morning; but, as we are ten in number, it makes but a slender meal, and it is barely sufficient to keep us from actual starvation. To stop, if possible, the sullen murmurings of our people, we have been reduced to the painful necessity of begging; but we might as well have addressed our petitions to the stones or trees—we might have spared ourselves the mortification of a refusal. We never experienced a more stinging sense of our own humbleness and imbecility than on such occasions, and never had we greater need of patience and lowliness of spirit. In most African towns and villages we have been regarded as demi-gods, and treated in consequence with universal kindness, civility, and veneration; but here, alas! what a contrast—we are classed with the most degraded and despicable of mankind, and are become slaves in a land of ignorance and barbarism, whose savage natives have treated us with brutality and contempt.

All ranks of people here are passionately fond of palm-wine, and drink of it to excess whenever they have an opportunity, which often occurs, as great quantities of it are produced in the town and its neighbourhood. It is a very general and favourite custom with them, as soon as the sun goes down, to hold large meetings and form parties in the open air or under the branches of trees, to talk over the events of the day, and make merry with this exciting beverage. These assemblies are kept up until after midnight; and as the revellers generally contrive to get inebriated very soon after they sit down to drink, the greatest part of the evening is devoted to wrangling and fighting, instead of convivial intercourse, and occasionally the most fearful noises that it is possible for the mind to conceive. Bloodshed and even murder, it is said, not unfrequently terminate these boisterous and savage entertainments. A meeting of this description is held outside the yard of our residence every evening, and the noise which they make is really terrifying, more especially when the women and young people join in the affray, for a quarrel of some sort is sure to ensue. Their cries, groans, and shrieks of agony, are dreadful, and would lead a stranger to suppose that these dismal and piercing sounds proceeded from individuals about to be butchered, or that they were extorted by the last pangs of anguish and suffering.

Last evening, Obie, in his showy coral dress, came barefooted to our hut, to inspect our books, and examine the contents of our medicine chest. His approach was announced to us by the jingling of the little bells which encircled his feet. He appeared greatly pleased with everything he saw, and looked aghast when informed of the powerful properties of some of the medicines, which ended in a fit of laughter. He expressed a strong desire to have a little, especially the purgatives; and as we treated the sultan of Yaoorie and family, so we treated him. Obie, was evidently fearful of our books, having been informed that they could 'tell all things'; and appeared to shrink with horror at one which was offered him, shaking his head, saying that he must not accept it, for that it was good only for white men, 'whose God was not his God!' The visit was of short duration.

We found King Boy in the inner yard of the king's house again today, and from his significant physiognomy we conjectured that he had something of consequence to communicate. Obie received us with his usual politeness and jocularity; but instantly directed his attention and discourse to King Boy, who maintained an earnest and pretty animated conversation with him for some time.

Shortly after the termination of the palaver, how transported were we to hear the last-mentioned individual explain himself in broken English to this effect: 'In the conversation which I have just had with Obie, I have been induced to offer him the goods which he demands for your ransom, on the faith that they be hereafter repaid me by the master of the brig *Thomas*, which is now lying in the First Brass River, and that the value of fifteen bars or slaves be added thereto in European goods, and likewise a cask of rum, as a remuneration for the hazard and trouble which I shall inevitably incur in transporting you to Brass. If you consent to these conditions, and on these only I consent to redeem you, you will forthwith give me a bill on Captain Lake for the receipt of articles to the value of thirty-five bars, after which you will be at liberty to leave this place, and go along with me, whenever you may think proper, agreeably to the understanding at present existing between Obie and myself.'

This was heavenly news indeed; and we thanked King Boy over and over again for his generosity and nobleness; for we were too much elated at the time to reflect on the exorbitant demands which he had imposed upon us. We immediately gave him a bill on Mr Lake. He wished to send it down to the brig, to know if it was good. This I had expected, so I told him that the *book* would be of no use unless we were sent along with it, and that the Captain would not pay it

King Obie and his wives.

before he had taken us on board the brig, on which he put it into his pocket-book.

Having sent our people on board Boy's canoe, we hurried after them immediately, and embarked at three in the afternoon. And thus terminated four of the most wretched days of our existence. Our own old leaky and shattered canoe we are unable to take with us, as it would detain us very much, from being so heavy to move along; the Damuggoo people will accompany us in their own, and everything is arranged for our departure at an early hour tomorrow.

The Brass canoe is extremely large and heavily laden. It is paddled by forty men and boys, in addition to whom there may be about twenty individuals, or more, including a few slaves and ourselves— so that the number of human beings will amount to at least sixty. Like Obie's war-canoes, it is furnished with a cannon, which is lashed to the bow, a vast number of cutlasses, and a quantity of grape and

other shot, besides powder, flints, etc. It contains a number of large
boxes or chests, which are filled with spirituous liquors, cotton, and
silk goods, earthenware, and other articles of European and other
foreign manufactures; besides abundance of provisions for present
consumption, and two thousand yams for the master of a Spanish
slaver, which is now lying in Brass river. In this canoe three men might
sit with ease abreast of each other. It has been cut out of a solid trunk
of a tree, and draws four feet and a half water, being more than fifty
feet in length. But it is so deeply laden that not above two inches of
the canoe is to be seen above the water's edge. With its present burden,
it would be impossible for her to sail on any river less smooth than the
Niger, and even as it is, when it comes to be paddled, there will be
danger of its being swamped. It is really laughable to reflect that the
canoe is supplied with two immense speaking-trumpets, which, considering the Stentorian lungs of the men of Brass, are entirely superfluous, and that she is commanded by regularly appointed officers,
with sounding titles, in imitation of European vessels, such as captain,
mate, boatswain, coxswain, etc, besides a cook and his minions.

Forest scenery, Niger delta.

XX

Eboe Town to Brass Town

November 12th.—A great tumult arose last night between the natives and the men of Brass, which might have had a serious and fatal termination, if the latter had not taken timely precaution to convey their canoe from the beach into the middle of the stream, whither the natives could not follow them. The natives had flocked down to the water's edge in considerable numbers, armed with muskets, spears, and other offensive weapons, and kept up a dreadful noise, like the howling of wolves, till long after midnight, when the uproar died away. During the night my brother experienced a sharp paroxysm of fever, which left him towards morning very languid and heartless. He was prevented from taking medicine, not only from our exposed situation, but likewise from its awkwardness and unpleasantness, originating from the number of people amongst whom we were literally jammed. King Boy slept on shore with his wife *Addizetta*, who is Obie's favourite daughter, and on her account we waited till between seven and eight o'clock in the morning, when she made her appearance with her husband—who we understand has embraced the present opportunity of making an excursion with her to his native country, to vary her life a little by a change of air and scene, and to introduce her to his other

261

wives and relatives residing at Brass. She has besides expressed a desire
to see white men's ships, and it is partly to gratify her curiosity in this
particular that she is going with us. At half past seven we pushed off
the Eboe shore, and for a little while, with forty paddles dashing up the
silvery foam at the same moment, we glided through the water with
the speed of a dolphin. To us it afforded no small gratification.

About ten in the morning a mess of fish, boiled with yams and plantains, was produced for breakfast. Before eating himself, Boy makes it
a practice of offering a small portion of his food to 'the spirits of the
river', that his voyage may be rendered propitious by conciliating their
good-will. Previous also to his drinking a glass of rum or spirits, he
pours a few drops of it into the water, invoking the protection of those
fanciful beings, by muttering several expressions between his teeth,
the tenor of which, of course, we do not understand. This religious
observance, we are told, is invariably performed whenever the Brass
people have occasion to leave their country by water, or return to it
by the same means; it is called a meat and drink offering, and is celebrated at every meal. A custom very similar to this prevails in Yarriba,
at Badagry, Cape Coast Castle, and along the western coast generally;
the natives of those places never taking a glass of spirits without spilling
a quantity of it on the ground, as a 'fetish'.

We stopped awhile at various little villages during the day to purchase yams, bananas, and cocoa-nuts; and the curiosity of their poor
inhabitants at our appearance was intense. They are chiefly fishermen
or husbandmen, and, notwithstanding our uncouth and remarkable
dress, they behaved to us without rudeness, and even with civility,
so that their inquisitiveness was not disagreeable. The villages that we
passed in the course of the day were very numerous, and distant not
more than two or three miles from each other on the banks of the
river. They were surrounded by more cultivated land than we have
seen this last fortnight; the crops consisting of yams, bananas, plantains, Indian corn, etc, etc, and we have not seen so much since leaving
Kacunda. The banks here seem to be well calculated for the growth of
rice, and every other grain that we have seen in the interior. The villages had a pleasing appearance from the river. The houses seem to be
built of a light-coloured clay, and being thatched with palm branches,
they very much resemble our own cottages. They are of a square
form, with two windows on each side of the door, but have no upper
rooms.

The villagers seem to be equally as distrustful as those above Eboe town, in trading with our people, for the men only came down with their yams and fish, and were armed with guns and swords. The fish they brought us consisted of cat-fish and shrimps, which had been smoked over a wood-fire, and when boiled were very palatable.

November 13th.—No two individuals in the world have greater reason to complain of disturbed slumbers or nightly watching than ourselves. Heretofore this has been occasioned chiefly by exposure to damps, rains, and dews, mosquito attacks, frightful and piercing noises, and over-fatigue, or apprehension and anxiety of mind. But now, in the absence of most of these causes, we are cramped, painfully cramped, for want of room, insomuch that, when we feel drowsy, we find it impossible to place ourselves in a recumbent posture, without having the heavy legs of Mr and Mrs Boy, with their prodigious ornaments of ivory, placed either on our faces or on our breasts. From such a situation it requires almost the strength of a rhinoceros to be freed: it is excessively teasing. Last night we were particularly unfortunate in this respect; and a second attack of fever, which came on me in the evening, rendered my condition lamentable indeed, and truly piteous.

It was not until two o'clock this morning that we arrived at a convenient place for stopping a while, to give the canoemen rest from their labour; and at day-break we launched out again into the river, and paddled down the stream. Without encountering anything remarkable, we passed the day in much the same manner as yesterday. We continued our course down the river until two hours after midnight, when we stopped near a small village on the east side of the river.

Sunday, November 14th—At five in the morning we again resumed our course down the river. In the course of the day we passed several sand-banks in the middle of the river, and our people ran the canoe aground on them purposely, to get into the water and to have a wash. The sun was exceedingly powerful, and they appeared to enjoy the water very much.

At seven in the evening we departed from the main river, and took our course up a small branch towards Brass Town, running in a direction about south-east by east from that which we had left.

At half-past eight in the evening, to our great satisfaction, we found ourselves influenced by the tide. We had previously observed an appearance of foam on the water, which might have been carried up by the flood-tide from the mouth of the river; but now we felt certain of being within its influence. Our track was through a narrow creek arched over by mangroves, so as to form a complete avenue, which in many places was so thick as to be totally impenetrable by the light above.

November 15th.—Through these gloomy and dismal passages we travelled during the whole of last night, without stopping, unless for a few minutes at a time, to disengage ourselves from the pendent shoots of the mangrove and spreading brambles, in which we occasionally became entangled. These luxuriant natives of the soil are so intricately woven, that it would be next to impossible to eradicate them. Their roots and branches are the receptacles of ooze, mud, and filth of all kinds, exhaling a peculiarly offensive odour, which no doubt possesses highly deleterious qualities. The reason adduced for not resting during the night, was the apprehension entertained by King Boy of being unable to overtake his father and brothers this morning, they having left the Eboe country the day before us. A certain spot had previously been fixed on by the parties for the meeting, and we arrived there about nine o'clock a.m., and found those individuals in three large canoes, with their attendants, waiting our arrival. Here we were introduced to the renowned King Forday, who, according to his account, is monarch of the whole country.

King Forday is a complacent venerable-looking old man, but was rather shabbily dressed, partly in the European, and partly in the native style. Like most savages, his fondess for spirituous liquors is extreme, and he drank large potations of rum in our presence, though it produced no visible effect either upon his manners or conversation.

Breakfast being over, the fetish priests commenced their avocations by marking the person of King Boy from head to foot with chalk, in lines, circles, and a variety of fantastic figures, which so completely metamorphosed him as to render his identity rather questionable, at the distance of only a few yards. His usual dress had been thrown aside, and he was allowed to wear nothing but a narrow silk handkerchief tied round his waist; on his head a little close cap was placed, made of grass and ornamented with large feathers. These we found were the wing feathers of a black and white buzzard, which is the fetish bird of Brass-town. Two huge spears were also chalked and put into his hands, and thus equipped his appearance was wild and grotesque in the extreme. The same operation was performed on the rest of the party, and the fetish priests were chalked in the same manner. Our own people were merely marked in the forehead, and ourselves, perhaps from being already white, though our faces were not a little tanned, were exempted from the ceremony.

At eleven a.m., we were ordered into King Forday's canoe to sit down with him. The old man asked us immediately in tolerably good English to take a glass of rum with him, and having seen us wondering at the strange appearance of King Boy and the rest of the party, gave us to understand that in consequence of no man having come down the river as we had, it was done to prevent anything bad happening to them.[1] We also understood from him that a certain rite would be performed to Dju-Dju, the fetish or domestic god of Brass-town, in honour of our coming. The tide was now fast returning, and preparations were made for proceeding to Brass-town. For this purpose the canoes were all arranged in a line, that of King Boy taking the lead, ourselves and King Forday in the next, followed by King Boy's brother, Mr Gun and the Damuggoo people in others, and in this order we proceeded up the river.

The whole procession formed one of the most extraordinary sights that can be imagined. The canoes were following each other up the river in tolerable order, each of them displaying three flags. In the first was King Boy, standing erect and conspicuous, his headdress of feathers waving with the movements of his body, which had been chalked in various fantastic figures, rendered more distinct by its natural colour; his hands were resting on the barbs of two immense spears, which at intervals he darted violently into the bottom of the canoe, as if he were in the act of killing some formidable wild animal under his feet. Under the bows of all the other canoes fetish priests were dancing and performing various extraordinary antics, their persons, as well as those of the people in them, being chalked over in the same manner as that of King Boy; and to crown the whole, Mr Gun, the little military gentleman, was most actively employed, his canoe now darting before and now dropping behind the rest, adding not a little to the imposing effect of the whole scene by the repeated discharges of his cannon.

In this manner we continued on till about noon, when we entered a little bay, and saw before us, on the south side of it, two distinct groups of buildings, one of which is King Forday's town, and the

[1] The people of the Niger delta still believe in the existence of a great variety of water spirits. For an account of their beliefs see Talbot, 1932, pp. 32–62. Talbot was told by one of his informants: 'All nations make juju when anything remarkable is seen in the river; for it is thought that the sight may be of one or other of the genii become visible to our eyes' (p. 34).

other King Jacket's town. The cannons in all the canoes were now fired off, and the whole of the people were quickly on the look out to witness our approach. The firing having ceased, the greatest stillness prevailed, and the canoes moved forward very slowly between the two towns to a small island a little to the east of Jacket's town. This island is the abode of the Dju-Dju, or grand fetish priest, and his wives, no one else being permitted to reside there. The canoes stopped near the fetish hut on the island, which is a low insignificant building of clay. The priest, who was chalked over nearly in the same manner as Boy, drew near to the water's edge, and with a peculiar air asked some questions, which appeared to be answered to his satisfaction. Boy then landed, and, preceded by the tall figure of the priest, entered the religious hut. Soon after this the priest came to the water-side, and, looking on us with much earnestness, broke an egg, and poured some liquid into the water, after which he again returned to the hut. The Brass men then rushed on a sudden into the water and returned in the same hasty manner, which appeared to us equally as mysterious as the rest of the ceremony.

After remaining at the island about an hour, during which time Boy was in the hut with the priest, he rejoined us, and we proceeded to Forday's town and took up our residence at Boy's house. In the extraordinary ceremony which we had just witnessed, it was evident that we were the persons principally concerned.

We saw with emotions of joy a white man on the shore whilst we were in the canoe, waiting the conclusion of the ceremony. It was a cheering and goodly sight to recognize the features of an European in the midst of a crowd of savages. This individual paid us a visit in the evening; his behaviour with perfectly affable, courteous, and obliging, and in the course of a conversation which we had with him, he informed us that he is master of the Spanish schooner which is at present lying in the Brass river for slaves. Six of her crew, who have been ill of fever, and are still indisposed, likewise reside in the town.

November 16th.—Of all the wretched, filthy, and contemptible places in this world of ours, none can present to the eye of a stranger so miserable an appearance, or can offer such disgusting and loathsome sights, as this abominable Brass town. Dogs, goats, and other animals, run about the dirty streets, half-starved, whose hungry looks can only be exceeded by the famishing appearance of the men, women, and children, which bespeaks the penury and wretchedness to which they are reduced; whilst the persons of many of them are covered with odious boils, and their huts are falling to the ground from neglect and decay.

Brass, properly speaking, consists of two towns, of nearly equal size, containing about a thousand inhabitants each, and built on the borders of a kind of basin, which is formed by a number of rivulets, entering it from the Niger through forests of mangrove bushes. One of them is under the domination of a noted scoundrel called *King Jacket*; and the other is governed by a rival chief, named *King Forday*. These towns are situated directly opposite each other, and within the distance of eighty yards; and are built on a marshy ground which occasions the huts to be always wet. Another place, called 'Pilot's town' by Europeans, from the number of pilots that reside in it, is situated nearly at the mouth of the First Brass River (which we understand is the '*Nun*' river of Europeans), and at the distance of sixty or seventy miles from hence. This town acknowledges the authority of both kings, having been originally peopled by settlers from each of their towns. At the ebb of the tide, the basin is left perfectly dry, with the exception of small gutters, and presents a smooth, and almost unvaried surface of black mud, which emits an intolerable odour, owing to the decomposition of vegetable substances, and the quantity of filth and nastiness which is thrown into the basin by the inhabitants of both towns. Notwithstanding this nuisance, both children and grown-up persons may be seen sporting in the mud, whenever the tide goes out, all naked, and amusing themselves in the same manner as if they were on shore.

The Brass people grow neither yams nor bananas, nor grain of any kind, cultivating only the plantain as an article of food, which, with the addition of a little fish, forms their principal article of diet. Yams, however, are freely imported from Eboe and other countries by the chief people, who re-sell great quantities of them to the shipping that may happen to be in the river. They are enabled to do this by the very considerable profits which accrue to them from their trading transactions with people residing further inland, and from the palm oil which they themselves manufacture, and which they dispose of to the Liverpool traders. The soil in the vicinity of Brass is for the most part poor and marshy, though it is covered with a rank, luxuriant, and impenetrable vegetation: even in the hands of an active, industrious race, it would offer almost insuperable obstacles to general cultivation; but with its present possessors the mangrove itself can never be extirpated, and the country will, it is likely enough, maintain its present appearance till the end of time.

The dwelling in which we reside belongs to King Boy; it stands on the extreme edge of the basin, and was constructed not long since by a carpenter, who came up the river for the purpose from Calebar, of which place he is a native; he received seven slaves for his labour. The man must have seen European dwellings, as this is evidently an attempt to imitate them. Its form is oblong, and it contains four apartments, which are all on the ground floor, lined with wood, and furnished with tolerably made doors and cupboards. This wood bears decided marks of its having once formed part of a vessel, and is most likely the remains of one which was wrecked, we hear, not long ago, on the bar of the river. The house has recently been converted into a kind of seraglio by King Boy, because he has, to use his own expression, 'plenty of wives', who require looking after. It also answers the purpose of a storehouse for European goods, tobacco, and spirituous liquors. Its rafters are of bamboo and its thatch of palm-leaves. The apartment which we occupy has a window overlooking the basin, outside which is a veranda, at present occupied by Paskoe and his wives. The whole of its furniture consists of an old oaken table; but it is supplied with seats made of clay. These, together with the floor, which is of mud, are so soft and wet, as to enable a person to thrust his hand into any part of them, without any difficulty whatever. One of the sides of the room is decorated with an old French print representing the Virgin Mary, with a great number of chubby-faced angels ministering to her, at whose feet is a prayer on 'Our Lady's good deliverance'. The whole group is designed and executed in very bad taste.

There are several huts opposite the town where the people make salt, after the rains are over: the water at present is brackish, from the effect of the rains; but in the course of two months, Boy tells us, that it will be quite salt, when they will again commence making it. It is an article of trade, and appears to be taken in large quantities to the Eboe market, where it is exchanged for yams, the cowrie shell not being circulated lower down the river than Bocqua.

Today I was requested to visit King Forday, and I accordingly complied with the summons. His house is about a hundred yards distant from that of King Boy, and on entering it I found him sitting half drunk, with about a dozen of his wives and a number of dogs, in a small filthy room. I was desired to sit down by his side, and to drink a glass of rum. He then gave me to understand, as well as he could, that it was customary for every white man who came to the river, to pay him four bars. I expressed my ignorance and surprise at this, but was soon silenced by his saying, 'that is my demand, and I shall not allow you to leave this town, until you have given me a *book* for that amount'. Seeing that I had nothing to do but comply with his demand, I gave him a bill on Lake, the commander of the English vessel, after which he said, 'Tomorrow you may go to the brig, take one servant with you; but your mate (meaning my brother) must remain here with your seven people, until my son, King Boy, shall bring the goods for himself and me; after this they shall be sent on board without delay.' Much as I regretted the necessity of parting with my brother, I was obliged to agree to this arrangement, and with the hopes of profiting by it, I told King Forday that we were all very hungry, and begged him to send us a fowl or two, which he promised to do.

It is now six in the evening, and the mean old king has sent us neither fowls nor yams. This is the most starving place that I have yet seen. Mr Gun has given us two meals since our arrival here, consisting of a little pounded yam, and fish stewed in palm oil, and for this he has the impudence to demand two muskets in payment. These fellows, like the rest on the coast, are a set of imposing rascals, little better than downright savages. We are told that they have absolutely starved three white men to death lately, who were wrecked in a slaving vessel, when crossing the bar.

A village in the Niger delta.

XXI

Brass Town to London

November 17th.—I had determined that one of our men should accompany me down the river; and at ten o'clock, having taken leave of my brother and the rest of our party, we embarked in King Boy's canoe, with a light heart and an anxious mind. Although distant about sixty miles from the mouth of the river, our journey appeared to me already completed, and all our troubles and difficulties I considered at an end. Already, in fond anticipation I was on board the brig, and had found a welcome reception from her commander—had related to him all the hardships and dangers we had undergone, and had been listened to with commiseration—already had I assured myself of his doing all he could to enable me to fulfil my engagements with these people, and thought ourselves happy in finding a vessel belonging to our own country in the river at the time of our arrival. These meditations and a train of others, about home and friends to which they naturally led, occupied my mind, as our canoe passed through the narrow creeks, sometimes wandering under avenues of mangrove-trees, and at others expanding into small lakes occasioned by the overflowing of the river. The captain of the canoe, a tall sturdy fellow, was standing up, directing its course, occasionally hallooing, as we came to a turn in the creek, to the fetish, and where an echo was returned, half a glass of rum, and a piece of yam and fish, were thrown into the water. I had never seen this done before; and on asking Boy the reason why he was throwing away the provisions thus, he asked, 'Did you not hear the fetish?' The captain of the canoe replied, 'Yes.' 'That is for the fetish,' said Boy; 'if we do not feed him, and do good for him, he will kill us, or make us poor and sick.' I could not help smiling at the ignorance of the poor creatures, but such is their firm belief.

At seven in the evening, we arrived in the Second Brass River, which is a large branch of the Quorra. We kept our course down it about due south, and half an hour afterwards, I heard the welcome sound of the surf on the beach. At a quarter before eight in the evening, we made our canoe fast to a tree for the night.

November 18th.—At five in the morning, we let go the rope from the tree, and took our course in a westerly direction up a creek. At seven we arrived in the main branch of the Quorra, which is called the river Nun, or the First Brass River, having entered it opposite to a large branch, which King Boy informed me runs to Benin.

About a quarter of an hour after we had entered the river Nun, we descried, at a distance before us, two vessels lying at anchor. The emotion of delight which the sight of them occasioned are quite beyond my powers of description. The nearest to us was a schooner, a Spanish slave-vessel, whose captain we had seen at Brass-town. Our canoe was quickly by her side, and I went on board. The captain received me very kindly, and invited me to take some spirits and water with him. He complained sadly of the sickly state of the crews, asserting that the river was extremely unhealthy, and that he had only been in it six weeks, in which time he had lost as many men. The remainder of his crew, consisting of thirty persons, were in such a reduced state, that they were scarcely able to move, and were lying about his decks more resembling skeletons than living persons. I could do no good here, so I took my leave of the captain, and returned into the canoe.

We now directed our course to the English brig, which was lying about three hundred yards lower down the river. Having reached her, with feelings of delight mingled with doubt, I went on board. Here I found everything in as sad a condition as I had on the schooner; four of the crew had just died of fever; four more, which completed the whole, were lying sick in their hammocks, and the captain appeared to be in the very last stage of illness. He had recovered from a severe attack of fever, and had suffered a relapse in consequence of having exposed himself too soon, which had nearly been fatal to him. I now stated to him who I was, explained my situation to him as fully as I could, and had my instructions read to him by one of his own people, that he might see I was not imposing on him. I then requested that he would redeem us by paying what had been demanded by King Boy, and assured him that whatever he might give to him on our account, would certainly be repaid him by the British government. To my utter surprise and consternation, he flatly refused to give a single thing, and ill and weak as he was, made us of the most offensive and shameful oaths I ever heard. 'If you think,' said he, 'that you have a —— fool to deal with, you are mistaken; I'll not give a b——y flint for your bill, I would not give a —— for it.' Petrified with amazement, and horror-struck at such conduct, I shrunk from him with terror. I could scarcely believe what I had heard, till my ears were assailed by a repetition of the same. Disappointed beyond measure by such brutal conduct from one of my own countrymen, I could not have believed it possible, my feelings totally overpowered me, and I was ready to sink with grief and shame. I returned to the canoe, undetermined how to act, or what course to pursue. Never in my life did I feel such humiliation as at this moment.

As there were no hopes that the captain of this vessel would pay any thing for us, I went on board again, and told King Boy that he must take us to Bonny, as plenty of English ships were there. 'No, no,' said he, 'dis captain no pay, Bonny captain no pay, I won't take you any further.' As this would not do, I again had recourse to the captain, and implored him to do something for me, telling him that if he would let me have only ten muskets, Boy might be content with them, when he found that he could get nothing else. The only reply I received was, 'I have told you already I will not let you have even a flint, so bother me no more.' 'But I have a brother and eight people at Brass-town,' I said to him; 'and if you do not intend to pay King Boy, at least persuade him to bring them here, or else he will poison or starve my brother before I can get any assistance from a man of war, and sell all my people.' The only answer I received was, 'If you can get them on board, I will take them away, but as I have told you before, you do not get a flint from me.' I then endeavoured to persuade Boy to go back for my people, and that he should be paid some time or other. 'Yes,' said the captain, 'make haste and bring them.' Boy very naturally required some of his goods before he went, and it was with no small difficulty I prevailed on him afterwards to go without them.

The captain of the brig now inquired what men I had; and on my telling him that I had two seamen, and three others, who might be useful to him in working his vessel, his tone and manner towards me softened a little. He agreed with me that they might be useful in getting the brig out of the river, as half of his crew were dead, and the other half sick, so I took courage and asked him for a piece of beef to send to my brother, and a small quantity of rum which he readily gave me. King Boy was now ready to depart, not a little discontented, and I sent my man into his canoe with the few things I had been able to obtain, and a note for my brother. I desired him to give Antonio an order on any English captain that he might find at Bonny, for his wages, and also one for the Damuggoo people, that they might receive the small present I had promised to their good old chief, who had treated us so well. At two in the afternoon King Boy left me, promising to return with my brother and people in three days, but grumbling at not having been paid his goods.

November 19th.—This morning Captain Lake seemed to be much better, and I ventured to ask him for a change of linen, of which I was in great want. He readily complied with my request, and I enjoyed a luxury which I had not experienced a long time. In the course of the morning I conversed with him about our travels in the country. Having laid all before him, as fully as I was able, and pointed out to him the bad opinion Boy would have of us, and the injurious tendency towards Englishmen in general that would result from not keeping our word with him, which it was in his power to enable us to do, I asked him to give me ten muskets for my bill on government. He had listened to my story with attention, but I no sooner advanced my wants, than, with a furious oath, he repeated his refusal, and finding him as determined as ever he had been, I mentioned it no more. He moreover told me, in the most unkind and petulant manner, 'If your brother and people are not here in three days, I go without them.'

In the middle of the day, the pilot, who had brought the vessel into the river, came on board and demanded payment for it. The pilot had no sooner made his business known than Lake flew into a violent rage, cursing him and abusing him in the most disgusting language he could use; he refused to pay him anything whatever, and ordered him to go out of the ship immediately. The pilot reluctantly went away, threatening that he would sink his vessel if he offered to leave the river without paying him his due. I was rather surprised to hear such language from the pilot, and doubted his meaning, till I found that he had a battery of seven brass guns at the town on the eastern side of the river near its entrance, which, if well managed, might soon produce that effect. This town is named Pilot's-town.

November 20th.—In the afternoon, the chief mate and three Kroomen were sent away by his direction to sound the bar of the river, in order to know whether there was sufficient depth of water for the vessel to pass over it. The pilot, who had been dismissed so peremptorily yesterday, was determined to have his revenge, and being naturally on the look out, had observed the movements of the boat. So favourable an opportunity was not to be lost; and accordingly, watching her, he despatched an armed canoe, and intercepted her return at the mouth of the river. The mate of the brig and one of the Kroomen were quickly made prisoners and conveyed to the Pilot's-town, and the boat with the remainder sent back with a message to the captain, that they would not be given up until the pilotage should be paid. Lake must have felt annoyed at this; but whether he did or not, he treated it with the greatest indifference, saying that he did not care, he would go to sea without his mate or the Krooman either, and that he was determined not to pay the pilotage.

Sunday, November 21st.—Nothing remarkable occurred today.

November 22nd.—My anxiety for brother's safety made me very unhappy, and I was on the look out the whole day for him and our men. Lake, observing the distress I was in, told me not to trouble myself any more about them; adding, that he was sure he was dead, and that I need not expect to see him alive again. 'If he had been alive,' said Lake, 'he would have been here by this time; tomorrow morning I shall leave the river.'

November 23rd.—This morning, to my great joy and to the mortification of Lake, the sea breeze was so strong that it raised a considerable surf on the bar and prevented us from getting out. This was an anxious time, and the whole of the day my eyes were riveted to the part of the river where I knew my brother must come, without my seeing anything of him. About midnight, I saw several large canoes making their way over to the west bank of the river, in one of which I imagined that I could distinguish my brother. I observed them soon after land, and saw, by the fires which they made, that they had encamped under some mangrove trees. All my fears and apprehensions vanished in an instant, and I was overjoyed with the thoughts of meeting my brother in the morning.

The captain of the brig, having observed them, suddenly exclaimed, 'Now we shall have a little fighting tomorrow; go you and load seventeen muskets and put five buck shot into each. I will take care that the cannon shall be loaded to the muzzle with balls and flints, and if there is any row, I will give them such a scouring as they never had.' He then directed me to place the muskets and cutlasses out of sight, near the stern of the vessel, and said to me, 'The instant that your people come on board, call them aft, and let them stand by the arms. Tell them, if there is any row, to arm themselves directly, and drive all the Brass people overboard.' This was summary work with a vengeance, and everything betokened that Lake was in earnest.

I could not help feeling otherwise than distressed and ashamed of leaving the Brass people in this manner, but I had no alternative.

November 24th.—This morning at day break I was on the look out for my brother, and observed him and the people get into the canoe. They were no sooner embarked than they all landed again, which I could account for in no other way, than by supposing that it was the intention of Boy to keep them on shore until he had received his goods. I was not long in this state of anxiety, for at about seven o'clock they embarked and were brought on board.

My brother's journal, which here follows, contains an account of his proceedings during the time we were absent from each other.

'*November 17th.*—This morning my brother, attended by one of our men, quitted this town with King Boy and suite, leaving the remainder of the party and myself behind, as hostages for the fulfilment of the conditions which we entered into with him in the Eboe country. For myself, though greatly chagrined at this unforeseen arrangement, I could not from my heart altogether condemn the framer of it, for it is quite natural to suppose that a savage should distrust the promises of Europeans, when he himself is at all times guilty of breach of faith and trust, not only in his trading transactions with foreigners, but, likewise in familiar intercourse with his own people.

'*November 18th.*—All our people complaining this evening of hunger, languor, and indisposition.

'*November 19th.*—The man that accompanied my brother to the brig in the river, returned this afternoon without him, and gave me a letter from my brother, [describing his reception by Captain Lake]. Nothing could exceed my regret and consternation on the perusal of this letter; and somehow, I almost dreaded to meet with King Boy. Well knowing how much it would influence his behaviour towards us, we had been careful to represent to that individual the thanks and cheering which he would receive from our countrymen the moment he should take us on board the English brig; that he would be favoured and caressed beyond measure, and receive plenty of beef, bread, and rum. His face used to shine with delight on anticipating so luxurious a treat; and he had uniformly been in a better humour after listening to these promises of ours, than anything else could have made him. The contrast between his actual reception on board the *Thomas*, to that which his own fancy and our repeated assurances had taught him to expect, was too dreadful to think on even a moment.

'The interesting moment at length arrived. We heard King Boy quarrelling with his women, and afterwards walking through their apartments towards ours, muttering as he went along. He entered it, and stood still. I was reposing, as I usually do for the greater part of the day, upon a mat which is placed on the seat of wet clay; but on perceiving him, I lifted my head without arising, and reclined it on my hand. He looked fixedly upon me, and I returned his glance with the same unshrinking steadfastness. But his dark eye was flashing with anger; whilst his upturned lip, which exposed his white teeth, quivered with passion. No face in the world could convey more forcibly to the mind the feeling of contempt and bitter scorn, than the distorted one before me. It was dreadfully expressive. Drawing up the left angle of his mouth on a parallel with his eyes, he broke silence with a sneering, long-drawn "Eh!" and, almost choked with rage, he cursed me; and in a tone and manner, which it is infinitely out of my power to describe, he spoke to the following effect: "You are thief man; English captain no will! You assured me, when I took you from the Eboe country, that he would be overjoyed to see me, and give me plenty of beef and rum; I received from him neither the one nor the other. Eh! English captain no will. I gave a quantity of goods to free you from the slavery of Obie; I took you into my own canoe; you were hungry, and I gave you yam and fish; you were almost naked; I was sorry to see you so, because you were white men and strangers; and I gave each of you a red cap and a silk handkerchief. But you are no good—you are thief man, Eh! English captain no will; he no will. You also told me that your countrymen would do this (taking off his cap and flourishing it in circles over his head), and cry Hurra, hurra, on receiving me on board their vessel; you promised my wife a necklace, and my father four bars. But Eh! English captain no will; he tell me he no will; yes I will satisfy your hunger with plenty more of my fish and yams; and your thirst will I quench with rum and palm-wine. Eh! you thief man, you are no good; English captain no will!" He then stamped on the ground, and gnashing at me with his teeth like a dog, he cursed me again and again.

'The fury of Boy having been somewhat appeased by my silence and submission, as well as by his own extraordinary and violent agitation, I ventured mildly to assure, on the strength of my brother's letter, that his suspicions were entirely groundless; that Mr Lake had certainly a *will* or inclination to enter into arrangements with him for the payment of his just demands; and that when he should convey our people and myself to the *Thomas*, everything would be settled to his complete satisfaction. He half believed, half mistrusted my words; and shortly afterwards quitted the apartment, threatening, however, that we should not leave Brass till it suited his own pleasure and convenience.

'It is really a most humiliating reflection, that we are reduced to the contemptible subterfuges of deceit and falsehood, in order to carry a point, which might so easily have been gained by straightforward integrity. But Lake's conduct has left us no alternative.

'*November 20th.*—King Boy has not visited us today, though we have received the customary allowance of four yams from his women.

'*Sunday, November 21st.*—This morning I dismissed the poor Damuggoo people with a note to the master of either of the English vessels lying in the Bonny river, requesting him to give the bearers three barrels of gunpowder, and a few muskets, on the faith of being paid for the same by his Majesty's government. They left Brass in their own canoe, quite dejected and out of heart; and Antonio went along with them on his return to his country, from which he has been absent two or three years. He is brother to the present, and son of the late king of Bonny.

'*November 22nd.*—Last evening King Boy, stripped to the skin, and having his body most hideously marked, ran about the town like a maniac, with a spear in his hand, calling loudly on his *Dju Dju*; and uttering a wild, frantic cry at every corner. It appears, that one of his father's wives had been strongly suspected of adulterous intercourse with a free man residing in the town; and that this strange means was adopted, in pursuance of an ancient custom, to apprize the inhabitants publicly of the circumstance, and implore the counsel and assistance of the god at the examination of the parties. This morning the male aggressor was found dead, having swallowed poison, it is believed, to avoid a worse kind of death; and the priest declaring his opinion of the guilt of the surviving party, she was immediately sentenced to be drowned. Therefore, this afternoon the ill-fated woman was tied hand

and foot, and conveyed in a canoe to the main body of the river, into which she was thrown without hesitation, a weight of some kind having been fastened to her feet for the purpose of sinking her. She met her death with incredible firmness and resolution.

'It is a kind of holiday here, and most of the Brass people, with their chiefs, are merry with intoxication. As well as I can understand, during the earlier part of the day they were engaged in a solemn religious observance; and since then King Forday has publicly abdicated in favour of Boy, who is his eldest son. I discovered those individuals in a court annexed to the habitation of the former, surrounded by a great number of individuals with bottles, glasses, and decanters at their feet; they were all in a state of drunkenness, more or less; and all had their faces and bodies chalked over in rude and various characters. Forday, alone, sat in a chair; Boy was at his side; and the others, among whom was our friend Gun, and a drummer, were sitting around on blocks of wood, and on the trunk of a fallen tree. The chairman delivered a long oration, but he was too tipsy, and perhaps too full of days, to speak with grace, animation, or power; therefore, his eloquence was not very persuasive, and his nodding hearers, overcome with drowsiness, listened to him with scarcely any attention. I had been sitting amongst the revellers till the speaker had finished his harangue, when I embraced the opportunity, as they were about to separate, of entreating King Boy to hasten our departure for the vessel. He was highly excited and elated with liquor, and, being in an excellent temper, he promised to take us tomorrow.

'*November 23rd.*—It required little time to take leave of the few friends we have at Brass, and we quitted the town not only without regret, but with emotions of peculiar pleasure—King Boy, with three of his women, and his suite, in a large canoe, and our people and myself in a smaller one.

'About nine o'clock in the evening we passed the "*Second Brass River*". From thence we could perceive, in the distance, the long-wished-for Atlantic, with the moon-beams reposing in peaceful beauty upon its surface, and could also hear the sea breaking and roaring over the sandy bar; which stretches across the mouth of the river. The solemn voice of ocean never sounded more melodiously in my ear than it did at that moment; O! it was enchanting as the harp of David. We presently entered the "*First Brass River*", where, at midnight, we could faintly distinguish the masts and rigging of the English brig in the dusky light, which appeared like a dark and ragged cloud above the horizon. To me, however, no sight could be more charming. It was beautiful as the gates of paradise, and my heart fluttered with unspeakable delight, as we landed in silence on the beach opposite the brig, to wait impatiently the dawn of tomorrow.

'*November 24th.*—This was a happy morning, for it restored me to the society of my brother, and of my countrymen. The baneful effects of the climate are strongly impressed upon the countenances of the latter. However, the crew of the Spanish schooner look infinitely more wretched; they are mere shadows or phantoms of men looking round for their burying-place.'

My brother had now joined me, and my station during the time the canoe was coming from the shore to the vessel had been by the cannon; it was the only one on board, but it had been loaded as Lake had directed, and pointed to the gangway of the brig, where the Brass people must come. Lake received my brother civilly, but immediately expressed his determination to dismiss Boy without giving him a single article, and to make the best of his way out of the river. A short time after his arrival, a canoe arrived at the beach with Mr Spittle, the mate of the brig, as prisoner, who immediately sent a note off to the captain, informing him that the price of his liberation was the sum demanded for the pilotage over the bar of the river. He said further, that he was strictly guarded, but that notwithstanding this he did not despair of making his escape if Lake could wait a little for him. The vessel had been brought into the river about three months before, but Lake would never pay the pilotage, and now all he did was to send Mr Spittle a little bread and beef. The amount demanded was about fifty pounds worth of goods, which it was quite out of the question that Lake would ever pay.

Meanwhile King Boy, full of gloomy forebodings, had been lingering about the deck. He had evidently foresight enough to suspect what was to take place, and he appeared troubled and uneasy, and bewildered in thought. The poor fellow was quite an altered person; his habitual haughtiness had entirely foresaken him, and given place to a humble and cringing demeanour.

Knowing how things were likely to terminate, we endeavoured to get Boy into a good humour, by telling him that he should certainly have his goods some time or other; the attempt was a complete failure; the present was the only time in his mind. We really pitied him, and were grieved to think that our promises could not be fulfilled. I rummaged over the few things left us from our disaster at Kirree, and

T   279

found to my surprise five silver bracelets wrapped up in a piece of flannel. I immediately offered these to him, along with a native sword, which being a very great curiosity, we had brought with us from Yarriba. Boy accepted of these, and my brother then offered him his watch, for which he had a great regard, as it was the gift of one of his earliest and best friends. This was refused with disdain, for Boy knew not its value; and calling one of his men to look at what he said we wished to impose on him in lieu of his bars, both of them, with a significant groan, turned away from us with scorn and indignation, nor would they speak to us or even look at us again.

Boy now ventured to approach Captain Lake on the quarter-deck, and with an anxious, petitioning countenance, asked for the goods which had been promised him. Prepared for the desperate game he was about to play, it was the object of Lake to gain as much time as possible, that he might get his vessel under way before he came to an open rupture. Therefore he pretended to be busy in writing, and desired Boy to wait a moment. Becoming impatient with delay, Boy repeated his demand a second and a third time. 'Give me my bars.'— 'I NO WILL!' said Lake in a voice of thunder, which one could hardly have expected from so emaciated a frame as his. 'I no will, I tell you; I won't give you a —— flint. Give me my mate, you black rascal, or I will bring a thousand men of war here in a day or two; they shall come and burn down your towns and kill every one of you; bring me my mate!' Terrified by the demeanour of Lake, and the threats and oaths he had made use of, poor King Boy suddenly retreated, and seeing men going aloft to loosen the sails, apprehensive of being carried off to sea, he quickly disappeared from the deck of the brig, and was soon observed making his way on shore in his canoe, with the rest of his people; this was the last we saw of him. In a few minutes from the time Boy had left the vessel the mate Mr Spittle was sent off in a canoe, so terrified were the Brass people that a man of war would come and put Lake's threats into execution.

At ten in the morning the vessel was got under way, and we dropped down the river. At noon the breeze died away, and we were obliged to let go an anchor to prevent our drifting on the western breakers at the mouth of the river. The rollers, which came into the river over the bar, were so high, that they sometimes passed nearly over the bow of the vessel. We had been obliged to anchor immediately abreast of Pilot's-town, and expected every moment that we should be fired at from their battery. The pilot, whom Lake had offended so much, is known to be a bold and treacherous ruffian. He is the same person who steered the brig *Susan* among the breakers, by which that vessel narrowly escaped destruction. The fellow had done this merely with the hopes of obtaining a part of the wreck as it drifted on shore. Another vessel, a Liverpool oil-trader, was actually lost on the bar by the treachery of the same individual. The treatment of the survivors of this wreck is shocking to relate; they were actually stripped of their clothes and allowed to die of hunger.[1]

Not long after we had dropped the anchor we observed the pilot, with the help of a glass, walking on the beach and watching us occasionally. A multitude of half-naked suspicious-looking fellows were likewise straggling along the shore, while others were seen emerging from a grove of cocoa-trees and the thick bushes near it. These men were all armed, chiefly with muskets, and they subsequently assembled in detached groups to the number of several hundreds, and appeared to be consulting about attacking the vessel. Nothing less than this, and to be fired at from the battery was expected by us; and there is no doubt that the strength and loftiness of the brig only deterred them from so doing.

November 25th.—The vessel rode very uneasily all night, in consequence of the heavy waves which set in from the bar. About eleven, we got under way, but were obliged to anchor again in the afternoon, as the vessel was not deep enough for the vessel to pass over the bar.

November 26th.—The wind favouring us this morning, we made another attempt at getting out of the river. We had already made some progress when the wind again died away, and the current setting us rapidly over to the eastern breakers, we were obliged to let go an anchor to save us from destruction.

The bar extends across the mouth of the river in the form of a crescent, leaving a very narrow and shallow entrance for vessels in the middle which is generally concealed by the surf and foam of the adjacent breakers.

[1] Macgregor Laird, who visited the Nun river in 1832, reckoned that 'the rapidity of the ebb-tide' was the cause of the wrecks at the mouth of the river rather than the wilful behaviour of the pilot. He was not able to find any trace of the battery, to which Lander had referred in his journal for 19 November (Laird and Oldfield, 1837, II, pp. 66–7).

Pilot's Town appears to occupy the same site as Akassa, a place well known in the latter half of the nineteenth century. One English trader described Akassa people as 'qualified to compare with the most degraded of the human race; they have villain, murderer and cannibal stamped across their baboon-like faces' (Whitford, 1877, p. 126).

November 27th.—We passed a restless and most unpleasant night. About eight a.m. a terrific wave struck the vessel with tremendous force and broke the chain cable.

We were riding by the kedge, a small anchor, which, however, was the only one left us, and on which the safety of the brig now depended. The breakers were close under our stern, and this was not expected to hold ten minutes—it was a forlorn hope—every eye was fixed on the raging surf, and our hearts thrilled with agitation, expecting every moment that the vessel would be dashed in pieces. A few long and awful minutes were passed in this state, which have left an indelible impression on our minds. Never shall I forget the chief mate saying to me, 'Now, Sir, every one for himself, a few minutes will be the last with us.' The tumultuous sea was raging in mountainous waves close by, their foam dashing against the sides of the brig, which was only prevented from being carried among them by a weak anchor and cable. The natives, from whom we could expect no favour, were busy on shore making large fires, and other signals, for us to desert the brig and land at certain places, expecting, no doubt, every moment to see her a prey to the waves, and those who escaped their fury to fall into their hands. Wretched resource! the sea would have been far more merciful than they.

Such was our perilous situation, when a fine sea-breeze set in, which literally saved us from destruction. The sails were loosened to relieve the anchor from the strain of the vessel, and she rode out the ebb-tide without drifting. At ten a.m., the tide had nearly ceased running out, and the captain determined on crossing the bar. At half-past ten a.m. he manned the boat with two of our men, and two kroomen belonging to the brig, and sent them to tow, while the anchor was got on board. With the assistance of the boat and good management, we at length passed clear over the bar on the edge of the breakers, in a depth of quarter-less three fathoms, and made sail to the eastward. Our troubles were now at an end; by the protection of a merciful Providence we had escaped dangers, the very thoughts of which had filled us with horror; and with a grateful heart and tears of joy for all his mercies, we offered up a silent prayer of thanks for our deliverance.

This river is by far the best place on the whole coast at which small vessels may procure oil, as it is the shortest distance from the Eboe country, where the best palm-oil is to be had in any quantity. The Eboe oil is pronounced to be superior to that of any other part of the country which is brought to the coast. The river is not much frequented, owing probably to its being unknown, and the difficulty of crossing the bar.

Sunday, November 28th.—Captain Lake agreed to land us in his boat at Fernando Po.[1]

December 1st.—The last two days were employed in making the passage to Fernando Po, and this morning, to our great satisfaction, we discovered the island. We were glad to get out of this vessel, for the unfeeling commander, notwithstanding that our men had rendered him every assistance in getting his brig out of the river, and had done everything required of them, afterwards employed every means he could think of, to annoy us and make us uncomfortable while we were with him. At night, when the people were sleeping, he would make his men draw water and throw it over them for mere amusement. There are many commanders as bad as he is on the coast, who seemed to vie with each other in acts of cruelty and oppression. The captain of the palm-oil brig *Elizabeth*, now in the Calebar river, actually white-washed his crew from head to foot, while they were sick with fever and unable to protect themselves; his cook suffered so much in the

---

[1] As a move in its campaign against the West African slave-trade, the British Government obtained in 1827 permission from the Spanish Government, the owners of the island, to establish a settlement on Fernando Po. The work of founding the settlement was entrusted to a naval officer, Captain Owen, celebrated for his surveys of the African coast and the first to point out the strategic importance of Fernando Po as a base for British warships engaged in anti-slavery patrols. The settlement, started in 1828, developed so rapidly that it soon appeared as a rival to Freetown in Sierra Leone. The British Government failed, however, to persuade the Spanish Government to cede the sovereignty of the island, and in 1833 it was decided to abandon the settlement. The Landers' lengthy account of Fernando Po has been omitted, as the island has been described by many other travellers. On the history of the British settlement see Dike, 1956, pp. 55–9, 65–6.

Owen left Fernando Po in 1829, being succeeded as Superintendent by an army officer, Colonel Nichols. Nichols was on leave in England, when the Landers arrived at Clarence. John Becroft (or Beecroft), the acting Superintendent, had an adventurous career behind and in front of him. Born in 1790 at Whitby in Yorkshire, he had joined the merchant service and been captured by a French privateer in 1805. He spent nine years in French captivity. After his release he returned to the merchant navy and took part in an expedition of Arctic exploration. In 1829 he accompanied Nichols to Fernando Po. He stayed on the island after the British Government's abandonment of the settlement, protected the interests of the Africans who had been attracted to Clarence and became 'in every respect uncrowned King of the island'. Between 1834 and 1849 he made a number of successful expeditions of exploration up the rivers of the coast. In 1849, by which time he had come to possess an influence on the coast such as no white man had ever before obtained, he was appointed the first British Consul to the Bights of Benin and Biafra, a post which he held until his death in 1854 (Dike, 1956, 'John Beecroft, 1790–1854').

In a letter to R. W. Hay at the Colonial Office, written on 7 January, Becroft briefly reported 'the happy arrival of Mr R. Lander and his brother ... after their successful mission into the interior of Africa' (C.O. 82/4, Becroft to Hay, 7 January 1931).

operation, that the lime totally deprived him of the sight of one of his eyes, and rendered the other of little service to him.[1]

In the afternoon we were happily landed at Clarence Cove, in the island of Fernando Po, where we were most kindly received by Mr Becroft, the acting superintendent.

It is more than probable, as we have now ascertained, that a water-communication may be carried on with so extensive a part of the interior of Africa, that a considerable trade will be opened with the country through which we have passed. The natives only require to know what is wanted from them, and to be shown what they will have in return, and much produce that is now lost from neglect, will be turned to a considerable account. The countries situated on the banks of the Niger will become frequented from all the adjacent parts, and this magnificent stream will assume an appearance it has never yet displayed. The first effect of a trade being opened will be to do away with the monopoly near the mouth of the river, which has hitherto been held by the chiefs of the lower countries. Steam-boats will penetrate up the river even as far as Lever, at the time of year in which we came down, and will defy the efforts of these monopolists to arrest their progress. The steam-engine, the grandest invention of the human mind, will be a fit means of conveying civilization among these uninformed Africans, who, incapable of comprehending such a thing will view its arrival among them with astonishment and terror, but will gradually learn to appreciate the benefits they will derive, and to hail its arrival with joy. In this case Fernando Po will become of still greater consequence, and will no doubt become a depot of considerable importance.

December 23rd.—The superintendent, Mr Becroft, invited me to accompany him in the *Portia*, colonial schooner, to the Calebar river, whither he was going to procure stock for the use of the colony. Being tired of Fernando Po, I accepted his invitation. My brother, being very ill, was unable to accompany us.

[1] Writing about the ships that came to purchase palm-oil in the Bight ports, Nichols, the Superintendent of Fernando Po, described 'the people on board' as being 'a very bad set, making use of falsehood and violence in all their transactions' (C.O. 82/7, Nichols to Hay, 31 January 1834). 'Most of the coast traders were among the abandoned desperadoes of their race and aptly nicknamed "palm-oil ruffians". They "were rude, uneducated men, who prided themselves upon coming in at the 'hawse-hole, and going out at the cabin windows'. Acts of wanton cruelty to white men, as well as to Negroes, have been handed down by generations of this fraternity" ' (Dike, 1956, p. 60, quoting Whitford, 1877, p. 288).

December 25th.—We anchored this morning off Ephraim Town, in the Calebar river.[1] On my way up the river, my attention was attracted by something of a very extraordinary appearance hanging over the water from the branch of a tree. My curiosity was excited by it, and I was at a loss to conjecture what it was. I did not remain long in suspense, for we soon passed sufficiently near it to enable me to discover that it was the body of one of the natives suspended by the middle, with the feet and hands just touching the water. So barbarous a sight quickly reminded me that I was again among the poor deluded wretches of the coast, although I had seen nothing so bad as this on my way down to the brig *Thomas*, in the river Nun. The natives of this place are pagans, in the most depraved condition, and know nothing of Mahomedanism, nor any other creed. They believe in a good spirit, who they imagine dwells in the water; and sacrifices such as that just mentioned are frequently made to him, with the idea of gaining his favour and protection. The object selected for this purpose is generally some unfortunate old slave, who may be worn out and incapable of further service, or unfit for the market; and he is thus left to suffer death either from the effects of the sun, or from the fangs of some hungry alligator or shark, which may chance to find the body.

It is usual with ships on their first arrival in the river, to be visited by Duke Ephraim, the chief of the town; a personage who is well known to the numerous Liverpool traders that frequent the river. As soon as we had anchored, I accompanied Mr Becroft on shore, and proceeded with him to the duke's residence, for the purpose of paying our respects to him. A walk of about ten minutes brought us to his house, and we found him in the palaver square which belongs to it, busily engaged in writing, and surrounded by a great number of his principal people. It was something unusual to find a native chief thus employed; but the large dealings which Duke Ephraim appears to

[1] The Efik people had created a number of towns as trading centres in the estuary of the Calebar river. The towns of Calabar were 'in fact a number of small republics, each with its own chief and council, united only by the Egbo confraternity, so far as they have joined it for mutual defence'. '*Egbo* is a secret association, under the patronage of a supernatural being of that name . . . It seems specially designed to keep women and slaves in subjection' (Waddell, 1863, pp. 313–14).

'*Efium*, called by the ships' captains *Duke Ephraim*, was the ruler of *Aqua-akpa* or New Town in the beginning of the century, and from him it came to be known by its present name. Under him it rose to its pre-eminence. He made the ships and persons of white men sacred in the country, under penalty of death, but guarded carefully against them forming settlements ashore, lest they should subjugate it.' Ephraim died in 1834 (Waddell, 1863, pp. 310–11).

have with the Liverpool merchants, accounts in some measure for this accomplishment, and the smattering of English he has obtained. His only pretensions to dress consisted in a smart, gold-laced hat, which he wore, and a handsome piece of silk tied round his loins. Duke Ephraim bears the character of being always very civil and attentive to the English, and of making himself very active in supplying their wants of live stock. He has formed a favourable opinion of them from the *fine things* they bring him, but his discernment goes beyond these; for the circumstance of slave vessels having been captured and taken out of the river by the boats of the English ships of war on the station, has impressed him with admiration of their boldness and courage, and given him a very exalted opinion of their power.

After a short time, we were desired to go up stairs into his best room, and we accordingly ascended about thirty or forty wooden steps, and entered a spacious apartment, when the sight that presented itself was of the most extraordinary description. The room, which was about thirty feet in length, by about twenty in breadth, was literally crammed full of all kinds of European furniture, covered with cobwebs and dust about half an inch deep. Elegant tables and chairs, sofas of a magnificent description, splendid looking-glasses, and prints of the principal public characters of England, as well as views of sea and land engagements, set in handsome gilt frames, beautifully cut glass decanters and glasses, glass chandeliers, and a quantity of other things, too numerous to mention, were all mixed together, in the utmost confusion. A handsome organ attracted our notice, and a large, solid, brass arm-chair, which an inscription on it announced was the present of Sir John Tobin, of Liverpool. Vain enough is the chief of his present. He exhibits this chair with the rest of his presents to the people, or any stranger who may happen to visit him, and allows them to feast their eyes, as he imagines, on the goodly sight; but such is his care and pride of them, that he will not allow them to be touched by any one; and his attendants are not permitted to approach them, even for the purpose of cleaning off the dust which has accumulated since their first arrival. The whole of this miscellaneous assemblage of goods are presents which have been made to the duke by merchants of Liverpool, as well as French, Spanish, and Portuguese traders.

Duke Town, or Ephraim Town, as it is known by both of these appellations, is situated on rather elevated ground, on the east bank of the river. From the appearance of it, I should conclude that its inhabitants amount to at least six thousand people. The duke's house is situated in the middle of the town, and, like the rest is built of clay. It consists of several squares, round each of which is a verandah, similar to the houses in Yarriba. The centre square is occupied by the duke and his wives, the others being the abode of his servants and attendants, which, all together, amount to a considerable number. Immediately opposite to the first square, which forms the entrance to his residence, stands a small tree, profusely decorated with human skulls and bones. The tree is considered by the people as fetish, or sacred; and is supposed to possess the virtue of preventing the evil spirit from entering the duke's residence. Near the tree stands the house which is inhabited by their priests, a class of beings certainly in the most savage condition of nature it is possible to imagine.[1]

Whether it may be with the idea of personifying the evil spirit they are so afraid of, I could not learn, but they go about the town with a human skull fastened over their face, so that they can see through the eye-holes; this is surmounted by a pair of bullock's horns; their body is covered with net, made of stained grass; and, to complete the whole, and give them an appearance as ridiculous behind as they are hideous before, a bullock's tail protrudes through the dress, and hangs down to the ground, rendering them altogether the most uncouth-looking beings imaginable. Sometimes a cocked hat is substituted for the horns, and the skull of a dog or monkey used, which renders their appearance, if possible, still more grotesque. Thus equipped, they are ready to perform the mysteries of their profession, which I had not sufficient opportunity to inquire into, but which are quite enough to enslave the minds of the people.

January 20th.—Since my first return to Fernando Po from the Calebar river, I have accompanied Mr Becroft there twice in the *Portia*. In this interval the *Caernarvon*, an English vessel, has arrived with government stores from England for the establishment, and as she is going to Rio Janeiro for a cargo to take back, and there seems to be no prospect at present of our getting away from this island by any other means, we have requested Mr Becroft to conclude an agreement for our passage to that place. About a week ago the brig *Thomas*, in which we came from the river Nun, touched at the island on her way home

---

[1] 'An object of universal reverence as a household idol was the *Ekpen yong*, a stick surmounted by a human skull, adorned with feathers and daubed with yellow paint.' The priests in their strange attire were the messengers of Egbo. Waddell, who worked in Calabar as a missionary in the 1840s, described the purpose of such a messenger. 'He represented the mysterious being who dwelt in the bush and executed his orders, but in reality was merely the agent of the native nobility' (Waddell, 1863, pp. 329, 258).

from the Cameroons—her commander Lake thinking that we should take a passage with him. We have now been here seven weeks, and would certainly stay seven more rather than put ourselves into his power again. After waiting three days at the island, he sailed about six o'clock in the morning, and had not got more than a mile from the anchorage, when a large vessel with long raking masts suddenly appeared from behind a part of the island, and was seen in pursuit of him. We observed this vessel fire several guns at him, which at length made him take in sail and wait. We have no doubt that this vessel was a pirate, and our suspicions were confirmed the next day by seeing the two vessels lying becalmed close to each other. There were no signs of them on the next day, and we saw nothing more of the *Thomas*.

Everything having been prepared for our departure, we embarked on board of the *Caernarvon*—Garth, commander, for Rio Janeiro. Mr Stockwell, the officer of marines, accompanied us on board. Our crew consists of seven European seamen, two free negroes, and one Krooman, besides the commander of the vessel and two mates.

Sunday, January 23rd.—At noon, Owen Williams, seaman, died.

January 27th.—The fever seems to be making great havoc among us.

Sunday, January 30th.—At two p.m., Wells, the captain's steward died. The crew are lying in different parts of the vessel ill with fever, in a helpless and most distressing condition. A general panic seems to have taken possession of them all.

February 4th.—Captain Garth was taken ill with fever, and John Williams, seaman, died.

Sunday, February 6th.—The chief mate taken ill with fever. So much are we reduced now, that the three black men, with my brother and myself, are all who are left to work the vessel, and only one of these, the Krooman, knows how to steer. Mr Stockwell is constantly employed in attending the sick.

February 7th.—Smith, seaman, died. In consequence of the sick state of the crew I have been constantly employed both day and night in working the ship. In addition to our troubles, the vessel is so completely overrun by rats, that it is quite impossible to stay below with any comfort; and as for sleeping there, it is out of the question.

March 14th.—Off Cape Frio. This evening our only Krooman fell into the sea. To have altered the ship's course would have endangered the masts and sails, and our small boat was so leaky, that it would not swim. We had no alternative, and were obliged to abandon him to his fate with the most painful feelings, and heard his cries nearly an hour afterwards.

March 15th.—We were becalmed all day, and found, by the decrease of the depth, that we were drifting close on towards the shore. Finding that we were drifting fast on the breakers, we made an attempt to get a long-boat out to save ourselves, as we expected the ship would be very soon wrecked, but we found that we could not muster sufficient strength to lift her over the side. At this critical moment, a breeze of wind from the land saved us from destruction, and enabled us to get the vessel under command.

March 16th.—The breeze favoured us, and at two p.m. we anchored in the harbour of Rio Janeiro.

March 17th.—This morning, we went to pay our respects to Admiral Baker, the commander-in-chief on the South American station, and made known to him our situation and anxiety to return to England. The Admiral received us in that kind and hospitable manner, which is a peculiar characteristic of a British seaman: he invited us to his table with his officers, and ordered us a passage in the *William Harris*, a government transport, which is to sail for England in a day or two.

Sunday, March 20th.—We sailed this afternoon for England, in the *William Harris.*

June 9th.—We arrived at Portsmouth after a tedious voyage, and gladly landed with hearts full of gratitude for all our deliverances.

June 10th.—Having left my brother at Portsmouth, I arrived in London this morning by the mail, and reported our discovery to Lord Goderich, his Majesty's Colonial Secretary.

EPILOGUE

The Brothers' Return to England and Richard Lander's Last Expedition

NEWS OF THE LANDERS' ACHIEVEMENT reached England before them, *The Times* publishing, with singular lack of éclat, on 24 May 1831, a letter from a naval surgeon in the Bight of Biafra reporting the discovery of the mouth of the Niger. A few weeks later, on 17 June, *The Times* printed a letter from John Lander to one of his brothers in Cornwall giving news of his arrival at Portsmouth. 'Richard enjoyed his health extremely well,' John wrote, 'but I suffered much from illness, and have been more than once on the borders of the valley of death.' A month later, however, Richard, who was staying in London, fell so 'dangerously ill' that his life was almost despaired of.[1] The paucity of newspaper comment suggests that little attention was paid, on the morrow of their return, to the achievement of these two 'unpretending young men', as one contemporary called them.[2]

But the Landers did not have to wait very long to reap some of the rewards of fame. On 6 July *The Times* wrote, 'We are glad to learn that Mr Murray has given Messrs Lander 1000 guineas for their journal.' John Murray was the most enterprising publisher of his day, with a special interest in works of exploration. His offer must have been accepted by the Landers with a measure of ironic satisfaction. Two years earlier Murray, on the advice of John Barrow, had turned down Richard's account, which John had largely rewritten, of his journey with Clapperton.[3] The Government proved less generous. Richard

---

[1] *The West Briton* (Truro), 15 July 1831, quoted in Rowe, 1952.
[2] Allen and Thomson, 1848, I, p. 18.
[3] Barrow acted as Murray's reader for many works of travel. In his report on Lander's book he criticized its 'deficiencies of style' and 'sins of egotism'; the sketch of the author's

received his bounty of one hundred pounds—a miserly sum compared with the rewards some explorers received—and was found a job in the Customs House at Liverpool. John, having been promised nothing, received 'not even the shadow of a reward' for his services.[1]

Later in the year Richard was honoured by the newly founded Royal Geographical Society and received the Society's first annual premium of fifty guineas. Lord Goderich made the presentation, 'accompanied by a few observations, most gratifying to his feelings'.[2] The following March the two brothers were received in audience by the King, who talked to them for an hour.[3] But it was in Liverpool rather than in London that the Landers found the clearest recognition of the importance of their achievement. Their 'splendid discovery was hailed with, if possible, more enthusiasm by mercantile than by scientific men. The long-sought for highway into Central Africa was at length found. To the merchant it offered a boundless field for enterprise; to the manufacturer, an extensive market for his goods; and to the energy and ardour of youth, it presented the irresistible charm of novelty, danger, and adventure,'[4] So wrote a twenty-three-year-old Liverpool businessman, Macgregor Laird, whose father, William Laird, with whom he had recently entered into partnership, was the founder of a famous firm of shipbuilders.

To young Laird and to other Liverpool merchants Richard Lander gave a glowing account of the 'ivory, indigo and other valuable produce' that might be 'collected in any quantity at a trifling expense'.[5] Convinced by his assurance, the merchants agreed to put up the capital for a company to be called the African Inland Commercial Company.[6] The Company was to finance a trading expedition up the Niger. The expedition was to be led by Richard Lander, with Macgregor Laird as one of the supercargoes and forty-five other Europeans, ship's officers, doctors, and sailors. It was to be transported up the Niger in two small steamships, the *Quorra* and the *Alburkah* (the Hausa word for 'blessing'), the latter vessel having the distinction of being the first sea-going

[1] C.O. 2/19, John Lander to Goderich, 14 April 1832.   [2] *Journal*, I, p. lxi.
[3] *West Briton* (Truro), 23 March 1832; quoted in Rowe, 1952.
[4] Laird and Oldfield, 1837, I, pp. 2–3.   [5] *Ibid.*, p. 4.
[6] The name of the company is given in C.O. 2/19, Forsyth to Hay, 7 April 1832.

life he considered 'utterly unimportant and uninteresting', the Zuma episode was 'in very bad taste', and the whole work was 'deplorably meagre in notices connected with the botany, zoology etc'. Barrow was a very able civil servant, but humourless and full of his own importance. (Barrow's report is in the possession of John Murray, Publishers; I am indebted to Mr J. G. Murray for permission to read it.)

vessel ever to be built of iron. At the confluence of the Niger and the Tshadda a permanent trading station was to be established. From the Government the promoters received no assistance, but a naval officer, Lieutenant William Allen, was attached to the expedition to make a survey of the Niger. To sanctify this commercial speculation, a higher purpose could not unreasonably be invoked. The development of 'legitimate commerce' on the Niger would strike 'a mortal blow to that debasing and demoralizing traffic which has for centuries cursed that unhappy land'. 'Under Providence' the promoters of the expedition 'aspired to become the means of rescuing millions of their fellow-men from the miseries of a religion characterized by violence and blood, by imparting to them the traits of Christianity'.[1]

The expedition left Liverpool in July 1832. On the Gold Coast Lander picked up old Pascoe, Jowdie, and Mina. By the middle of October they had reached the mouth of the Nun river. The debt which Lander had incurred with King Boy had already been paid by another trader, Captain Townson, but Boy received a special reward in various handsome presents sent out by the Government, together with a Highland uniform, complete with kilt, provided by Macgregor Laird's father.[2] In the course of the previous year, Boy had succeeded in obtaining the journal which Richard Lander had lost at Kirree; this he sold to a Captain Townson for an alleged £200. Lander obtained the journal from Townson, but lost it again, presumably in the skirmish of January 1834, before anyone else had seen it.[3]

'King Boy and King Forday,' Lander wrote to Hay at the Colonial Office, 'were very glad to see me again and say I am no man but a devil.'[4] Assured of the Brassmen's support and protected by their own formidable armament, the two steamships began to ascend the river. Before reaching Aboh there was a spot of trouble. One of the ships' boats was fired on. 'We found it necessary to chastise the natives,' Lander wrote, 'and destroyed the town.' No doubt the incident arose from a 'misconception', possibly the villagers were 'regular robbers';[5] nevertheless the incident was an uneasy augury for the future. At Aboh, however, all was joy and welcome. Lander made a splendid entry into the town, 'wearing a general's uniform with a feather in his cocked hat that reached almost to the ground'. Pascoe and Jowdie followed

[1] Laird and Oldfield, 1837, I, pp. 3–4.
[2] C.O. 2/19, Lander to Hay, 26 October 1832; Roose to Hay, 3 June 1833. Laird and Oldfield, 1837, I, p. 71.
[3] Laird and Oldfield, 1837, I, pp. 63, 71.
[4] C.O. 2/19, Lander to Hay, 26 October 1832. [5] *Ibid.*, 9 November 1832.

him, dressed in soldiers' jackets, while Boy provided an escort of fifty canoes. From Obi, who struck Laird as 'the most intelligent black man I have yet met with', they received a most cordial reception; the chief 'displayed towards us the very essence of gentility in the most lively attention to our wants and comforts'. His behaviour and character contrasted strongly with that of the people of the delta, whom Laird regarded as 'thoroughly debased, demoralized and degraded'. This contrast led him to the chastening reflection that 'intercourse between civilized and savage nations has hitherto been productive of anything but good to the latter'.[1]

There was a vast quantity of palm-oil to be purchased at Aboh, but Lander was determined only to start trading higher up the river. So far the journey had been made with little difficulty; after leaving Aboh, things began to go seriously wrong. Lander's leadership came to be disputed by other members of the expedition. 'The officers that were sent out with me,' Lander told Hay, 'were a set of most unruly fellows';[2] later he found cause to complain of the 'scandalous manner' in which he had been treated by Laird.[3] Laird, however, had good reason to suspect Lander's judgment. The river was not easy to navigate, and the *Quorra* became stuck for several weeks near the confluence. The powerful Ata of Igala, on whom Lander paid a ceremonial visit in his capital at Idah, resented the white men's arrival. Although his canoes were not strong enough to attack the steamships, his hostility was always to be feared. Indeed, old Pascoe died on his orders, poisoned, as the Ata himself confessed, by one of his servants.[4] The amount of ivory produced by the natives was disappointingly small. Worst of all, shortly after leaving Aboh, the Europeans were struck by 'the jungle fever'. Within a few weeks half the white men were dead. For a time Lander found himself the only European not incapacitated by disease.[5]

After spending several months at the confluence, Lander decided to return by canoe to the mouth of the river in order to procure fresh stores from Fernando Po. By the end of July he was back at the steamships. He returned to find that Laird, who had visited the famed Funda during his absence, had decided to return with the *Quorra* to England. Lander's own hopes of achievement still ran high. Accompanied by

[1] Laird and Oldfield, 1837, I, pp. 97, 101, 107.
[2] C.O. 2/19, Lander to Hay, 9 May 1833.
[3] C.O. 82/6, Nicholls to Hay, 2 May 1833.
[4] On Pascoe's death, Laird and Oldfield, 1837, I, p. 250; II, pp. 8, 224.
[5] C.O. 2/19, Lander to Hay, 9 May 1833.

Surgeon Oldfield, he decided to take the *Alburkah* up the Tshadda to see if the river was in fact, as many of the natives reported, an outlet of Lake Chad. After travelling one hundred miles up this completely un-explored river, the impossibility of obtaining provisions and the evident absence of any opportunities for trade forced him to turn back. So Lander took the ship up the Niger, revisited many of the places where he had stayed in his earlier journey, and at length reached Raba, whose people were thus enabled to witness an extraordinary sight in 'the arrival of a British steam-vessel constructed of iron'. On his earlier journey Lander had not set foot in the town; now he was received politely by the Fulani ruler. Engine trouble prevented the *Alburkah* from reaching Bussa.[1]

By now the ship's stores were exhausted, so Lander decided to take it back to Fernando Po. He reached the island in November. Needing a supply of cowries for bartering with the natives and finding that none were to be obtained locally, Lander went on to Cape Coast Castle, leaving Oldfield to take the *Alburkah* up the Niger once again. By the middle of January Lander was back, his purchases completed, and set off up the river. His own words, taken from a letter to Colonel Nichols, the Superintendent of Fernando Po, provide the best account of the incident that followed.

> Having to proceed into the interior with goods in one boat, and two canoes man'd with four Englishmen, seventeen Blackmen, one woman, her child, and two boys, we met with a most desperate attack at 2 p.m. on the 20th of Jany from the natives near Hiammah[2] about one hundred miles up the Niger. The savages had assembled on both banks, also on a small island, for the purpose of attacking us where the river was very narrow. About a quarter of a mile ahead of us there was a great many war-canoes stationed. I felt so confident of all the natives being friendly to me, that the crew-men (Krumen) were tracking the boat up. The current being very strong she unfortunately got aground, and in a moment we received a volley of musketry like a shower of rain from the island and the mainland, which kill'd two of my men, wounded myself and three others. No sooner did they commence their fire than the war canoes which were waiting round the point came with all despatch to conquer us; seeing ourselves completely sur-rounded by numbers, and not having a chance of returning the fire, we

---

[1] Oldfield's account of this expedition occupies most of the second volume of Laird and Oldfield, 1837.

[2] Angiama is the correct name of the place; it was visited by Baikie in 1854 (Baikie, 1856, p. 323).

were obliged to abandon the boat, and make an escape in the canoe. After receiving the wound I was very faint, and in the hurry of the moment, the woman and child (Mrs Brown whom I was taking up to her husband) and one boy who was wounded, were forgotten until it was too late to return. Had we remained ten minutes longer, not a soul would have been alive. We were now followed by a great number of war-canoes, and with them we kept up a running fight for five hours. In this engagement we lost John Thompson, late second mate of the cutter *Crown*, who was shot through the head, and four blackmen wounded. Total 3 killed and seven wounded. . . . I have lost all my papers both private and public. . . . I fear if these savages are not chastised immediately it will never be safe to go up in a boat or canoe. I am afraid some white men have a hand in this, as they were placed in so formidable a position and their numbers I suppose about 8000 or 10,000 all armed with muskets and swords, Bonny, Benin and Brass people. They gave up the attack at 8 o'clock p.m. We pull'd all night and reached the Crown, cutter, at 4 o'clock p.m. next day.[1]

To this account some details were added by a young English doctor named Moore, who was with Lander at the time of the attack. On their way up the river they had run into King Jacket, a relative of King Boy; 'his eyes sparkled with malignity, as he said in his own language, "White men will never reach Eboe this time."' During the fight Moore described Lander as behaving with great gallantry, 'cheering on his men', though himself 'seriously wounded'. At the end, when the canoe had passed out of reach of the pursuers, he performed a characteristic gesture. Standing up in the canoe, 'he waved his hat and gave a last cheer in sight of his adversaries. He then became sick and faint from loss of blood, and sank back exhausted.'[2]

Describing the attack in a letter sent to Oldfield from the River Nun on 22 January, Lander wrote of himself as being 'wounded, but I hope not dangerously, the ball having entered close to the anus and struck the thigh-bone: it is not extracted yet'.[3] On 25 January he reached Fernando Po. There a week later, at two-fifteen on the morning of 2 February, in the house of Colonel Nichols, he died.[4] To the last he had retained something of that 'natural cheerfulness' which had made him a 'general favourite' among the garrison of the island.[5]

[1] C.O. 82/7, Lander to Nichols, 24 January 1834, enclosed in Nichols to Hay, 31 January 1834.
[2] Huish, 1835, pp. 770-2.
[3] Laird and Oldfield, 1837, II, p. 252.
[4] C.O. 82/7, Nichols to Hay, 2 February 1834, postscript to 31 January 1834.
[5] C.O. 82/4, Becroft to Hay, 7 January 1831; Huish, 1835, p. 772.

He was buried in a simple grave, unmarked by any memorial, in the cemetery at Clarence, the main settlement on Fernando Po.

Nichols was anxious to avenge Lander's death, but it was not until the beginning of May that he was able to visit the Nun river. There he met King Boy, who told him that Lander's attackers were a 'lawless set' at enmity both with Aboh and with Brass. They had justified their attack on the grounds that 'the river was theirs and white men should not go up'. Their numbers, Boy reckoned, could not be more than one hundred and eighty, not the eight or ten thousand that Lander had imagined. Boy had already succeeded in ransoming Mrs Brown—the wife of one of the Africans on the *Alburkah* —and her child and told Nichols that he was anxious to avenge Lander's death by destroying the offending town, killing all the men and enslaving the women. Nichols said that he would be content with a more modest punishment.[1] But though he took the opportunity of his visit to sign a treaty of friendship with King Boy, no campaign against the people who had attacked Lander was ever undertaken. Nichols himself was under orders to return to England and was engaged in dismantling the settlement at Fernando Po, which the Government, unable to buy the island from its Spanish owners, had decided to abandon.

Richard Lander's wife and daughter received a pension from the Government. John Lander, who had taken over his brother's post in the Customs, survived him by only five years. He died in London on 16 November 1839, leaving a wife and three children.

No sooner had the news of Lander's death reached Truro than a public meeting was held in the town. A sum of money had been raised to make a presentation to the two brothers; this sum, it was now agreed, should be put to a fund for erecting a memorial to Richard Lander. The memorial took the form of an imposing column, erected in one of the main streets of the town. It was surmounted some years later by a statue of the explorer, the work of a well-known local sculptor, Nevill Burnard.

Nearly a century was to pass before Lander received a memorial in Africa. In 1911 an appeal was started to raise funds for a memorial to both Park and Lander in the form of an obelisk to be erected at one of the mouths of the Niger, where it might also serve as a light-house. This project proved too expensive; instead, it was decided in the 1920s to build a monument at Jebba Island, where the road and rail bridge

[1] C.O. 82/7, Nichols to Hay, 4 May 1834.

crosses the Niger.[1] The site is excellent, even if the monument itself, put up by the Public Works Department, is rather dull. On the monument is a plaque with these words:

To Mungo Park 1795 and Richard Lander 1830,
who traced the course of the Niger from near its
source to the sea.
Both died in Africa for Africa

[1] *Journal of the Royal Geographical Society*, LXVIII (1926), p. 456; LXXIV (1929), p. 470.

Richard Lander's burial place, Fernando Po.

Richard Lander's Instructions

Downing Street, 31st December 1829

Sir,

I am directed by Secretary Sir George Murray to acquaint you, that he has deemed it expedient to accept the offer which you have made, to proceed to Africa, accompanied by your brother, for the purpose of ascertaining the course of the Great River which was crossed by the late Captain Clapperton on his journey to Soccatoo; and a passage having been accordingly engaged for you and your brother on board the *Alert*, merchant vessel, which is proceeding to Cape Coast Castle, on the western coast of Africa, I am to desire that you will embark directly on board that vessel.

In the event of your falling in with any of his Majesty's ships of war on the coast of Africa, previously to your arrival at Cape Coast Castle, you will prevail on the master to use every endeavour to speak with such ship of war, and to deliver to the officer commanding her, the letter of which you are the bearer, and which is to require him to convey yourself and your brother to Badagry, to present you to the king, and to give you such assistance as may be required to enable you to set out on your journey.

You should incur as little delay as possible at Badagry, in order that, by reaching the hilly country, you may be more secure from those fevers which are known to be prevalent on the low lands of the sea-coast. You are to proceed by the same road as on a previous occasion, as far as Katunga, unless you shall be able to find, on the northern side of the mountains, a road which will lead you to Funda, on the Quorra or Niger, in which case you are to proceed direct to Funda. If, however, it should be necessary to go as far as Katunga, you are to use your endeavours to prevail on the chief of that country to assist you on your way to the Quorra, and with the means of tracing down, either by land or water, the course of that river as far as Funda.

On your arrival at this place, you are to be very particular in your observations, so as to enable you to give a correct statement—

1st. Whether any, and what rivers fall into the Quorra at or near that place, or whether the whole or any part of the Quorra turns to the eastward.

2nd. Whether there is at Funda, or in the neighbourhood, any lake or collection of waters, or large swamp; in which case you are to go round such lake or swamp, and be very particular in examining whether any river flows *into* or *out* of it, and in what direction it takes its course.

3rd. If you should find that at Funda the Quorra continues to flow to the southward, you are to follow it to the sea, where, in this case, it may be presumed to empty its waters; but if it should be found to turn off to the eastward, in which case it will most probably fall into the Lake Tshad, you are to follow its course in that direction, as far as you can conceive you can venture to do, with due regard to your personal safety, even to Bornou, in which case it will be for you to determine whether it may not be advisable to return home by the way of Fezzan and Tripoli: if, however, after proceeding in an easterly course for some distance, the river should be found to turn off towards the south, you are to follow it, as before, down to the sea. In short, having once gained the banks of the Quorra, either from Katunga, or lower down, you are to follow its course, if possible, to its termination, wherever that may be.

Should you be of opinion that the Sultan of Youri can safely be communicated with, you are at liberty to send your brother with a present to that chief, to ask, in the king's name, for certain books or papers which he is supposed to have, that belonged to the late Mr Park; but you are not necessarily yourself to wait for your brother's return, but to proceed in the execution of the main object of your mission, to ascertain the course and termination of the Niger.

You are to take every opportunity of sending down by the coast a brief abstract of your proceedings and observations, furnishing the bearer with a note, setting forth the reward he is to have for his trouble, and requesting any English person, to whom it is presented, to pay that reward on the faith that it will be repaid him by the British Government.

For the performance of this service, you are furnished with all the articles which you have required for your personal convenience, during your journey, together with a sum of two hundred dollars in coin, and in case, upon your arrival at Badagry, you should find it absolutely necessary to provide yourself with a further supply of dollars, you will be at liberty to draw upon this department for any sum not exceeding three hundred dollars.

During the ensuing year, the sum of one hundred pounds will be paid to your wife, in quarterly payments, and upon your return a gratuity of one hundred pounds will be paid to yourself.

All the papers and observations which you shall bring back with you, are to be delivered by you at this office, and you will be entitled to receive any pecuniary consideration which may be obtained from the publication of the account of your journey.

I am, Sir, &c. &c.

(Signed) R. W. Hay.

To Mr Richard Lander.

The text of the instructions is printed in the Introduction to the Landers' *Journal*, Vol. I, pp. lii–lvii. R. W. Hay was Under-Secretary of State at the Colonial Office and responsible for African affairs.

APPENDIX II

The Landers' Equipment

THE LANDERS' EQUIPMENT was divided between presents and trade goods to be used for purchasing food and repaying hospitality and stores for their personal use.

The presents included fifty yards of Staff Sergeants' scarlet cloth, one hundred and ten mirrors (one hundred being of 'inferior quality'), fifty razors, one hundred combs, fifty thousand assorted needles, one hundred Dutch pipes, and two 'medals, silver, large'.

The personal stores included one round tent, mattresses, sheets and blankets, and cooking equipment. Food-stuffs were limited to tinned soup, six pounds of tea, ten of coffee, and twenty of sugar. An elaborate supply of medicines was provided, ranging from submuriate of mercury to sulphate of quinine; remarks on the use of the medicines were written out by Sir John Webb, the director-general of the ordinance medical department. Fire-arms were limited to two fowling-pieces and two brace of pistols.

The value of the presents was estimated at £260, of the personal stores at £96. The equipment was packed in seven panniers and three valises, together with two bales of cloth, one case for the guns, and two cases for the medicine. The total weight of all the stores was about half a ton.

(A 'List of Stores' and 'List of Medicines and Surgical Materials' is given in the *Journal*, III, pp. 343–54. There is another slightly different list in C.O. 2/18.)

Bibliography

1. WORKS ESPECIALLY CONNECTED WITH THE LANDERS

Bishop, 1953. Morchard Bishop. 'The Niger, the Manservant, and the Printer' in *The Cornhill Magazine*, No. 997. London. 1953.

Clapperton, 1829. Commander Clapperton. *Journal of a Second Expedition into the Interior of Africa. To which is added, the Journal of Richard Lander from Kano to the Sea-Coast, partly by a more Easterly Route.* London, 1829.

Huish, 1836. Robert Huish. *The Travels of Richard and John Lander, into the Interior of Africa, for the Discovery of the Course and Termination of the Niger; from Unpublished Documents in the Possession of the late Capt. John William Barber Fullerton, Employed in the African Service; with a Prefatory Analysis of the Previous Travels of Park, Denham, Clapperton, Adams, Lyon, Ritchie, &c. into the hitherto unexplored Countries of Africa.* London, 1836.

This volume has two title-pages, on the first of which the date is given as 1835.

Laird and Oldfield, 1837. Macgregor Laird and R. A. K. Oldfield. *Narrative of an Expedition into the Interior of Africa, by the River Niger, in the Steam-Vessels Quorra and Alburkah, in 1832, 1833, and 1834.* London, 1837. 2 vols.

Lander, 1830. Richard Lander. *Records of Captain Clapperton's Last Expedition to Africa: with the Subsequent Adventures of the Author.* London, 1830. 2 vols.

Rowe, 1952. Ashley Rowe. A series of articles on the Landers. *The West Briton.* Truro. January, 1952.

Tregellas, 1884. H. W. Tregellas. 'Richard Lander', in *Cornish Worthies.* London, 1884.

2. OTHER WORKS

Abadie, 1927. M. Abadie. *La Colonie du Niger.* Paris, 1927.

Allen and Thomson, 1848. Captain W. Allen and T. R. H. Thomson. *A Narrative of the Expedition to the Niger River in 1841.* London, 1848. 2 vols.

Allison, *Odu*, n.d. Philip Allison. 'The Last Days of Old Oyo', in *Odu*, No. 4, Ibadan, n.d.

Baikie, 1856. W. B. Baikie. *Narrative of an Exploring Voyage up the Rivers Kwora and Binue in 1854*. London, 1856.

Bargery, 1957. G. P. Bargery. *A Hausa–English Dictionary*. London, 1957.

Barth, 1890. Henry Barth. *Travels and Discoveries in North and Central Africa*. London, 1890. (Second and abridged edition.)

Bascom, 1960. William Bascom. 'Lander's Route through Yoruba Country', in *Nigerian Field*, Vol. XXV, Worcester, 1960.

Campbell, 1955. M. J. Campbell. 'Borgu Journey', in *Nigeria Magazine*, No. 49, Lagos, 1955.

Dike, 1956. K. Onwuka Dike. *Trade and Politics in the Niger Delta 1830–1885*. London, 1956.

Dike, 1956. K. Onwuka Dike. 'John Beecroft, 1790–1854', in *Journal of the Historical Society of Nigeria*.

Fage, 1962. J. D. Fage. 'Some Remarks on Beads and Trade in Lower Guinea in the Sixteenth and Seventeenth Centuries', in *Journal of African History*, Vol. III, No. 2, London, 1962.

Hastings, 1926. A. C. G. Hastings. *The Voyage of the Day Spring*. London, 1927.

Ifemasia, 1962. C. C. Ifemasia. 'The "Civilizing" Mission of 1841', in *Journal of the Historical Society of Nigeria*, Vol. II, No. 3, Ibadan, 1962.

Ilorin Gazetteer. *Gazetteer of Ilorin Province*. Compiled by K. V. Elphinstone. London, 1921.

Johnson, 1957. Samuel Johnson. *The History of the Yorubas*. Lagos, 1957.

Kontagora Gazetteer. *Gazetteer of Kontagora Province*. Compiled by E. C. Duff. London, 1920.

Lucas, 1948. J. O. Lucas. *The Religion of the Yorubas*. Lagos, 1948.

Lupton, 1962. K. Lupton. 'The Death of Mungo Park at Bussa', in *Nigeria Magazine*, No. 72. Lagos, 1962.

Meek, 1937. C. K. Meek. *Law and Authority in a Nigerian Tribe*. London, 1937.

Metcalfe, 1962. G. E. Metcalfe. *Maclean of the Gold Coast*. London, 1962.

Moorehead, 1960. Alan Moorehead. *The White Nile*. London, 1960.

Nadel, 1942. S. F. Nadel. *A Black Byzantium*. London, 1942.

Newbury, 1961. C. W. Newbury. *The Western Slave Coast and Its Rulers*. Oxford, 1961.

Niven, 1958. C. R. Niven. *A Short History of the Yoruba Peoples*. London, 1958.

Park, *Everyman Ed. The Travels of Mungo Park*. *Everyman's Library*. London, n.d.

Talbot, 1932. P. Amaury Talbot. *Tribes of the Niger Delta*. London, 1932.

Thomson, 1890. Joseph Thomson. *Mungo Park and the Niger*. London, 1890.

Trimingham, 1959. J. Spencer Trimingham. *Islam in West Africa*. Oxford, 1959.

Waddell, 1863. Hope Masterton Waddell. *Twenty Nine Years in the West Indies and Central Africa*. London, 1863.

Whitford, 1877. John Whitford. *Trading Life in Western and Central Africa*. Liverpool, 1877

Willett, 1960. Frank Willett. 'Investigations at Old Oyo, 1956–57: An Interim Report', in *Journal of the Historical Society of Nigeria*, Vol. II, No. 1, Ibadan, 1960.

Willett, 1960. A. Frank Willett. 'Ife and its Archaeology', in *Journal of African History*, Vol. I. No. 2, Cambridge, 1960.

3. MANUSCRIPT SOURCES

In the Public Record Office, London

C.O. 2/16 and 17. Clapperton's last expedition. 1825–28.

C.O. 2/18. The Landers' expedition. 1829–31.

C.O. 2/19. Richard Lander's last expedition and other papers. 1832–36.

C.O. 82/1–9. Fernando Po. 1828–42.

In the Cornwall County Record Office, Truro

A few letters and papers, mainly written by John Lander between 1831 and 1839, have recently been deposited at the Cornwall County Record Office at Truro by Mr and Mrs W. Birnie (descendants of John Lander's wife, Mary Livett). They do not include an original journal of the Lander brothers. For information about these papers I am indebted to the County Archivist (Mr P. L. Hull).

Place-Name Index and Gazetteer

This index is confined to place-names mentioned by the Landers in the text of this edition of their *Journal*. Where it has been possible to identify the place-name used by the Landers with a modern town or village, the modern name has been given in parenthesis. All modern names have been taken from the map of Nigeria in 15 sheets, scale 1:500,000. Place-names mentioned in the introduction, epilogue, or foot-notes are given in the general index, together with detailed references to the more important places given here.

General Index